Teaching Religion and Film

AMERICAN ACADEMY OF RELIGION

TEACHING RELIGIOUS STUDIES SERIES

SERIES EDITOR
Susan Henking, Hobart and William Smith Colleges

A Publication Series of
The American Academy of Religion
and
Oxford University Press

TEACHING LEVI-STRAUSS
Edited by Hans H. Penner

TEACHING ISLAM
Edited by Brannon M. Wheeler

TEACHING FREUD
Edited by Diane Jonte-Pace

TEACHING DURKHEIM
Edited by Terry F. Godlove Jr.

TEACHING AFRICAN AMERICAN RELIGIONS
Edited by Carolyn M. Jones and Theodore Louis Trost

TEACHING RELIGION AND HEALING
Edited by Linda L. Barnes and Inés Talamantez

TEACHING NEW RELIGIOUS MOVEMENTS
Edited by David G. Bromley

TEACHING RITUAL
Edited by Catherine Bell

TEACHING CONFUCIANISM
Jeffrey L. Richey

AMERICAN ACADEMY OF RELIGION

Teaching Religion and Film

EDITED BY
GREGORY J. WATKINS

OXFORD
UNIVERSITY PRESS

2008

OXFORD
UNIVERSITY PRESS

Oxford University Press, Inc., publishes works that further
Oxford University's objective of excellence
in research, scholarship, and education.

Oxford   New York
Auckland   Cape Town   Dar es Salaam   Hong Kong   Karachi
Kuala Lumpur   Madrid   Melbourne   Mexico City   Nairobi
New Delhi   Shanghai   Taipei   Toronto

With offices in
Argentina   Austria   Brazil   Chile   Czech Republic   France   Greece
Guatemala   Hungary   Italy   Japan   Poland   Portugal   Singapore
South Korea   Switzerland   Thailand   Turkey   Ukraine   Vietnam

Copyright © 2008 by The American Academy of Religion

Published by Oxford University Press, Inc.
198 Madison Avenue, New York, New York 10016

www.oup.com

Oxford is a registered trademark of Oxford University Press

Library of Congress Cataloging-in-Publication Data
Teaching religion and film / edited by Gregory J. Watkins.
    p. cm.—(Teaching religious studies)
Includes bibliographical references and index.
ISBN 978-0-19-533598-9
1. Motion pictures—Religious aspects.
2. Motion pictures—Moral and ethical aspects.
3. Religion—Study and teaching.   I. Watkins, Gregory J.
PN1995.5.T37 2008
791.43'682—dc22   2007040450

9 8 7 6 5 4 3 2 1

Printed in the United States of America
on acid-free paper

The manuscript for this volume happened to be completed a couple of days after the death of Ingmar Bergman. A classroom screening of Bergman's The Seventh Seal *my freshman year of college had a profound impact on me. Having come to college from a small farming town in Idaho, I had no idea such a movie was possible. My now deep and abiding interest in the connection between religion and film started with that screening. I dedicate this volume to the memory of Ingmar Bergman.*

Preface

This project was inspired by a suggestion from Diane Jonte-Pace, whom I would like to thank. I had just been hired to teach a class on religion and film at Santa Clara University. Fresh from the publication of her own volume in the AAR Teaching Series, *Teaching Freud,* Jonte-Pace encouraged me to consider doing the same for religion and film. The idea was slow to take hold. I was only starting to understand how to tackle the intersection between religion—that diverse and complicated area of human culture and experience—and the extremely powerful medium of film. But by way of the classroom (and with thanks to my many curious and thoughtful students at Santa Clara and Stanford) I quickly began to see the intellectual and pedagogical promise of bringing religion and film together. Part of that promise comes from the fact that we, as a scholarly community, are just beginning to discover the many ways we can investigate and teach this intersection. Indeed, part of the enjoyment of teaching this material is that our challenges as scholars can be shared in the classroom—the students can play a role in the investigation by telling us who they are as movie viewers and what they find themselves thinking and feeling when they watch a movie.

However, I also learned that very little material was available on the pedagogical challenges in the religion and film classroom. Finally, with Jonte-Pace's invitation in mind, I tested the waters by asking a few well-known names in the field (whom I did not know personally) whether they would be interested in contributing to such a volume. From the very start, the contributors to this book accepted the invitation enthusiastically—and I thank them for the hard work they put into this wonderful collection of essays. I would also like to thank Susan Henking, the AAR Teaching Series editor, for her friendly and informative support throughout this process, from the numerous proposal drafts to final OUP approval, as well as Cynthia Read and Meechal Hoffman at Oxford University Press for their patient guidance during the publication process. Finally, I would like to thank Carol Hoke for such excellent work in the editing of the manuscript, editing which so many of the contributors to this volume went out of their way to praise.

Contents

Contributors

Alice Bach is professor of Catholic studies at Case Western Reserve University. She is the author of *Women, Seduction, and Betrayal in Biblical Narrative* (1997) and editor of *Semeia 74: Biblical Glamour and Hollywood Glitz* (1996), which includes her articles " 'Throw Them to the Lions, Sire': Transforming Biblical Narratives into Hollywood Spectaculars" and "Calling the Shots: Directing Salomé's Dance of Death."

William L. Blizek is professor of philosophy and religion at the University of Nebraska at Omaha. He is a founder of the *Journal of Religion and Film* and a former cochair of the AAR Group on Religion, Film, and Visual Culture. He is presently preparing *Companion to Religion and Film* for Continuum Books of London.

Richard M. Carp is chair of the Department of Interdisciplinary Studies at Appalachian State University and has research interests in the spaces between religion, performance, and anthropology. Recent publications include "Art, Education, and the Sign(ification) of the Self" (2004) and "Integrative Praxes: Learning from Multiple Knowledge Formations" (2001).

Gayatri Chatterjee is a teacher of film studies and has written the award-winning *Awaara* (1992) and *Mother India* (2002), part of the British Film Institute's film classics series.

Francisca Cho is associate professor of Buddhist studies at Georgetown University. Her research focuses on East Asian Buddhism as expressed through aesthetic media. In addition to articles on Buddhism and film, her publications include *Embracing Illusion: Truth and*

Fiction in the Dream of the Nine Clouds (1996), which examines Buddhist philosophy in the medium of fiction, and *Everything Yearned for: Manhae's Poems of
Love and Longing* (2005), a translation and study of Buddhist poetry.

Christopher Deacy is head of religious studies at the University of Kent, where
he specializes in applied theology. He is the author of *Screen Christologies:
Redemption and the Medium of Film* (2002), *Faith in Film: Religious Themes in
Contemporary Cinema* (2005), and (co-authored with Gaye Ortiz) *Theology and
Film: Challenging the Sacred/Secular Divide* (2008). Deacy is a member of the
American Academy of Religion, Interfilm, and the UK Theology, Religion, and
Popular Culture Network Group.

Michele Desmarais is associate professor of religious studies at the University
of Nebraska at Omaha. She serves as associate editor of the *Journal of Religion
and Film* and participates in the journal's annual "Report from Sundance."
Her book, *Changing Minds,* is forthcoming from Motilal Banarsidass Press,
New Delhi, India.

Gregory Grieve is assistant professor of religious studies at the University of
North Carolina at Greensboro and has research interests in religion, art, and
visual culture. Recent writings include *Retheorizing Religion in Nepal* (2006)
and "The Rubin Museum of Art: Re-framing Religion for Aesthetic Spirituality" (2006) in the *Journal of Material Religion*.

Amir Hussain is associate professor in the Department of Theological Studies
at Loyola Marymount University in Los Angeles. Specializing in the study of
Islam, he focuses on contemporary Muslim societies in North America. He
was cochair of the Religion, Film, and Visual Culture group of the American
Academy of Religion and now serves as co-chair of the Contemporary Islam
consultation. His latest book, an introduction to Islam for North Americans, is
titled *Oil and Water: Two Faiths, One God* (2006).

John C. Lyden is professor and chair of the religion department at Dana College in Blair, Nebraska. He is the author of *Film as Religion: Myths, Morals, and
Rituals* (2003) and is also the editor of *Enduring Issues in Religion* (1995). He has
also published numerous articles on religion and film, interreligious dialogue,
and popular culture and is cochair of the Religion, Film, and Visual Culture
Group of the American Academy of Religion.

Irena S. M. Makarushka currently serves as associate dean for the College of
Liberal Arts at Towson University in Maryland, where she has taught an
honors seminar on evil. A former associate professor of religion at Bowdoin
College, she served as chair of the religion department and taught courses in
the philosophy of religion, Western religious thought, religion and culture, and
film and the visual arts. Her publications include *Religious Imagination and*

Language in Emerson and Nietzsche (1994) and more than a dozen articles and chapters in books. She also wrote a monthly column, "Education Matters," for a Baltimore publication, *Smart Woman.*

Clive Marsh is principal of the East Midlands Ministry Training Course at the University of Nottingham and a local preacher in the Methodist Church of Great Britain. He has edited and written many books, including *Explorations in Theology and Film* (with Gaye Ortiz 1997), *Christianity in a Post-atheist Age* (2002), *Cinema and Sentiment* (2004), *Christ in Focus: Radical Christocentrism in Christian Theology* (2005), *Christ in Practice: A Christology of Everyday Life* (2006), and *Theology Goes to the Movies* (2007).

Ellen Ott Marshall is associate professor of ethics at Claremont School of Theology and Claremont Graduate University's School of Religion in Claremont, California. She is a contributing editor of *Choosing Peace through Daily Practices* (2005) and the author of *Though the Fig Tree Does Not Blossom* (2006) and *Christians in the Public Square: Faith that Transforms Politics (2008).* She has also published essays on welfare reform, the use of film to teach ethics, and the United Methodist Church's response to war.

Jolyon Mitchell is senior lecturer in theology, ethics, and communication at New College, Edinburgh University, where he teaches courses in film and religion. He is a former BBC World Service producer and journalist. His publications include *Visually Speaking* (1999), *Mediating Religion* (2003, co-edited with Sophia Marriage), *Media Violence and Christian Ethics* (2007), and *The Religion and Film Reader* (2007, co-edited with S. Brent Plate). He is coeditor of the Media, Religion, and Culture monograph series with Routledge.

Gaye Williams Ortiz teaches communication studies at Augusta State University, Augusta, Georgia. Her publications include (with Clive Marsh) *Explorations in Theology and Film* (1997), *Literature and Theology: Re-thinking Reader Responsibility* (with Clara Joseph 2006), and *Theology and Film: Challenging the Sacred/Secular Divide,* written with Chris Deacy (forthcoming in 2008). She is also a fellow of York Saint John University, where she was senior lecturer in theology and religious studies and head of cultural studies.

Conrad Ostwalt is professor of religion at Appalachian State University. He is coeditor, with Joel Martin, of *Screening the Sacred: Religion, Myth, and Ideology in Popular American Film* (1995) and the author of *Secular Steeples: Popular Culture and the Religious Imagination* (2003).

S. Brent Plate is associate professor of religion and the visual arts at Texas Christian University. He is author/editor of several books, including *Blasphemy: Art That Offends* (2006); *Walter Benjamin, Religion, and Aesthetics* (2004); *Representing Religion in World Cinema* (2003); and *The Religion and*

Film Reader (2007). He is also managing editor of *Material Religion: The Journal of Objects, Art, and Belief.*

Gregory J. Watkins is a lecturer and resident fellow in the Program in Structured Liberal Education at Stanford University. He is the author of "Seeing and Being Seen: Distinctively Filmic and Religious Elements in Film" (*Journal of Religion and Film* 1999). Also a filmmaker, Watkins has an MFA in film production from the University of California at Los Angeles.

Teaching Religion and Film

Introduction: Teaching Religion and Film

Gregory J. Watkins

The study of religion has always been both vexed and blessed by the fact that it is a "field" and not a "discipline." While those of us working in religious studies have rarely been able to defend our scholarly pursuits except from the standpoint of a discipline (e.g., sociology, anthropology, philosophy, psychology, aesthetics), it is religion's resistance to the constraints of a single field of study that encourages a certain intellectual fascination with the subject, as well as an invitation to think truly creatively and even to question the disciplinary constraints themselves. Such theoretical latitude is no less the case when the field of religious studies intersects with the discipline of film studies.

Though the youngest of all of the arts, cinema has quickly become the most powerful art form in history, and academic conversations about the relationships between religion and film have proliferated in the past two decades. This growth has been driven in part by students' changing intellectual sensibilities. Today's students generally embrace (and sometimes expect) multimedia approaches to course material, and the dynamic and cross-disciplinary power of film makes it an inviting option for almost any class. And with many films tackling explicitly religious material, it is hard to resist the opportunity to bring them into the classroom. However, combining the complex nature of religious studies with the still-growing popularity and creative diversity of films is a complex task. This volume makes significant strides in the field by giving readers both a sense of the pedagogical challenges of using films in religious studies and theology classrooms and an indication of the tremendous theoretical range that is developing with respect to this intersection of art, culture, and tradition.

Growth in the Field

The panel offerings at the American Academy of Religion (AAR) annual meeting over the past decade reflect this expanding academic interest in the field of religion and film (I thank William Blizek for providing the figures quoted here). Started in the mid-1990s as a consultation, the first "religion and film" meeting consisted of an audience of about 35 people who came to listen to three papers (the presenter of a fourth paper failed to appear). For the past several years, the Religion, Film, and Visual Culture Group has routinely presented two regular sessions with five papers each and often an extra session of five papers on a special topic. For each of these three sessions, the group attracts 150–200 audience members (for a total of 500–600 per annual meeting). Furthermore, the group receives more paper proposals each year than it is able to accept, and these figures do not include the occasional paper on some aspect of film-related media that is presented at other gatherings.

The number of people who come to hear these papers is particularly telling. While AAR and Society of Biblical Literature (SBL) members are undoubtedly interested in hearing about religious studies approaches to film and visual culture, I think the large turnout is partly due to the fact that many members are using films in their courses—they want to hear what scholars think about film, and they want to consider how they are using film in their own classrooms. In other words, the number of nonspecialists working with film in their classrooms probably exceeds that of nonspecialists who are focusing on almost any other single topic within religious studies.

Another indication of this growing interest is the popularity of the *Journal of Religion and Film* (*JRF;* http://www.unomaha.edu/jrf/). Founded in 1997 by William Blizek and Ronald Burke, *JRF* has published considerably more than two hundred articles and reviews and is currently registering an average of thirty-five hundred hits per month (2008). As a final mark of the increasing importance of this field, we are starting to see the publication of books devoted to the introduction of religion and film studies in general (see, for example, Melanie J. Wright's *Religion and Film: An Introduction* [2006]). Although this volume has an express interest in pedagogy, it aims equally at giving the reader a broad introduction both to thinking about the teaching of religion and film and to representing the range of work that has already emerged and continues to take shape in the pages of this very volume.

Pedagogical and Theoretical Value of the Volume

Although the field of religion and film has been in need of a volume on pedagogy, I have also recognized a unique opportunity to present not only the range of theoretical orientations to that intersection but the latest developments in theory as well (even in the thinking of those whose work in the field has already become foundational). In short, the pedagogical issues are closely tied to the theoretical approach one takes in putting together a course that uses film to reflect on religion (or, conversely, uses religion to consider film). If this volume succeeds in helping teachers of religion and film, it will be principally by way of giving insight into the range of theoretical approaches available in this field, such that the design of a religion and film course (or even just the occasional use of film in a religious studies or theology classroom) promotes greater clarity and depth of content—a benefit to both teacher and student. Indeed, as I argue in my own chapter in the volume, presenting the many ways in which the study of religion and the medium of film can be brought together can itself make for a very rich classroom experience.

Organization of the Volume

The organization of the volume reflects the general breakdown of the kinds of work one can find in this emerging field. Of course, the chapters themselves do not always fit precisely into the divisions suggested by the table of contents, but the categories are a useful orientation to the theoretical terrain of religion and film.

Establishing Shot: Viewing the Field of Religion and Film

The volume starts with an orientation to the field and then presents a chapter about one of the most important current topics in theoretical work. In chapter 1, "What Are We Teaching When We Teach 'Religion and Film'?" Blizek and Desmarais report on a survey of four general approaches to the use of film in a class on religion: (1) using religion to interpret movies (what some call the "theological" approach); (2) using movies to critique religion; (3) using movies to promote religion; and (4) using movies to expose cultural values (or what some call the "ideological" approach). Blizek has already had an important impact on this field with his leadership in the AAR's Religion, Film, and Visual Culture Group, as well as his role in founding the valuable *Journal of Religion and Film.*

With this chapter, he and Desmarais offer an overall view of the field and guide the reader through a consideration of each approach, highlighting both theoretical and pedagogical issues. The basic divisions are undeniable, though the language any particular writer in the field uses to describe and discuss them can vary considerably. Indeed, the categories Blizek and Desmarais utilize greatly help to explain the organization of this volume by grouping the chapters into the "religious traditions," "religious studies," and "values" approaches. Moreover, these groupings can be important even if one is teaching within a narrowly construed version of one of them because they also describe the range of *reactions* students might have to the films in class. That is to say, whatever our intentions as teachers, it can be helpful for us to know that students might be construing the material in the different ways outlined in this chapter. Keeping these divisions in mind can help a teacher navigate those reactions.

Conrad Ostwalt's chapter, "Teaching Religion and Film: A Fourth Approach," has in the background Ostwalt's own early and foundational contribution to the field as coeditor, with Joel Martin, of *Screening the Sacred: Religion, Myth, and Ideology in Popular American Film* (1995). As Ostwalt and Martin saw it then, there were at least three fundamental approaches to criticism in the religion and film intersection: theological, mythical, and ideological. Though Ostwalt offers a thumbnail sketch of that tripartite approach, I strongly encourage readers to look at the introduction and conclusion to *Screening the Sacred* for a fuller discussion. In chapter 2 Ostwalt describes what he calls a "fourth approach," which is best seen not as a refinement of the tripartite division but rather as an introduction to a qualitatively different method. As Ostwalt explains, the three approaches to religion and film criticism in *Screening the Sacred* depend on seeing film as *reflecting* ideas in particular ways. In contrast, the "fourth way" is an entirely new method. As Ostwalt puts it, "I have since felt it necessary to supplement the book's pedagogical content with a fourth approach, one that focuses more on the uniqueness of film." He calls this process "sensory criticism" because it focuses on the carefully separated visual and audible elements of movies. In addition, Ostwalt does a wonderful job of describing specific classroom exercises for making the most of this new technique.

One of the pleasant surprises of putting together this volume has been that several of the chapters echo the kind of shift in orientation that Ostwalt reports in his own thinking. I believe it is safe to say that there is a general interest in moving beyond (or at least adding to) what might be called strictly literary approaches to this intersection; that is to say, the tools we use as religion specialists to critique texts have served us well, but they may not be the only (or even the best) tools when the object of study is the religious dimension of film (see especially the chapters by Cho, Carp, and Marsh).

Film and the Teaching of Religious Traditions

This part of the volume tackles the use of film when teaching both from *within* a particular tradition (what Ostwalt would call theological criticism) and *about* a particular tradition. Needless to say, with even one of these purposes in mind, this volume could include only a small sample of the myriad possibilities. Fortunately, a great deal of exemplary work has already been done on these topics (and many of the chapters here point the reader to some of them), so my goal is to provide either representative work that is not easy to find or work that stretches the boundaries of what has already been done.

Chapter 3, "Teaching Biblical Tourism: How Sword-and-Sandal Films Clouded My Vision," by Alice Bach, is a great example of this effort to add new insight to current work. In the field of religion and film, no single subject has been mined so much as connections between the Bible and film, often by way of explicit "textual" overlap between Bible stories and movie stories. Bach has made significant contributions to that area (note the extensive bibliography she offers in the appendices to her chapter). But Bach has since experienced a profound transformation with respect to the "sword-and-sandal" approach to Bible and film, as well as a new strategy for the use of film in the religious studies classroom—namely, a transition to the use of documentaries and other visual media in a course on the Israeli/Palestinian conflict. Her chapter is therefore instructive on many different levels: What are the pedagogical dangers of traditional Bible and film course offerings? How are narrative films different from documentaries and television news media, and what is at stake in choosing between them? What makes for a "critical viewer" in each case?

By contrast, chapter 4, Gayatri Chatterjee's "Designing a Course on Religion and Cinema in India," is the kind of wonderfully rich and sustained effort that advances our knowledge of the use of film to teach about religion in India because so little has been written on the subject. Because work in this particular area is rare and relatively piecemeal, I feel especially fortunate to have Chatterjee's contribution. I am sure it will quickly become a foundational work for thinking about religion and film in India. Although specialists on religion in India will no doubt find her topic rewarding, I encourage nonspecialists to read the chapter as well; even without specific knowledge of religion or cinema in India, one comes away from the chapter with a fresh sense of the possibilities for interactions between religion, culture, and cinema.

Chapter 5, "Buddhism, Film, and Religious Knowing: Challenging the Literary Approach to Film," by Francisca Cho, sits a bit less comfortably in this "religious traditions" section. Cho's specialty is Buddhism, and her article, titled "Imagining Nothing and Imagining Otherness in Buddhist Film," in *Imag(in)ing the Other: Filmic Visions of Community* (1999) had a powerful impact on my thinking when I was learning my way around this kind of material. Buddhism poses many interesting challenges to the consideration of religion and film, not the least of which is the fact that "theological" approaches are problematic since the idea of "theology" has such a complicated currency in Buddhist studies. What is more, in contrast to Jewish and Christian theological approaches, the doctrinal rigidity of sacred stories is much less fixed. At the same time, however, the challenges Buddhism in general poses to the largely literary approach to religious studies in Western academia have allowed both Buddhist filmmakers and Buddhist-oriented critics of film "to show things that wouldn't otherwise be seen" (to borrow Godard's famous phrase for understanding what film should be doing). Cho does a commendable job of explaining what a Buddhist approach to this topic can teach us about the broader relationship between religion and film. In other words, her chapter does not focus entirely on the intersection of film and the Buddhist tradition, but its insights have their source in the particular challenges of studying that tradition. The chapter is especially rich in that Cho draws a connection between her specific argument about religion and film and our thinking about pedagogy in the humanities generally.

Chapter 6, "The Pedagogical Challenges of Finding Christ Figures in Film," by Christopher Deacy, deals with a Christian theological approach head on. As editor of *Screen Christologies: Redemption and the Medium of Film* (2002) and author of *Faith in Film: Religious Themes in Contemporary Cinema* (2005) and the forthcoming (with Gaye Ortiz) *Theology and Film: Challenging the Sacred/Secular Divide* (2008), Deacy has also had a major impact on the field. As he points out here, one of the challenges of the theological approach is the apparent ease with which one can search for correlations between religious narratives/imagery and movie narratives/imagery, and the hunt for Christ figures in movies is certainly leading the pack. Such projects can reach absurd limits, to the point that either Christ figures are simply in the eye of the beholder or the correlations are so flat as to be uninteresting. With so much of that kind of mediocre work going on, Deacy asks these key analytical questions: When is theology an integral part of a film, and when is it brought to a film? To address these challenges of method, he encourages us to push theological considerations beyond Christ typology and into a deeper examination of both the concept of the movie as a whole and its theological implications. With Deacy's approach, we can ask, for example, "Is it more important from the perspective of Christian theological criticism that a character is Christ-like in certain typological features or that the movie as a whole is misogynistic?" Once again—as is the case in many of the chapters—the questions of theory and method can themselves be the subject of classroom inquiry; in this case, students could come to see the power and potential of typological correlations at the same time that they discover the limitations of "hunting for type" and start to explore the rich theological alternatives to that approach.

As with Chatterjee's chapter, that by Amir Hussain, "Film and the Introduction to Islam Course," presents more basic points of reference for the use of film when the subject is Islam. Most of the current work on this particular intersection of religion and film focuses on the representation of Muslims in popular movies and on television (see, for example, Rubina Ramji's "From *Navy Seals* to *The Siege:* Getting to Know the Muslim Terrorist, Hollywood Style" (*Journal of Religion and Film* 9[2], 2005). Indeed, as Hussain points out, any approach to Islam and film in contemporary classrooms has to tackle the prejudicial power of the images of Muslims in contemporary popular movies and television. He deftly guides us through that challenge by recounting his own classroom experiences and teaching strategies. Hussain also urges us to consider the many factors related to student population and institutional context that can profoundly affect the way in which these issues are handled in the classroom. I hope that the day will soon come when the burden of such a class will not involve countering the harmful characterizations found in the mass media (and indeed when the content of so many current movies will not be principally tied to overly self-conscious portrayals of Muslims or Islam, whether positive or negative).

Clive Marsh's chapter, "Is It All about *Love Actually?*: Sentimentality as Problem and Opportunity in the Use of Film for Teaching Theology and Religion," presents a compelling argument for putting the role of the sentiments in students' reactions to popular movies at the center of a strategy for connecting Christian theology to movies. Marsh teaches Christian theology in both secular institutions and seminary settings, or, as he puts it, he teaches theology *through* the use of film and teaches *about* Christian theology. That the teaching strategy he presents here can apply to both settings (as well as to any number of other venues) is part of what I find so exciting about this chapter.

Marsh contends that films can bring "live" material into the classroom by way of the sentiments they elicit. The general point is that teachers of religion need to consider both the cognitive and the affective elements of movie watching. Marsh's methodological recentering of the sentiments not only aids the teaching of theology but also has the advantage of bringing a process of reflection to the usually unimpeded consumption of visual media by this generation of students. A central dynamic point of contact between religious systems and film, he argues, is that they are both engaged in meaning making. Although the larger purposes of the class vary, a religion and film course can focus on what a religious tradition has to say about love (for example) and what the products of popular culture are saying about the same subject—and do so with the human sentiment that movies provoke, thereby initiating and energizing the process.

The next chapter, "Women, Theology, and Film: Approaching the Challenge of Interdisciplinary Teaching," by Gaye Williams Ortiz, discusses the challenges of introducing another theoretical enterprise into the religion and film equation—in this case, feminist studies. Needless to say, the theoretical and methodological complications quickly multiply as the juggling of theology, film theory, and feminist theory extends into the specific difficulties of feminist theology and feminist film theory. By discussing her experiences while teaching a course on this subject, Ortiz shares her wisdom with respect to the pedagogical challenges and provides many references to helpful films and texts. What I find especially exciting about this chapter is Ortiz's assertion that academic development must accompany personal growth (a central tenet of feminist pedagogy) and that the use of movies can facilitate that objective.

The Religious Studies Approach

The Religious Studies approach is a catchall phrase, to say the least. Nonetheless, this section draws a helpful distinction between approaches to religion and film oriented toward certain religious traditions and those whose academic inquiries into the nature of religion are less tradition bound. In a formal sense, many such projects adopt the same practices and navigate the same pitfalls of the theological method discussed earlier and just as often draw crude correlations between a particular theory of religion and its cinematic manifestation (see a more complete discussion of this distinction in my article "Seeing and Being Seen: Distinctively Filmic and Religious Elements in Film" (*Journal of Religion and Film* 3[2], 1999). However, very important studies are being done in this area as well, and this technique works best when a rich conversation takes place between the "religion side" and the "film side" rather than when the former is directly mapped onto the latter. The chapters here are good examples of the rewarding possibilities of that dialogue.

Richard Carp, in his chapter, "Seeing Is Believing, but Touching's the Truth: Religion, Film, and the Anthropology of the Senses," reports on the use of ethnographic film in the religious studies classroom. This choice of film genre stands in contrast to the prevailing practice of using popular movies. However, the real point of Carp's argument is his emphasis on the *limitations* of ethnographic films. He argues that they are insufficient on their own and in fact can be misused if not properly contextualized within other theoretical frameworks. Carp maintains that the success of visual media in modern Western culture (and the attendant bias that to *see* something is to have obtained its principal truth) makes the use of ethnographic film a difficult option (but one that is also full of promise, if appropriately carried out). Carp's approach puts ethnographic film in the context of (1) "sensorial anthropology," whose advocates contend that "the world disclosed by 'our' senses is not necessarily the one revealed by 'theirs,' " and (2) film theory as it relates to the anthropology of perception. Though film is sorely limited in capturing sensory complexity (and actually perpetuates the emphasis on an especially narrow sense of the visual in modern Western culture), Carp maintains that ethnographic film can nonetheless be used to open students to an understanding of the crucial role of "sensory modalities" and the different worlds those modalities make available for interpretation in the understanding of religion. His description of student exercises both inside and outside the classroom provide clear guideposts for incorporating this approach into the reader's own teaching.

From the start, one of the guiding ideas of this volume was to avoid as much as possible in-depth discussions of particular films, both to ensure an emphasis on the teaching aspects of religion and film and to promote the shelf life, as it were, of these chapters—it would be a shame if pedagogical or theoretical insights are buried in the analysis of a specific film whose relative importance fades or becomes too dated for students to tolerate. Of all of the chapters in the volume, Gregory Grieve's contribution, "There Is No Spoon? Teaching *The Matrix,* Postperennialism, and the Spiritual Logic of Late Capitalism," comes the closest to moving beyond that principle, but I think it is a valuable addition for the following reasons. First, *The Matrix* has sparked more discussion of its religious significance than any other film, with the possible exception of Mel Gibson's *The Passion of the Christ* (though I would put the *Passion* discussions almost entirely in the camp of theological criticism, whereas *The Matrix,* with its famously eclectic references to religion and philosophy, raises issues in the general understanding of religion). In other words, it is likely to remain of interest to teachers and students for some time to come.

Second, Grieve's analysis of the film is among the best I have read, both in making a cogent survey of its many types of interpretation and also in offering a deeply compelling analysis. Third, Grieve uses this extremely popular and what I would call literate movie (in that it self-consciously draws on many religious and philosophical ideas) to construct an argument about a distinctively contemporary form of modern Western religiosity that Grieve calls *postperennialism.* His analysis could serve as a program for sustained investigation of this movie in a classroom setting. *The Matrix* is so rich and inviting that one could spend a good deal of time unpacking it. This would give students a chance to work through its many layers while developing their own interpretation, including what the movie might say about new religious forms in their immediate context.

Finally, in a sense Grieve's argument serves as a counterbalance to several other chapters in this volume that argue for a less discursive, less literary, less cognitive approach to religion and film. *The Matrix,* as Grieve makes clear, would richly reward a genuinely discursive, literary investigation in the classroom, one that weaves together many different theoretical threads (e.g., of postmodernism, perennial philosophy, Marxism, Buddhism, and gnosticism) while entertaining the proposition that the movie as a whole and the response to it describe a distinctively contemporary form of religiosity.

Another contributor to this volume, John Lyden, has also had a significant impact on the field with the publication of his book *Film as Religion: Myths, Morals, and Rituals* (2003). His chapter here, "Teaching *Film as Religion,*" provides important classroom observations that go hand in hand with the thesis of his book. Disgruntled with the loose connections that are often drawn between theology or religious traditions and popular film (especially when these efforts aim to diminish popular culture in comparison to religious tradition), Lyden insists on the need to see popular culture on its own terms. He also maintains that many features of popular culture (in this case, the specific role and power of movies) are analogous to religion. Lyden highlights four categories for thinking about this relationship: myths and literalism, the relation of real to ideal, sacrifice, and liminality and catharsis. He makes a strong case for getting students to see the religious dimensions of the otherwise cultural commonplace of moviegoing, both for the insight it gives them into their own cultural practices and the understanding they gain about religion generally.

Another significant contributor to the field (especially as editor of *Representing Religion in World Cinema* [2003] and *The Religion and Film Reader* [2007]), S. Brent Plate pursues a project similar to Lyden's and finds an integral connection between religion and the cultural activity of moviegoing. Drawing on the theoretical work of Peter Berger and Nelson Goodman, Plate's chapter, "Filmmaking and World Making: Re-Creating Time and Space in Myth and Film," shows how students can discern the world-making activities of both film and religion by comparing the formal structures of each. As Plate puts it, "World making, like filmmaking, is an active intervention into the space and time of the universe. It is the performative drama in which we humans partake when we attempt to make meaning of the spaces, times, and people that make up our lives." Plate provides a possible program for investigating this thesis by taking us through just such an analysis of *Star Wars* and *The Matrix.* Furthermore, he contends that understanding this particular cinematic function leaves students in a better position to engage in criticism both of a movie as a movie and of its cultural values—or to be a better critic of the worlds movies make for us.

This part concludes with my own chapter, "Introducing Theories of Religion through Film: A Sample Syllabus." I walk the reader through a course I teach that uses films to get at major theories of religion while exploring the nature of the medium itself. In brief, the course is designed as an investigation of a guiding question: If film is in some measure a distinctive art form (if there are elements of film that cannot be found in any other art form), does it make possible new types of religious expression and experience? To answer this question, one would need to determine both what religion is and what is distinctive about film, and those investigations represent the bulk of the intellectual work in the class. The details of the syllabus aside, the course I describe represents my conviction that the project of determining what is uniquely possible in film as it relates to religion can be as productive—pedagogically and theoretically—as investigating what film has in common with other arts or with religion itself.

The Values Approach

The "values approach" has to do with organizing the work that is already out there. It involves surveying the literature that many of the works on religion and film take as their starting point. It also examines the proposition that the various articulations of general cultural values necessarily overlap with religious territory. One of the more important and early works taking this approach is Margaret R. Miles's book *Seeing and Believing: Religion and Values in the Movies* (1996), in which Miles functions as a cultural critic with respect to some American blockbuster movies. In short, the values approach represented here argues that the question "How should we live?" is the umbrella inquiry, as it were, that religion and culture generally undertake to answer. I argue that this is ultimately so tenuous a connection to religion that religion need not have a special status in the conversation; why not just call this cultural criticism? And yet, the sources, contours, and challenges of human values have clearly been in the province of all religious traditions, and this approach works best when the associations between cultural products (movies) and religious traditions are carefully considered. Again, the scholarly and pedagogical possibilities of this technique are many, but the chapters presented here are representative of the kind of good work being done with this method, especially when the relationships are organized around central themes—evil versus good, moral agency, and violence versus peacemaking.

I first learned of Irena Makarushka when, as a graduate student, I came across her wonderful book, *Religious Imagination and Language in Emerson and Nietzsche* (1994). Knowing her work would be sharp and insightful, I was delighted to discover she was doing work on religion and film. Makarushka stays true to form with her chapter, "Touching Evil, Touching Good." As with Grieve's chapter, Makarushka analyzes a particular film, *Crash*. However, the nature of her analysis and the pedagogical points she makes can give readers the tools for doing similar work with any number of classroom approaches. Makarushka considers evil and good by investigating racism in *Crash* and its

relationship to alienation, confession, and redemption, drawing on an examination of evil by Paul Ricoeur for its theoretical foundation (a method that
could be used to make connections to many different movies). As Makarushka
points out, a course that proceeds along these lines would introduce students
to "evil as a complex dimension of human experience." The thrust of the
argument with respect to pedagogy is that "Reading films critically increases
the likelihood that students will move beyond either/or, black/white dichotomies toward a more integrated understanding of the problem of evil."

Ellen Ott Marshall's chapter, "Teaching Ethics with Film: A Course on the
Moral Agency of Women," describes a course in feminist ethics that asks what
difference gender makes in our understanding and analysis of moral agency.
This chapter has a thematic link with the chapter by Ortiz, though many of the
differences between them relate to the distinction between a theological and a
values approach. Specifically, Marshall supports her inquiry with the long
philosophical tradition of investigating moral agency (drawing on the likes of
Aristotle, Kant, and Rawls), while arguing that these issues rise to the level of
the expressly religious by way of "human experiences of the sacred." Marshall
skillfully articulates the ways in which films can play an important role in such
a course by giving students common frames of reference in the representation
of human drama and experience. This allows them to claim their own subjective positions with respect to the issues at hand. Her argument is also
noteworthy for its self-awareness with respect to the role teachers play in
representing the authors and the works we teach: "We all have ideologies and
commitments that shape the way we order material for a class, represent a
viewpoint during a lecture, or frame a text or film with secondary material." We
should not overlook, Marshall argues, the analogous elements of filmmaking
and course design, and we should be willing to question the assumptions and
effects of both.

Author of *Media Violence and Christian Ethics* (2007) and coeditor (with
S. Brent Plate) of *The Religion and Film Reader* (2007), Jolyon Mitchell turns his
expert eye on the challenges and rewards of examining genocide in the religious studies classroom. Though this chapter focuses on a single film, *Shooting
Dogs* (2005), and its specific historical context, the 1994 genocide in Rwanda,
Mitchell does a remarkable job of bringing to light the many different lines of
inquiry available when teaching this subject. While the movie concentrates on
genocide (and in this case explicitly considers Christian theological questioning by means of a character who is a priest), Mitchell shows just how textured
a thorough classroom consideration of genocide can be. Teachers and students
can discuss the interplay between history and filmmaking (from history to
story to production to reception), as well as the nature of film itself (e.g., what
are the creative, moral, and theological challenges of representing violence in
film—or of representing peace, for that matter?). Mitchell skillfully commu-
nicates the wealth of pedagogical potential first by examining the themes of
absence, ritual, and presence in *Shooting Dogs* and then by considering the
moral issues (e.g., witnessing, viewing, remembering) of genocide. He maintains that this kind of careful consideration can have a transformational effect

on students: "My contention is that film education, at its best, can assist students in developing a more critical understanding of the difficulties of attempting to depict genocide cinematically, the related religious and theological issues, and the wider problems and values of cinematic brutality. Undertaken in a creative, supportive, and imaginative environment, film education that focuses on understanding films about genocide may even inspire students to consider ways of living that will promote a more peaceful world."

REFERENCES

Cho, Francisca. 1999. "Imagining Nothing and Imagining Otherness in Buddhist Film." In *Imag(in)ing the Other: Filmic Visions of Community,* ed. S. Brent Plate and David Jasper, 169–96. Atlanta: American Academy of Religion.

Deacy, Christopher. 2001. *Screen Christologies: Redemption and the Medium of Film.* Cardiff: University of Wales Press.

Lyden, John. 2003. *Film as Religion: Myths, Morals, and Rituals.* New York: New York University Press.

Makarushka, Irena. 1994. *Religious Imagination and Language in Emerson and Nietzsche.* New York: Palgrave Macmillan.

Martin, Joel W., and Conrad E. Ostwalt Jr., eds. 1995. *Screening the Sacred: Religion, Myth, and Ideology in Popular American Film.* Boulder, Colo.: Westview.

Miles, Margaret. 1996. *Seeing and Believing: Religion and Values in the Movies.* Boston: Beacon.

Mitchell, Jolyon. 2007. *Media Violence and Christian Ethics.* New York: Cambridge University Press.

Plate, S. Brent, ed. 2003. *Representing Religion in World Cinema.* New York: Palgrave Macmillan.

Ramji, Rubina. 2005. "From *Navy Seals* to *The Siege:* Getting to Know the Muslim Terrorist, Hollywood Style." *Journal of Religion and Film* 9(2).

Watkins, Gregory J. 1999. "Seeing and Being Seen: Distinctively Filmic and Religious Elements in Film." *Journal of Religion and Film* 3(2).

Wright, Melanie J. 2006. *Religion and Film: An Introduction.* London: Tauris.

PART I

Establishing Shot

Viewing the Field of Religion and Film

I

What Are We Teaching When We Teach "Religion and Film"?

William L. Blizek and Michele Desmarais

Everyone these days, it seems, is interested in religion and film. But what are they really interested in? The phrase "religion and film" refers to so many different kinds of interests and activities that it is difficult to know what you might find when you encounter something called "religion and film." In this chapter we identify four of the most popular topics in the field of religion and film. We also say something about them as the subject of courses in higher education.

Among authors of books and articles on religion and film, four issues seem to be more popular than any others by, we contend, a wide margin. These are the use of (1) religion to interpret movies, (2) movies to critique religion, (3) movies to promote religion, and (4) movies to expose cultural values. We are not able to say which of these is the most popular. It may be that one will eventually become predominant, but at the moment all four seem to be roughly equal in popularity. We can say, however, that some of these interests are more suitable for certain kinds of institutions of higher education than others.

Using Religion to Interpret Movies

For the most part, movies are stories, and stories (unlike lectures or sermons) are open to interpretation. We regularly interpret stories according to the author's intentions. Sometimes we figure one out by reference only to the text—independently of the author's intentions. At other times we might unravel a text not in and of itself but in its historical context. We frequently hear of Marxist interpretations, psychoanalytic (Freudian) interpretations, or, more recently, feminist interpretations. All of these ways of understanding stories are as applicable to tales on film as they are to those on paper.

To this list of methods of interpreting stories we now add religion. That is, by using religion or religious ideas to make sense of movies we can give new meanings to them—ones that we would not find by any other means. When we interpret a story according to Marxism, the movie becomes an expression of Marxism. When we utilize a feminist perspective, the movie becomes an expression of feminist thinking. Similarly, when we analyze a movie from a religious perspective, it becomes an expression of that religion or of some part of it.

For those whose interest is in using religion to explore movies, the kind of movie that best serves this purpose is a typical Hollywood film. What looks like the usual secular movie is given new meaning when religion serves as the method of interpretation. When a film is seen as a religious picture, then religion does not give new meaning to the movie; rather, religion is the film's primary meaning. Those who use religion to understand film are interested in discovering a meaning that is not the movie's primary or obvious message.

Miloš Foreman's *One Flew over the Cuckoo's Nest* (1975) is a good example of a movie that is given new meaning by the application of religion (McEver 1998).[1] One conventional interpretation is that it demonstrates the appalling state of mental health care in the United States in the late fifties and early sixties. Another generally accepted reading is that it shows us how we *should* and *should not* treat human beings. The evil Nurse Ratched represents the controlling of other people "for their own good," while R. P. McMurphy treats others with respect by allowing them to make their own decisions.

However, some viewers have noticed that McMurphy shares important characteristics with Jesus. McMurphy is betrayed by Billy Bibbit: Billy falsely tells Nurse Ratched that McMurphy made him have sex with "that woman." Billy, like Judas, then commits suicide, although he does so by slitting his wrists rather than by hanging himself. McMurphy is then crucified: In this case he is given a frontal lobotomy, which destroys his personality. Nonetheless, McMurphy rises from the dead, as Big Chief takes McMurphy with him to Canada. Big Chief's courage, provided by McMurphy's spirit, brings with it a kind of salvation as Big Chief escapes the asylum.

By applying the Christian story of Jesus to *One Flew over the Cuckoo's Nest*, we come to see the meaning of the movie as the significance of the Christian story—someone dies for our sins and in doing so offers us salvation. Clearly the movie and the Christian stories are not exactly the same, but they are sufficiently parallel for us to see that the movie's point is the Christian message of Jesus dying for our sins, arising from the dead, and making salvation possible.

Another movie that has been given new meaning by applying religion is Oliver Stone's *Platoon* (1986). One conventional interpretation sees the movie as just one more story about the horrors of war. Another describes it as an antiwar film, and a third sees the movie as depicting the battle between good and evil, in which the evil we struggle against is present in us all.

However, Avent Childress Beck (1995, 44–54) applies the entire Christian story—from the two creation stories in Genesis all the way to the Apocalypse—to Stone's movie. In early Genesis we find a condition of chaos and formlessness from which the world is created. Early in *Platoon* we find a similar chaos and confusion from which the elements of the story emerge. In Revelation we find the risen Christ doing battle with the Beast. In the movie we find Chris (the Christ figure) doing battle with Barnes (the Beast, who is evil incarnate). In between, other elements of the movie parallel portions of the Christian story, including the death and resurrection of Jesus. At the end of Revelation Christ ascends into heaven, and the Kingdom of God is upon us. In the movie, Chris ascends symbolically in the medevac helicopter—and the Kingdom of God is upon us.

Platoon retells a much larger Christian story than that in *One Flew over the Cuckoo's Nest*. Applying religion brings new meaning to what might otherwise be seen merely as a war (or an antiwar) tale or as another story about the battle between good and evil. Beck (1995) goes so far as to claim that, although we find the war disturbing, in watching the movie "we are treated to balms of religious myth"; in the case of *Platoon,* these "balms" are the ordered familiarities and emotive comfort of the Christian narrative.

Probably the most popular movie to date to be given religious interpretation is *The Matrix* (1999), written and directed by the Wachowski brothers, Andy and Larry. *The Matrix* generated so much religious interpretation so quickly that it may sound odd to talk about conventional interpretations. However, one might see *The Matrix* as nothing more than a good sci-fi movie or another motion picture about the battle between good and evil.

The Matrix, however, obviously calls for religious interpretation. First, Frances Flannery-Dailey and Rachel Wagner (2001, ¶ 4) claim that the main character, Thomas Anderson, "is overtly constructed as a Jesus figure." Called "Neo," Anderson is "the One." Although he is killed, he comes back to life. It is prophesied that Neo will return to the matrix. Moreover, it is Anderson who battles the representatives of evil and brings about the possibility of salvation. *The Matrix* has all the earmarks of another Jesus story.

However, Flannery-Dailey and Wagner introduce us to elements that make us see the movie more in terms of gnostic Christianity than orthodox Christianity. In gnosticism, there is one supreme God but also a second, malformed deity who breathes the divine spark into human beings. The result is that the divine spirit is trapped in a material body. Fortunately, salvation comes in the form of *gnosis,* or knowledge imparted by a redeemer.

Artificial Intelligence (AI) has created a computer simulation program that enslaves humanity by providing it with an illusory perception of reality called "the matrix." Obviously AI is the malformed deity, and it has trapped humanity in the matrix. However, Neo escapes the matrix, discovers that it is not real, and returns with this knowledge to set others free or provide salvation.

Whichever version of Christianity might be more applicable to the movie, *The Matrix* can also be given a Buddhist interpretation. Buddhism teaches that human suffering is the result of our ignorance and desire, which trap us in a cycle of birth, death, and rebirth in the world (the matrix). Escape from this cycle is possible through enlightenment, which is the discovery of another plane of existence without desire and suffering. Neo achieves enlightenment and returns to the material world to make enlightenment available to those trapped in the world of desire and suffering. It is not difficult to see how *The Matrix* might be considered an expression of Buddhism (Fielding 2003).

Finally, and in a somewhat different direction, consider *The Mexican* (2001), directed by Gore Verbinski and starring Brad Pitt and Julia Roberts (Matalon 2001). *The Mexican* can be viewed as a mystery/thriller or as a love story. However, according to Guy Matalon, the story of *The Mexican* parallels the book of Esther. The Hebrew Bible presents two different explanations of the relationship between God and human events. In one view, God is in complete control of all events and intervenes directly in human affairs, an intervention that God reveals. In the other view, God is also in control of human affairs and intervenes in them, but God's handiwork is not revealed to humans. Human beings have a sense that God is at work in the world but do not have any direct evidence of what God is doing.

Matalon claims that the book of Esther expresses the second view, in which God's intervention is not revealed. Haman punishes Mordechai and all of the Jewish residents of the Persian Empire. However, in the end, Haman himself is punished, and the decree to punish the Jews is repealed. No mention is made of God's bringing about this change, but it is clear that this could not have happened by accident—it must have been God's handiwork.

In *The Mexican*, the main character, Jerry Welbach, is asked to retrieve an expensive pistol known as "the Mexican"; if he fails, he will die. In Jerry's pursuit of the Mexican, one seemingly random event after another occurs, and these are what make the story interesting. In the end, however, all of these incidents, while seeming to be random, result in the outcome desired by Margolis, the mob boss. Margolis wants to return the gun to its rightful owner, who hopes to free the soul entrapped in the weapon so that it can return to the angels. At the end of the movie we learn that the seemingly accidental events have served a greater purpose, but the characters in the film are never shown the hand of God at work. No mention is made of God's bringing about the outcome, but it is clear, at least to the viewer, that it could not be the product of chance—it must have been God's handiwork.

These four examples depict people who have tried to give new meaning to a movie by using religion as an interpretive mechanism. The first two use Christian stories to show that the movies provide parallel tales. This is also true for the Christian interpretation of *The Matrix*. The second two examples show a parallel between the movie's perspective and that of a particular religion—at least this is true when we apply Buddhism to *The Matrix*.

Let us consider two important questions that relate to the use of religion to interpret movies. First, how closely must a movie follow a religious story or perspective before we can say that it warrants a religious interpretation? There is no precise answer to this question. This is not, after all, a case of matching fingerprints. The answer will differ for different people with different interests.

For some, finding that a character in the movie dies and comes back to life might be sufficient to claim that this is the story of Jesus. Others may require more similarities, and others may insist on a great many correspondences.

All of this depends to some extent on an individual's interests. If someone wants to claim, for example, that a secular movie was retelling a Christian story, then a few parallels might suffice. Others, however, may require many similarities. If only a few likenesses are required, then some people may not find the interpretation at all interesting. If a careful comparison shows many connections, then some people may believe this investigation is worth following.

The second question has to do with whether finding parallels between movies and religious stories or ideas fully captures the idea of using religion to interpret movies. Since the entire field of religion and film is just in its infancy, we might expect a much more thorough consideration of the nature of "using religion to interpret the movies" to yield a variety of other activities that fall under this rubric. Furthermore, we might find that movies express religious ideas in a wide variety of ways, even though all of these would be considered storytelling. These descriptions constitute a starting point in the process of discovering how religion can be used to interpret film.

Using Movies to Critique Religion

The flip side of applying religion to movies is, of course, applying movies to religion. We may ask not only what religion can tell us about movies but also what movies can tell us about religion. In this case, however, we are following in a long tradition that considers the social purposes of art. One of the expectations we have of the arts is that they will comment on or provide a critique of society or culture. Since religion is a part of culture, we can expect the arts in general and movies in particular to offer a critique of religion as well as they would any other aspect of culture.

That movies comment on religion seems obvious. Many movies—from Antonia Bird's *Priest* (1994) to Mel Gibson's *Passion of the Christ* (2004), from Martin Scorsese's *Last Temptation of Christ* (1988) to Leo McCarey's *Going My Way* (1944) and Norman Jewison's *Agnes of God* (1985)—have given us a wide variety of commentary on religions.[2] Interestingly, however, using movies to critique religion seems to be of much greater interest to filmmakers than to religious studies scholars, who appear much more interested in using religion to interpret movies than they do in using movies to critique religion. Perhaps they believe that critiquing religion through textual analysis, argument, or theory is more appropriate to their task even if the movies mentioned earlier belie the exclusivity of argument, theory, and textual analysis.

Bear in mind that a critique of religion is not necessarily critical or negative. To critique a religion is to analyze it and comment on both its contributions to culture and the problems it may create within a culture. One message of Antonia Bird's *Priest* is that the doctrine of the sanctity of the confessional can generate great harm for individual human beings. However, one point of Bruce Beresford's *Tender Mercies* (1983) is that religion can play an important role in turning one's life around.[3] One implication of *Going My Way* is that the formal hierarchical church often fails to deal effectively with the real problems that human beings face, and one underlying idea of *Agnes of God* is that science can take us only so far in understanding the mysteries of the universe.

Additionally, movies that critique religion are generally those that we would call religious movies. Generally speaking, they would not be considered secular movies. It would be possible, of course, to see George Lucas's *Star Wars* (1977) or Robert Zemeckis's *Contact* as secular films, but part of their story is a critique of religion.[4]

As examples of movies that critique religion, let us begin with four that span a period of fifty years and yet have a similar critique of the Roman Catholic Church. In *Going My Way*, the official church (hierarchical, rule governed, image conscious) is represented by Father Fitzgibbon. The church is failing financially, seems disconnected from the lives of its parishioners, and has little impact on the community around it. Enter Father O'Malley (played by Bing Crosby). Father O'Malley represents the community of believers, as opposed to the hierarchical structure of the official church. O'Malley dresses casually, enjoys sports, and does not seem to take the rules seriously. He connects with the parishioners, effects changes in the lives of people in the neighborhood, saves the church from financial disaster, and even brings Father Fitzgibbon's mother, whom Fitzgibbon has not seen in twenty years, over from the old country. The message of this movie is clearly that what is important in God's eyes is not the church's official structure, its rules, or its image but rather what the church does for others—how it helps others live better lives.

In Roland Joffe's *The Mission* (1986), the community of believers is represented by a number of missionaries in South America, and the official church is represented by the bishop.[5] The missionaries' concern is with the salvation and the well-being of the Indian tribes that participate in the missions. The bishop's concern, however, is with the political situation in Europe: How can the church best get along with the government of Spain? In the 1750 Treaty of Madrid, Spain cedes part of South America to Portugal, including the seven Jesuit missions and the Indians they serve. The official church agrees to the treaty in order to protect itself in Spain even though it knows the Portuguese will destroy the missions and enslave the Indians. The official church thereby abandons both the Indians and its own missionaries for political gain. The message of this movie is that what is important in God's eyes is what the church does for others— in this case how it protects the Indians from slavery and death.

In John Duigan's *Romero* (1989), a Salvadoran priest, Oscar Romero, represents both the official church and its community of believers.[6] As the movie begins, Romero carries out his religious work in a formal way, following the rules and being obedient to those in authority. He is a moderate who will not rock the boat. Because he is a safe choice, he is named archbishop. As the military dictatorship of El Salvador becomes more repressive, however, Romero's conscience forces him to take a stand against the insurgents' brutal suppression. He is transformed from an unassuming, compliant priest (official church) to the conscience of a nation (community of believers). The message of the movie is clearly that the official church collaborated in the brutal suppression of the Salvadoran rebels by failing to speak out against the government and its policies and practices. The community of believers, represented by Archbishop Romero, does God's will by standing up to the dictatorship. (The actual Archbishop Oscar Romero was assassinated in March of 1980 while saying mass.)

Finally, in Antonia Bird's 1994 movie, *Priest,* Father Matthew symbolizes the community of believers, and Father Greg (along with the bishop) stands for the official church. The irony of this is that Father Greg fails to save a young girl from sexual assault because he believes that he must maintain the sanctity of the confessional (official church), and he continues a homosexual relationship with a man he has met in a bar (contrary to the official church policy). Because Father Greg and Father Matthew celebrate communion together at the end, the message of the movie is that the community of believers is more important than the official church. The bishop and even some of the parishioners leave the service, but the young girl Father Greg could not save stands before him to take communion as the sound track plays "You'll Never Walk Alone."

All four of these movies can be seen as criticizing the official church in various ways and promoting the importance of the community of believers over church doctrine, hierarchy, and image. One might be tempted to say that they represent a protestant critique of the Roman Catholic Church, but *Romero* is a product of Paulist Pictures, and Father Daniel Berrigan served as an advisor to the director in the making of *The Mission.* So, while the analysis may be protestant in nature, it is also a critique brought to bear by Roman Catholics.

A different kind of critique comes into play in Bae Yong-Kyun's 1989 movie, *Why Has Bodhi-Dharma Left for the East?*[7] The most unusual feature of this 135-minute film is that dialogue occurs in only six or seven scenes, and even then it is sparse.

When our students watch this film, it does not take long for them to become restless. We assume that they are thinking, "Okay, what's the plot?" or "When will the action start?" or "What the hell is this?" Watching *Bodhi-Dharma* is not their usual movie-viewing experience. However, they will not get up and walk out of the classroom—it is an assigned movie, after all. They want more information, more action, and more plot, and they want it now, but they do not get what they want. The movie is not for entertainment. Rather, its purpose is to expose the students to an element of Zen Buddhism with which they are not familiar: living in the present or in the moment. The movie might be called a visual explanation of this important idea in Zen Buddhism.

We assume that after only about fifteen or twenty minutes our students' minds begin to wander. They start thinking about things that have happened or may happen in the future. They are now living outside of the moment—in the future or the past. They are not living in the present. What the movie provides, then, is an experience that is the opposite of what is an important element of Zen Buddhism. By showing the opposite (or giving the students the experience of the opposite), the movie points to this significant component of Zen Buddhism—living in the present. As a result, students may not immediately learn to live in the present, but they begin to recognize that they are living in either the past or the future (and therefore not the present), and they may at least wonder what it would be like to live in the now. We take this to be a positive critique because the movie, by its very nature, explains one of Zen Buddhism's valuable concepts in an experiential way.

Another movie that provides a critique of religion is Robert Duvall's *The Apostle* (1997).[8] Duvall wrote, directed, starred in, and bankrolled *The Apostle,* thereby giving it a very personal touch. Duvall wanted to give an accurate representation of a particular kind of evangelical Christianity with which he was familiar. He believed that earlier movies dealing with evangelical Christianity (such as Richard Pearce's *Leap of Faith* [1992][9] and Richard Brooks's *Elmer Gantry* [1960][10]) had portrayed evangelical Christianity in a stereotypic and an unflattering manner (these movies would be considered criticisms of evangelical Christianity). However, Duvall did not want to do the opposite and simply show evangelical Christianity in a positive light.

Duvall thus selected Sonny (or the Apostle E. F., as Sonny came to be known) as the character to critique this version of Christianity. Using Sonny, Duvall shows both positive and negative aspects, both the potentials and the dangers of evangelical Christianity. On the positive side, evangelical Christianity reaches out to those in need and offers people an opportunity to turn their lives around. On the negative side, it can be used to manipulate people for an evangelist's personal benefit. After having to leave his old church, Sonny establishes a new one. In doing so he is transformed from a manipulator into a man who cares for others and uses his religion to both sustain himself and enrich the lives of others.

These films provide a variety of critiques of particular religions. The four that are critical of the Roman Catholic Church all comment on what they see as its negative aspects. *Bodhi-Dharma* shows us (and even allows us to experience in a sense) a positive element of Zen Buddhism. Finally, Robert Duvall comments on evangelical Christianity by demonstrating how it can help people and how it can be used (or misused) for the benefit of the evangelist.

Religion Uses the Movies

One of the most popular interests in religion and film is the use of movies to encourage people to be better practitioners of their particular faith. We believe that aspect is better described as an interest rather than a methodology because it includes many different techniques. Indeed, if one's goal is to change people's lives, then whatever works counts as using movies to promote better religious practice. This means that even if the connection with a particular film is tenuous, that movie may nevertheless inspire better religious practice. Because the basic interest here is in how people live and how one can affect their behavior, an element of subjectivity is at work that is not present in the methodologies discussed earlier. The interpretation of *Platoon,* for example, requires one to identify a number of elements in the movie and relate them to aspects of the Christian story. Or, in discerning the message of *Priest,* one will have to specify certain elements of the movie so that others can also understand its message. On the other hand, if something in a movie influences one to be a better person of faith, then nothing else is required—no one else has to see the same thing.

When people use movies to encourage faith, the movies may be secular or religious. We have chosen two secular films and one religious movie for consideration. Moreover, we have selected a secular movie that promotes faith in two quite different ways. We hope that these samples will give the reader an indication of what is at work when movies are used for this objective, but we realize that many different examples are also available.

In his book, *Faith and Film,* Bryan Stone takes the Apostle's Creed as an organizing principle for his consideration of movies (Stone 2000, 22). The first words of the creed are "I believe," and Stone asserts that the 1997 Robert Zemeckis movie, *Contact,* is a movie about belief. *Contact* is the story of a zealous radio astronomer, Ellie Arroway (played by Jody Foster), who is searching for intelligent life elsewhere in the universe. Arroway does not believe in God because she is convinced that no empirical evidence of God exists. Because of her conviction, she is not allowed to travel into outer space even though she is the first to discover evidence of intelligent life there. Circumstances change, however, and Arroway is given the opportunity to travel into outer space, where she makes *contact* with intelligent life. However, when she returns to earth she can produce no objective evidence to support her claim. She is now the believer, but her belief is not based on evidence that she can share with others.

How does Stone use the movie to promote religion? He first raises questions about faith and belief and then offers his own understanding of what they should mean to the practice of Christianity. He contends that "faith is always a combination of believing and acting—together" (Stone 2000). Faith means not only holding particular beliefs but also having a loyalty to God that requires us to live in a Christian manner. Once we understand that "I believe," the first words of the Apostle's Creed, really means that we are committed to both holding particular ideas *and* living life in a particular way, we will become better Christians.

However, how are Stone's views of belief and faith connected to *Contact* since they are not the opinions expressed in the movie? Stone might explain the relationship between the movie and being a better Christian in the following way: "If I can get people to watch this movie [Stone admits that this is not a religious movie], then they will begin to think about faith and belief, and when they do, I can introduce my own ideas about faith and belief, which will help people better practice their religion." Movies get us thinking about particular ideas, and when we begin to consider these ideas in particular ways, we can live our lives as better Christians.

In her book, *Finding Meaning at the Movies,* Sara Anson Vaux (1999) claims that *Contact* is interesting because it does not ask three important questions: Is there life after death? Is scientific exploration ethical? What kind of God is implied in the question "Do you believe in God?" Vaux goes on to answer these questions: Whether there is life after death can be answered only by both science and religion. The money we spend on space exploration could be better spent on fighting hunger and poverty here on earth. The kind of God we are interested in is not a God of power but "a God who prizes gentleness and innocence, who welcomes the shamed" (81).

Again, the connection between the movie and living life as a practicing Christian is an odd one. Clearly, Vaux believes that if we accept her answers to the questions she has posed, we will be better Christians. However, these are not the answers the movie gives; indeed, the movie, Vaux notes, does not even ask these questions. The exhortation to be a better Christian (whatever this means to Stone and Vaux) might not be found in the movie, but it is "inspired," "suggested," or "provoked" by it. Movies stimulate us to think about things, and if we consider those things in the ways that Stone and Vaux suggest, we will become better Christians.

Bryan Stone also applies his principle, the Apostle's Creed (specifically, the issue of "I believe in . . . the forgiveness of sins") to another secular movie, Tim Robbin's *Dead Man Walking* (1995).[11] In the movie Stone identifies two different quests in relation to forgiveness. The first is the desire to be forgiven. The second is the need to forgive. In *Dead Man Walking*, the first quest is that of Matthew Poncelet, a racist, white inmate on death row who has been convicted of the murder of a teenage boy and the brutal rape and murder of the boy's girlfriend. The second quest is that of the parents of the murdered children—forgiving the unforgivable. Sister Helen Prejean (played by Susan Sarandon) provides an example of forgiving to the parents, and in forgiving Matthew Poncelet she provides him with an opportunity to seek forgiveness.

Given these elements, Stone then describes what the New Testament says is expected of us with regard to forgiveness. He claims that a core Christian belief is that there is a "two-way relationship between offering forgiveness and experiencing forgiveness" (2000, 172). Christians must forgive because they themselves have been forgiven. Forgiveness is not dependent upon other factors such as justice or benefits to society. But those who do not forgive will not be themselves forgiven, which is an element of forgiveness that is frequently ignored. Stone goes on to say that, since the accurate idea of forgiveness as found in the New Testament is a harsh one and can be costly to the forgiver, some people cheapen the idea by trying to make it more palatable.

Since it would be difficult to say that Stone's complex views on forgiveness are the same as those that make up the message of the movie, we can again say only that the movie provides an opportunity for discussing ideas of forgiveness and that, through that discussion, we can arrive at an accurate Christian view of forgiveness. This, then, enables us to be better Christians.

Our final example of the use of religion to encourage faith is Mel Gibson's *The Passion of the Christ*. There is a significant difference between Gibson's reason for making the movie and the uses to which it was purportedly put in the marketing campaign that surrounded its release. For Mel Gibson, life was not going well at the time, even though he was experiencing great acting, directing, and financial success. When Gibson returned to reading Scripture, he focused upon the suffering of Jesus. If Jesus could suffer this much for him, then surely he could live a better life. The suffering of Jesus made such an impression on Gibson that he indeed turned his life around.

The reason for making the movie, then, was for Gibson to share with others his experience of contemplating the suffering of Jesus. He would share it with others through the medium he knew best: film. He believed that when others were also confronted with Jesus's suffering, they would want to be better Christians as well. This is clearly a case of making a movie with the intention of affecting the lives of the audience and encouraging them to become more heartfelt Christians.

Gibson may also have imagined the movie as a tool for evangelism in that it might inspire people to convert to Christianity. However, the push for evangelism by others seems to have come after the controversy over the film's accuracy and anti-Semitism. Many people believed that the movie needed to be defended against criticism, and, as is often the case in American culture, the best defense is success—financial success. So, as part of the marketing campaign for the movie, people were told to take a friend to see the film so that the friend might be converted to Christianity. This evangelical ploy differs from Gibson's interest in sharing his experience with others, but both uses encourage religious practice, whether that means improving one's faith and practice or taking up the practice to begin with.

One interesting feature of using movies to encourage religious practice is that different people can use movies in a number of ways to encourage a variety of practices. Again, this interest in religion and film introduces a kind of subjectivity not to be found elsewhere.

The preceding examples provide a very limited account of how movies can be used to promote religion, but they are not exhaustive. Nevertheless, we hope that they will help the reader to recognize other ways of using movies to endorse religion and to distinguish between the use of film to promote and critique religion and the use of religion to interpret movies.[12]

Using Movies to Expose Cultural Values

The fourth popular link between religion and film is what we call the cultural values connection. In *Screening the Sacred*, Joel Martin and Conrad Ostwalt (1995) devote a third of their book to what they call ideological criticism. For Martin and Ostwalt, movies present an ideology—a point of view on some element of our experience. This perspective may not be readily recognizable in the movie, but it may exert considerable influence on the audience. The purpose of studying movies, then, is to expose the hidden beliefs of movies, especially those that concern the status of women, race, sexual identity, and possibly social issues such as global warming, immigration, and poverty.

We have no problem with people's efforts to uncover or expose the ideologies or biases of movies. Moreover, we believe that movies influence the ways in which people think and behave. Indeed, they can have a very powerful effect on their audiences even if we do not believe that movies should be censored in a free society. However, it is productive to examine the relationship between exposing cultural values and religion. In what way would uncovering cultural values in films constitute a connection between religion and film?

The answer lies in the fact that most religions espouse some values and discourage others. Sometimes the principles of a religion are compatible with the popular values of a culture, and sometimes they are seriously at odds with them. When religious and popular cultural values conflict, it is important for religions to reveal those popular standards in movies, especially because they may influence people without their recognizing it. By exposing differing values in movies, religions promote their own ideals and encourage people to live their lives in accordance with them.

Since the very early days of film, religion and movies have had an uneasy relationship when it comes to promoting particular values or actions. From 1934 to the late 1960s the Catholic Church's Legion of Decency controlled the content of films and determined the degree of sex or violence allowed in movies by rating them. When the Legion decided that a movie was unacceptable, it gave the film a rating of "C," for "condemned." Consequently, all Catholics were forbidden from seeing such movies, and the loss of this audience frequently meant that a movie fared poorly at the box office. This financial leverage gave the church considerable influence over the content of movies.

The movie industry now monitors itself through the Motion Picture Association of America (MPAA), which is not a religious organization but plays a role similar to that of the Legion of Decency. The MPAA's rating system uses letters and numbers to indicate what material will be found in a particular movie, thus providing potential viewers with information about the content of films.

Various other groups (some political and others religious) also speak out about the content of movies. Many religious organizations attack something called "Hollywood values." Sex, drugs, and violence, for instance, are often identified as contrary to these groups' basic values. When these associations claim to speak for all Americans, they mean that the elements of certain movies are contrary to American values.

However, in the religious studies literature, most of the writing is not about sex, drugs, and violence but rather about race, ethnicity, gender, and sexual identity and, in some cases, immigration, poverty, global warming, or the effects of globalization. This demonstrates that various religious communities have diverse cultural, social, or moral values. Because they have a strong interest in promoting certain principles and discouraging others, it is understandable that they pay special attention to those that films endorse.

In some sense, this may be an instance of religion using the movies. In this case religion exposes values espoused by the movies that are contrary to those of a given religion or religious group. In doing so, religion is attempting to discourage particular values and advocate others. The difference here is between religion using the movies to *encourage better spiritual practice* on the part of believers and religion using movies to *expose cultural values* so that everyone conforms more to the religious communities' values.

One example of a movie that exposes cultural values is *Thelma and Louise* (1991; directed by Ridley Scott).[13] In this film two women start out on a vacation and end up on a remarkable adventure. Moving from vacation to adventure is the result of Thelma's beating and attempted rape in the parking lot of a bar where the women have stopped for a drink. Louise shoots and kills Thelma's attacker, and now the women find themselves on the run. The various twists and turns seem to be the result of men behaving badly toward women, and the impression we form is of a society in which women are treated much worse than men.

The movie ends with Thelma and Louise driving their car into the Grand Canyon. The message seems to be that it is better to die than to return to a world where one will always be dealt with like a woman. Undoubtedly, the ending is strong stuff, and it makes sense only if one has seen for oneself the variety of ways in which women are treated poorly in our culture. Depicting the ways in which this takes place exposes the gender bias in our society. Religious groups that support equal treatment for men and women can use the movie to show how we ought not to behave.

Another example is Brian Gilbert's *Not without My Daughter* (1991).[14] In this movie the main character, Betty Mahmoody, marries an Iranian doctor, with whom she has a child, Mahtob. Things do not go well for the doctor in the United States, so he tells Betty that they will go and visit his family in Iran. When they get there, the doctor decides to stay permanently and will not let his daughter return with Betty to the States. Betty Mahmoody has essentially been kidnapped. All of the doctor's family support the husband's decision and work to prevent Betty and Mahtob from leaving the country. Nevertheless, Betty finally escapes Iran with Mahtob, and at the end of the tale she arrives at the U.S. embassy in a different (unspecified) country, where the American flag serves as the background for the scene.

For those who wish to use movies to expose cultural values, this is not a story about a woman who is tricked into leaving her own country but is about one who escapes to freedom. This is a film about good Americans and bad Iranians, bad Arabs, bad Muslims, or even bad Middle Easterners. The movie allows the viewer to choose whom to see as the bad guys, who are, of course, despicable; their behavior is backward, antifreedom, and anti-American. Betty cannot escape without the help of some Iranians, but their number is so small compared to the bad Iranians that their description has little impact on the viewer's conception of Iranians in general (e.g., Muslims, Arabs). In fact, even one of the Iranians who is helping Betty to escape tries to molest her on the trip.

This is in essence a propaganda film in which Americans are shown to be wonderful people and Iranians are portrayed as barbaric and inhumane. The problem here (i.e., the reason such values need to be exposed) is that most Americans get their information about the Middle East from television and movies, and these sources make it appear that all Middle Easterners are horrible human beings at best and, at worst, not human beings at all. (This can be understood as a counterexample to Al Jezzera television, which regularly shows Americans as contemptible people. Al Jezzera is many Muslims' only source of information about the United States.)

Since some religious communities want everyone to see others as human beings, these groups aim to expose movies that show others as evil and less than human. (These same groups may also wish to show that not all Americans are good. Consider the torture of enemy combatants by the U.S. military.)

For those who wish to use movies to reveal cultural ideals, the task is most frequently to uncover values that the viewer may not be aware of when watching a movie. (The audience may see a particular story as a thriller or a tale of intrigue without recognizing the other principles the movie is espousing.) Furthermore, such disclosure is necessary because these values are contrary to those of particular religious groups.

In some sense, the use of movies to both expose cultural values and promote religious practice has an ethical connection. In both cases, those who use movies want others to behave differently or to act rightly (as determined by the religious community). In the first instance, the religious community speaks to its own members through movies (although they also may seek converts through this process). In the second case, the group speaks to the entire world, exposing undesirable cultural values and encouraging everyone to reject them.

Religion, Film, and Higher Education

We have identified four of the most popular interests in the relationship between religion and film. Given the extensive and growing attention to this field, many colleges and universities have added courses on the topic to the curriculum, and many more are likely to be included in the near future.

So, we return to the title of this chapter: What are we teaching when we teach religion and film? The answer is, of course, that different scholars are teaching a variety of things. Some are teaching students to interpret movies using religion or religious ideas, and others are helping them to find in movies a critique of religion. Still others are assisting students to become better practitioners of their religious faith, while others are facilitating their discovery of the cultural values that movies express. These principles may not be obvious at first glance, but they may have a significant impact upon how movie audiences go about living their lives.

We would like to draw a distinction between the academic and the religious study of religion and film. Roughly speaking, teaching students to interpret film using religion and religious ideas and helping them to better understand religions through their critique of films constitute the academic study of this subject. Using movies to promote religious practice or faith is the religious study of this field. Moreover, using movies to expose cultural values can be considered either the academic or the religious study of religion and film. This last method falls more fittingly into one category or the other depending upon the extent to which the study is tied to the practice of particular religious communities. One can expose cultural values without any reference to religion at all, as we mentioned earlier, in which case uncovering them in movies seems more of an academic study. However, one can disclose cultural values as part of one's religious practice or religious obligation, and doing so would more appropriately be considered the religious study of religion and film.

There are, of course, many different kinds of colleges and universities throughout the United States, Canada, and Europe. Some are public colleges and universities funded by tax dollars. Such institutions should maintain a careful separation between the study and the practice of religion. For them, the religious study of religion and film seems inappropriate because it is more like religious *practice* than *study*. (We personally encourage the study of religion on the campuses of public colleges and universities.) For private or religious colleges and universities (and seminaries), any of the four popular interests seem fitting. Students who attend these schools expect that religious practice will be a part of their educational experience. Therefore, since tax dollars do not fund these institutions, we believe that teaching religion and film as either an academic or a religious enterprise would not be problematic.

NOTES

1. Starring Jack Nicholson, Louise Fletcher, and William Redfield and directed by Miloš Forman, *One Flew over the Cuckoo's Nest* is based on Ken Kesey's 1975 novel with the same name. It won Academy Awards for best picture, best actor (Jack Nicholson), best actress (Louise Fletcher), best director (Forman), and best screenplay adapted from other material (Lawrence Hauber and Bo Goldman).

2. Directed by Antonia Bird, *Priest* stars Linus Roache, Tom Wilkinson, Robert Carlyle, and Cathy Tyson. Mel Gibson directed *The Passion of the Christ*, starring James Caviezel and Maia Morgenstern, and Martin Scorsese directed *The Last Temptation of Christ*, starring Willem Dafoe, Harvey Keitel, and Barbara Hershey. *Going My Way*, directed by Leo McCarey and starring Bing Crosby and Barry Fitzgerald, won Academy Awards for best picture, best actor in a leading role (Crosby), best actor in a supporting role (Fitzgerald), best director, best music, original song, best writing, original story (McCarey), best writing, and screenplay (Frank Butler and Frank Cavett). Directed by Norman Jewison, *Agnes of God* stars Jane Fonda, Anne Bancroft, and Meg Tilly. *Latter Days* was directed by C. Jay Cox and stars Steve Sandvoss, Wes Ramsey, and Jacqueline Bissett.

3. *Tender Mercies* stars Robert Duvall, Tess Harper, Betty Buckley, and Wilford Brimley. Directed by Bruce Beresford, it won Academy Awards for best actor (Duvall) and best original screenplay (Horton Foote).

4. George Lucas directed *Star Wars*, which stars Mark Hamill, Harrison Ford, Carrie Fisher, and Alex Guinness. *Contact* was directed by Robert Zemeckis and stars

Jodie Foster, Matthew McConaughy, Tom Skerritt, Angela Bassett, James Woods, and John Hurt.

5. *The Mission* was directed by Roland Joffee and stars Robert DeNiro and Jeremy Irons.

6. *Romero* stars Raul Julia and was directed by John Duigan.

7. *Why Has Bodhi-Dharma Left for the East?* was directed by Bae Yong-Kyun.

8. Robert Duvall directed and stars in *The Apostle*. Others starring are Farrah Fawcett, Miranda Richardson, and John Beasley.

9. *Leap of Faith* stars Steve Martin and Debra Winger. It was directed by Richard Pearce.

10. Directed by Richard Brooks, *Elmer Gantry* stars Burt Lancaster and Jean Simmons. It was based on Sinclair Lewis's 1960 novel by the same name.

11. Based on the 1995 book with the same name by Sister Helen Prejean, CSJ, *Dead Man Walking* stars Susan Sarandon and Sean Penn. It was directed by Tim Robbins.

12. Films also provide a religious community in diaspora with a way to communicate and reaffirm shared beliefs and values. The immensely popular masala (Bollywood) films, whose primary purpose is entertainment, nevertheless fulfill this role for many nonresident Indians. Themes in these movies often reaffirm beliefs such as karma and cultural practices such as arranged marriage (or at least the importance of parental blessings on a love match). Characters tend to conform to the standards of beauty or heroism enunciated in the *Natya Shastra*, a treatise on classical Indian drama. In all, the films provide, as Suketu Mehta observes, "the cheapest round-trip ticket home" and give parents a chance to expose their children to "Indian values" (2004, 351).

13. *Thelma and Louise* stars Susan Sarandon, Geena Davis, Harvey Keitel, Michael Madsen, Christopher McDonald, and Brad Pitt.

14. Sally Field and Alfred Molina star in *Not without My Daughter*.

REFERENCES

Beck, Avent Childress. 1995. The Christian Allegorical Structure of *Platoon*. In *Screening the Sacred: Religion, Myth, and Ideology in Popular American Film*, ed. J. W. Martin and C. E. Ostwalt Jr., 44–54. Boulder, Colo.: Westview.

Fielding, Julien. 2003. "Reassessing *The Matrix/Reloaded.*" *Journal of Religion and Film* 7(2). Omaha: University of Nebraska–Omaha. http://www.unomaha.edu/jrf/Vol7No2/matrix.matrixreloaded.htm (accessed November 19, 2007).

Flannery-Dailey, Frances, and Rachel Wagner. 2001. "Wake Up! Gnosticism and Buddhism in *The Matrix*." *Journal of Religion and Film* 5(2). Omaha: University of Nebraska–Omaha. http://www.unomaha.edu/jrf/gnostic.htm (accessed November 19, 2007).

Martin, Joel W., and Conrad E. Ostwalt Jr., eds. 1995. *Screening the Sacred: Religion, Myth, and Ideology in Popular American Film*. Boulder, Colo.: Westview.

Matalon, Guy. 2001. "Esther and *The Mexican*." *Journal of Religion and Film* 5(1). Omaha: University of Nebraska–Omaha. http://www.unomaha.edu/jrf/esther.htm (accessed November 19, 2007).

McEver, Matthew. 1998. "The Messianic Figure in Film: Christology beyond the Biblical Epic." *Journal of Religion and Film* 2(2). Omaha: University of Nebraska–Omaha. http://www.unomaha.edu/jrf/McEverMessiah.htm (accessed November 19, 2007).

Mehta, Suketu. 2004. *Maximum City: Bombay Lost and Found*. New York: Vintage Books (Random House).

Stone, Bryan P. 2000. *Faith and Film: Theological Themes at the Cinema*. Saint Louis: Chalice Press.

Vaux, Sara Anson. 1999. *Finding Meaning at the Movies*. Nashville: Abingdon Press.

2

Teaching Religion and Film: A Fourth Approach

Conrad Ostwalt

The power of film to teach about religion first came to my attention while I was teaching a New Testament class nearly twenty years ago. As the semester wound down and the class began reading John's revelation, a student asked a question about the movie *The Seventh Sign*. It soon became apparent that more of the class had seen the movie than had read Revelation, and much of what the students knew about the Christian Apocalypse had been informed more by *The Seventh Sign* than their reading of the Bible. We had to do some serious unpacking before we could discuss the book in class, but I believe in some ways the students continued to see the apocalyptic text in terms of the movie.

Some years later my colleague Joel Martin and I edited a book, *Screening the Sacred: Religion, Myth, and Ideology in Popular American Film* (Martin and Ostwalt 1995). The book maintains that films form, support, and transform cultural beliefs and values that society holds to be important (some of these are even of ultimate importance). That volume explores the values and beliefs expressed in many popular films of the day. Our basic goal was to demonstrate that films do not have to have obvious religious content in order to function religiously in either an individual or a corporate manner. We also wanted to explore the use of film as a pedagogical tool in religion classes. Toward that end, we organized the book around three approaches: theological, mythological, and ideological. These methods of teaching religion and film have served as pedagogical tools since the publication of that book.

The tripartite approach to studying religion and film in *Screening the Sacred* evolved as a way to balance conceptual approaches to religious studies. The three methods deal with the way most film and religion criticism is organized. Theological criticism places the interpretation of film in the context of traditional religious and theological categories and terms; mythological criticism tends to understand the religious functioning of film in terms of universal archetypes; and ideological criticism views the meaning of film in relation to sociocultural narratives and truths (ibid., chapter 1; Ostwalt 2003, 148–49).

While these three techniques have served well to introduce students to religious studies through the medium of film, I have since felt it necessary to supplement the book's pedagogical content with a fourth approach, one that focuses more on the uniqueness of film. Such an approach not only seeks to understand what is unique about how film, as a cultural product, interacts with or functions in the religious dimension but also uses some simple pedagogical techniques to demonstrate the various ways film *functions* religiously rather than simply *reflecting* religious content. It addresses the visual and auditory character of film as primary components. Many religion and film studies, including my own, have been informed by theories and methods of textual criticism that either largely ignore the visual and auditory or understand these characteristics from the perspective of textual and narrative elements. Even the ubiquitous movie review tends toward the textual as a way of describing a film's quality.

Such a situation has perhaps been inevitable, considering the way film and religion studies have developed within the field of religious studies and the way film reviews are produced and considered. Much of the early work in religion and film was done by scholars trained in theological and narrative studies, so early in the development of interest in the hermeneutic of film, a textual bias emerged as an interpretive standard. As a result, plots, character development, settings, and an authorial viewpoint tend to dominate the way religion and film scholars analyze films in the classroom. Of course, this is a legitimate way to proceed since films have a narrative component. Even when scholars and teachers attempt to get at the unique layers that the film medium brings to narrative (for example, rather than dealing with the author of a book as the primary creative source, film study forces us to look at directors, screenplay writers, and even actors as sources of creative layering) (Martin and Ostwalt 1995, 153; Weaver 1996; Ostwalt 2003, 150–51), the focus has remained on narrative considerations of plot, character, setting, and point of view. What happens then is that the unique elements of a film prop up its narrative qualities. The screenplay writer and the director take on authorial intent; special effects and animation aid in creating the settings; camera angles, lighting, colors, and direction become various points of view; and all of this takes on a narrative quality.

As I have said, there is nothing wrong with this, and narrativizing film is appropriate but inadequate. New pedagogical methods must investigate the unique qualities of film *apart from*—not *as part of*—its narrative elements. Thus, these new teaching techniques should explore what film can add to the study of religion and culture in its uniqueness as an art medium. Jann Cather Weaver has been looking into this potential with her work on the visual aspects of film. Weaver differentiates between *seeing* a film and *watching* one. For Weaver, "seeing is a disciplined task, not confined to the ocular function of sight. Rather, seeing is the critical discipline of delving beneath surface . . . to engage a film in this intentional, participatory visual discipline" (1996). Picking up on Weaver's thread, I want to produce, along with *seeing,* a companion attempt to teach students to *hear*—not just *listen to*—the auditory component of the film experience. When a parent says to a child, "Do you *hear* what I am saying?" the parent is asking whether the child is actively understanding the meaning of the words and not just listening to the sound. My goal is to provide classroom techniques that guide students in *seeing* and *hearing* critically just as we teach them to read critically with textual subjects. This endeavor must first recognize and take seriously the fact that film is more than narrative and that it represents a complex and integrated audiovisual participatory event that includes an interpreted narrative.

Therefore, I am promoting a type of visual-auditory criticism that highlights the unique components of film, apart from its more familiar recognition as a narrative form. Movies are more than just another way to tell a story. Rather, their sophisticated sensory component makes them more participatory and thus requires a more participatory method of study. I call this fourth type of criticism (beyond the textual-based theological, mythological, and ideological approaches described earlier) "sensory criticism." The goal is to incorporate a wide range of sensory experience into the understanding of how films may function religiously.

Why do we need such an approach? First, it would enable us to better appreciate the multisensory character of film. Religion and film study is not just about religion. Although it is fundamentally about film and its uniqueness as a cultural product, it involves more than the concept of film as a multisensory medium. It is also about religion, and because religion itself may be more sensory than textual, it deserves a sensory methodology that recognizes the role of sensory input in religious functioning. While religious studies, especially in the Western tradition, sometimes trick us into thinking that religion and religious authority are primarily textual, in reality, religion functions on a variety of experiential levels, and when the experiential component of religion is part of the equation, one might argue that religion is more sensorial than textual. Thus, such a method will help us understand how films function differently from texts by providing a more participatory, sensory experience that more closely mimics religious experience. This technique will also help the student appreciate the sensory component of religious experience.

The advantages of this sensory method become more apparent if we distinguish between substantive and functional understandings of religion—an important differentiation to make in the classroom. Substantive approaches are concerned with the essence and the truth of religion and religious claims. As such, they are served well by creeds, orthodoxy, and right visions and are often represented by texts. However, to understand religion functionally, we are concerned not with its truth claims but rather with how it orders life and functions within individual and cultural frameworks. In this instance we are better served by rituals, symbols, and experiences, some of which might be supplementary (or even contrary) to the substantive definition of religion. For example, one might substantively understand God as a sovereign, a single entity who demands complete allegiance. At the same time, one could functionally incorporate religion into everyday life through dependence on various types of "good luck" activities and charms (Albanese 1999, 6–8). The substantive claim to a sovereign God is asserted intellectually and textually, whereas functional religion asserts itself through experience.

Most students in university classrooms seem to understand religion substantively. However, the academic study of religion mostly looks at religion functionally, at least in part because, in state-supported schools, religion must be taught from a nonconfessional perspective. Thus, to look at how religion functions rather than at its essence represents a more appropriate way to proceed in the university classroom. The irony is that much of this teaching from a functional perspective is based upon texts. As a result, we have methods and sources that do not match well. I am speaking mainly anecdotally, but the evidence on which I base these assertions comes from twenty years of teaching, studying textbooks and syllabi, and supervising religious studies students. The use of film gives religious studies scholars a source material that is more effective at achieving a functional understanding of religion because film is more sensory and experiential, just as a functional understanding of religion is more sensory and experiential. Films not only give us examples of the ways stories can serve religious ends (i.e., ritualistically) but also provide a medium for communicating the ways in which religion functions in society.

The use of film gives the teacher supplementary source material, as well as an innovative technique for supporting students as they learn how to understand religion functionally rather than substantively. In addition, by training students to *hear* and *see* rather than *listen* and *watch,* instructors can encourage students to apply critical skills not just to reading but also to other sensory stimuli, which makes learning more participatory overall. Thus, the use of film in the classroom goes far beyond entertainment to introduce innovative approaches that are particularly well suited for the religious studies classroom.

Sensory Criticism

To develop a sensory critical approach when dealing with film, one must move beyond textual critical touchstones. For example, although examination of the interaction between screenplay/narrative (textual theory) and directorial intent (auteur theory) might provide interesting insights, the goal of sensory criticism is to transcend these concerns and get behind the creative source and narrative qualities of film. To make a connection to narrative theory, what one is after (with sensory criticism) is perhaps more akin to what is known as *reader reception criticism,* although here it would be more rightly understood as "viewer reception" or "viewer response." In particular, sensory criticism deals with the viewer's responses to the film's visual and aural qualities.

In addition to this focus, sensory criticism is adept at explicating the functional workings of religion. There are many ways in which film (and other objects of culture, for that matter) might function religiously. Normally, when one focuses on a functional understanding of religion, the relevant categories are ones that are familiar to religious scholars. For example, rituals, myths (especially participatory myths), and symbols all create the experiential quality of transcendence—taking one beyond oneself in time and space. Rituals and symbols provide religious meaning. In sensory criticism of film, one focuses on the ritualistic (participatory) and symbolic visual/aural qualities in order to discover and understand a meaning-granting function of film in cultural context.

How do sound and image enhance the mythic quality of filmic experience? And why would we treat the visual and auditory elements as more significant than the narrative quality of film? For one thing, we need to deal with these aspects as primary if they are to escape the supportive status they tend to maintain in relation to narrative, director, actor, and so on. Even beyond that, image and sound play a more important role in our experience of film, religion, and reality than many of us realize. In this sense, the unique characteristics of film as a medium that incorporates both of these stimuli make it very effective at creating cultural myths and individual experiences.

One becomes acutely aware of the power of sound by watching young children react to startling or unknown noises. For example, many youngsters are frightened by thunder. What is it about thunder that creates fear instead of surprise? The first startling thunderclap produces a sensory jolt, a momentary rush of adrenaline from the surprise. But why do subsequent peals of thunder, even when they are preceded by flashes of lightning, still scare some young children? From the child's perspective, the sound is loud, it has an unknown origin, it cannot be tied in any real sense to something immediate that produced it, and it is menacing. Even though children, through experience, know that thunder will not hurt them, they still react with terror. Aural experiences of all sorts produce bodily reactions that seem beyond our control. Movies can incorporate sound and silence to create the same visceral reactions that children experience with thunder.

We are all familiar with the creepy sounds in horror films that can provoke certain reactions in viewers. Sounds can create predictable responses long after we rationalize that what we hear on a movie soundtrack is just part of the movie and not connected to our reality. We sublimate certain reactions to particular sounds, or we associate them with our own reality, and by doing so, we have predictable responses when we hear them. Recently I was listening to a radio interview with Trevor Cox, a professor of acoustical research at the Acoustic Research Center, who conducted a study on disagreeable sounds. His work suggests that humans find sounds unpleasant in part because of a deep connection to the survival instinct. For example, the sound of sniffling is displeasing because we associate it with disease. This, of course, helps explain the child's reaction to thunder. Cox found that the sound of someone vomiting produced the number-one negative reaction to sounds in the study (2007). As the clip was played, I found myself gagging simply from listening to the sound of vomiting. Why should we react so viscerally to the sound of retching coming over the radio? We are all familiar with the sensations we feel when we hear fingernails scraping on a chalk board. And we know that certain sounds can produce a sense of calm, just as others produce unpleasant sensations. A sensory-auditory criticism not only evaluates the effects of sounds on the listener but also encourages the critical analysis of this effect. What happens when we hear these sounds, and how does this play into the hermeneutics of film analysis? Of course, we can also ask the same things about the use of sound in religious ritual and experience. Questions such as these, when students are challenged to critically examine the effects a soundtrack might have on them as viewers, teach them how to critically *hear* the sounds of film.

Sensory-auditory criticism would also pay careful attention to the role of music in movies. Whether haunting dissonance, cheerful melodies, or soulful chords—music can stir the emotions and heighten viewers' experience. When it is skillfully and creatively combined with visual elements, the result can be quite powerful. Religious ritual often incorporates music in order to stimulate an emotional response to rites or symbols. In the same way, music can evoke certain reactions to the myths reenacted in films or to their visual images. As a teenager, I experienced a fight-or-flight response whenever I heard the music of Bill Conti on the *Rocky* soundtrack, particularly when it was accompanied by the images of athletic pursuit or fighting in the movie. How often does music move us to tears, raise our spirits, and perpetuate our blues? It has the power to intensify emotion and perhaps even to create it.

When I was writing *Secular Steeples: Popular Culture and the Religious Imagination* (Ostwalt 2003), evidence from multiple sources and disciplines suggested that music is particularly effective at expressing or challenging ideologies and at intensifying feelings, values, and beliefs. Bennett (2001), Scott (1990), and Spencer (1993) state that music can operate collectively, socially, and even politically. Certainly it operated in this manner in the folk and protest music of the 1960s and 1970s. Evidence also suggests that music intensifies behaviors and beliefs, especially when combined with images in the form of music videos (Rich et al. 1998; Kalof 1999; Wald 1998). Thus music, both alone and with images, can be a powerful force individually and collectively, reinforcing and strengthening feelings, emotions, values, beliefs, and behaviors. This is evident in religious and filmic uses of music, where music can function religiously to aid in transcending through participation in the creative process. If we can learn to *hear* critically, we can not only ask questions about why this happens but also examine what is happening when we ourselves are involved.

In addition to sounds, symbols can be objects or images, and the power of movies is based in part upon the director's ability to create images. Movie making allows the creation and presentation of both realistic and surrealistic images (pathway to the transcendent). The power of images gives film one of its distinctive traits as a medium and is one of the most obvious ways in which movies are distinct from literary narrative. Images can have great impact partly because of our tendency to believe what we see even if we can rationalize the obvious truth that what is happening on the screen is not reality. Still, if we see it on the screen, we are mesmerized into believing that it could happen or that it depicts something that actually did happen. We carry some realist assumptions with us when we watch films. Therefore if we want our students to be critical viewers—*seers* of film rather than merely *watchers*—we need to train them to recognize the ways in which images affect us and create a kind of contrived truth through presentation.

Religious studies scholars are familiar with the power of images through their study of fetishism and iconography. In religious studies, "fetishes or charms are material objects believed to embody supernatural powers that aid or protect the owner" (Lehmann and Myers 1997, 278). Fetishes represent power and often promise magical abilities. In the same way that objects can be made into fetishes, images can also function as fetishes and bestow a religious power on their viewers. In addition, fetishistic images can work through disavowal, as Slovoj Zizek points out, by providing substitutes for one's unrealized desires (2005, 50). As substitutes for our desires and ideals, fetish objects and images can shape the way we view society and thereby help us create countersocial or individual fetishistic realities. When we say that the movies provide a type of escapism, we are describing an alternative view of reality or individuality—a fetishistic reality—that is powerful and meaningful. Filmic images can empower, support, challenge, and help construct our assumptions about ourselves and our world. This is the power of icons. An image is iconic if its meaning goes beyond the actual thing or reality it represents and receives uncritical devotion because of the power it represents. Uncritical watchers of film can be fooled by the iconic power of images.

We can see this dynamic with images when we consider voyeurism. By viewing images, the voyeur experiences gratification. We often associate voyeurism with sexual gratification, but we can apply this concept to the viewing of all sorts of images. The desire to view the macabre, for example, or the drive to view violent images played out on screen represents another type of voyeuristic desire that affects the viewer viscerally. The voyeuristic nature of one's viewing demonstrates a potentially strong association between feelings and perceiving, between desire and watching. The visual alone (or in combination with other sensory experience) can stimulate deep and powerful emotions. In this light, the power of film to titillate, scandalize, shock, or excite becomes apparent.

Films give us the freedom to watch what is unavailable in common experience. They can be intemperate in their visual representation of behaviors or experiences that are beyond the mundane. Violence, mutilation, graphic sexuality, superhuman acts—all of these (and more) are played out visually in the films we watch, and this inundation of images gives movies a particular type of aesthetic power over viewers' senses.

We see the voyeuristic urge everywhere in the contemporary consumption of movie and television images. Reality TV provides vicarious adventures for viewers; crime dramas graphically display mutilated, autopsied, and otherwise disfigured bodies; slasher films and other movies inundate the screen with violence and bloodshed; sexual excess is defined by ratings and codes; bucolic settings and beautiful people challenge our aesthetic perceptions. The viewer as voyeur seeks gratification in the consumption of these images. To be a critical viewer, a *seer* rather than a *watcher,* we must critically assess the way in which images exploit our voyeuristic urges and how this dynamic affects our perceptions of reality.

Religions have often tapped into voyeuristic desire to define the divine. Moses catches a glimpse of God; Krishna reveals divine awesomeness to Arjuna; Paul is blinded by the divine revelation; and the Apocalypse is unveiled bit by bit. *Seers* in religious traditions reveal what is otherwise unavailable, and the revelation is a powerful source of knowledge. The religious voyeur needs revelation, an image, an icon to represent the source of power. Perhaps this is why Mel Gibson's film *The Passion of the Christ* has had such a powerful effect on conservative and evangelical Christians. For the Christian voyeur, the film was not violent; rather, it was graphically realistic, confirming through visual representation a central theological component of certain strains of Christianity—the suffering of Christ. The sadism displayed during the scourging scene, for example, gives the Christian voyeur a visual depiction of unimaginable suffering and reinforces a central tenet of the faith. One devout fan of Gibson's film expressed it this way: "I think everybody should see it. You read the Bible like it's a fairy tale. It's a true story; it really happened. It gives life meaning" ("U.S. Audiences See Gibson's 'Passion'" 2004). For this viewer and no doubt many more, *seeing* the suffering made it real in a way that reading the narrative never had.

Images are powerful because of our realist assumptions. "Seeing is believing," says conventional wisdom. Or we might say that seeing either confirms or challenges our reality constructions and can either authenticate or help deconstruct our imagined visions of the world. Images are powerful, too, because of our tendency to invest fetishes and icons with power. Icons symbolize things beyond themselves. They lead to transcendence, and when they transfix us, whether in art or on the silver screen, we participate in the transcendent as well. Images are powerful because they can stimulate voyeuristic desire and uncover sublimated need. They support our beliefs through symbolism, transcendence through iconography, and power through voyeurism. In short, they aid the experiential in ways that texts alone cannot and thus are akin to religious experience.

Sensory criticism of film is appropriate if we are to critically assess the power of movies to shape, challenge, and create values, feelings, and beliefs. In particular, aural and visual stimulation is an important component of our appropriation of film. Aural and visual stimulation is also important to religious experience. The sensory experience of the auditory and visual operates in certain ways to affect us, and if students are to be critical interpreters of film and religion, they need to be sensitized to how sound and sight work through film in experiential and compelling ways. Let us look at some examples of how to introduce a sensory critical perspective in the classroom.

Images

To train students to become critical consumers of images, we need to explore the richness of their visual lives. Surrounded by television, movies, video games, cell phones, the Internet, and the like, today's students have had their lives enriched by images in ways that previous generations did not. This fact alone makes it imperative that we investigate the critical reception of these powerful motivators. How does one learn to *see* images critically and thus incorporate a visual critical method into the study of religion and film? Two simple strategies have worked well for me. The first includes taking a close look at the power of images in films that purposively employ familiar iconic or religious images to underscore an already-known narrative or remake a familiar myth. When participating in a close viewing, students are encouraged to compare the ways in which the images in a movie differ from preconceived images associated with a story, one that is based either on imagination or on some other medium for communicating the images. It is often helpful to view a scene first with no sound as a way to focus on the visual. Students are frequently familiar with watching images on a soundless track while performing other tasks, so they are in some ways not unfamiliar with this technique. However, they are less familiar with basing interpretive assessment on the visual, which leads to a second exercise.

I regularly have students view clips from movies with no sound and then challenge them to make a hermeneutic assessment based solely on images (this can be combined with the comparative technique described earlier). This exercise encourages them to rely on the visual stimuli and to note how much is missing when the soundtrack is turned off. In both cases, images produce a dreamlike state for the *seer*, a perceptual unconsciousness of the stories being played out on the screen. The goal for sensory criticism is to bring this perceptual process into consciousness, thereby facilitating the critical reception of images.

Janice Rushing has beautifully described the character of filmic image in relation to the unconscious: "[Films have] the visual form of the dream.... Films are to the cultural unconscious what dreams are to the personal unconscious" (1993, 2). If Rushing is right and the images of film can tap into the cultural unconscious and cultural archetypes, then Jann Cather Weaver's attempts to create a method for *seeing* allows students to practice visual criticism with the goal of uncovering the invisible in the visible—to disclose the hidden in the obvious. As I mentioned earlier, students and teachers of religion are already familiar with this process through their study of fetishes and icons. The same approach might be transferred to the study of film as a cultural icon. Particularly in a highly visual culture, where movies play a prominent role, it is imperative to train *seers* who have the ability to critically assess images displayed with great realism, for these images are partially responsible for constructing meaningful and meaning-laden myths.

Films may use images to underscore, remake, or in some way make relevant an already existing mythology and place it meaningfully in a contemporary context. In order to help students grasp this, the instructor may start with a film that tells a familiar story and examine in detail how the film highlights certain images in order to bring the myth into stark consciousness. An obvious example of this is again Mel Gibson's *The Passion of the Christ*. For whatever else it represents, Gibson's film is rich in imagery; employing special effects, Gibson has created for the screen the sufferings and torture of Christ with a level of disclosure unmatched in art, story, or motion pictures.

Much can be done with a film like *The Passion*, which, from an aesthetic perspective, is groundbreaking. From an aural perspective, ancient languages enrich the film, and from a visual perspective, the radical portrayal of sadistic torture takes this retelling of the Christian story to a level previously unachieved. For the purpose of exploring a visual criticism, I limit this discussion to the scene in which Roman guards torment the Christ. Whether viewing the scene in a movie theater or with students, one undeniably finds the scene difficult to watch. In order to highlight only the visual, students might view the scene with the sound turned down. Yet, even without hearing the wrenching sounds of torture, many students avert their eyes.

Virtually every student in my classes at the public university where I teach is familiar with the Christian Passion story, and nearly all have seen Gibson's film. So when I ask them to reflect upon their knowledge of the story before and after watching the clip, one would assume they would report little difference. Nevertheless, when they view the scourging scene without sound, they often report intensified feelings, probably because their attention is so focused on the visual stimuli. Before we watch the scourging scene, we discuss the violence and the extent of mutilation it depicts. We even have a discussion about the obvious—the fact that the images are not real and that the torture scene is a product of filmmakers' amazing ability to manipulate special effects and makeup. Then the students sit transfixed, yet are unable to avoid responding viscerally to the mutilation scenes on the screen.

As an observer, I have concluded two things from watching others view this scene. First, for many Christian believers, this scene remakes the Christian Passion story on the strength of the visual alone. Even though many people are familiar with the story from the minimal description in the gospels, a lifetime of accumulated reenactments of the various scenes of scourging and crucifixion, and Christian artwork through the centuries, this familiarity still does not prepare one for Gibson's work. The suffering of the Christ and the effect on the believer are sometimes made more real by watching this film. Thus, *The Passion*, through its effective visual presentation of suffering and mutilation, remakes the Christian myth. The graphic presentation made possible by technology renders the myth-making process effective in a way not felt since perhaps the traveling flagellants of medieval Europe. Once sound and context are removed from the scourging scene, fruitful discussion on the ability of image to produce a reassessment of one's response to the story can take place. With students, it is important to note the primary role the image plays in creating or re-creating the story, not the other way around. Even when familiar with the narrative, students are still affected by the images—the scourging scene in essence puts "flesh" on the "bones" of a familiar narrative. Armed with this graphic illustration, students are then better able to critically assess other films.

Second, this exercise brings into relief the power of sensory experience. Once again, students are familiar with the story and are adequately forewarned (many have already seen the movie before classroom observations and exercises take place). Nonetheless, the mutilation scenes in the scourging of Christ still have dramatic effects. When questioned, students begin to assess the sensory experience in new ways. They report having a sympathetic response to the sensory stimuli; they feel the power such response can exert; and they notice the sympathetic response taking control of their own rational reaction. All of these guided observations create within students a growing awareness of the effects of sensory input, and they become more attuned to the way in which visual input plays a role in their reception of the film.

A rich body of literature on auteur theory explores the role of the director as the main creative force in film, and certainly the movie director manages much of the visual imagery with creative intent. No one disputes the director's power to fix the film viewer's gaze in specific ways to produce certain responses. Nevertheless, the director is in some ways a master of manipulation—but not of source. The source is sensory, and a sensory criticism that involves exercises that help students isolate visual and auditory stimuli and has them critically assess these stimuli can be effective, especially when used in conjunction with auteur theory and other critical approaches to the study of film and religion.

The exercise with *The Passion* is helpful because students can gauge their reactions to sensory stimuli while viewing a story and a movie with which they are familiar and which has obvious religious content. I have found it productive to follow this exercise with a similar approach but using a film and a story with which students are less familiar and which has religious content that is subtle rather than obvious. For this purpose I have sometimes had students examine the movie *The Legend of Bagger Vance*. This film, directed by Robert Redford, is a beautifully made aesthetic film based on the book by Steven Pressfield (screenplay by Jeremy Leven). The film and book rely on a twin myth, so to speak, that uses the metaphor and mythology of golf (complete with incarnations of Bobby Jones and Walter Hagen) to highlight an ancient Hindu myth.

The film chronicles the story of Bagger Vance (Bhagavan), who mysteriously materializes and then vanishes but in the interim helps Rannulph Junuh—R. Junuh (Arjuna)—find his "authentic swing" (authentic self). The story is a retelling of the great Hindu epic, the *Bhagavad Gita*. The central moment for Junuh in finding his swing comes when Bagger and Junuh stand on the tee box, surveying the course. Bagger instructs Junuh "to *see* the field," a process that involves a visionary experience that leads Junuh to find the harmony of his authentic swing and self. The film is a wonderful tool for exploring Hindu concepts such as dharma and bhakti. But even more so, focusing on the visionary experience helps students learn to *see* critically. The scene I have just described highlights that visionary experience from Junuh's perspective.

Most students in my classes are unfamiliar with both Hinduism and the movie, *The Legend of Bagger Vance*. Thus, in contrast to the scourging scene from *The Passion*, they come to view the visionary scene in *Bagger Vance* without a context. As before, I first turn off the volume. Afterward I instruct them to describe the short scene, which produces a variety of responses. Even though the students understand that something transcendent is being depicted (imaged), they are hard pressed to explain what it is. They see the scene without Bagger Vance's accompanying instruction, so they are forced to use their imagination with little context to help them. The unfamiliar image provides a way for them to explore the concept of discipline and heightened seeing, which in turn leads to a metaphorical description of visual criticism. The visionary experience, presented on film without accompanying sensory input, requires students to be aware of the possibility not only of enhanced vision (the point of the scene) but also of a heightened hermeneutic.

One final exercise for exploring a visual critical approach again involves viewing short clips without sound. For classroom discussion, I chose two scenes: one I expected would be familiar to students (from *Matrix Reloaded*) and one I believed would be unfamiliar (from *Luther*). I instructed my students to focus on the visual attributes of the scenes and to pay special attention to the costuming and setting. I asked them to take notes in two columns: The first column would include descriptions of costumes and settings, and the second would note their reactions to these visual elements. Their comments would be organized as follows:

description   reaction

I then screened short clips from each movie. The scenes have visual similarities and even broad parallels in terms of action. Many of the students were familiar with the plot and scene from *Matrix Reloaded*, yet only one recognized the story of Worms from *Luther*. Even so, they made a number of interesting descriptions and assessments. They noticed that the costumes belonged to different times and places (one to medieval Europe and the other, the future). Moreover, they recognized similarities between the two scenes. From their knowledge of one film and the visual aspects of both, they were able to accurately describe some of the purposes behind the costuming and settings.

Both movies are stories of revolution—the one recounting Martin Luther's courageous stand against the sixteenth-century Roman Catholic Church and the other Neo's revolution against automatons that have stripped society of individual freedom. Both heroes restore a type of civil and individual liberty. The scenes we watched without sound are Luther's appearance at Worms and his refusal to recant his writings and Neo, Trinity, and Morpheus appearing before the Merovingian. In both scenes, the hero, clad in robes or a long black overcoat, appears before a council or an authority and his court. The debate in each involves free will, power, and control, but of course the students do not hear the debate upon first viewing.

When asked to deconstruct the visual elements, students invariably home in on costume symbolism, relative positions of the principal characters, facial expressions, and the like and surmise that the scene has something to do with authority and challenges to it. The comparison of the visual aspects—one a sixteenth-century setting and the other a futuristic, postmodern situation—reveals that the films share certain visual features. The exercise illustrates how effectively visual elements in films support and communicate the narrative. By showing these isolated clips out of context and without sound, the examination of the images takes precedence over other critical aspects.

By learning to isolate images from context, narrative, and sound, students hone their critical *seeing* and are often amazed at how insightful either they are as interpreters or directors are as auteurs. In either case, this productive exercise provides a starting point for teaching critical *seeing*, which can then be built upon by using other critical techniques and narrative analysis. The narratives of all of these films are powerful ones for investigation in a class on religion and film, but by performing the visual exercises first, this critical tool is not lost to the story, characterization, or other components of the film. The value of this type of exercise becomes even more pronounced when applied as an auditory critical method.

Sound

In studying film criticism, one can find an abundance of work on image, auteur, and other factors that influence the visual quality of movies. Less is available on the auditory aspects of films once the issue of music is exhausted. Postmodern culture is quite visual, as I mentioned earlier, and the critical perspective of scholars and students alike tends to the visual. Thus, the auditory quality of films is often overlooked, and the role of sound in the process of dream and myth making is underrated. The goal of sensory criticism is to encourage students to analyze as many sensory components of a film as possible from new perspectives. In order to do this visually, one isolates images from context, narrative, and sound.

The same technique can be applied to highlight the aural component of a film and sometimes produces even more dramatic results. In order to encourage students to think critically about the auditory components of the films they view—to *hear*, not just *listen to*, a film—one can lead students in experiencing the soundtrack of a film divorced from context, narrative, and visuals. The most common way to do this is to focus on the soundtrack. For this to be effective, one must choose a soundtrack that in some way adds value to the narrative. A second technique is to find clips in which the dialogue is missing and which may or may not have a musical accompaniment. The lack of dialogue helps to separate the clip from context and narrative. In either case, the method is to separate the soundtrack from the context and then to analyze the music or other sounds without the benefit of images or an organizing story. Finding such clips can be an arduous task, but the reward is worth the effort.

First, the role of music in filmmaking has long been recognized as important. Music often plays such a central role that it can sometimes eclipse the film itself. This makes sense because music by itself has the capacity to stir emotion and feeling. I first recognized the role of music as part of the film experience when, as I noted earlier, my teenage emotions were energized whenever I heard the signature music from the soundtrack of the movie *Rocky*. After purchasing the album and reading the words on the cover, I realized that music, image, and story could work together more effectively than they perhaps could separately. Sylvester Stallone, star of the film and author of the screenplay, summarized his reaction to the music that became a hallmark of the film. "When I wrote the script for 'Rocky,' I wanted passion music. I wanted a symphony of powerful men . . . of lonely women . . . of love . . . of courage . . . of dignity cast in bronze" (Stallone 1976). There it is—a statement connecting music to emotion, to metaphor, and even to the visual.

To draw attention to the power of music to evoke emotion, we might employ a whole list of films and a little imagination. For example, Andy Trudeau analyzes the music in the movie *The Village* and describes a musical score that incorporates solo violin music, which, because it is so tender, brings a sense of peace in the midst of chaos (2005). Commenting on short clips from various points in the soundtrack, Trudeau explains how the violin music adds an emotional element to the score. By being superimposed on the love story, the violin motif counters the more chaotic and supernatural elements of the movie and soundtrack. In this way, the score itself changes the "texture" of the film (ibid.). I suggest that you have your students listen to Trudeau's commentary (available at NPR.org) and then let them listen to the music at various points in the film (first without and then with visuals). This will help them analyze the type of scene the music accompanies. They will learn, in Trudeau's words, to *hear* motifs and textures of the film through the soundtrack. Then they will be able to make astute critical judgments about the music, its intended effect, and even what might be occurring at that point in the movie (in broad terms, of course). Additionally, since this music is without lyrics, the assessments are again without much context, illustrating to students how effectively music can convey meaning.

A second way of proceeding in auditory criticism is to find clips that may or may not have music, have no (or else very little) dialogue, and have other sounds that convey meaning. When such clips are presented without other sensory input, the exercise can be quite enlightening. I first experimented with this technique using a beautifully crafted film that few students knew, *The Black Stallion*. The richness of the film's auditory element became apparent to me only when my daughter was watching the movie in the back seat of the car while our family was on a road trip. While I drove and listened without benefit of the visuals, I became aware of several extraordinary portions of the film that passed with few or no words but provided a wealth of auditory information. After the trip I watched the film (I was already familiar with it) and focused on the specific sections I had noticed in the car. One scene was of Alec and the horse shipwrecked on the beach; a second was of Alec and the horse swimming in the lagoon; and a third involved Alec and the horse racing to victory. Watching these scenes after listening to them, I was stunned. I then played portions of these same scenes to a class without the visuals and asked them to make certain assessments. The description of the classroom experiments follows.

The Black Stallion, a movie based on the book series, plays off the mystery and mythology of the horse. In this film the horse represents transcendent, magical power that is symbolized in the horse figurine that Alec carries as a fetish and is brought to reality in a race against the fastest horses available. The Black, as the horse is called, is Arabian, has no papers (no legitimacy), "saves" a young boy (Alec) and an aging trainer, vanquishes his opponents, and is known publicly as the "mystery horse." Because the film is full of mythological symbolism, one could easily use this movie in a course on religion and film as the object of close critical analysis. The Black Stallion is also useful for highlighting the way in which aural aspects of movies can contribute to their effectiveness.

For the exercise with students, I began with a discussion of the sensory effects of films and the way they can relate to ritualistic observance more effectively than texts. We talked about how sensory input and experience allow ritual to connect an individual to a larger narrative and become part of it. Ritual retells a story in such a manner that the participating believer becomes part of a sacred story. Sensory experience of ritual allows the believer to transcend and merge with the sacred story. I suggested to my students that something similar happens with the sensory input of a film—that the senses invite the *seer* and the *hearer* to become part of the story. I lowered the lights and placed the cover on the film projector. I instructed the students to listen carefully and critically. In order for this to be a guided exercise, I asked them to take notes specifically on the sounds, the feelings engendered by the sounds, and possible narrative or visual images accompanying the sounds. I instructed them to put these notes in columnar form with three columns across the page.

description   feelings   narrative/images

Then I played three short clips and had the students complete the columns for each clip. The first is a remarkably beautiful scene that begins with Alec and the horse swimming/dancing in crystal-clear waters. This part of the scene is shot underwater to peaceful music and has a ballet quality of grace and elegance. The latter part of the scene, which shows Alec learning to ride the horse in the water and on the beach, is accompanied by more energetic music. The second clip shows the horse saving Alec from a snake on the beach. The third clip is of the horse race at the end of the movie. I repeated this process with each of the three short scenes. Following each clip, the class members discussed their notations on the aural presentation and created a collective note on the clip. As the students discussed their entries, I re-created them on the board in columnar form. Two observations emerged: First, individual notes on descriptions, feelings, and images were remarkably similar from student to student, and second, simply by using the sounds, the students were able to re-create a very accurate assessment of the context (narrative, visual, and other aspects). For brevity, I summarize the results for two of the clips: the swimming/dancing scene and the horse race scene.

Many students provided detailed descriptions of the music from the water scene; they isolated instruments and described the type of music, its rhythms, and its development (evolution or movement). Some of the students noticed the surf undertone at the end of the clip. Many described the music as earthy or naturalistic, sweet, and domestic. Virtually all noted that it began peacefully and elegantly and transitioned abruptly, boldly, and thunderously to ballroom or adventure music before returning to calm music. The predominant reaction was of soothing music that transitioned to heroic music before winding down and merging with surf sounds.

The descriptions of feelings were even more interesting, and again reactions were similar across the class. Students reported feeling calm, relaxed, whimsical, peaceful, and playful during the early portion of the clip. These feelings then gave way to excitement, exhilaration, celebration, and even trepidation during the more thunderous section of the music. Some of the students described their hearts racing or having feelings of anxiety. Finally, the denouement evoked a sensation of resolution or triumph.

What was startling was how closely the students' visions of images matched the images on the screen. This is particularly interesting since none of the students reported having seen the film before, and none could identify the film from the exercise. They entered various items in the third column, but here are some of the more striking ones: During the early portion of the clip (accompanied by the peaceful music, when Alec and the horse are playing in the water), one student imagined a girl riding a horse; another pictured a child frolicking or playing by the ocean; many predicted dancing, ballet, or other rhythmic movement; a few visualized a scene in nature; yet more predicted characters drifting or floating or children skipping. For the more energetic portion of the scene (when Alec is learning to ride), they overwhelming expected images of frenetic movement, racing, or travel. Finally, as resolution occurred, they imagined the portrayal of arrival (e.g., from a journey) or accomplishment (Alec has mastered the skill and now rides with arms outstretched). The predicted images correlate very closely to the actual ones, which shocked the students.

While analysis of these exercises can yield rich results, I want to highlight two observations from this experiment. First, the close critical examination of just the audio portion allowed students to accurately assess the emotional impact and the visual content of the scene in question. The exercise demonstrated with significant impact how the sound not only supported other aspects of the film and story but also helped to *create* certain feelings and conditions of the narrative. Thus, the senses are primary in film and not just secondarily related to the story. Second, the close critical examination of the auditory portion of this scene emphasized a threefold structure of the scene that is not readily apparent when one examines the visual portion alone. The structure is mythological as journey, departure, and return. As such it provides a structural parameter for considering the rest of the narrative within this threefold framework. In other words, the auditory analysis (sensory critical analysis) provides a framework for studying the narrative, not the other way around.

While repeating the experiment with the other short clips mentioned earlier, I found that the sound experiment applied to the match race scene is particularly helpful. The race scene is again without dialogue (and, like the water scene, virtually without words of any kind) but is rich in sound. There is a calm period prior to the clanging of the bell that signals the beginning of the race. During the event, one hears hooves pounding the ground, heavy breathing, crowd noises, the announcer in the background, and music. The students describe these noises in column one with great accuracy, and, given the crowd and announcer, most of them recognize this as a horse race. But they also notice and describe a pattern in which the breathing, running, crowd, and announcer noises build to a frenzy before dissolving into a peaceful musical section that sounded familiar to the students.

In column two, the students described their feelings associated with each of these sections. Fear, anxiety, triumph, power, and suspense gave way to a peaceful, soothing mood during the music portion and transitioned to the triumphant sounds at the end of the scene. None of that is surprising, given the nature of the scene. In the third column, the students were (predictably) able to describe the visual and narrative aspects of the horse race. However, a couple of students made an insightful observation here. They recognized the music from the earlier clip in which Alec is riding bareback on the beach and accurately predicted a flashback to that scene. During the music portion of this scene, both the audio and the visual dissolve to that scene on the beach, where Alec rides bareback with arms outstretched in freedom and joy.

This is a transcendent moment in the film: In the midst of the race the story returns to the crucial moment that defines the essence of Alec's relationship to the Black and the connection of the Black to magical power. By making this connection, the students recognized the role of sound and music in establishing this transformative instant. Horse and boy transcend to a moment beyond time and are delivered to triumph and freedom. As the film returns them to the race, the Black, with Alec on his back, crosses the finish line, and Alec's arms are again outstretched in victory. Here students make the association between sound and the senses in general and to ritual, whose purpose is to bring the believer to participate in the sacred story; the sounds of the film transport the characters and the viewer to a place of transcendence and sacredness.

Finally, I mention one brief sound experiment related to *The Black Stallion*. After playing and discussing the match race scene with my students, I also played the auditory portions of race scenes from two other horse race movies, *Dreamer: Inspired by a True Story* and *Seabiscuit*. I allowed a comparative analysis because each movie has a horse race scene that follows the conditions I was looking for (lots of sound but few words), and each film chronicles a journey of outcast characters from failure to triumph. Mythologically, all three movies represent resurrection stories, and the magical horse becomes the vehicle for a life-affirming resurrection. In *Black Stallion*, a fatherless child, an aging trainer, and a horse that has no identity are all healed through victory; in *Dreamer*, a failed horse trainer, who is estranged from both his father and his daughter, and a jockey who is afraid to race find redemption by rehabilitating and winning with an injured horse named Dreamer. In the process, the estranged relationships are healed. In *Seabiscuit*, a horse owner who had lost his child, a down-and-out trainer, and an aging, battered jockey rehabilitate an injured horse and win the biggest race of their careers. Each of these stories features broken characters and broken horses who together achieve victory and resurrection. There are many other similarities as well, but the key here is that comparison of the race scenes, beginning with a sensory critique, allows students to feel and hear the story of redemption before they see it.

Conclusion

My previous work with Joel Martin described three types of critical approaches to religion and film: theological, mythological, and ideological (Martin and Ostwalt 1995). At the time and since then, we have called for further critical approaches to the study of religion and film that address shortcomings of these and other methods. The history of religion and film studies has been dominated by narrative methodology, including the three approaches listed earlier. This chapter is an attempt to provide a fourth approach, one that moves beyond narrative methods for studying film. I do not suggest that narrative methods are inappropriate or ineffective but mention that they can be used in conjunction with the approach outlined here: a sensory critical methodology.

It is difficult for scholars in religious studies to divorce methods of analysis from narrative, so I have shifted the focus away from text and toward ritual. Ritual participation, therefore, provides a metaphor for a sensory criticism. Sensory participation in ritual helps the believer to become part of a sacred story; sensory analysis in film criticism allows one to set the story in a sensory context, not the other way around. In order to approach sensory aspects of film as primary and not derived from the narrative of the film, I have chosen to separate sound and image from the story of the film and to guide students in focusing their senses on the critical task.

The guided exercises I have discussed are designed to break both the student's and the teacher's dependence on narrative. A sensory criticism involves decontextualizing image and sound—removing them from the context of the story. This at first may seem a strange tactic for religious studies scholars since much of what religious studies involves is contextualizing. We teach our students to study traditions in the context of culture and society; to study texts in the context of time and place; and to study individual beliefs in the context of psychological forces. With sensory criticism, we need to first divorce the sensory aspects of film from narrative context in order to more fully appreciate the power of the sensory during the film-viewing process. There is ample time to recontextualize later by considering how sound, image, and story work together. Thus this is not a deconstructionist method as much as it is a decontextualizing and recontextualizing approach that emphasizes the sensory.

In any event, the study of film in the context of religious studies provides teachers and students fascinating opportunities to examine belief, behavior, and ritual in both a corporate and an individual setting. A sensory method more closely mimics religious experience in the incorporation of sensory experience to knowing. It challenges us to be *seers* (not just *watchers*) and *hearers* (not just *listeners*). As *seers* and *hearers* we better appreciate not only the richness of religious experience but also the depth and beauty of movies, which offer us a complex and meaning-laden experience.

REFERENCES

Albanese, Catherine L. 1999. *America: Religions and Religion,* 3d ed. Belmont, Calif.: Wadsworth.

Bennett, Andy. 2001. *Cultures of Popular Music.* Philadelphia: Open University Press.

Cox, Trevor. 2007. "A Tour of Some of the World's Worst Sounds." NPR, *Talk of the Nation.* February 12.

Kalof, Linda. 1999. "The Effects of Gender and Music Video Imagery on Sexual Attitudes." *Journal of Social Psychology* 139(3): 378–85.

Lehmann, Arthur C., and James E. Myers. 1997. *Magic, Witchcraft, and Religion: An Anthropological Study of the Supernatural,* 4th ed. Mountain View, Calif.: Mayfield.

Martin, Joel, and Conrad Ostwalt, eds. 1995. *Screening the Sacred: Religion, Myth, and Ideology in Popular American Film.* Boulder, Colo.: Westview.

Ostwalt, Conrad. 2003. *Secular Steeples: Popular Culture and the Religious Imagination.* Harrisburg, Penn.: Trinity Press International.

Rich, Michael, Elizabeth R. Woods, Elizabeth Goodman, S. Jean Emans, and Robert H. DuRant. 1998. "Aggressors or Victims: Gender and Race in Music Video Violence." *Pediatrics* 101(4) (April): 669–74.

Rushing, Janice. 1993. "Introduction to 'Evolution of the New Frontier' in *Alien* and *Aliens:* Patriarchal Cooptation of the Feminine Archetype." Paper presented at conference. Fayetteville, Ark., September 1.

Scott, James C. 1990. *Domination and the Arts of Resistance: Hidden Manuscripts.* New Haven, Conn.: Yale University Press.

Spencer, Jon Michael. 1993. *Blues and Evil.* Knoxville: University of Tennessee Press.

Stallone, Sylvester. 1976. *Rocky.* Album jacket, original motion picture score. United Artists UA-LA694-G.

Trudeau, Andy. 2005. Interview by Sheila Kast. "Listening to the Movies: Oscar-nominated Music, Part 2: Fantasy and Fright. *The Village* and *Harry Potter.*" NPR, February 20.

"U.S. Audiences See Gibson's 'Passion.'" 2004 (February 24). http://www.cnn.com/2004/SHOWBIZ/Movies/02/24/film.passion.audiences.reut/index.html (accessed November 20, 2007).

Wald, Gayle. 1998. "Just a Girl? Rock Music, Feminism, and the Cultural Construction of Female Youth." *Signs: Journal of Women in Culture and Society* 23(3) (Spring): 585–610.

Weaver, Jann Cather. 1996. "Discerning the Religious Dimensions of Film: Toward a Visual Method Applied to *Dead Man Walking.*" Conference of American Academy of Religion, New Orleans, November.

Zizek, Slavoj. 2005. *Interrogating the Real: Selections 2005,* ed. Rex Butler and Scott Stephens. London: Continuum.

FILMS CITED

Black Stallion, The (Carroll Ballard, director, 1979)
Dreamer: Inspired by a True Story (John Gatins, director, 2005)
Legend of Bagger Vance, The (Robert Redford, director, 2000)
Luther (Eric Till, director, 2003)
Matrix Reloaded (Andy Wachowski and Larry Wachowski, directors, 2003)
Passion of the Christ, The (Mel Gibson, director, 2004)
Rocky (John G. Avildsen, director, 1976)
Seabiscuit (Gary Ross, director, 2003)
Seventh Sign, The (Carl Schultz, director, 1988)
Village, The (M. Night Shyamalan, director, 2004)

PART II

Film and the Teaching of Religious Traditions

3

Teaching Biblical Tourism: How Sword-and-Sandal Films Clouded My Vision

Alice Bach

About ten years ago I was delighted that I could incorporate so-called sword-and-sandal films, particularly from the Hollywood film factories of the fifties, into my teaching of Scripture. Students enjoyed them, and visual culture teaches the sharpening of narrative observation. It felt avant garde to be teaching visual culture instead of source criticism. Imagine Victor Mature playing a curly-haired Samson, at once hulking and heart-breakingly dumb. And Hedy Lamarr as a stereotypic bad-girl flirty Delilah who remarked about her own performance, "Any girl can be glamorous. All you have to do is stand still and look stupid." Clearly this kind of material is more popular for undergraduates and gets better class ratings than a course in biblical writers, possibly named J, D, E, and P.

What we see in practice, however, when broad categories like the sciences, humanities, and social sciences are supposedly bridged, are courses billed as interdisciplinary, and they are if you consider that a religion professor who has some interest in visual arts is teaching the Art of William Blake or a psychologist is putting forward Scorsese's heroes as case studies. However, such courses are not really interdisciplinary because both are taught by people trained in one discipline who are essentially amateurs in another. Now *amateur* means one who loves, thus Bible and film produced a sweet combination for me. I was fully aware, even at the beginning of the delicious sound of interdisciplinarity, that the term applied to a professor trained in one discipline who was an amateur in another field. Although possibly late to the dance, my own university now offers small undergraduate seminars in which a philosopher teaches evolution theory and a historian traces the history of the pizza pie. The idea is that students will see the integration of knowledge and be able to synthesize data in unusual ways. But what I learned is that I was re-affirming the "truthiness" of biblical narratives by showing visual adaptations that were merely retellings, not analytic reformations of the stories.[1]

That Scholars of the Bible and religion have been incorporating film study into their work is not a sudden move. There were a few considerations of the connection between the two beginning with the moralizing concerns of Henry James Forman (1933) and Raymond Moley (1938). However, in the past handful of years, a scholarly interest in Bible and film has steadily grown and runs parallel to the development of both cultural studies and the elevation of popular culture to academic heights. The goal of this chapter is not to review the "usual" films since many articles by biblicists are widely available. Rather, I examine the reciprocal and heuristic relation of the spectator to the work. The uses of history, whether it be biblical history or American pioneer history, are not fixed but become the "pre-text" to a fashioning of a new narrative; as such, they create an intertext between the religious and cinematic interpretations. For too long I followed the narrative line by not creating enough tension be-tween biblicism and the intentions of the narrative preservers. It took the arguments of Christian and Jewish religious Zionists to show me the danger of this position.

Similar to other cultural forms, movies have the potential to reinforce, to challenge, to overturn, or to crystallize religious perspectives, ideological as-sumptions, and fundamental values. Films can bolster or challenge our soci-ety's norms, guiding narratives, and accepted truths. Films can and do perform religious and iconoclastic functions in American society. When films present religious motifs and themes, an academic response would include an inves-tigation into whether traditional religious teachings are present, whether any of the common forms of expression normally associated with religion are present, and whether religious symbols are invoked.

A second current has been formed by a wave of biblicists and scholars of that broader epithet known as "religious studies," which uses biblical tropes as

---

Teaching Film in 2001: Apocalypse Then

This course will focus on the cultural use of biblical figures, primarily in film. First, we will focus upon movies as myth, indicate the place of these myths in American culture, and finally [discuss] how the cinematic image has continued the populari-zation of biblical image and intertwined it with the American myth. We will examine the "sword-and-sandal" films of the fifties, [specifically,] how the films differ from or imitate the biblical narratives on which they are based and reflect the American cold war period. Second, we will evaluate a number of Jesus movies, from biopics to interpretative films. Finally, we shall look at several American film genres, such as the Western, which weave male Christ figures into their ideology, and recent films with female Christ figures. There will be some cinema theory, but the course is pri-marily one in which we shall "read" film as a reflection of changing American theological beliefs and tropes.

heuristic tools in analyzing films. While I understand Owens's claim that allegory in a postmodern sense exists "in the gap between a present and a past" (Owens 1983, 68), I have trouble reconciling my own readerly location in this gap between sign and meaning with the biblical texts, where sign and meaning overlap. Too often the comparisons between contemporary films and biblical tropes in recent collections attempt such a false unity, one that endeavors to bridge an unbridgeable gap. I find McLemore's (1995) effort to trace this connection between filmic and social representation in David Lynch's surrealistic film *Blue Velvet* compelling on a theoretical level. That is, she presents the various contemporary concepts of allegory, as well as the reactions to Lynch's complex and elusive work. However, a sophisticated understanding of the codes in the biblical narratives is lacking in her discussion of the possible allegorical interpretation of *Blue Velvet* as "Christian typology, replete with Jeffrey as the angelic choirboy, Adam in the garden, and Sandy as his Eve" (ibid., 136). Nowhere does she admit to the over-the-top quality of such an interpretation.

Students are not disturbed by the time gap between biblical time and cinematic time. When looking at cartoons as mindless as Veggie Tales,[2] my students laugh at the familiarity of cartoon figures without wondering why young David is a kaffiyeh-wearing brussels sprout attacking (successfully, of course) a very warty pickle Goliath. As I continued to teach film, I realized that students needed media analysis before they could analyze the agenda of the filmmakers (other than the Veggie guys, who chose vegetables as characters because they could not draw limbs). Visual presentations by human actors did not challenge students to be suspicious of biblical narratives.

Jesus Christ, Celluloid Superstar

Talk about a slippery slope. Jesus films are fraught with theology, ideology, sentimentality, pageantry, and sophistry.[3] I am certain that it is a losing battle to talk about one's favorite or the most effective Jesus films, sometimes called biopics, especially with scholars who are still wrestling with images of the historical Jesus. What students need to understand up front is that they are not learning about Jesus in geographic Galilee, in the hills surrounding Bethlehem, in Jerusalem. Most likely they are seeing (in American sword-and-sandal films) the hills between Los Angeles and Santa Barbara. Visual culture tends to underscore or implement a vision of reality; thus, a film with a clean-shaven, blue-eyed European Jesus fighting swarthy Semitic Pharisees seems natural and influences images of the biblical figure of Jesus. Thus, time winds backward, with the cinematic Jesus influencing the reader/viewer's mental image of the biblical version of the narrative.

Not surprisingly, one's favorite Jesus film often tells us a great deal more about the spectator than the film itself. One person's faith is another person's fantasy. For instance, one of my colleagues thinks Monty Python's *Life of Brian* (1979) is brilliant, while another hums along with *The Greatest Story Ever Told* (1965). Full of self-revelation, I am willing to admit my own strong connection to Martin Scorsese's *The Last Temptation of Christ* (1988). Lest you think you have me typed, dear reader, I also love some of the great pious films such as *The Diary of a Country Priest* (1951), Henry Koster's *The Robe* (1953), Henry King's *The Song of Bernadette* (1943), and a film that defies categorization, Franco Zeffirelli's *Brother Sun, Sister Moon* (1972). Showing these films to students without secondary analysis can often result in meatier discussions than offering other critics' analyses. It is easier for students to evaluate the filmmaker's agenda by comparing several films with similar narratives. Not incidentally, students are so familiar with Mel Gibson's violent secular films that his emphasis on the Passion narrative and the elimination of the rest of the Jesus's life in *The Passion of the Christ* (2004) seemed to them "like Gibson in *Braveheart.*" Simply put, it seemed like Mel Gibson theology—more *Lethal Weapon* than Sermon on the Mount. Accustomed to horror and torture films, the students were uninterested in the media concerns that the film was anti-Semitic on one side and that it would bring new conversions to Catholicism on the other.

The greatest example of how film can illuminate and extend the Gospels is surely *Vangelo secondo Matteo* [The Gospel according to Saint Matthew], directed by Pier Paolo Pasolini (1964). This is clearly my own biased view, but fortunately it is shared by Lloyd Baugh, whose chapter "The Masterpiece: The Gospel according to Saint Matthew" (1997, 94–108) provides both excellent background on Pasolini as a creative artist and a crisp analysis of the Italian filmmaker's portrait of Jesus. Baugh focuses on Pasolini's representation of the Matthean Jesus as a human rather than a divine hero, one who is much more distant from the people and his disciples than the Matthean figure. Cutting to the bone, Baugh argues that Pasolini sees an irritable Jesus, one not well integrated into human society. "Solitary, aloof, he is a kind of biblical intellectual, who, despite an intense desire to be organically linked to the people, cannot breach the immeasurable gap between them" (ibid., 104). Baugh argues, and I think rightly, that Pasolini's Jesus is an extreme figure who discomforts many interpreters of the film but that the severity of the film's interpretation is in keeping with the radical nature of the Gospel. Pasolini's broken-faced peasants are much closer to a Gospel peasantry, I suspect, than the bland Hollywood peasants or even the Bronx-voiced disciples of Scorsese. Baugh also notes the nuances of Pasolini's Jesus: "When Jesus heals the leper, there is a marvelous warm exchange of smiles between him and the man; and when Jesus cures the cripple, he smiles at him and later he even speaks gently and reasonably to the Pharisees. During his triumphal entrance into Jerusalem, Jesus is anything but solemn. He is clearly enjoying himself and participating in his popular manifestation" (ibid., 103).

There is something so fitting in Pasolini's hollow-cheeked, slight, Mediterranean Jesus that it resonates with my own internal portrait. After seeing one of these Jesus films, particularly the Pasolini or the Scorsese movie, one never reads the Gospels in quite the same way again. One proof of the spectator's power in interpreting film is that the so-called New York accents found in the Scorsese film sounded normal to me (a native New Yorker) and the tough-guy Judas (played by Harvey Keitel) finally gave me a "henchman/ betrayer" figure who was simultaneously intimate and inimical, one who brought a depth and complexity to Judas that I had never understood. In addition, the scoring of the Congolese "Missa Luba" for the final scene of Pasolini's film is a success. The pounding drums and the women's joyful cries pick up the ultimate triumph as they approach the tomb. As the drumbeat picks up urgency, so does the message of the Gospel, as death is silenced by the fierce, harsh music of the victory of the risen Christ. What better visual interpretation of the triumph of the embattled Matthean community could there be than Italian peasants, sure-footed on rocky terrain, in a fight against hostile forces? This good triumphing over evil narrative brings us full circle—to the American Western and its unyielding landscape.

The American Western situates the hero in this life: more the figure of the incarnate Jesus than the heavenly Christ. The Western hero is concerned only with keeping the peace on the range, in the saloon, and at the garrison. He is not looking toward an afterlife, only a well-ordered roundup and a patient wife in bonnet and gingham, so different from the rustling silks of the saloon gal. The Western hero assures us of harmony between human beings and the unforgiving stretch of nature. The male hero suppresses feeling, kills what he must, and seems to walk through a mythic landscape without relating to women, to Indians, or even to his horse. Similar to biblical storytelling, the focus is upon the moral hero, his code of conduct, and his standard of judgment. The story is expected to influence the audience's moral beliefs. The shepherds of traditional biblical narrative have become cattle ranchers. There are still great celebrations at harvest time; stories are told around campfires. Women are subservient and devote themselves to growing food and raising children. Today, the classic American Western is out of vogue. There is, however, still a parallel with the land of Israel. There, the pioneers, full of idealism and hungry for land, are the Israeli settlers. The Indians they fight are the Palestinians.

Three years ago I went to Jerusalem for several weeks, and for the first time I lived on the West Bank. Although I had been to scholarly conferences in Tel Aviv and Jerusalem during the past decade, I had never visited Bethlehem, Ramallah, or Hebron. Nor had I visited Jewish settlements. Moreover, my time frame of events in Jerusalem and other biblical sites ended in roughly the third century CE. All that changed during that first summer. Here are several images that stand out in my memory: standing in the sun for hours, waiting to pass through a checkpoint; visiting the Christian peacemakers team in Hebron, where the settlers at Kiryat Arba threaten Palestinian citizens daily; standing with the "Women in Black" in Jerusalem a few Fridays; and meeting with Machsom Watch, Israeli women of a certain age who monitor checkpoints and document soldiers' behavior toward Palestinian citizens.

I returned to the United States with grave images of Occupation tumbling through my mind. Within weeks I had fashioned PowerPoint presentations of Palestinian issues and was eager to show them to anyone who would watch. Few people were interested. Colleagues did not want to get involved with either the difficult framing of the problem or the possibility of charges of

---

Teaching Film in 2007: Paradise Now

Class negotiation on the final status of the West Bank, in which individuals/teams represent various stakeholders (self-appointed or otherwise), for example, Likud, Labour, Peace Now, the U.S. State Department, American Israel Public Affairs Committee (AIPAC), Christian Zionists, the Palestinian Authority, residents of the Old City (Muslim, Jewish, Christian), residents of Bethlehem, Ramallah, and Hebron, and the Israeli settlers living in the West Bank, Hamas, the EU, those with Palestinian identity cards, and those with Jerusalem residency cards.

Adopting the perspective of the stakeholder, which will, of course, require *extensive research,* each student or team of students will present an *outline, a bibliography, and two drafts* of position papers on the "final status of Palestine, the state of Israel, and/or the final status of Jerusalem." After a student/team presents a position paper, the other "stakeholders" will, from their designated perspectives, offer critiques of the proposals. Those critiques should be taken into account in the final draft of the paper. Each person will write a paper, to be turned in at the end of the semester, including all the elements described above. Class will also struggle with question of which voices will and should be heard in order to guarantee a viable solution. An ongoing process; class will devote at least one hour of class time each week for eight weeks on "negotiations."

Note: I am grateful to Jennifer Glancy of LeMoyne College, who taught a course with a similar, ongoing class assignment and shared her teaching experience and syllabus with me.

---

anti-Semitism if they questioned Israeli politics. My friends did not seem any more moved by my pictures of Palestine than I was by theirs of the melting glaciers off Alaska.

As a result, I decided to teach a course called "Whose Land Is It Anyway?: Palestinian and Israeli Issues from Biblical Times to the Present." I would have an audience, and if I were successful, I would gain allies in enlivening this issue on our campus.

Fashioning a syllabus was difficult, especially attempting to "balance" this course. In fact, with no other course on Palestine history, life, culture, or literature being taught at the university (but a generous offering of courses in Jewish studies), what exactly is meant these days by "academic balance"? "Balance" is a code word perhaps for agenda or for point of view. As most scholars agree, there is no innocent presentation of a topic, only a willingness to discuss varying perspectives. Thus, making clear to students my own political and social position, which I do in all my courses, I needed to be Israeli on some days and Palestinian on others. I had to learn to argue credibly that any accounting of the last forty years cannot put all the moral failures on the Israeli side. The continued support by the Palestinian majority of political forces (first embodied in the Palestinian Liberation Organization (PLO) until it changed its line in 1993, now in Hamas), which rejects the right of Israel to exist as a Jewish state, has played fast and loose with the justifiable fears of the Jewish people, whose experience of statelessness (including that in Arab and Islamic countries) was always coupled with second-class status of roughly apartheid dimensions, special taxes, and vulnerability to occasional (in Arab lands) or systematic (in Christian lands) violence, murder, rape, and then genocidal policies.

There were, of course, Palestinian perspectives that needed to be represented in class. The Occupation brought us to consider other "occupations" we might have studied: from the U.S. government's dealing with Native Americans to the French government's treatment of Algerians to the Soviets' handling of Afghans to the Chinese government's dealing with Tibet to the Iraqis' conduct toward the Kurds. The Israelis behaved with arrogance and insensitivity toward Palestinians, sought no integration or economic advancement for the Palestinian people (yes, the refugees were far better off in Jordan than they were in the West Bank in the 1990s), and attempted to balance the growing popularity of the PLO by encouraging the growth of Hamas. In the most cynical move of that sort in the past years, Israel withdrew troops and settlers from Gaza in 2005 while refusing to negotiate with the PLO's moderate, peace-oriented leader, Abbas, thus allowing the Hamas forces to claim credit for the Israeli withdrawal ("we drove them out with force, not with the weakness of the Abbas/Fatah strategy of negotiated peace"), which contributed to the electoral victory of Hamas in 2006.

My university colleagues (some who knew me and others who had just heard about my course) questioned the readings listed on the syllabus. The major complaint was that they were too leftish.[4] My colleagues were correct. The majority of the readings were books written by Jewish/Israeli writers who were sympathetic to Palestine issues. I hoped that the media assignment of reading the Web sites of *Ha'aretz*, an Israeli newspaper, and *Al Jazeera*, an Arab-based news organization covering the same political issues, would help students understand the passions of the players in this ongoing narrative. At the request of a student I added the *Jerusalem Post* to our daily readings.[5]

I emphasized media analysis because I have learned that students must be able to identify the ways in which political strategies play themselves out in print, electronic media, and, of course, documentary films, which were the third focus of the course. Each student was required to choose a general topic (e.g., Hamas versus Fatah, the security fence or the apartheid wall, a one-state or a two-state solution). The goal was to evaluate the bias, propaganda, truthiness, and positive or negative impact on the student as reader. One media choice was to be from an Israeli perspective and another from a Palestinian viewpoint.

Documentary films were central to the course, but we did not attempt to combine scripted and visual views until after we had sharpened our analytic skills in evaluating print and electronic media. While many excellent films certainly obey the traditional "rules" of documentaries, nonfiction films do much more than simply document the facts of our world. Even though the main distinction between documentaries and other films is that the former use available historical evidence and attempt to portray reality rather than invent it, even the choice of topic is a revelation of the filmmaker's subjectivity. In an avant-deconstruction world, one might assume that documentarians did not express their own opinions or personal feelings. Like historians and anthropologists, their work was considered to be objective. Critical analysis has shown the subjectivity of the gaze. Film, like any other constructed model, is an inherently imperfect substitute for reality. Possibly because it is more immediately available to the human mind than scholarly texts, our class discussions after watching these films (see appendix C) were the most impassioned. Students expressed thoughts of being tricked by the filmmaker. What they had seen looked real, yet it could *not* be real because if those bulldozers were genuine, then the Palestinians *were* trapped. What if it were all staged? What if documentaries are a clever form of propaganda?

All semester we struggled with form and content. We recognized the following elements of documentaries:

> *reenactments*: Some reenactments use actual people and places, whereas others use actors.
>
> *animation and special effects*: These are often employed as a means of communicating the parts of a story that a camera cannot capture, including a subject's dreams, memories, and imaginings. They are clearly not reality.
>
> *altered timelines*: Very few documentaries adhere to an exact chronology of scenes. Because the final film shows only a very small percentage of the total footage shot, many actions and quotes are necessarily taken out of context. Shuffling the order of scenes and dialogue is acceptable, even necessary, for coherence. This notion was the most difficult for student aficionados of "reality TV shows" (e.g., *Big Brother, The Bachelor, Project Runway, Super-Nanny.*) Could it be that these shows were scripted by means of altered timelines and the selective use of footage—just like the documentaries?
>
> *editing and omissions*: Sometimes portions of a story are omitted because a subject is too complicated to present every episode comprehensively in less than two hours. Filmmakers might also be willing to sacrifice some credibility with scholars in order to produce a film that is understood and well received by a wider audience The relative importance of each part of a story is always the filmmaker's subjective decision.

During the semester we watched about a dozen documentaries (some during informal "dinner and doc" extra classes), and the number of topics grew to exceed what we had expected (see appendix C). I next discuss our favorite three in some detail in the hope that others will be encouraged to include them in their teaching of the current Israeli and Palestinian conflicts.

Paradise Now

Filmed under extraordinary duress in Nablus, Nazareth, and Tel Aviv, this intensely powerful movie neither romanticizes nor demonizes its characters, who would rather die than live in grinding poverty and despair. Filmmaker Abu-Assad instead shows the forces, both external and internal, that drive two best friends to embrace what they regard as political martyrdom. At times as nerve wracking as any thriller, *Paradise Now* is first and foremost a compelling, character-driven film that skillfully blends the personal with the political. According to an interview with Abu-Assad in the press notes, the film's location manager was kidnapped by a militant Palestinian group (the late Palestinian President Yasser Arafat intervened to secure his safe return), land mines exploded near the actors during filming, and gunmen ordered everyone to leave Nablus. The final shooting took place in Nazareth. The scenes are so realistic that I felt that I had made a U-turn on that road, too! *Paradise Now* is a great suspense movie that offers numerous discussion topics. It also provides a sense of life behind the Occupation wall—or security fence, depending on who is talking. Crisscrossing the borders and avoiding checkpoints by taking circuitous routes is probably more exciting for those of us who have driven those rocky roads than for those who are used to smoothly crafted chase sequences in hyped-up Porsches.

The Iron Wall

Ze'ev Jabotinsky and other Zionist leaders requested an independent Jewish Legion force that would be sponsored by the mandatory government and empowered to defend citizens against Arab rioters. It soon became apparent that the mandated government would agree only to a mixed Jewish and Arab force under British supervision. Given the lack of zeal that Arabs and British soldiers showed in defending Jews against rioters, Zionists felt that this force would be inadequate. Indeed, British protection proved to be insufficient during the riots of 1929. However, the mainstream Zionist leadership also understood that a Jewish Legion was not forthcoming from the British and that they would have to be content with a small, illegal Hagannah force and whatever protection the mandated police force would provide. Adamant on this point, Jabotinsky published a polemic that defended the right to a mandate-sponsored self-defense force for Jews, which he described as an "iron wall." His words inspired (if one can use that term) the title of the film:

> We all demand that there should be an iron wall. Yet we keep spoiling our own case, by talking about "agreement" which means telling the Mandatory Government that the important thing is not the iron wall, but discussions. Empty rhetoric of this kind is dangerous. And that is why it is not only a pleasure but a duty to discredit it and to demonstrate that it is both fantastic and dishonest. I am optimistic that they will indeed be granted satisfactory assurances and that both peoples, like good neighbors, can then live in peace. But the only path to such an agreement is the iron wall, that is to say the strengthening in Palestine of a government without any kind of Arab influence, that is to say one against which the Arabs

will fight. In other words, for us the only path to an agreement
in the future is an absolute refusal of any attempts at an agreement
now.[6]

Occupation 101

This film forms the cinematic backbone of my course on Palestine. *Occupation 101*, a 2006 documentary film by Sufyan Omeish and Abdallah Omeish, is thought provoking and powerful. Although it focuses on both the current and historical causes of the Israeli-Palestinian conflict, it seems a bit outdated. *Occupation 101* attempts to present a comprehensive analysis of the facts and hidden truths surrounding the never-ending controversy and dispels many long-perceived myths and misconceptions. Many viewers will disagree with this analysis, of course.

The film also details life under Israeli military rule, the role of the United States in the conflict, and the major obstacles that stand in the way of a lasting and viable peace. The roots of the conflict are explained through the firsthand experiences of leading Middle East scholars, peace activists, journalists, religious leaders, and humanitarian workers whose voices have too often been suppressed in U.S. media outlets.

The film covers a wide range of topics, including the first wave of Jewish immigration from Europe in the 1880s, the tensions of 1920, the 1948 war, the 1967 war, the first Intifada of 1987, the Oslo Peace Process, settlement expansion, the role of the U.S. government, the second Intifada (2000), the apartheid wall, and the Israeli withdrawal from Gaza, as well as many heart-wrenching testimonials from victims of this tragedy. Some of the best material for classroom use is contained in the extras on the DVD: historical photos and footage from the Pathé News Archives (from the 1900s, 1940s, and 1967), international law, home demolitions, victims of conflict, the chain of victimization, Israeli awakening, and much more. My students were most affected by historical footage from testimonies from Bethlehem University, humanitarian actions by the International Solidarity Movement, and the all-too-realistic Jenin Refugee Camp destruction.

Occupation 101 features opinions from some of the most credible Middle East scholars, historians, peace activists, journalists, and humanitarian workers, including Albert Aghazarian, Rabbi Arik Ascherman, Noam Chomsky, Cindy Corrie, Craig Corrie, Richard Falk, Paul Findley, Neta Golan, Jeff Halper, Amira Hass, Rashid Khalidi, Ilan Pappé, Gila Svirsky, and Alison Weir. If you do not recognize these names, you need to watch the film.

Unbiblical Tourism

My video for the pictures of biblical tourism has turned dark. Perhaps documentaries are the answer. No more meet-cute-Samson-and-Delilah movies—unless one wants to rewrite Samson as the first suicide bomber. The calendar says it is 2008, the sixtieth anniversary of the founding of Israel and of the Nakba, the Palestinian catastrophe. Walking through the Occupied territories, one can almost feel biblical: no refrigeration, electric fans, television, or lights to study and read by; no regular water supply, as that is dependent upon a flickering, irregular supply of electricity. Walking through the state of Israel, one can still be a tourist and enjoy the air-conditioned, wi-fi restaurants and shops selling Cuban cigars and fluffy Turkish towels; one can buy electronics of every size and kind. One observes satellite dishes and carefully tended olive trees growing in the medians of smooth Israeli highways that lead to settlements with swimming pools and strip malls. We can only imagine the world that Hollywood called Palestine.

There are those who see what the tourists do not. Journalist Amira Hass reminds her readers of the devastation in Gaza: "The experiment was a success: The Palestinians are killing each other. They are behaving as expected at the end of the extended experiment called 'what happens when you imprison 1.3 million human beings in an enclosed space like battery hens'." Not much of an ad for tourism.

Appendix A: Films Taught from Traditional Biblical Perspectives

Sword-and-Sandal Films (Old Testament Narratives)

The Bible (1966)
David and Bathsheba (1951)
Samson and Delilah (1949)
Solomon and Sheba (1959)
The Story of Ruth (1960)
The Ten Commandments (1956)

Jesus Films

Gospel according to Saint Matthew (Pasolini 1964)
The Greatest Story Ever Told (1965)
Jesus of Montreal (1989)
Jesus of Nazareth (Zeffirelli 1977)
King of Kings (deMille 1927, 1953)
The Last Temptation of Christ (Scorsese)
The Life of Brian (1977)
The Passion of the Christ (Gibson 2004)

Figuring Jesus

Babette's Feast (1987)
Dead Man Walking (1995)
Shane (1953)
Star Wars (1977)
La Strada (1954)

Appendix B: Films Taught from a Theological Perspective

Female Jesus Figures

Babette's Feast (1987)
Dead Man Walking (1995)
La Strada (1954)

Christ Figures in Trouble

Cool Hand Luke (1967)
One Flew over the Cuckoo's Nest (1975)
Shane (1953)
Star Wars (1977)

Scandalous Jesus Films

The Last Temptation of Christ (1988)
Life of Brian (1979)

Religious Films without Peer

Blade Runner (1982)
Gospel of Matthew (Pasolini) (1964)
Metropolis (1927)

Appendix C: Top Ten Documentaries (Palestine and Israel)

Arna's Children (2003; Danniel Danniel and Juliano Mer Khamis)
Death in Gaza (2004; James Miller)
Gaza Strip (2002; James Longley)
The Iron Wall (2006; Mohammed Alatar)
Jenin, Jenin (2002; Mohammed Bakri)
Paradise Now (2005; Hany Abu-Assad)
Peace, Propaganda, and the Promised Land (2004; Sut Jhally and Bathsheba
    Ratzkoff)
Rana's Wedding (2003; Hany Abu-Assad)
Stolen Freedom: Occupied Palestine (2005; Tony Kandah)
Wall (2004; Simone Bitton)

Appendix D: Books That Might Engender Controversy

Abunimah, Ali. 2006. *One Country: A Bold Proposal to End the Israeli-Palestinian
    Impasse.* New York: Metropolitan.
Finkelstein, Norman. 2007. *Beyond Chutzpah: On the Misuse of Anti-Semitism and the
    Abuse of History.* Berkeley: University of California Press.

Pappé, Ilan. 2006. *Ethnic Cleansing of Palestine*. Oxford, UK: Oneworld.

————. 2006. *A History of Modern Palestine: One Land, Two Peoples*, 2d ed. New York: Cambridge University Press.

Said, Edward. 1996. *Peace and Its Discontents: Essays on Palestine in the Middle East Peace Process*. New York: Vintage.

Salaita, Steven. 2006. *Anti-Arab Racism in the USA: Where It Comes from and What It Means for Politics Today*. London: Pluto.

————, and Peter Gran. 2006. *The Holy Land in Transit: Colonialism and the Quest for Canaan*. Syracuse, N.Y.: Syracuse University Press.

Appendix E: Bibliography I (Attach to Syllabus for Background)

Arabs in America

Dinnerstein, Leonard, Roger L. Nichols, and David M. Reimers. 2003. *Natives and Strangers: A Multicultural History of Americans*. New York: Oxford University Press.

Elaasar, Aladdin. 2003. *Silent Victims: The Plight of Arab and Muslim Americans in Post 9/11 America*. Bloomington, Ill.: AuthorHouse.

GhaneaBassiri, Kambiz. 1996. *Competing Visions of Islam in the United States: A Study of Los Angeles*. Contributions to the Study of Religion. Westport, Conn.: Greenwood.

Gher, Leo A., and Hussein Y. Amin. 2000. *Civic Discourse and Digital Age Communications in the Middle East*. Civic Discourse for the Third Millennium. Stamford, Conn.: Ablex.

Haddad, Yvonne Yazbeck, Jane I. Smith, and Kathleen M. Moore. 2005. *Muslim Women in America: The Challenge of Islamic Identity Today*. New York: Oxford University Press.

Hanania, Ray. 2005. *Arabs of Chicagoland*. Chicago: Arcadia.

Marschner, Janice. 2003. *California's Arab Americans*. Sacramento: Coleman Ranch.

Read, Jen'nan Ghazal. 2003. *Culture, Class, and Work among Arab-American Women*. New Americans series. New York: LFB Scholarly Publishing.

Salhi, Zahia Smail. 2006. *The Arab Diaspora: Voices of an Anguished Scream* (Routledge Curzon Advances in Middle East and Islamic Studies). New York: Routledge.

Shain, Yossi. 1999. *Marketing the American Creed Abroad: Diasporas in the U.S. and Their Homelands*. New York: Cambridge University Press.

Suleiman, Michael. 2000. *Arabs in America*. Philadelphia: Temple University Press.

Terry, Janice. 2003. *U.S. Foreign Policy in the Middle East: The Role of Lobbies and Special Interest Groups*. London: Pluto.

Jerusalem

Benvenisti, Meron. 1998. *City of Stone: The Hidden History of Jerusalem*. Berkeley: University of California Press.

————. 2002. *Sacred Landscape: The Buried History of the Holy Land since 1948*. Berkeley: University of California Press.

————. 2007. *Son of the Cypresses: Memories, Reflections, and Regrets from a Political Life*. S. Mark Taper Foundation Book in Jewish Studies. Berkeley: University of California Press.

Appendix F: General Bibliography for Bible or Religion and Film

Babington, B., and P. W. Evans. 1993. *Biblical Epics: Sacred Narrative in the Hollywood Cinema*. New York: Manchester University Press.

Bach, Alice. 1996. "Calling the Shots: Directing Salomé's Dance of Death." In *Semeia 74: Biblical Glamour and Hollywood Glitz*, ed. Bach, 103–26.

———, ed. 1996. *Semeia 74: Biblical Glamour and Hollywood Glitz*. Special issue. Atlanta: Scholars Press.

———. 1997. *Women, Seduction, and Betrayal in Biblical Narrative*. New York: Cambridge University Press.

———. 2004. *Religion, Politics, Media in the Broadband Era*. Sheffield, UK: Sheffield Phoenix.

———. 2006. "Film." In *The Blackwell Companion to the Biblical Culture*, ed. John F. A. Sawyer. Malden, Mass.: Blackwell Publishing.

Baugh, Lloyd, S. J. 1997. *Imaging the Divine: Jesus and Christ Figures in Film*. Kansas City: Sheed and Ward.

Bliss, Michael. 1995. *The Word Made Flesh: Catholicism and Conflict in the Films of Martin Scorsese*. Lanham, Md.: Scarecrow.

Boyd, Malcolm. 1958. *Christ and Celebrity Gods: The Church in Mass Culture*. Greenwich, Conn.: Seabury.

Butler, Ivan. 1969. *Religion in the Cinema*. New York: Barnes.

Campbell, Richard H., and Michael R. Pitts. 1981. *The Bible on Film: A Checklist, 1897–1980*. Metuchen, N.J.: Scarecrow.

DeMille, Cecil B. 1959. *Autobiography*, ed. Donald Haynie. Englewood Cliffs, N.J.: Prentice-Hall.

———. 1993. *Soul in Suspense: Hitchcock's Fright and Delight*. Metuchen, N.J.: Scarecrow.

Exum, J. Cheryl. 1996a. "Bathsheba Plotted, Shot, and Painted." In *Semeia 74: Biblical Glamour and Hollywood Glitz*, ed. Bach, 47–74.

———. 1996b. *Plotted, Shot, and Painted: Cultural Representations of Biblical Women*. Sheffield, UK: Sheffield Academic Press.

Facey, Paul W. 1974. *The Legion of Decency: A Sociological Analysis of the Emergence and Development of a Social Pressure Group*. New York: Arno.

Forman, Henry James. 1933. *Our Movie-Made Children*. New York: MacMillan.

Forshey, Gerald E. 1992. *American Religious and Biblical Spectaculars*. Westport, Conn.: Praeger.

Glancy, Jennifer. 1996. "The Mistress and the Gaze: Masculinity, Slavery, and Representation." In *Semeia 74: Biblical Glamour and Hollywood Glitz*, ed. Bach, 127–46.

Gunn, David M. 1996. "Bathsheba Goes Bathing in Hollywood: Words, Images, and Social Locations." In *Semeia 74: Biblical Glamour and Hollywood Glitz*, ed. Bach, 75–102.

Holloway, Ronald. 1977. *Beyond the Image: Approaches to the Religious Dimension in the Cinema*. Geneva: World Council of Churches (in cooperation with Interfilm).

Hurley, Neil P. 1978. *The Reel Revolution: A Film Primer on Liberation*. Maryknoll, N.Y.: Orbis.

Ketcham, Charles B. 1976. *Federico Fellini: The Search for a New Mythology*. New York: Paulist Press.

———. 1986. *The Influence of Existentialism on Ingmar Bergman: An Analysis of the Theological Ideas Shaping a Filmmaker's Art.* Lewiston, N.Y.: Mellen.

———. 1992. *"One Flew over the Cuckoo's Nest:* A Salvific Drama of Liberation." In *Image and Likeness: Religious Visions in American Film Classics,* ed. Mays, 145–52.

Konzelman, Robert G. 1972. *Marquee Ministry: The Movie Theater as Church and Community Forum.* New York: Harper and Row.

Koosed, Jennifer L., and Tod Linafelt. 1996. "How the West Was Not One: Delilah Deconstructs the Western." In *Semeia 74: Biblical Glamour and Hollywood Glitz,* ed. Bach, 167–82.

Kreitzer, Larry J. 1993. *The New Testament in Fiction and Film.* Sheffield, UK: JSOT Press.

———. 1994. *The Old Testament in Fiction and Film: On Reversing the Hermeneutical Flow.* Sheffield, UK: Sheffield Academic Press.

Lucano, Angelo L. 1975. *Cultura e religione nel cinema.* Turin, Italy: ERI.

Makarushka, Irena. 1995. "Women Spoken For: Images of Displaced Desire." In *Screening the Sacred: Religion, Myth, and Ideology in Popular American Film,* ed. Martin and Ostwalt, 142–51.

Marsh, Clive, and Gaye Ortiz, eds. 1998. *Explorations in Theology and Film: Movies and Meaning.* Malden, Mass.: Blackwell.

Martin, Joel W., and Conrad E. Ostwalt Jr., eds. 1995. *Screening the Sacred: Religion, Myth, and Ideology in Popular American Film.* Boulder, Colo.: Westview.

Martin, Thomas M. 1991. *Images and the Imageless: A Study in Religious Consciousness and Film,* 2d ed. London: Associated University Presses.

May, John R., ed. 1992. *Image and Likeness: Religious Visions in American Film Classics.* New York: Paulist Press.

———, and Michael Bird, eds. 1982. *Religion in Film,* 1st ed. Knoxville: University of Tennessee Press.

McLemore, Elizabeth. 1995. "From Revelation to Dream: Allegory in David Lynch's *Blue Velvet,*" in *Screening the Sacred: Religion, Myth, and Ideology in Popular American Film,* ed. Martin and Ostwalt, 134–41.

Miles, Margaret. 1996. *Seeing Is Believing: Religion and Values in the Movies.* Boston: Beacon.

Moley, Raymond. 1938. *Are We Movie Made?* New York: Macy-Masius.

Ostwalt, Conrad E. 1995. "Hollywood and Armageddon: Apocalyptic Themes in Recent Cinematic Presentation." In *Screening the Sacred: Religion, Myth, and Ideology in Popular American Film,* ed. Martin and Ostwalt, 55–64.

Owens, Craig. 1983. "The Discourse of Others," in *The Anti-Aesthetic: Essays on Postmodern Culture,* ed. H. Foster, 57–82. Port Townsend, Wa.: Bay Press.

Phy, Allene Stuart. 1985. *The Bible and Popular Culture in America.* Philadelphia: Fortress.

Schaberg, Jane. 1996. "Fast Forwarding to the Magdalene." In *Semeia 74: Biblical Glamour and Hollywood Glitz,* ed. Bach, 33–46.

Scorsese, Martin. 1989. *Scorsese on Scorsese,* ed. David Thompson and Ian Christie. Introduction by Michael Powell. London: Faber and Faber.

Scott, Bernard Brandon. 1994. *Hollywood Dreams and Biblical Stories.* Minneapolis: Fortress.

Zeffirelli, Franco. 1984. *Franco Zeffirelli's Jesus: A Spiritual Diary.* San Francisco: Harper and Row.

Appendix G: Bibliography for Jewish American Films

Because there are so many recent, ethnically oriented books on film, I have made separate lists for the categories of Jewish American and African American films. I have also appended the category of feminist film criticism since these theories are fundamental to ways of seeing film and character. With apologies to those who care about such things, I have placed books on Jesus and specifically Christian interpretations in the general Bible or Religion and Film section.

Avisar, Ilan. 1988. *Screening the Holocaust: Cinema's Images of the Unimaginable.* Bloomington: Indiana University Press.

Bartov, Omer. 1996. *Murder in Our Midst: The Holocaust, Industrial Killing, and Representation.* New York: Oxford University Press.

Cohen, Sarah Blacher, ed. 1983. *From Hester Street to Hollywood: The Jewish-American Stage and Screen.* Bloomington: Indiana University Press.

Colombat, André. 1993. *The Holocaust in French Film.* Metuchen, N.J.: Scarecrow.

Desser, David, and Lester D. Friedman. 1993. *American-Jewish Filmmakers: Traditions and Trends.* Urbana: University of Illinois Press.

Erens, Patricia. 1984. *The Jew in American Cinema.* Bloomington: Indiana University Press.

Fox, Stuart. 1976. *Jewish Films in the United States: A Comprehensive Survey and Descriptive Filmography.* Boston: G. K. Hall.

Friedman, Lester D. 1982. *Hollywood's Image of the Jew.* New York: Ungar.

———. 1987. *The Jewish Image in American Film.* Secaucus, N.J.: Citadel.

Friedman, Regine Mihal. 1983. *L'image et son Juif: Le Juif dans le cinéma nazi.* Paris: Payot.

Insdorf, Annette. 1983. *Indelible Shadows: Film and the Holocaust.* New York: Random House.

Koch, Gertrud. 1992. *Die Einstellung ist die Einstellung: Visuelle Konstruktionen des Judentums.* Frankfurt am Main: Suhrkamp.

Kritzman, Lawrence D., ed. 1995. *Auschwitz and After: Race, Culture, and "the Jewish Question" in France.* New York: Routledge.

Santner, Eric L. 1990. *Stranded Objects: Mourning, Memory, and Film in Postwar Germany.* Ithaca, N.Y.: Cornell University Press.

Stevens, Matthew. 1992. *Jewish Film Directory: A Guide to More than 1200 Films of Jewish Interest from 32 Countries over 85 Years.* Westport, Conn.: Greenwood.

Appendix H: Bibliography for African American Films

Bobo, Jacqueline. 1995. *Black Women as Cultural Readers.* New York: Columbia University Press.

———. 1991. "Black Women in Fiction and Nonfiction: Images of Power and Powerlessness." *Wide Angle* 13(3–4/July–October): 72–73.

Bogle, Donald. 1973. *Toms, Coons, Mulattoes, Mammies, and Bucks: An Interpretive History of Blacks in American Films.* New York: Viking.

Cham, Mbye B., and Claire Andrade-Watkins, eds. 1988. *Blackframes: Critical Perspectives on Black Independent Cinema.* Cambridge, Mass.: MIT Press.

Cripps, Thomas. 1978. *Black Film as Genre.* Bloomington: Indiana University Press.

————. 1977. *Slow Fade to Black: The Negro in American Film, 1900–1942*. New York: Oxford University Press.

Dash, Julie. 1992. *Daughters of the Dust: The Making of an African American Woman's Film*. New York: New Press. Includes screenplay for the film.

Diakite, Madubuko. 1980. *Film, Culture, and the Black Filmmaker: A Study of Functional Relationships and Parallel Developments*. New York: Arno.

Friedman, Lester D., ed. 1991. *Unspeakable Images: Ethnicity and the American Cinema*. Chicago: University of Illinois Press.

Fusco, Coco. 1988. *Young, British, and Black: The Work of Sankofa and Black Audio Film Collective*. Buffalo, N.Y.: Hallwalls Contemporary Arts Center.

Guerrero, Edward. 1993. *Framing Blackness: The African American Image in Film*. Philadelphia: Temple University Press.

hooks, bell. 1993. *Black Looks: Race and Representation*. London: Turnaround Press.

Maynard, Richard A., ed. 1974. *The Black Man on Film: Racial Stereotyping*. Rochelle Park, N.J.: Hayden.

Nesteby, James R. 1982. *Black Images in American Films, 1896–1954: The Interplay between Civil Rights and Film Culture*. Washington, D.C.: University Press of America.

Reid, Mark A. 1993. *Redefining Black Film*. Berkeley: University of California Press.

Silk, Catherine. 1990. *Racism and Anti-racism in American Popular Culture: Portrayals of African-Americans in Fiction and Film*. Manchester, UK: Manchester University Press.

Weisenfeld, Judith. 1996. "For Rent, 'Cabin in the Sky': Race, Religion, and Representational Quagmires in American Film." In *Semeia 74: Biblical Glamour and Hollywood Glitz*, ed. Bach, 147–66.

Additional Resources for Early African American Cinema

African American Film Heritage video series: *Go Down, Death; Lying Lips; Moon over Harlem; Scar of Shame*. Facets Video, Chicago.

Marcelline, Ashley. 1994. *Ashley Marcelline's Black Film and Video Guide*. Thornhill, Ont.: Black Cinema Network.

Tyler, Texas, Black Film Collection: *Where Is My Man Tonight? The Vanities; Souls of Sin; Murder in Harlem; Midnight Shadow; Juke Joint; Girl in Room 20; Broken Earth; Boogie-woogie Blues; By-line Newsreel*.

Appendix I: Bibliography for Feminist Criticism and Women in Film

Berenstein, Rhona. 1996. *Attack of the Leading Ladies: Gender, Sexuality, and Spectatorship in Classic Horror Cinema*. New York: Columbia University Press.

Byars, Jackie. 1991. *All That Hollywood Allows*. Chapel Hill: University of North Carolina Press.

Carson, Diane, Linda Dittmar, and Janice R. Welsch, eds. 1994. *Multiple Voices in Feminist Film Criticism*. Minneapolis: University of Minnesota Press.

Clover, Carol J. 1992. *Men, Women, and Chain Saws*. Princeton, N.J.: Princeton University Press.

Cook, Samantha. 1992. *Women and Film Bibliography*. London: British Film Institute.

De Lauretis, Teresa. 1984. *Alice Doesn't: Feminism, Semiotics, Cinema*. Bloomington: Indiana University Press.

———. 1990. *Film and the Primal Fantasy—One More Time: On Sheila McLaughlin's She Must Be Seeing Things*. Milwaukee: University of Wisconsin–Milwaukee, Center for Twentieth-century Studies.

———. 1987. *Technologies of Gender: Essays on Theory, Film, and Fiction*. Bloomington: Indiana University Press.

———, and Stephen Heath, eds. 1980. *The Cinematic Apparatus*. New York: St. Martin's.

Doane, Mary Ann. 1987. *The Desire to Desire*. Bloomington: Indiana University Press.

———. 1991. *Femmes Fatales*. New York: Routledge.

———, Patricia Mellencamp, and Linda Williams, eds. 1984. *Re-vision: Essays in Feminist Film Criticism*. Frederick, Md.: University Publications of America.

Erens, Patricia, ed. 1979. *Sexual Stratagems: The World of Women in Film*. New York: Horizon.

Jayamanne, Laleen, ed. 1995. *Kiss Me Deadly: Feminism and Cinema for the Moment*. Sydney: Power Publications.

Kaplan, E. Ann. 1992. *Motherhood and Representation: The Mother in Popular Culture and Melodrama*. New York: Routledge.

———, ed. 1990. *Psychoanalysis and Cinema*. London: Routledge.

———. 1983. *Women and Film: Both Sides of the Camera*. New York: Methuen.

———. 1980. *Women in Film Noir*, rev. ed. London: BFI.

Locke, Maryel, and Charles Warren, eds. 1993. *Jean-Luc Godard's* Hail Mary: *Women and the Sacred in Film*. Foreword by Stanley Cavell. Carbondale: Southern Illinois University Press.

Mayne, Judith. 1990. *The Woman at the Keyhole: Feminism and Woman's Cinema*. Bloomington: Indiana University Press.

McCreadie, Marsha. 1983. *Women on Film: The Critical Eye*. New York: Praeger.

Mellen, Joan. 1974. *Women and Their Sexuality in the New Film*. New York: Horizon.

Modleski, Tania. 1992. *Feminism without Women: Culture and Criticism in a "Postfeminist Age."* New York: Routledge.

———. 1988. *The Women Who Knew Too Much: Hitchcock and Feminist Theory*. New York: Methuen.

Mulvey, Laura. 1989. *Visual and Other Pleasures*. Bloomington: Indiana University Press.

Penley, Constance, ed. 1991. *Close Encounters: Film, Feminism, and Science Fiction*. Minneapolis: University of Minnesota Press.

———. 1988. *Feminism and Film Theory*. New York: Routledge.

———. 1989. *The Future of an Illusion*. Minneapolis: University of Minnesota Press.

———. 1993. *Male Trouble*. Minneapolis: University of Minnesota Press.

———. 1991. *Technoculture*. Minneapolis: University of Minnesota Press.

Pietropaolo, Laura, and Ada Testaferri, eds. 1995. *Feminisms in the Cinema*. Bloomington: Indiana University Press.

Rushing, Janice Hocker. 1995. "Evolution of the 'New Frontier' in *Alien* and *Aliens*: Patriarchal Co-optation of the Feminine Archetype. In *Screening the Sacred: Religion, Myth, and Ideology in Popular American Film*, ed. Joel W. Martin and Conrad E. Ostwalt, 94–117. Boulder Colo.: Westview.

———. 1983. "The Rhetoric of the American Western Myth." *Communications Monographs* 50: 14–32.

Silverman, Kaja. 1988. *The Acoustic Mirror: The Female Voice in Psychoanalysis and Cinema*. Bloomington: Indiana University Press.

———. 1992. *Male Subjectivity at the Margins*. New York: Routledge.

Smith, Prudence. 1984. *Women and Film Bibliography*. London: BFI Education.

Stoddard, Karen M. 1983. *Saints and Shrews: Women and Aging in American Popular Film*. Westport, Conn.: Greenwood.

Thumim, Janet. 1992. *Celluloid Sisters: Women and Popular Cinema*. London: Macmillan.

Vincendeau, Ginette. 1987. "Women's Cinema, Film Theory, and Feminism in France." *Screen* 28(4/Autumn): 4–18.

———, and Berenice Reynaud, eds. 1993. *Vingt ans de théories féministes sur le cinéma: Grande-Bretagne et Etats-Unis*. Courbevoie, France. Reprint of *CinemAction* 67.

Walker, Janet. 1993. *Couching Resistance*. Minneapolis: University of Minnesota Press.

NOTES

1. "Truthiness" is a Stephen Colbert neologism.

2. For a lengthy analysis of my irritation with this tasteless "vegetable soup" made from biblical scraps, see my *Religion, Politics, Media in the Broadband Era,* chapter 4.

3. Portions of this section appeared in slightly different form in my article, "Film."

4. Students kept a journal of daily readings of *Ha'aretz* and *Aljazeera.net*. The course readings were from the following books:

Bornstein, Avram S., *Crossing the Green Line between Palestine and Israel (The Ethnography of Political Violence)*

Finkelstein, Norman, *Beyond Chutzpah: On the Misuse of Anti-Semitism and the Abuse of History*

Gish, Art, *Hebron Diary*

Hass, Amira, *Drinking the Sea at Gaza*

Pappé, Ilan, *A History of Modern Palestine: One Land, Two Peoples*

Reinhart, Tanya, *The Road Map to Nowhere: Israel/Palestine since 2003*

Sizer, Stephen, *Christian Zionism: Road-Map to Armageddon*

Stein, Rebecca, and Ted Swedenburg, eds., *Palestine, Israel, and the Politics of Popular Culture*

Reporters without Borders, eds., *Israel/Palestine: The Black Book*

5. By the fifth week of class, students had developed their own preferred list of websites to troll daily for updates of Israeli and Palestinian happenings:

http://a-mother-from-gaza.blogspot.com/
http://www.electronicintifada.net
http://www.ipsc.ie
http://joeskillet.livejournal.com/
http://www.maannews.net
http://www.machsomwatch.org
http://news.bbc.co.uk/2/hi/middle_east
http://www.palsolidarity.org
http://tabulagaza.blogspot.com/

6. First published in Russian under the title "O Zheleznoi Stene in Rassvyet" on November 4, 1923. Published in English in the *Jewish Herald* (South Africa) on November 26, 1937. For the complete article see http://www.mideastweb.org/ IronWall.htm (accessed November 21, 2007). Jabotinsky was a dyed-in-the-wool European colonialist who swallowed whole the Euro-American cultural colonialism and racist clichés that were common in that era. Paleontology texts speculated that Africans and Australian aborigines belonged to a different, inferior species, and popular novels and movies ridiculed Jews, Africans, and other minorities. Jabotinsky conceived of Zionism as a colonial enterprise in the same vein as colonization of the United States or Australia, with Arabs from Palestine serving as placeholders for the indigenous people of North America and the aborigines of Australia.

4

Designing a Course on Religion and Cinema in India

Gayatri Chatterjee

This chapter addresses the challenge of designing and teaching an undergraduate course on religion and cinema in India. Film and religious studies departments in American universities usually offer this topic as part of a general course on Indian cinema or in combination with other disciplines such as the media studies and the study of popular culture and popular visual art. Courses may compare American and Indian film and religion or deal with the representations of gods and sex—or the sacred and the profane in cinema.[1] Importantly, the number of courses exclusively on religion and cinema in India is very low, if not nil. If this is the case and if one is designing a course in this context, one must first survey and prepare the "land."

Many Religions in India

The usual focus of most courses and studies has been Hinduism—even if that is not specifically stated. There is no one religion that could properly be called Hinduism—no single text, Godhead, or prophet. The monolithic term *Hinduism* becomes necessary only in the context of encounters with other religions—not only Islam and Christianity but also those that have developed as distinct teachings through a history of debate with orthodox Hinduism, namely Buddhism and Jainism. In her book (the first on this topic in the English language), Rachel Dwyer provides one reason for the noninclusion of Islam in film studies: This religion does not allow representation; thus, because there are no gods and goddesses or stories connected with them, there can be no "Islamic" films (Dwyer 2007). In the chapter titled "The Islamicate Films," Dwyer provides examples of movies in which Muslims are the main protagonists and Islamic and Sufi ideas and aesthetics provide the subtexts.

Two films by Saeed Mirza are crucial to any study of Islam in India. The first, *Salim Lagde Pe Mat Ro* (1989; in Hindi), is about the difficulty of being a Muslim in Bombay. After Salim's father loses his job following the closure of a textile mill, the family members find odd jobs to keep the family going; but Salim turns to petty theft and crime. *Salim Lagde Pe Mat Ro* cautions Muslim youths against taking the easy way out. Six years later Mirza made the remarkable *Naseem* (1995; in Hindi), which ends with Bombay burning after the demolition of the Babri Mashjid (in the northern city of Ayodhya). On that same day the elderly grandfather (played by progressive writer and poet Kaifi Azmi) also passes away; it is as though, with this death, an era comes to an end. However, he has succeeded in instilling democratic and progressive values in his granddaughter, Naseem, but not in his grandson.

Indian Catholic Christians have always been avid worshippers of iconic images. Images and rituals are an integral part of church services, which are both performative and participatory. Representations of biblical characters and saints, as well as narration and performances about their lives, have been important to the religious practice of Indian Catholic Christians. Christianity is very much represented in Indian films—even in secular movies in which religion is not a dominant theme.[2] Many popular films show Hindu protagonists seeking moments of peace in the quiet of a church, for example in *Dilwale Dulhaniya Le Jayenge* (Aditya Chopra 1995). Additionally, we have the romantic (or melodramatic) hero imagined as a crucified Christ, as in *Pyaasa* (Guru Dutt 1959). At times, orphaned heroes are sheltered in a church and brought up as Christians, for example in *Amar Akbar Anthony* (Manmohan Desai 1977).

However, with some exceptions, films with a Christian hero or heroine are rare. In *Esthappan* (1978; in Malayalam), by Govindan Aravindan, villagers believe Esthappan [Stephan] can work miracles; the village priest both protects and admonishes this man, who at various times appears to be a crazed artist, a bemused prophet, or an eccentric.[3] In a manner that is gentle, affectionate, penetrating, and also humorous, this marvelous film explores common folks' need for believing in extraordinary happenings, their habit of reading meanings into events they see but do not fully comprehend, and the growth of strong individuality in the midst of everyday life. Because of Aravindan's interest in both the close interrelationship between reality and illusion and the construction of myths, the film ends with a statement about storytelling, representation, and performance.

Purushan, the main character in *Amma Arian* [*Report to Mother*] (John Abraham 1985; in Malayalam), is on his way from Kerala to Delhi in the pursuit of his career. On his way he sees the dead body of a young man, Hari, which he finds strangely familiar. Wanting to know why someone his age would commit suicide, Purushan begins a search among all those who knew Hari—the actual hero of the film. During this journey, the audience becomes well acquainted with much of Kerala's political history. At the end of the film,

Purushan, accompanied now by a dozen men of various age groups, goes to tell Hari's mother of her son's death. They must wait, however, because she is in church attending the baptism of a male infant.[4]

Strangely, India has not produced many Buddhist films, a rare example of which is the silent *Prem Sannyas* [*The Light of Asia/Die Lichte Asiens*] (Franz Osten 1929) on the life of Buddha.[5] Based on a long poem by Edwin Arnold, it is a well-crafted film with a German crew and many Indian artists in the capacity of art director and actors. Full of Orientalist imagery, the film begins with a group of foreign travelers in Bodhgaya listening to Buddha's story from a local ascetic.

Many Hinduisms

Insofar as this chapter treats the theme of religious expression in India, I discuss primarily diverse aspects of Hinduism. I do so, in part, in order to survey and address existing trends. However, this is a provisional approach. The study of all religions and the history of diverse strands of religious expression as they developed together in modern India would be the ideal basis of a course. In this chapter I develop what would be an ideal course for me, too. Ramkrishna Paramahansa, the prominent nineteenth-century Bengali devotee of the goddess Kali, often said that, when it comes to religion, there are "as many paths as there are viewpoints."[6] The saying became popular among exponents of religious reform and modernization in India. Quite in accordance with this spirit, Indian films normally do not claim the existence of any single religion called Hinduism.[7] In the world of cinema, too, there are as many films as there are ways and viewpoints and vice versa.

However, some films clearly represent a certain binary emerging within the Hindu fold: the ritualistic Brahmanic way, exemplified by the Vedic fire sacrifice *(yajna)* and based on Sanskrit texts, as opposed to *bhakti,* or mode of devotion, in which the relationship between God and humans is seen as intimate and participatory and which is based on local languages, literatures, performances, and the arts. Attempting to establish a flow from the Vedic/Brahmanical religion to bhakti, the barefoot filmmaker G. V. Iyer created *Adi Shankaracharya* (1983; in Sanskrit), *Madhavacharya* (1986, in Kannada), and *Ramanujacharya* (1989; in Tamil).[8] Iyer shows these religious figures as deeply and passionately theist and at the same time as eclectically creating new formulations. In tune with contemporary trends and understandings of religion and history, Iyer does not represent the miraculous events featured in the hagiographies of these religious leaders.

Language, Religion, and Cinema

Discussions of Indian religion and cinema as usually conducted in Anglo-American universities focus mainly on Hindi films made in Bombay; they begin with or are confined to the study of two genres: the mythological and the devotional. For the study of the mythological, the main example is usually *Jai Santoshi Maa* (Vijay Sharma 1975; in Hindi); the second is typically *Sant Tukaram* (Damle and Fattelal 1936; in Marathi). Both these films are popular with audiences and important for film studies; but the latter is in the Marathi language, not in Hindi, and is imbued with the spirit of regional Maharashtrian devotionalism. This example points to the need for the inclusion of non-Hindi films in Indian cinema courses and for the expansion of the canon of films usually presented. The studies of both religion and cinema in India must cross language borders. Not only devotional literature and music but even the mythological stories written in Sanskrit are locally inflected and also have a transregional distribution.

Perhaps a typical Indian film on religion does not follow the argumentative modes exemplified by the three religious leaders in Iyer's films, but many carry vestiges of those modes. Additionally, they engage in modern debates about religion in local as well as pan-Indian nationalist discussions. For example, if we examine the devotional films made in Bangla, Tamil, or Marathi, we find them significantly different. *Sant Tukaram* is representative of Maharashtra in the 1930s and differs in instructive ways from a later Hindi film of the same title and about the same character (Rajesh Nanda, 1963). At the same time, it contains some contemporary and pan-Indian themes and concerns (and thus is popular elsewhere in India). Given the scope of this chapter, the phrase "Indian cinema" means films made in all Indian languages. Even if the Hindi film market were larger than that of Tamil and Telegu (the exact figures are lacking), that would not justify presenting only films made in Hindi within the framework of a course on "Indian cinema." However popular the tendency of stressing the products of the Hindi-language industry, or "Bollywood," may have become among academics who design survey courses on Indian cinema, it is impossible to do so when it comes to the topic of religion. That approach would risk portraying religion in India as a monolithic and relatively homogeneous phenomenon.

A Brief Survey of the Current Study of This Topic

Courses on religion and cinema typically begin with the mythological and the devotional and then turn to more contemporary, popular Hindi films such as *Amar Akbar Anthony* (Manmohan Desai 1977; in Hindi) to show how religion is often a subtext in mainstream, entertainment-oriented films (Rotman, Elison, and Novetzke, in process). At times more recent films dealing with problems related to religion and society are chosen; examples are *Mr. and Mrs. Iyer* (Aparna Sen 2005; in Bangla) and *Fanaa* (Kunal Kohli 2005; in Hindi) for the Hindu-Muslim conflict and *Rang De Basanti* (Rakesh Mehra 2006; in Hindi) for (terroristic) nationalism and religion. Satyajit Ray's Bengali film *Devi* (1960; in Bangla) has been a longtime favorite for unpacking complex social and psychological issues traditionally expressed in an Indian context through religious idioms.

Syllabi that begin by introducing the two genres (the mythological and the devotional) and then add other disciplines are following a traditional chronology or trajectory of Western film studies—that is, from the classical genre study to more recent methods utilized by anthropology, reception theory, and cultural studies. This could be an effective strategy for designing short courses, but I suggest first that we widen the field of vision in order to better encompass the vast landscape out there and, second, that we scrutinize the assumptions upon which the established strategies of studies of these topics are based.

The Importance of the Indian Middle Class

In India the birth of cinema coincided with the birth of the vast middle classes in the cities and innumerable towns, both large and small. And so cinema, to begin with, is very much part of middle-class activity and the awakening of the time. More films in India are critical (or even reformative) of religious practices than those that fully endorse them. For a full understanding of this project, one must focus on the religious reform movements—another middle-class activity of that period—which finds strong articulation in films.

This in turn would mean reformulations of the category of the individual as spectator and new dynamics within and between the private and public spheres in the country. The history of the middle class in India is not isolated from those of the other classes and caste factors; rather, Indian cinema is strongly characterized by the many shifts in the classes and the castes (and other matters related to tribe, race, and gender). This chapter envisions and designs longer courses that can provide students with a wider knowledge and a deeper understanding of cinema and religion in India in a historical perspective.

Some Binaries within Pluralities

Before we engage with the two genres commonly studied, we need to be familiar with other issues regarding binaries and pluralities. Some courses look at religion only in terms of popular culture. Certain teachers like to include art cinema examples such as Satyajit Ray's *Devi*; whereas some do not make these distinctions. A course on religion and cinema must negotiate a binary that is formal, and that distinguishes *popular* and *art* cinema.

In *Devi* the young and beautiful Dayamayee (henceforth "Daya") lives with her in-laws, who belong to a traditional and decadent feudal family. She is fully engaged in serving her widower father-in-law, Kalikinkar Ray, while her husband, Umaprasad, attends college in Calcutta. One day Kalikinkar dreams that Daya is an incarnation of the goddess Kali and begins to treat her as a living *devi* (the female aspect of the divine), who is adored and prayed to. When a poor, critically ill child revives because of her "blessings," Daya's fame as a goddess spreads across the country, but when she cannot similarly "save" Kalikinkar's grandson (from another son), she is damned. On the surface, the film takes a critical look at religious and feudal practices in early twentieth-century British Bengal and at the propensity of rich and poor alike to believe in and live by superstitions. It also offers other interesting issues worthy of exploration. Kalikinkar's act is quite clearly explained as the subconscious sublimation of his libido, which has been restored by the sight of this young beautiful woman. On the other hand, though Umaprasad learns modern ideas (thanks to his English teacher, a social reformer who has converted to Christianity), he is totally ineffective against his feudal father.[9] Modernity in the colonial period might have provided ways to escape the extremely rigid, mundane existence available to most, but it did not pave paths for transcendence into a fully satisfying self hood. Umaprasad convinces Daya that she is human and should escape with him to Calcutta. On the way there she sees a discarded wooden structure by the riverbank, which a few months ago had carried the mud idol of goddess Durga, whom everyone had worshipped. Daya stops and exclaims to her husband, "What if I were a goddess!" She has always been treated like a doll (a word that is repeated several times); transformed to a *goddess* now, could she return to being a *doll* or a discarded wooden frame? Distraught by her experiences, Daya runs away and disappears into the early morning mist (Ghosh 1992).

There is a common perception that art films are critical of religion and that popular films are not. On the other hand, Ravi Vasudevan has pointed out that two popular-cinema or studio genres, the *social* and the *devotional,* present social critique and that they were meant "to displace the mythological and the superstitious and irrational culture it founded" (Vasudevan 2000). If we follow this logic, there is no difference between art and commercial studio films when it comes to movies that are critical of religion. Extending the argument, we must conclude that if only art films are critical of religion, the popular devotionals films must be pro-religion; moreover, if the devotionals carry social criticism, they must be art films and not belong to popular cinema.[10] If one thinks along argumentative lines, other anomalies might surface and disturb the way we usually think of cinema. Finally, when we disturb familiar thoughts we see several sets of binaries making up a scene of plurality.

Multiplicity and Plurality

The two words *multiplicity* and *plurality* offer the prerequisite keys to designing a course on religion and cinema. The rich diversity of this topic is what we must take into account (later we may need to move to a subsequent stage that can be understood as a period of depletion or loss of that diversity). Religion and cinema separately are vast enough topics; together they constitute a mind-boggling field that can also embrace other areas of study such as philosophy, poetics, sociology, and history—and particularly the histories and studies of visual and narrative cultures in India and beyond.

Indian cinema draws on rich and complex, not to mention obsessive, traditions of storytelling that are deeply entrenched in South Asian communities. More or less familiar with the tales, audiences enjoy their retelling; habituated with the oral traditions' allowance for different versions and renditions, they accept changes made in the story; they are aware that story elements and characters are often vehicles for some discourse or comment upon contemporary affairs. Meditation and contemplation, verbalization, analysis, and modification are necessary components of both religion and cinema.

Thus, the most important challenge of designing this course is that not only must one negotiate a series of binariesnot only must one make the students aware of the plurality of the Indian situation, but one must also be able to graft the films and their studies onto these binaries and pluralities. This is crucial to any study of cinema in India. To familiarize students with notions of multiplicity and plurality vis-à-vis the Indian situation in only one lecture is one thing, but to integrate the idea and supporting facts throughout a course is another matter. One might be required to present a binary in one class and a contradictory binary in the next or to link the sets of binaries with the grand narrative of multiplicity-plurality. Having said this, I now examine the two genres that are widely pervasive in Indian film studies and religious studies that offer short courses in religion and cinema. These two film genres—the mythological and the devotional—are often treated as binary opposites.

Genre Studies, Indian Cinemas, and Indian Religions

Film industries used genre headings such as mythology and the devotional to advertise films (in media such as English-language newspapers, handbills, and posters).[11] Some genre heads or titles for Indian such as the "mythological" or the "historical" were borrowed from Hollywood, and some such as the "devotional" or the "*Sant* film" were indigenous.[12] During the period of silent films in the twenties the nomenclature was quite complete. These terms were picked up again by film reviewers (film writing in journals and newspapers started appearing on a regular basisin the thirties) and retained by film scholars (from the seventies on).[13] Some scholars of Indian cinema (e.g., Rajadhyaksha, Madhava Prasad) have pointed out that Indian cinema does not—or cannot—have precise genres (as Hollywood does).[14] Though the situations in the United States and India are very different, it is useful to read the American elaboration and critiques of genre study while engaging in Indian cinema studies; several scholars of American cinema have been problematizing genre studies very effectively in the past few decades (e.g., Neal; Altman 1999). Paul Willemen has notes how most scholars agree that cinematic genres are, in fact, simply marketing categories presenting product lines. He argues that cinema is perceived as an industry and so the profusion of books of American and other genre cinema. But the over emphasis is also due to intractable problems in film theory and, from there, to cultural theory in general and problems of poetics in particular (Willemen 2006).

Rachel Dwyer (2007) has divided her book on religion in Indian cinema into four chapters. One is on the Islamic films (as mentioned earlier), while two others are devoted to the mythological and the devotional. Importantly, she titles her book *Filming the Gods,* and it is only in the subtitle that she announces the book is about religion. Clearly, Dwyer has paid particular attention to specific aspects of the cinematic expression of religious themes associated with popular Hinduism and cinema in India. In this chapter I discuss other aspects, but I begin by taking a critical look at the two genres, both as the foundation of a course syllabus and also in terms of problematizing a genre-informed study of religion and cinema.

The Mythological

The mythological genre, to put it plainly, is about representing the Hindu gods. A typical narrative weaves together various exploits of gods and goddesses; a god's relationship with other gods; their perennial conflict with the *asuras* (demons or "antigods"); and their interestingly codependent relationship with mortals. The genre adapts stories from the classical epics, the *Rāmāyana* and *Mahābhārata,* and the various *Purānas* (canonical texts of mythological literature) as found in different local and regional versions. Not all mythological films have the same relationship with the source text. It is a rewarding experience when the studies of some films lead us to the multiple aspects of these texts and their diverse histories: religious, political, economic, and sociological. These are texts that discuss morality and ethics in the light of changes that each historical epoch brings about. Inasmuch as these texts represent India's vibrant storytelling traditions, we can see films as continuing those customs as well.

It is often noted that the mythological dominated the Indian film industry during the silent period; in the thirties, the two important genres were the social and the devotional. The majority of films in the silent period were mythological, but as we proceed, something unexpected will often break into an easy historiography and make things complex—as in this case. There are two films vying to be the "first full-length feature film made in India": *Pundalik* (P. R. Tipnis 1912) and *Raja Harishchandra* (D. G. Phalke 1913).[15] The first is about a *bhakti* saint from the southern region of Karnataka who is reputed to have founded the Vitthala temple at Pandaharpur in Maharashtra. The second is sourced from a story in the *Mahābhārata* about the legendary/mythical king of Kashi (Banaras, in the present-day north Indian state of Uttar Pradesh), who was known for his truthfulness and exemplary conduct. The story recounts the personal sacrifices he makes in order to placate the sage Durvasha and maintain *dharma.* These narratives are examples of the tendency of both genres, which remain historically intertwined (Dwyer 2007).

Most mythological films made by D. G. Phalke have been well studied (Rajadhyaksha 1987; Schulze 2003; Dwyer 2007).[16] The work of the other, equally important silent filmmaker from Maharashtra, Baburao Painter, also demands attention (some of his films have recently been found and included in the collections of the National Film Archive of India, located in Pune). Painter was trying for greater realism in his films, including those in the mythological or devotional genres. *Murliwala* (1927) is about Krishna as a boy and includes Radha as an important protagonist. Because she is much older than he, her love for him is a combination of parental love *(vātsalya)* and erotic love. In this film, the spiritual attainment of Radha and her husband is as important as the miraculous feats of young Krishna. *Murliwala* mixes the mythological and the devotional and brings together that which belongs to the regions both above and on the earth.

However, the mythological had other uses as well. In Maharashtra, theater often depicted veiled (in religious terms) or at times explicit political messages; in the late colonial period several theater personalities were jailed, and plays were banned. Filmmakers picked up these plays, at times changed the titles, and diluted the allegorical political content in order to produce entertaining films; however, audiences recognized the hidden messages and cheered.[17] When Krishna tamed Kaliya, in D. G. Phalke's *Kaliya Mardan,* people stood up and shouted anti-British slogans. In *Bhakta Bidur* (Kantilal Rathod 1921), the character of Vidur was made to resemble Mahatma Gandhi and wore the Gandhi cap; consequently, the film was banned in some parts of the country. However, most filmmakers were cautious (for financial reasons) and yet eager for their works to be marketable and released unhindered. *Sairindhri* (Baburao Painter 1920) was inspired by Khadilkar's famous banned play, *Keechak Badh,* but the film did not meet with the same fate.[18] *SriKrishna Janma* [The Birth of Krishna] (D. G. Phalke 1918) advocates a Hindu nationalist policy of bringing together all of the castes under one banner, that of Hinduism in general and Krishna Bhakti in particular. An intertitle cites Krishna's famous advice to Arjuna in the *Bhagavad Gita,* "Abandon all other paths and follow me."[19]

The fantasy element, an obvious ingredient of the popularity of mythological films, has been criticized for being escapist and regressive and for proliferating superstitions and moribund social systems. However, their tremendous popularity across India demands closer study. In Bombay, director Babubhai Mistry has been depicting miraculous events (*camatkār* or *tilsim*) for the past six decades. With his scriptwriters, he gathers stories from diverse religious and language resources and speaks fondly of his sources of inspiration in the *Purānas* (in particular the *Matsya-Purāna* and the *Shiva-Purāna*). Scenes of battles between the gods and the *asuras* or of devotees having their wishes miraculously granted, as shown in his films, are indeed close to the Sanskrit Puranic texts.[20] Mythological films have also yielded numerous love stories (e.g., Nala-Damayanti), so one cannot say that Puranic or epical texts yield only religious films. The story of Nala and Damayanti finds special mention here as this mortal couple repeatedly defeats many gods and demigods.

The Devotional

Bhakti, or devotional, films are based on biographies and hagiographies of historical, semi-legendary, and legendary devotees (and poets).[21] At times, a devotional also embraces local and national issues and can be considered an allegory as well. It might even attempt to redefine religious practices in India or in a particular region. At the same time, the most important feature of a devotional remains fixed in every film: an individual's or a community's love of God.

The New Theatres of Calcutta, a pioneering film company, was particularly famous for making movies based on devotees of historical or semilegendary figures; two bilingual movies, *Chandidas* (Nitin Bose 1932/1934; in Bengali and Hindi) and *Bidyapati/Vidyapati* (Devaki Bose 1937; in Bengali and Hindi), have become the most famous films in the history of Indian cinema. The two main features of these movies are the belief that spirituality is coterminous with poetic creation and the conviction that devotion is real and good only when associated with love for humanity. A line from one of Chandidas's verses reverberates in them: "Man is above [superior to or more important than] all else; nothing beyond [man]."[22] However, other films in the Bengali language are also important for a study like this—for example, *Bhagawan Shri Krishna Chaitanya* (Devaki Bose 1954)—because of their research and thought content.

Similarly, the celebrated Prabhat Film Studio, based in Pune, made a number of films (called the "*sant* films of Prabhat") based on the legends surrounding the *vārkari* saint-poets *(sant-kavi)* of Maharashtra.[23] A close look at *Sant Tukaram* shows what a devotional film is often about: issues of love and humanity; the hagiography of a saint-poet; aspects of the local history; social criticism and religious debates. But over and above everything else, devotional films are about one's love for God. The most important feature of mythological films, as commonly perceived, is that they represent or film the gods. But so do the devotional films. We cannot talk of *Sant Tukaram*, for example, without mentioning its representation of the god Vitthala. To the extent that it offers representations of the gods, the devotional crosses genre boundaries and enters the mythological.

Continuing in this vein, we see more than half a dozen representations of miracles in *Sant Tukaram*. If one believes that the mythological films promote superstitions because they depict miraculous happenings, then *Sant Tukaram* must also do so. As we speak about these two genres, we will see their boundaries crumble and the field opening up to the vast multiplicity of Indian history and reality. We could make a distinction, though: In the mythological, gods and goddesses are the principal protagonists, whereas in the devotional a mortal is the protagonist.

Like typical mythological films, the devotional films too can be based on the *Purānas*. A devotional in that case would resemble a mythological film and would have scenes of miraculous happenings (e.g., *Bhakta Prahlad, Bhakta*

Dhruva).[24] Prahlad, Dhruva, and Vidur are early examples of *puranic* heroes as devotees. Another mythological character, Narada, is considered one of the earliest legendary writers of a bhakti text; a colorful ascetic character, Narada is popular with filmmakers and audiences and has occurred in scores of films.

Sant Tukaram makes several departures in the hagiography it draws upon. Against the common knowledge that he had two wives and six children, Tukaram here has one wife, one son, and one daughter—the picture of a modern nuclear family.[25] His representation as a lone individual engrossed in his poetic creation also goes against contemporary accounts that he was always in a crowd singing and dancing.[26] These and similar examples demonstrate how the story is made modern or relevant to the contemporary, but they do not mean the film is in any way not *religious*. It does not blindly use tradition for the service of nationality and modernity but critiques tradition from within itself and from certain modernist, reformist positions (Geeta Kapoor 1987/2000).

In one tradition of belief, Tukaram's wife, Jijai, was "shrewish," based on six or more verses in which Tukaram rebukes her for being materialistic and not understanding spiritual matters. In the film, Jijai bitterly scolds her husband and his god for not providing for the family; her words constitute a criticism of those who are religious without being productive and responsible to the family. The actors act in befitting manners—she is earthy, open, and passionate, while he is gentle, graceful, and captivated by his creative and spiritual energy.[27] Applying their knowledge of Maharashtra, the filmmakers show Jijai as a true devotee of a local goddess, Mangal-aai. Fierce in her own belief, Jijai remains (along with the villainous Brahman Salomalo) unproselytized until the end. Thus, there are three tiers of religious people here: the Brahmans, who represent the institutional power of religion; Tukaram, who founds a sort of religion of the people, a religion of love and equity; and Jijai, who represents the marginal (e.g., women, the low caste people, poverty-stricken rural India) and follows an inferior form of religious practice. The first two representations of a miracle happen not to Tukaram but to his wife. Audiences hugely enjoy seeing Jijai in proactive moods, scolding both her husband and his god.

The reasons behind such narration-representation also lie within the tradition of bhakti discourse and narration: Tukaram's deity, Vitthala, responds to Jijai because (a) the gods love a true devotee; (b) Vitthala feels a special bond of affection for Tukaram's wife and children; (c) gods—like heroes—love to placate an angry heroine *(kupitā nāyikā);* and (d) just as the gods love to test the devotee, they too like a devotee to test and admonish them. The appeal of the two sequences is enhanced each time Vitthala does something to help Jijai or her family, but she attributes her good fortune to her own goddess and rebukes her husband's god more vehemently, which causes Vitthala to laugh and gleefully resume his childlike form.

Local religious traditions have never been fully submerged into translocal, Sanskritized forms of worship, nor have they ever been properly represented in cinema—this film is an important exception. As individual films are studied in detail (deviating from the practice of studying and understanding films in clusters), a class is better situated to align with the theoretical trends of the social sciences. *Sant Tukaram* is a film well suited to teaching how Indian civilization can be understood in terms of an interplay between *great* (trans-local, elite, Sanskritized, Brahmanical, institutionalized) and *little* (local, sub-altern, vernacular, low caste, informal) traditions. Interestingly, cinema too could be better appreciated in those terms.

Going beyond Genre

A study centered on the mythological and the devotional does not pay enough attention to the plurality of mainstream Hinduism in the modern period. The formation of Indian cinema coincided with the growth of the Indian middle class and the peak period of social and religious reform at the time of nationalism. Until the sixties and even later, Indian films were heavily characterized by the motifs of the societies' and the social leaders' engagement with religious reform. This cannot be understood through the conventional binary of blind, dogmatic superstition and religiosity (or in other words, backward-ness) versus social critique, rationalist negation of religion (or, in other words, modernity). The films retain the discursive nature of religious narratives and conduct social criticism while staying within the bounds of religious faith.

The accent is on the shaping of the modern individual—self-probing and self-critiquing, weaned away from explicit dependence on God but with a strong desire for self-realization and various modes and formulations of transcendence. Although perhaps not ostensibly religious, these individuals are morally and ethically superior. They pray not for the augmentation of wealth, health, and physical protection but for the attainment of abstract inner qualities and betterment of character.[28] Interestingly, the two epics often furnish the inspiration for such discourses and lend to film narratives; it should be possible to design a teaching module that would explore the cinematic modernizations of epic themes and narratives.

Storytelling and Performance: Two Major Sources

The *Mahābhārata* and the *Rāmāyana* were edited and translated into the local languages all through the medieval period. The storytelling and performative habits of people in this part of the world grew even stronger as these two texts were recited, listened to, and performed. During these activities, local stories would slip in, making up yet other versions.[29] It is now quite well known that the *Rāmāyana* exists in many different versions (Richman 1991); we need to study the numerous ways performance is linked to that story of the creation of texts and bring that understanding to cinema.

Since the inception of cinema, films have drawn from the repertoire of stories found in the two epics in many different adaptations; in turn, these films have also given rise to newer variations. The *Rāmāyana* can be told as a simple chronological story, and so every decade has seen movies based on the entire epic *(sampūrna)* or a part of it. For example, Ram and Seeta's marriage is the main topic in the Telegu *Seeta Kalyanam* (Narasimha Rao 1934; Bapu 1976); both versions have been extremely popular and are significant examples of Telegu cinema. *Sampurna Rāmāyana* [The Complete Ramayana] (Babubhai Mistry 1961) is a milestone in the history of the Hindu mythology. Released in the year of the Quit India movement, *Bharat Milap* (Vijay Bhatt, 1942, in Hindi) sent a message to the British rulers: Just as good brother Bharat had continued the good rule *(rām-rājya)* in the absence of Rama, so Indians are capable of taking up self-rule *(swarāj)*.[30] All of these films are revived periodically on television, and their videodiscs have a steady market.

At times the *Rāmāyana* has helped continue traditional values and reinstate religious and social injunctions in newer (and more regressive) *avatār* through a film; at other times it has provided innovative visual and narrative motifs to cinema through films with wholly new interpretations of the epic. In *Kanchan Seeta* (G. Aravindan 1976; in Malayalam), Rama and Laksman are dark-skinned people from south of the Vindya Mountains, marking their constant association with marginal tribal groups. In this film we see Lakshman's wife, Urmila, a marginalized figure in the epic; she admonishes her husband for being fascinated by the Aryans and encouraging the Aryan and non-Aryan separation. The film-Rama's death as he walks into the river Sarayu signifies the hero's union with nature as Sita—as opposed to his former civilization-building and war-making activities.

Another startling example of the retelling of the *Rāmāyana* is *Subernarekha* (Ritwik Ghatak, 1964, in Bangla). Displaced during the partition of Bengal, young Seeta comes to Calcutta (in West Bengal, India) from a village in East Bengal (now Bangladesh). Soon her elder brother, Ishwar, takes a job as manager of a rice mill situated on the banks of the river Subernarekha (in an area that was formerly in the state of Bihar; now it is Jharkhand). For Seeta, this is yet one more move toward another "new home" in a locale that resembles the world during early civilization: dense forest, sandy riverbanks, and tribes fishing with their primitive nets. However, there is also an abandoned airstrip and a ruined clubhouse the British had built during World War II. History and myth mix continually in any stage of a civilization—not all levels or layers are comprehensible to everyone in the same way.

One day Seeta walks happily in this new play area singing a song by Rabindranath Tagore about sunlight and clouds playing hide and seek on a beautiful spring day. Suddenly there appears a *bahurūpī* (one who earns money by parading around in disguises) dressed as the goddess Kali. Scared, Seeta runs blindly away and hugs the half-crazed former mill manager, who happens to be coming in her direction. The *bahurūpī* takes off his protruding metal tongue (part of the makeup) and says, "I did not mean to scare her. She had happened to come my way." Common people do not intend to but become witnesses to and participants in violent historical events. The Kali image has been variously created over centuries of brutal histories; today she is familiar and well loved. Her iconography (skulls, weapons, the fierce/gentle look) is comprehensible and even a means of livelihood for some. However, Seeta and the manager can make little meaning out of the scattered iconography of contemporary history—in the process of turning mythical (Ghatak 1987; Rajadhyaksha 1975).

The mill manager asks Seeta whether she knows the story of the "original Seeta," who is her namesake. Upon learning she does not, the he says, "Once while ploughing the fields, King Janak of Mithila found a little girl. Seeta came from the earth, and many years later she returned to her mother earth. All that happened in between make up the story of the *Rāmāyana*." Turning the epic into *Seetayan,* the maverick-genius filmmaker suggests the story of civilization as a series of migrations—just as the epic Seeta had experienced her entire life. The film-Seeta experiences constant relocation. She marries a man named Abhiram, but both die horrible deaths in events associated with the violence in Calcutta in the postpartition years. People are fashioned after some mythical past and then tossed around by the contemporary.

A typical Bollywood film, *Lajja* (Rajkumar Santoshi 2001) provides another spectacular use of the epic. That women in India continue to suffer in various ways under patriarchy is not new, but what is unique in the film is that its heroine gains such an understanding by traveling across the country and meeting other Seetas—characters who go by other names of the epic heroine: Vaidehi, Maithili, Janaki, and Ramdulari.

Disgusted with the immoral ways of her husband, Raghu, Vaidehiruns away from her New York penthouse; however, her parents in Bombay refuse to take her back and instead encourage her to return to her husband. On learning that Raghu (another name for Rama) wants to do away with her after acquiring the child she is carrying, Vaidehi runs away to Nagpur. In order to escape the goons her husband has sent after her, she mingles with Maithili's guests and family, as Maithili is about to be married—but ultimately refuses to do so. The groom's father insists on receiving the entire amount of dowry money before the wedding. Then, with Raghu's thugs close on her heels, Vaidehī takes off again.

She now visits a smaller town and enters a lower-middle-class milieu. Here she meets Jānaki, the lead actress in a local Nautanki-style theater company, and the two women form a deep friendship that cannot last. Jānakī is cruelly abused both by the theater owner and her lover, a coactor. Even her audience brutalizes her, as an inebriated Jānaki (playing Seeta in a play) refuses to follow the script and jump into a fire; instead, she gives an impassioned speech about the condition of women in India. The last stop in Vaidehi's journey is a tribal village, where the oppressed Ramdulari has mobilized the village women through education, computers, and small loans for private enterprises. The film also depicts men who are not oppressive or cruel; take, for example, the lovable thief who offers money to supplement Maithili's dowry or the fierce *dacoit* (worshipper of the Mother Goddess Kali) who is determined to take revenge on the overlord who has incarcerated both Ramdulari and him. The end provides the ever-popular, conventional, happy ending. Raghu finally realizes the worth of his wife, Seeta, and they return to New York.

Similarly, some adaptations of the *Mahābhārata* attempt only to reproduce the stories traditionally, whereas some are consciously modern in their interpretation. The realist *Kaliyug* (Shyam Benegal, 1980; in Hindi) is a story of rivalry between two business families in Bombay. Epical in scope, *Tarang* (Kumar Sahni, 1984; in Hindi) touches upon several histories: the nationalist leaders, now corrupted or dissipated in postindependence India; the failure of the once-active labor movement at the time of the widespread closure of Bombay's mills and factories; the suppression of socialism; and the rise of extreme Marxist groups. Sahni follows historian D. D. Kosambi in seeing the correlations between myth and history. In the end, the principal woman protagonist is visualized as Urvashi, the celestial dancer, and the weak scheming hero as Pururava, the mortal mythical king she had fallen in love with. The story sourced from the *Rig Veda* points toward the ruthless growth of the masculine principle in the shaping and development of human civilization; humanity then is in danger of forever losing its feminine principle. For both of these films, money is the modern-day religion under capitalism, leading to decay and the destruction of family and society.[31]

Other Important Sources

The case of the *Purānas* is a little different in that they might not yield grand narratives, epic fashion, but they contain many short tales that can be narrated, performed, or used in order to weave new tales. The stories vary as they occur in the different *Purāna* collections, so this is another good example of the long-established Indian practice of repeating a story with a number of variations. Which version is narrated depends on what the narrator-performer chooses or what is available. As the stories are related, they are annotated, elaborated, and interpreted, and they serve as vehicles for conveying moral-ethical dictates, teaching, or solving psychosociological (and even philosophical) quandaries relevant to the social context.

Indian films might seem to tell the same story over and over again; but, seen this way, one might form a different perspective on that phenomenon. A course on religion and cinema in India becomes important in furthering the understanding that Indian narrative traditions come from the proper perusal and continual recasting of ancient and medieval texts.

The Discursive Nature of Performance

An aspect of narration-performance associated with medieval storytelling sessions is that the stories were related through prose (in the local languages) and songs were composed to explain the events. Songs elaborate on the discourse in the tale. In the sphere of popular religion, the art of delivering didactic discourse through song was perfected by itinerant, socially marginal singers and cult members (e.g., the Bauls and fakirs of Bengal). In their case, songs do not always expand the talk; indeed, the converse can also occur, with the talk elucidating the content of the songs. Those popular modes of *kīrtan* and *kathā* have been integrated within contemporary Indian storytelling traditions and have influenced films.

Following Western dramatic modes, it is often said of Indian cinema that songs dilute the story and dramatic content. However, a proper look at popular Indian studio films from the thirties through the fifties or the art cinema of filmmakers such as Ritwik Ghatak reveals how songs are used for discursive purposes.[32] Indian cinema is linked to historically established discursive, narrative, musical, and performative practices, all of which dovetail. This is not to say that art, music, or storytelling belong to religion alone; indeed, as many secular circumstances give rise to these as do religious ones. However, in this chapter we are looking at cultural traditions that arise from religious thoughts and practices and shape cinema in India.

To Show and Tell—and to Listen

Performance, narration, music, and art in India are often drawn from religious texts and are integral to religious rituals, particularly in Hinduism. To understand one is to understand the others. To recount *(kīrtan)* and listen to *(śravan)* events from the lives of gods and goddesses, saints and humans (as well as animals, celestial beings, demons, and others) is as important as other rites and rituals. Reading, recitation, and performance of different texts while repeating, elaborating on, interpreting, and changing them are integral to this practice—and not merely reading a written text verbatim.

It is necessary to *show* in order to *tell.* For many Indians, the experience of cinema has been an extension of previous ways of narrating that incorporate depictions of gods and sages, kings and queens, devotees and lovers. Narrative performance traditions involving multimedia experiences—paintings, puppets, shadow plays, and magic lantern shows—can be seen as the prehistory of cinema in India (Chabria 1994). Narration and oral traditions have been closely linked to a long history of painting in iconic and narrative modes in the ancient and medieval periods; such associations continued through lithographs and calendar art in the colonial period (Pinney 2004). The practice of book illustration—in the case of handwritten manuscripts in the past and books in the print era—is also relevant in this context (Chatterjee 2004). All of this points to the complex relationship between *visuality* and *aurality,* regardless of whether treated as separate or mutually related. At times, seeing or hearing is as if one is totally incorporeal but constituted of just one sense; for example, in some songs we might find that the devotee has opened his eyes and *spread them out* over the path his god is coming by and is waiting. Listening to Krishna's flute is all that another devotee desires. Tagore too has sung about a lover/devotee "spreading" her or his hearing (*śravan*) in the path that the beloved/god would take and arrive one day. A popular song attributed to the seventeenth-century bhakti saint Meera-bai is a prototype for many others.

She has heard his footsteps, so she is climbing up the flights of stairs (signifying spiritual advancement).

Pictorial Traditions, Iconicity, and Cinema

With this we come to an important aspect of Indian cinema: iconicity. Several films demonstrate rich and complex relationships between iconicity and narrativity. Pointing out the important act of a devotee's visiting and seeing an idol in a temple, scholars have discussed Indian cinema in terms of *darśana,* or visual worship, and associated issues such as iconicity and frontality (Kapur 1987; Vasudevan 1993; Lutgendorf 2006).

If religious stories and discourses are rivers that flow, change course, and pick up new tributaries, then icons are frozen moments of narratives. A devotee gazing at a deity in a temple is linked through *some story* to the *God in that form.* By altering a story (e.g., introducing new visual and narrative elements), filmmakers bring in contemporary issues, and the old tale gets a new lease of life. Thus, the iconic image often acts as a springhead of a new story, theme, and discourse.

Iconic images in films are preceded and followed by other iconic or narrative images of the film. Consequently, these images and those in posters or calendars generate meaning and feeling in different ways. Additionally, cinematic icons are invested with *time* (shot duration) and *movement* and require different verbalizations. The flip side of the iconic image in cinema is the *narrative image* (which has been a historically distinctive feature of Indian painting traditions); a rich site for analysis is presented by the juxtaposition of these two kinds of images in cinema through the editing process.

To understand this, we return to *Sant Tukaram,* which begins with two shots—two iconic images of the god and the devotee. The first is a full frontal image of the idol of Vitthala (along with consort Rakhumai) against an empty background with nothing to indicate where the deity is situated, whereas the set and property in the second shot indicate that Tukaram may be in a temple or a house. Tukaram's image is constructed at an angle to the camera. The two shots run for about five minutes, the images do not change, and there is no movement within the frame. The visual composition and juxtaposition of the images of the god and the devotee put the audience in a triangular relationship with them (Cutler 1987).[33] Furthermore, juxtaposition like this does not initiate the story along the lines of "one day Tukaram was sitting alone in front of his God singing his compositions." Instead, the shots place the film and its audience in the tradition of bhakti (devotional worship) and a contemplative viewing mode (Chatterjee 2004). The images are accompanied by an original composition by Tukaram about his god being constantly in his mind and the focus of his contemplation.

This is a brilliant use of a devotional song as iconic. Hearing (or *śravana*), which is important in religious and philosophical traditions, needs fresh verbalization also because of the significance of singing in Indian religious and performative modes and now in films.[34] Many Indian song traditions, like *kīrtan* and *kathā* (mentioned earlier), as well as *bhajan* and *ārtī*, consist of descriptions of gods and their praise and the narration of stories associated with their deeds and events (*karma*). Didactic discourses and religious debates are also important, and such songs are sometimes quite long. Interestingly, *Sant Tukaram* does not begin with a traditional song of praise (*stava*) dedicated to the god but with one that speaks of the devotee's cultic devotion to and relationship with meditation and attention. Rather, the film *ends* with a song describing the god Vishnu, who concludes the narrative by sending a celestial vehicle to transport Tukaram to the heavens (one could say that this devotional movie thus ends as a mythological film).

The Participatory Dimension of Literary, Performative, and Artistic Practices

Singing, recitation, discourse (*kathā*), and plays by individuals and groups take place in allotted spaces. At times an entire city becomes a stage for the performance, and the urban populace joins in—not only observing but also participating, as in the case of the *Rāmāyana* performances in the holy city of Banaras (Schechner 1983; Kapoor 1990). At the root of the word *bhakti* lies the meaning "to share." Even the silent films depicted crowds singing in praise of the gods, and according to contemporary reports, audiences at such moments would spontaneously start chanting the name of the god led by the musicians whom the exhibitor or the production company had hired. Touring companies took the films to small towns and villages. Similarly, audiences traveled and camped in fields or stayed with local families. At times, they began the day with worship, recitation, and chanting, ending with a screening of the film at night. As in a *kīrtan* or *bhajan* session, members of the audience distributed and shared food (*prasād*). Often the venue of film projection resembled a fairground, but then, habituated to narrative-performative modes of religion, the film audiences did not lack in attentiveness.

Most narrative-performance sessions occurred at night, when the performers could take advantage of light and shadow techniques, and they thus prefigure the cinematic experience. Long hours and a formal alternation between celebration and concentration are characteristic of Hindu ceremonials, and it is no accident that film viewing in India tends to replicate those features.[35] It is a common belief that when a performance is arduous, extends over long hours, or lasts all night, audiences are transported to a different state of being and feeling; thus, film producers and distributors stipulated that their films must be quite long.

The participatory nature of the Indian audience is often remarked upon and could be considered a cliché, but it is important to note that this factor guides the formal aesthetics of performances in many ways. Therefore, more recent theoretical approaches (most notably reception theory) must be combined with a thorough historical and anthropological contextualization of the formal, structural aspects of Indian cinema relative to their antecedents in religious observance and performance traditions.

Religion, Art, and Artifact

The study of audience reception opens up the topic of religion and cinema to other academic discussions and ideological positions For example, a student might think or read "high class" whenever Hindu texts and art practices are mentioned. But art and performances do not come from or belong uniquely to priestly classes, kings, and nobles; they belong every bit as much to the artisan classes. Very curiously, this has remained a neglected area of the social and cultural history of India. It is a characteristic irony of Indian scholarship that, even as scholars avow a critical attitude toward Brahmin hegemony, they tend to be obsessively attentive to it.[36]

It is not enough to think only of those who avail themselves of art as consumers; we must also consider those who produce it (and so it is unwise to think that art belongs only to the rich and powerful). Studies of audience reception must be strengthened by production history. What is needed is not to think of art only as *fine art* but also as art that is linked to everyday life. The creation of art is a part of the human activity of community formation, as well as the tendency to rule and subjugate. Art is seen as an individual activity, but it must also be seen as practices specific to family, community, race, and language groups. Just as societies and civilizations exist at very different levels and stages of formation, codification, and hierarchy, so too do religion and art.

Formal, structural, thematic, and stylistic motifs from performances by artisan-artists graced court practices. Arts practiced by lower-caste and tribal artisans, once adopted by kingly and aristocratic patrons, became developed within classical court culture. The same would also disseminate outward and be found in peripheral corners of the land. As in the case of Indian languages, there is constant upward and downward mobility of artistic motifs, crossing class, caste, and racial borders. A sociological grounding is necessary for a class on religion and cinema, be it in any part of the world. In India, certain re-formulations of Western social-scientific theories may become necessary.

The legend of Tansen, the court singer of the Mughal emperor Akbar, going to learn music from the Hindu sage Haridas is discussed in terms of Muslim-Hindu relations. However, the oral and painting traditions have emphasized the trope of Tansen traveling from the *palace* to the *hut* of Haridas and picking up musical motifs in order to enrich his classical repertoire. Indian cinema regularly shows that music (at times allegory for the other arts) belongs to the poor, the common folk, the *vulgaire,* and the nomadic. Students could be shown medievalpaintings of the meeting between Tansen and Haridas—a favorite topic with painters.

Baiju-Bawara (Vijay Bhatt 1952; in Hindi) depicts a tiered world of music and religion in India and illustrates how at times music might enjoy mobility across the classes.[37] Baiju is a Hindu man who wishes to avenge himself upon Tansen. As a child, Baiju witnessed this proud courtier insulting and inadvertently causing the death of his father, an itinerant singer. Now Baiju wants to use music as a tool of revenge. It so transpires that Gauri (a woman who rows the village ferry) becomes his muse and teaches him that music must never be dissociated from the common folk (in fact, all classical music arises from folk forms) and that artists must never forget their simple origin even though they may have experienced the riches and social prominence associated with success. The film ends as Baiju revokes his violent vow and instead dies together with his beloved. Another way to quickly appreciate how the *classical* often cites the *folk* is to listen to Indian classical or art music and songs of nomadic folk singers of Rajasthan, where the categories of *folk* and *classical* and other distinctions constantly break down.[38]

We appreciate *Sant Tukaram* better when we discover that three types of music were used in this film: the *ovi* form (the songs women sing while working at home, in the fields, or elsewhere); Tukaram's own songs, which are short versions of *vārkari* music (which in turn emerged from the folk tradition and combined with both devotional and classical music).[39] The third kind is made up of the pretentious Brahmin Salomalo's songs, which are prototypes of Marathi stage music and avidly borrow from classical music (which could also be termed art music).[40]

Narrative Structure

The common Western idea of film narrative must undergo many changes when one studies the Indian film narrative structure, which is mainly episodic with many ruptures—extradiegetic elements, performative items, and so on.[41] More or less familiar with the film's themes and contemporary societal issues disguised within the narrative, audiences enjoy the retelling of the familiar tale—and with the particular *rasa* (taste or flavor) the film can successful create (Mishra 1985).

Sant Tukaram runs more than one narrative thread throughout, as is the case in many Indian films. One of these has to do with a contemporary debate about where a *bhakta* should pray and meditate: in his house, in the temple, in the forest, or within his heart. In the film, we first see Tukaram all alone, praying at home; then he goes to the temple, where he is turned away; finally he goes to his favorite spot for meditation, the Bhandara hills. Then he gets an agricultural job, and here, for the first time, we see throngs of devotees joining him—an episode and direct representation derived from the contemporary thought that God is found wherever common folks are engaged in work: "Work is worship."[42] Working for daily wages, Tukaram receives his share of the crops as payment in the evening. When he asks for some sugar cane for his children, he receives plenty but distributes all but two pieces to the children in the street. His children are beside themselves with joy at getting only one stick of sugar cane because they have not learned to want more than they need. After this point, much of the film is devoted to questions of work, payment, and property (e.g., how much to keep, how much to give away), as well as the nature and consequences of charity.

The villainous Brahman Salomalo may be seen as more important to the narrative structure since he is instrumental in placing the requisite obstacles in front of Tukaram (i.e., the devotee is tested in the path of bhakti). These obstacles come in the form of a prostitute, a Brahman, the king (Shivaji), and the Muslim ruler of the neighboring kingdom of Chakan. The segmentation of the film follows aother logic too. Tukaram is forbidden entry into the temple; he loses his house; his books of verses *(abhangs)*, which are dearer to him than his life, are thrown into the river Indrayani (the reason for this is that, according to orthodox dogma, a low-caste man is not permitted to dispense religious teachings of his own). However, the goddess of the river hands back the drenched manuscripts *(bhiki vahi)*. Twice a year, millions of devotees carry these books to and from Tukaram's village (Dehu) and the Vitthala temple in Pandaharpur (the practice continues even today).

The Problem of Representation: Narration as Reflected in Religion

Of the many links between cinema and Hinduism, the most obvious corresponds to the Hindu belief in a manifest godhood *(saguṇa)* that exists in some anthropomorphic or human form *(rūpa)*, possesses properties or qualities *(guṇa)*, and engages in various activities *(karma)*.[43] The history of the belief in a monotheistic God and in a body of pantheistic gods and goddesses is ancient and cyclic. At times, the monotheistic God becomes the principal God—at once paramount and separate from the pantheon of *gods*. At times, the monotheistic idea of a God who appears on earth as an *avatār* and enters into human relationships with the mortals has predominated; other heavenly gods and goddesses then must interact with this God-on-earth from time to time, thus blurring the line between earth and the heavens (Calasso 1999).

If God is one and indivisible, without form and attribute; if the existence of the mortals is nothing but illusion *(advaita)*, then representation is not encouraged. Though the *Vedas* mention gods, Vedic India saw no production of images. This tendency of aesthetic sparseness is still extant as a teaching taken to heart by many Brahmans. The habit of making representations of gods in human form becomes an integral part of Bhakti practices because God is seen to have form *(rūpa)* and properties or qualities *(gūṇa)* and to be engaged in action and event *(karma)*. Each form, quality and event would give rise to new name and iconography and produced a new image. Philosophers and religious practitioners saw Man and God as variously related. Such thoughts, debates, and production of narration-representation have frequently contributed (as we will later see) to the representation of cinematic heroes and heroines.

Belief, Representation, and Modernity

The belief system, based upon more abstract discourses about God as formless *(nirguṇa)* but nevertheless realizable (as well as somewhat attainable) through meditation and contemplation, was behind the formation of many religious reform movements during the period of Indian nationalism, such as the Brahmo Samaj in Bengal or the Arya Samaj in the North. Such thoughts are often articulated in films through dialogues and songs. And several such film songs have become popular as school songs, for example the two Hindi songs "Give me the strength of mind" from *Guddi* (Hrishikesh Mukherjee, 1971) and "Oh Lord we pray to you" from *Do Aankhe Barah Haath* (V. Shataram, 1957). In several Vedic texts this formless god (or divine principle) is believed to be manifest in people in an abstract fashion.[44]

What is relevant here is that in the modern period the beliefs in a formless god, the contemplative mode of worship, and the idea that people are godlike— are brought back in order to recast and formulate a superior (renaissance) modern human being. In the Indian context, tradition means something belonging to the past and existing through documentation and memory, as well something existing in the present. The Western idea of a tradition and the linear journey from tradition to modernity does not apply in the Indian situation (Raghuramaraju, forthcoming). Various models are operating here, and they could clarify particular situations: cyclic, spiral, and linear, as well as the one I introduced earlier, the mathematical set.

In the modern period maHindu reformers who were formulating this new way of being religious or spiritual dispensed with the belief in miracles, superstitions, and other aspects of religion deemed unacceptable to a rational, modern person. The story of religion in this period is a perpetual balancing act between rationality and faith—and all shades of beliefs and engagement with practice.[45] Because films contain or are made with all of these colors and shades, the study of that history is essential to a proper understanding India and Indian cinema.[46]

Religion, Love, and Sex

On one hand religious reformers in India borrowed from the Vedic and Upanishadic texts (attempting to make the practice of religion more meditative and less ritualistic), and on the other hand they adopted bhakti practices and discourses (attempting to introduce modern notions of universal love, community, and gender equity into everyday life). All forms of worship would now be informed by the bhakti mode. On the other hand, they borrowed from the aspect of Bhakti in which heterosexual romantic love is the model upon which religious talks are based.[47] So a branch of the devotional way of bhakti *(madhurā-bhakti)* makes human love—heterosexual, romantic, ideal—an analogy for god-love and vice versa.[48] Accordingly, gods and mortals engage in loving and acting/playing with divine (*līlā*) and/or mortal partners, forhuman love is sweet as honey (*madhu*); bhakti that emulates human love is similarly sweet enjoyable and fulfilling. Full of *rasa*, it fills the lover/devotee with various emotional juices; colorful and plural, it tints or dyes him/her in the color of the beloved or God. Behind many beliefs, practices, stories, paintings, and songs lies what Tagore explains simply: "We make god our beloved and turn our beloved into god."[49] The New Theatres of Calcutta made several devotional films on the saint-poets who wrote about the love between Radha and Krishna— the main source of *madhura-bhakti*.[50] Thus it is interesting and important that, in the beginning of the film, the hero of *Bidyapati/Vidyapati* (Devaki Bose 1937; in Bengali/Hindi) is not yet fully cognizant of this truth. On the other hand, all other important protagonists are capable of immense love: The king and queen of Mithila love each other very much; a young girl, Anuradha, loves the God Krishna—and they all love the poet passionately. There is also a blind singer and Krishna worshipper who facilitates these many permutations of love relationships. All impart to Vidyapati their *knowledge* of love through their actions, speech, and songs. It is as if the poet must gather together these loves and attain the spiritual state necessary for his poetic creation. He can excel in his poetic creation and his spiritual quest only when he fully belongs to this special community of lovers and after he has fully realized that "above all Man is Truth, none beyond that."

This line actually belongs to another poet, Chandidas, whose legend was portrayed in the film *Chandidas* (Nitin Bose 1932/1934; in Bengali and Hindi) by the New Theatres. Rami the washerwoman encourages Chandidas, a local schoolteacher, to compose verses about the love between Radha and Krishna. When she frustrates the local feudal lord Zamindar's efforts to possess her sexually, he, in revenge, maligns Chandidas because of the latter's association with the "low-caste woman." The local priest instructs the poet to go through ritual purification. Initially the poet agrees to it until he hears Rami's scream: "Poet, you have admitted to purification!" Chandidas then realizes that he was about to abandon his true path, which is the path of love.[51]

These films refer to the practice of *parakīyā*, according to which love outside marriage was considered better than marital love *(svakīyā)*, for one marries for creature comfort and for the sake of begetting children, whereas in the former one unites with a woman so that both can experience God. Representations of heterosexual love within and without marriage converge in *Vidyapati* to create a world of *total love*. However, in both films the heroes are ultimately chaste as they believe in *prema* (divine love) but not *kāma* (sexual love).[52] Often in such films, the female protagonist is the museand instrumental in keeping the hero on his path of devotion; and in that sense she is a guru. The hero suffers from moral and emotional ambivalence and is crisis ridden, but she is capable of total love and surrender.

Many apparently secular films by the New Theatres of Calcutta, like *Devdas*, draw heavily upon visual and narrative motifs of poetry and paintings influenced by *madhurā-bhakti*. In turn, many later movies draw from the New Theatre films—for example, in *Pyaasa* (Guru Dutt 1961; in Hindi), the heroine's faltering steps; her half–closed, unseeing eyes *(ardha-unmīlita)*; the pearls of sweat on her forehead—are iconography of Radha as a heroine. In the song-picturization *(aaj sajan mujhe)*, the heroine climbs several flights of stairs while following the hero (the camera, too, climbs with her to the terrace where he is standing and at one point seems to soar to some *transcendental heights*, as if it were). In *Kagaz Ke Phool*, a filmmaker, Suresh Gupta, is trying to make a film titled *Devdas*, but he cannot find a suitable heroine, someone who is not a glamorous star. The film bears clear reference to *Devdas* by P. C. Barua, to its lead actress, Jamuna Barua, and to Indian cinema before it succumbed to the "star system."

Many Indian films acclaim marital love, and the marriage of Shiva and Parvati is the model in many secular movies, with marital love as the topic. Many film narratives show young lovers who are confused about their love and find emotional and spiritual sustenance from an older married couple.

Examples of male heroes as *superior men* striving for or equaling the divine are important to a discussion of religion and cinema in India. Such films are popular with audiences but are usually neglected in the classroom. Brilliant examples like *Uttarayan* (Agradoot 1967; in Bangla) could be revived for such studies. In this film Mr. Sen loses his business during the Second World War, and his son dies during the London bombing. Prabir Chatterjee, a man of immense charm and unknown antecedents, befriends the Sen family. When Sen's daughter Sulekha falls in love with Prabir, the possibility of an intercaste marriage for his daughter does not bother Mr. Sen.[53] Fascinated by a life of recklessness, Prabir joins the war as a civil engineer; and one day he is astounded to see his double in a poor driver named Ratan Bhattacharya (Uttam Kumar). The resemblance between the two is purely physical and perhaps derives from their Brahman ancestry. Ratan represents a traditional, ritualistic India; Prabir, however, has no interest in gods and religions. Ratan has joined the war simply to earn money to support his wife, who is superior to him in all respects and deserves better. However, the superior hero Prabir has left his fiancé in order to expand his horizons and be tested on many grounds. Ratan dies as the war ends on August 16, 1946. Back in Calcutta and posing as Ratan, Prabir quietly serves the riot-torn city—the war has ended, but there are communal riots on the eve of the India's independence. Prabir is led to believe that Sulekha has married a former lover, and so does not see her; One day, he saves her from some Muslim rioters but pretends not to know her.

Sulekha traces Prabir to Ratan's house; Ratan's mother has just passed away, and he is performing all of the rituals expected of a "son." Sulekha is puzzled, seeing him in his religious garb, and angry, thinking Prabir has not only tricked her but is also taking advantage of Ratan's literate and beautiful wife by cohabiting with her. The latter explains everything to her (shown in a flashback): that when Prabir arrived merely to convey the news of Ratan's demise, the family and neighbors had taken him for the deceased man. Prabir felt unable to leave because he did not want to destroy their impression and push Ratan's blind, ailing mother to sure death. That night Ratan's wife came for the reunion befitting a husband and wife but soon realized a stranger was in her bed. On hearing his story, she urged him to stay on until the imminent death of the old woman. By drawing on an incident from her past, she resolved the problem of how to continue dressing as a married woman even though she is now a widow.[54]

Foreseeing her future as a widow, her astrologer father—before her wedding to Ratan—had *married her* to a stone that stands for and is worshipped as Vishnu.[55] Because she is married to God, she can never be a widow How-ever, she decides to sleep in the *pujā* room and permits Prabir to sleep in the conjugal bed—no one need know of this deception. But then Ratan's wife falls in love with Prabir—as she had never loved her husband. She tells Prabir she has seen in him the "shadow of the most-superior-man or *puruśottam* [another name for Krishna]." For her, there was then a triple marriage: to God (in the form of the stone); to an ordinary good man, Ratan; and to a superior man in whom she saw the reflection of God. As for Prabir, this experience is a lesson on how love can be ennobling, something he would have liked to learn but is incapable of. He could never embody God, but he can quietly obey Ratan's wife as if he could. In fact, this woman's perception of him as a man of higher qualities makes him realize for the first time how ordinary he actually is. The film ends with Ratan's wife keeping the stone on the steps of the river Ganges and stepping into the water to end her life. The ordinary hero and the heroine, Prabir and Sulekha, would now unite as an ordinary couple, leading their ordinary lives—or perhaps not so ordinary, after this extraordinary experience.

A very important by-product of love-as-worship, the dialectic of desire and renunciation is the topic of many films. At times this produces simple binary characters as in *Chitralekha* (Kidar Sharma 1964; in Hindi). It may also create a more complex psychospiritual drama between the *desire to desire* and the *desire to not desire,* as in *Jogan* (Kidar Sharma 1951; in Hindi).[56] This film also points to the need to study carefully certain tendencies of visual construction in Indian cinema. A unique aspect of Indian cinema, the extensive use of the two-shot, which shows two people in a single frame, is the cinematic continuation of the importance of the deity-as-couple or the couple-as-deity (Chatterjee 2004). As we study these films we also realize the need to develop a psy-choreligious study of the *self and the other,* which might not fully conform to Western psychoanalytical theories. In terms of audience construction, too, such films are important for scholars of cinema and religion because they exhibit another important tendency of Indian movies: to inhibit easy audience identification with either or both the characters forming the couple. This is accomplished by restraining from adopting usual (Western) methods of image construction, avoiding the shot counter-shot, over-the-shoulder-shot, point-of-view shots, and eye-line matching. Additionally, such studies would also open up several crucial questions that relate to feminist criticism in different ways and add importantly to Western feminist thought.

Corporeality and Religion

The visualization of the human body in these motion pictures draws upon the importance of corporeality in bhakti—and also in all marginal cults that constitute an interface between bhakti and Nath, or bhakti and Tantric ways, etc. The daily rituals of bathing, dressing, and feeding the deity are important devotional devices; and gazing upon the deity is a necessary and not a disembodied act. Corporeality influences several aesthetic principles in Indian films; to take this into account would be to take Indian film aesthetics beyond the centrality of visuality as explained through the concept of *darśan*. Many films, for example, show their reluctance to use close-ups (absent in medieval Indian painting traditions); often in a movie the focus is not on the face and the eyes, but on the entire body, oron other body parts e.g., the feet.

The symbology of women's bodies and body parts is more complex as the meaning might swing between adoration and desire; the desire to possess and violate; and transcendence from one's human confines to higher realms. Men's bodies register adoration in a more uncomplicated way; for example, the shoulders and the bare upper half of the body are meant to evoke attributes such as generosity and a sense of responsibility. Men's bodies could be erotic, but eroticism in this case is not associated with the desire to violate, disfigure, and destroy, as is the case with women's bodies and their representation in cinema. The lower and higher equations (i.e., thoughts that revolve around the sacred and the profane or the debased) continue to be crucial, but these are in need of deeper thought and wider research.

Religion, Money, and Cinema

Like love and sex, another centuries-old Indian concern is wealth. The *Mahabharata* is a treasure trove of such thoughts and discussions. The characters discuss the importance of money (in particular, grandfather Bhishma, who goes so far as to say that one is of no consequence if one has no money).[57] This might seem strange to those who are used to religious people being secretive about the role of money in life and about the various connections between money and religious institutions and activities.[58] As I write this I reflect on the ancient wisdom of the three *vargas*, or the emphasis upon the close association between *dharma*, *kāma*, and *artha*.

Dharma refers to the moral-ethical-social laws, earthly duties, or life's various imperatives. It is the natural and innate properties of the living; it is also culturally produced tendencies. *Artha* refers to money or wealth, which enables one to earn one's living, pursue happiness, and attain social prominence; it also refers to the meanings of human speech and actions We could say *artha* is the set of values with which things are endowed.[59] *Kāma* is desire—all desires in general and sexual desire in particular. *Kāma* can be used in the sense of the affect men and women share when they form a couple; it is the base (both basic and low) emotion that keeps the humans engrossed in earthly matters. All three are important for human happiness, and the pursuit of happiness is an important civilizational discourse in India (or in any civilization past and present for that matter). Several texts elaborate upon the three *vargas* that everyone (i.e., members of the upper castes) needs to learn and put to "proper" use.[60] The *Mahabharata* argues each of these separately and comparatively and is a complicated compendium of thoughts carried out by its numerous but important protagonists. For example, Bhima, the second Pandava brother, argues for the supremacy of *kāma*: "Without *kāma* there is no desire for *artha* and without *kāma* there is no wish for *dharma*, for without *kāma* there is none who desires—therefore *kāma* is the best—from *kāma* happiness arises." The *Manusmriti*, seen as the most important influence on the final codification of the Hindu society in India, advises one to follow all three together. The *Purānas* and the puranic tales are simple and straightforward in their articulation of desires and needs.

A short story in three verses in the *Brihadāranyak Upanishad* has influenced many later stories (5.1–3). This is one instance of the construction and flow of desires down the ages—students could look for others. Three sorts of progeny—gods, men, and antigods—live with Father Prajapati Brahma during their (celibate) student days. At the completion of their period, each group requests (on three separate occasions), "Master, tell us something." In response, Brahma utters the consonant *d* each time and then asks, "Did you understand?" The gods believe the father has asked them to be *dānta*, that is, to exercise restraint in all matters; the mortals interpret it as the father's advice to them to be *datta*, or generous givers; while the antigods believe the father has advised *dayaddham*, for them to "be full of pity."[61] To each reply the father says, "Yes, you have understood it well!" Even today religious people are advised to learn and practice these same virtues.

Interestingly, these words later become a general plea—save me, give me, have pity on me, and help me—in the *Purānaic* and local language texts. Men go to sages and gods, or gods and sages go to the higher trinity of Brahma, Vishnu, and/or Shiva with similar entreaties for favors and help. More interestingly, in many stories the request is for the deity to restrain the enemy—another king, another god, or (more commonly) the antigods. The influence of the Puranic stories on the local tales is a neglected area of studies—something that would be important to film studies.

Another set of vernacular texts that articulate collective desires are the various *vrata*, *kathā*, or *kāvya* stories. The *vrata* is a form of worship with antecedents in a particular locale and people. A special feature here is that the gods that people pray to do not belong to the pantheon of Vedic and post-Vedic gods but are uniquely local or regional. A group of films centers around the tradition of the *vrata* or *kāvya* stories, and a special characteristic is that the local god or goddess finds a place in the pantheon of Hindu gods.[62] These are particularly important for the study of the articulation and creation of contemporary social desire. *Jai Santoshi Maa* (Vijay Sharma 1975; in Hindi) belongs to this genre and is one of the most popular, religious Indian films and also the most discussed by scholars.[63] In this movie a minor goddess, Santoshi, is worshipped by a mortal woman named Satyavati, much to the chagrin of the consorts of the trinity Brahma, Vishnu, and Maheshwar (or those gods in feminine form). Satyavati's successful worship of Santoshi and the latter's reconciliation with the three upper-class goddesses indicate the upward mobility of middle-class women—both actual and aspirational. Through such stories the *vrata* films register shifts in social classes, all emerging now as consumers. The worship of the goddess became a huge social phenomenon in the postfilm decades, when thousands of women observed the *vrata* of Santoshi Maa in real life. However, a recent version of *Jai Santoshi Maa* has failed at the box office. We might ask whether the mythological has died (Vardhan 2005).[64] Alternatively, perhaps the remake lacks what the earlier version had (and so our study continues).

The formation and consolidation of wants and needs happen during daily worships, special rituals, and festivals (all conducted with some definite desire) in the pattern of a transaction between the devotee and the god. In the daily worship mode, the god is propitiated—bathed, fed, and praised. Special rituals are like special banquets, where many other gods are invited to join in. They are often identified by their castes (as in the case of Kshatriya, the sun god), profession and artisanship (as in the case of Vishvakarma, the god of the artisans), and race (as in the case of Kubera, who can also be a single god attached to wealth and its protection). At times a family might make space for a minor local goddess in order to avert nearby mishaps (e.g., Manasa is prayed to for protection against snakebite, or Seetala is worshipped for protection against smallpox or other virulent diseases). And then there are the marginal antigods and ghosts, who are not allowed to attend; they are offered a little token that is served outside the house and then request to leave without causing harm to the family. The society of the gods is patterned after human society.

Important to these customs is the fact that one must offer the gods material objects and thus spend money—only then will they grant one's wishes.[65] Prayers and songs are filled with various pleas or cries of "give" or "grant."[66] For the past three decades, ritualistic practice in India has been combining with modern-day consumerism. Films amply exhibit new desires that consumerist societies and states are able to create if not fulfill. In tune with the state of the market economy, some movies also produce new desires in audiences. To fully understand today's religious films as completely reconciled with the business of the accumulation of wealth, we need to study early connections between religion and money—with monarchical, mercantile, and feudal affluence. It is important to note cinema's concern with material desire and fulfillment if one wants to trace the way Indian films have developed through the growth of unbridled consumerism and a globalized market economy. One could, for example, make a chronological survey of the period that extends from *Devdas* (P. C. Barua 1935) to *Devdas* (Bimal Roy 1955) and to *Devdas* (Sanjay Leela Bhansali 2002) and see how the discourse of love becomes attached to the display of money and material goods. In the first film, the heroine is dressed simply throughout; when she gets an opportunity to do so, she gives away all of her jewels and continues to live simply even though she is married to a rich man. At the same time, she manages the finances of the home (it is a large household) and the estate. She is active in community work: She helps to build temples, hospitals, and schools, and she hosts community meals.[67]

In the nationalist period religion was meant to help create modern individuals who could better serve both the community and the nation. "Simple living, high thinking" was a motto of that period. The obsessive display of "high living" in recent films marks the making of the individual under the spell of the state and market forces without any sense of control. The question would be whether money has replaced religion today and how much the films indicate that.

Religion, Power, and Politics

Mythological films from Tamil Nadu and Andhra Pradesh merit special attention for their close contact with political development and changes in these states (Pandian 1992; Vardhan 2005). Actors of the mythological here have enjoyed unimaginable popularity; they have been identified with the gods and had temples built with their idol inside; they have also become political leaders (four actors have become the chief ministers of the two states). In Andhra Pradesh, N. T. Ramarao became just such a "living god" when he played Krishna or the deity of the Tirupati temple.[68] At times, after a visiting a deity in the temple (that is, after having a *darshan* of the god), devotees ended their pilgrimage with a *darshan* (or a visit in order to have glimpse) of Ramarao.[69] However, the familiar formulation of "audience identification with the movie hero" is put to the test when confronted with the fact that Ramarao also acted and endeared himself as Ravana and other "villains" of Hindu mythology. One reason for this, of course, is historical. The Aryan and Dravidian question has made it possible for actors in the south of India to act in any role and be identified as both Aryan and Dravidian; the choice depends on what message is imparted through the character: one of morality or a critique of the northern obsession with Aryan supremacy in India.

Additionally, ancient dramatic theories advocate that the actor not be rigidly attached to one particular affect but serve as a "container" for all emotions: cruelty, kindness, romantic love, bravery or devotion. This is a component of the ancient Indian dramatic theory of the *rasa:* If a performance must inspire many different feelings in the audience's heart, then an actor must be able to perform in all kinds of roles.

Scholars have applied the *rasa* theory to Indian films (Mishra 2002). And with this we come to another reason for the popularity of the mythology films: their traditional and/or devotional music. Film music adds to several of the cinematic factors mentioned earlier: its discursive property invigorates the theme and narrative; it enhances the meaning, feeling, and *rasa* of the performance; it is an important component of episodic narratives, which is in synch with the fact that music and *rasa* may be enjoyed serially (Lutgendorf 2006). The topic of cinema and religion makes possible fresh verbalizations about the auditory aspect of motion pictures.

Tamil mythological and devotional films have liberally used traditional musical compositions by medieval saints like Thyagaraja or important national leaders like Subramanyam Bharati. Additionally, the voices of important contemporary singers like Papanasham Shivam or Sundarambal as actors or playback singers have added to their popularity.[70] *Avvaiyar* (S. S. Vasan 1953) is a Tamil film about a woman *sant* (belonging to either the ancient Sangam or the medieval Kamban period). The established singer Sundarambal plays the fearless devotee. Her tremendous popularity was a result of her personality, powerful singing, and austere presence.[71] On the other hand, M. S. Shubha-laxmi was trained as a singer and an actress; her beauty and sensuality con-tributed to the persona of Meera-bai, whom she plays in the bilingual *Meera* (Elis Duncan, 1943; in Tamil and Hindi). Throughout her life, Shubhalaxmi remained an icon of devotion and music for the whole of India and not merely Tamil Nadu. She is considered as *the face of India*, at once traditional and modern, local and pan-nationalist, an individual, as well as a family and com-munity member.

Besides making mythological and devotional movies, Tamil cinema has also significantly critiqued mainstream religious practices and has been de-voted to the creation of the Tamil identity (separatist and/or antibrahminical); and all of this has taken place against the backdrop of the Tamil Nadu's political history. Important writers joined the industry in large numbers, writing scripts with the intention of making cinema a popular tool for the mobilization of the people; consequently, they introduced rhetorical dialogues (at times even speeches) in their films. The founder of the DMK (Dravida Munnetra Kazhagam, or literally the Davidian Progress conference) party, C. N. Annadurai, gave rise to the "DMK film propaganda genre" through his scripts and dialogues (Rajadhyaksha 1995). Protégé M. Karunanidhi scripted *Parashakti* (1952), which ends when a man (Gemini Ganeshan) sets out to take revenge on the temple priest, who has raped his sister. Ganeshan first speaks from behind the idol, producing the illusion that the deity is speaking to the people in the temple. Then he emerges, declares that the deity is "mere stone," and delivers a speech on society's various misdeeds.

The deification of Tamil stars like M. G. Ramachandran and Ganeshan or the Kannada superstar Rajkumar (in Karnataka) came about as they played good and bad characters in progressive or deeply religious films in which they promoted or denounced blind faith and superstition. Finally, it is the star persona that takes over the minds and hearts of the people, creating a phe-nomenon that is not fully understood. People's politics in such cases conflate with their devotion to the star, and it is difficult to determine which is more prominent: religion or politics.[72]

A Different Course on Religion and Cinema in India

A teacher might want to design a course that differs somewhat from what I have discussed and perhaps begin with the effect of the collapse of religion on money, power, and politics. The course could be based upon the realization that religious fundamentalism is on the rise all over the world, that religion has always been a tool in the hands of a few who wish to contain and control people (the large population of India is an important factor here), and that religion has often turned to the use of weapons to harm others. The course might look into how religion in India, because of its close relationship with matters of love, sex, and marriage, often leads to wrongdoing and consequently produces a surfeit of representation of such transgressions in films.

A companion piece that exposes the darker side of *dharma*'s attachment to *kāma* and *artha* would surely make this chapter more complete. Religion may very well have initially been built upon ignorance and superstition, but I contend that this view of the "primitive past" and the idea of history as linear is largely informed by the European colonial spirit (and is incorrect by many Western standards). Religion has been used for the purpose of elevating the standard of human existence; it has also been used by some people in order to suppress some others—films register both the tendencies.[73] While working with Indian ancient material, one finds instead dual human tendencies running in parallel: to acquire-build-rule and to seek meanings behind the mysteries of natural human and divine creations so that human life becomes sweeter or more pleasant. It could very well be that the idea that religion is ennobling, individuality forming, and philosophically inquiring was carefully superimposed on those tendencies. I agree that it is possible to begin the teaching of religion either way (for example, by showing religion as civilization building tool or by stressing upon the fact that many people have an innate desire for transcendence of some sort) and come to the other (for example, by showing the role of religion in most the drama of struggle the acquisition of money power and sex). However, my argument for beginning this way is that cinema in India largely addresses the former way of engaging with religion and criticizes people who put religion to *wrong* use. One could adopt herethe analogy of architectural drawings: when a new building is to be constructed on the foundation of a former structure two drawings on tracing paper are placed one on top of the other and then removed for individual consideration.

Finally, it is often said that today's American students identify more with contemporary films; my personal experience of teaching in the United States has taught me that this is not necessarily true. For example, students were thrilled with a fifties' film like *Jogan*. I believe that students and teachers are increasingly eager to explore more than the usual films discussed in books and classes. I have tried to expand the choices, and whenever possible I have mentioned the availability of the films. Because more and more movies are coming out in subtitled DVD format, my intention was to promote the study of newer films so that distributors are encouraged to make still more movies available. Because of the nonavailability of subtitled DVDs, teachers like to use recent movies and are then obliged to design a course "backward." From looking at numerous course syllabi and talking to teachers who have attempted that, I have learned that it is not a very productive approach.

Acknowledgments

I am grateful to Christian Novetzke, Gene Thursby, Ram Bapat, Madhavi Kolhatkar, William Elison, Ashish Rajadhyaksa, Andy Rotman, Urmila Bhirdikar, Rohini Sahni, Vishnu Vardhan, Philip Lutgendorf, Jyotirmaya Sharma, and Laurie Patton for helping me with information and ideas or for shaping up the manuscript at various stages.

NOTES

1. I have studied more than a dozen syllabi of courses offered between 2004 and 2006.

2. In Kerala the history of Christianity dates back to the pre-Vatican first century AD. Christians are as much a part of the everyday reality in Kerala as are the Mappila or Mophla Muslims, who began settling along the Indian coasts around 8 CE as Arab traders plied the oceans.

3. Aravindan's films are available for viewing only in the National Film Archive of India (*Vastuhara* is preserved in the Kerala State Chalachitra Academy). His documentary on spiritual leader J. Krishnamurthy, *The Seer Who Walked Alone,* is available for sale in video format at the Films Division in Bombay. Considering the importance of this director's works, I discuss films that are not readily available.

4. During the editing of the film, Abraham told the editor *Bina Paul* that he had imagined Hari as having a mixed religious background—his mother a Christian, and his father a Hindu. Paul conveyed this to me during a conversation.

5. Unfortunately, D. G. Phalke's *Gautam Buddha* has been lost. An important film, *Angulimala* (Vijay Bhatt 1960), financed by the Thai government, has recently come out in DVD format. The small number of films featuring Buddhism is strange, considering the importance of Buddha and his thoughts while India was going through social and religious reform. The representation of Buddha and Buddhist motifs recurs often in the films of the nationalist period and the early decades after independence. For example, Rabindranath Tagore's play *Natir Puja* was turned into a movie (by Nitin Bose for Aurora Films) and started the trend of showing a dancing girl as a rebellious worshipper. Sreemati disobeys the royal order that no one must pray at a Buddha's *stūpa* in the kingdom; she dances in prayer and is ultimately beheaded.

6. After trying all other religions, he concluded that the worship of Kali was the best way of attaining self-realization and/or unity with God. The quoted sentence, however, has mostly meant the tolerance of other religions—the actual meaning of secularism in India.

7. Only in the last few decades have we discerned an increased effort to define a monolithic image of Hinduism for nationalist and jingoist purposes.

8. Shankaracharya (tenth century AD; Kerala) is credited for consolidating Hinduism, unifying a vast landscape (now known as India), and propagating the theory of nondualism between human beings and God. However, because people's lives in the world are mere illusions (maya), Shankaracharya also introduced institutionalized asceticism in Hinduism (so that people can overcome maya). Ramanujacharya (eleventh–twelfth century AD; Tamil Nadu) was an important bhakti leader who promoted *viśista-advaita-vad,* or the view that humans (the knowers) and God, the supreme knowable, are separate but ultimately the same. The world is real, but nothing exists

apart from Brahaman. Madhvacharya (thirteenth–fourteenth century AD; Karnataka) was another realist who advocated that humans and God must be essentially different and separate. The body and the materiality of the world are important, for without them, human beings cannot know God—God is knowable only through humankind—or the guru, who in that sense is more important to a common person than God is.

9. Indian films have quite obsessively shown men as emasculated—in those made not only in the colonial period but also in the immediate postindependence period. This seems to be fully in consonance with the arguments of Partho Chatterjee (Chatterjee 1993), who states that in the colonial period Indian men suffered from a loss of power in the public sphere. Consequently, Indian societies created several sets of social binaries, in which "home" emerged as the seat of all that is traditional and sacred and which women were believed to embody, while being confined in the home. Interestingly, many films of these early decades show young Indian men, recently awakened to modern liberal thoughts, as powerless against the previous generation and the female characters as more rooted and spiritual than their male counterparts.

10. Japan is an important example since Japanese masters Yasojiru Ozu, Kenji Mizoguchi, Akira Kurosawa, and others made films *within* the studio system. The art-popular divide must be revised as we study Indian films.

11. It is interesting to note the terms the regional-language papers used for film advertisements. For the Telegu film industry in Hyderabad they were "pauranic" and "bhakti."

12. The saint-poets of medieval Maharashtra were called "sant" and so the Marathi devotional films are often designated as "Sant films."

13. Over time, one realizes how much research remains to be conducted in each field. Thus students may develop future interests if the teacher makes them aware of lacunae in the field.

14. Madhava Prasad and Rajadhyaksha in classroom lectures.

15. The *Encyclopaedia of Indian Cinema* (1995) lists *Pundalik* as the first film. Incidentally, the intertitles of these films appeared in many languages. Those released in Bombay would have been in Hindi, Urdu, English, and Gujarati.

16. These films are available for viewing (even though few exist in complete form) at the National Film Archive of India; a few silent-era films have been produced by the British Film Institute in DVD format; some of these are available in the United States with individual teachers who are always eager to make copies available.

17. During the post–World War I era, the years between the two world wars, and the post–World War II period, the Indian economy was violently rocked. The talk of profit and loss quickly replaced nationalistic talks of reform and other aspirations.

18. The connection between religion and politics has been very strong in Tamil Nadu and Andhra Pradesh, stronger even than in Maharashtra and Gujarat.

19. *Sarva dharmam parityājyam māmekam śaraṇam braja.*

20. Mistry takes pride in the way he achieved success in those days of limited means, before the advancement of digital technology and computer-generated images. For many, such images are religious in nature, whereas more sleek contemporary images are considered to belong to other genres such as science fiction.

21. By "semilegendary" I mean a poet whose works are known but whose historical existence is not supported by accepted historical evidence.

22. *Shawbaar upore manush satto; taahar upore naai.*

23. Some of these films are available on DVD and have English subtitles; some are available in VCD format.

24. Many films were made with these titles and on this topic; one would have to see how many and which versions are available.

25. One could argue that the film begins after the death of his beloved first wife, and so there is only one wife. However, the film definitely goes against the fact, and common knowledge has it that Tukaram had six children.

26. The entire body of literature on the "saints" that appeared with the advent of the printing press shows that writers and thinkers were widely referring to Western literature. Modern writers described Tukaram as "graceful" and compared him to Wordsworth and Keats or called him the Socrates of India; his wife, Jijai, however, was depicted as a shrewish Xanthippe (Ranade 1933/1987).

27. Remarkably, contemporary reviewers and scholars have discussed the acting style of the actor playing Tukaram as *realistic* and that of the actor playing Jijai as *stylized*. They have also discussed whether the depictions of miracles go against the aesthetics of good cinema, which should be realistic.

28. Perhaps this is better appreciated if such films from the early decades are compared with films made after the mideighties, when the trend is all but gone.

29. The medieval history of India needs more investigation. There is a belief (voiced within postcolonial studies) that Indian texts were revived by colonial scholars and administrators and that Indian tradition is thus fully recast in the colonial period. The story of the revival of traditional Hindu texts in the Muslim courts is important in this context. The medieval rulers encouraged and enjoyed storytelling sessions and performances of plays and initiated the translations of several Sanskrit texts.

30. The film hailed as the first Indian feature, *Ayodhyacha Raja* [The King of Ayodhya] (1913) can also be seen as a reminder to the British government of how Indian kings of yore carried out dharma.

31. A recent addition to films drawn from the *Mahabharata* is *The Shadow of the Dog* (Girish Kasavalli 2005).

32. One could also study the plays of Rabindranath Tagore in this context.

33. Accordingly, the factor of identification operates very differently in many Indian films. A discussion would contribute greatly to film studies in general.

34. Also see my analyses of the opening sequences of *Devdas* (P. C. Barua 1936) and *Jogan* (Kidar Sharma 1951), in which the song fully establishes the film's discourse rather than its narrative (Chatterjee 2004).

35. Western film scholars have long talked of the experience of viewing films in the dark in terms of its psychological impact on audiences. To think of religion and cinema is to enlarge this and delve into questions of cognition, contemplation, and celebration.

36. The sculptor Meera Mukherjee cast gigantic metal sculptures with contemporary topics after training with tribal-artisan *dokra* artists. She conducted research on Vishwakarma, the god of the artisan. In fact, several modern Indian artists have also thought along this line—which is very different from the new style and discourse of "primitivism" that Western artists have introduced. Urmila Bhirdekar's work on Indian music too is reflective of this.

37. The Hindu-Muslim dynamics in these films are not about any monolithic concept of an Islamic India; rather, they point to the fact that in India the Mughals are seen as benign rulers, unlike the Afghans, Pathans, or Turks. That Tansen wishes to learn music from a Hindu ascetic or accept defeat at the hands of a poor man is indicative of the Mughal rulers' policy of religious tolerance. Of course, the films ultimately prove the victory of Hindi film music over all else—but then that is *another story*.

38. For this, one must do some archival work on the periods before the era of the gramophone. Several films use nomadic music illustrative of this point—for example, *Duvida* or *The Desert of a Thousand Lines,* both by Mani Kaul.

39. The musical compositions were kept short (about two minutes long) because they are being used in a film and because the songs could be made into records and sold separately.

40. Ashok Ranade has introduced five categories in the history of music: primitive, folk, devotional, art or classical, and modern. He has written and lectured widely on this, and a synopsis of his thesis occurs in his recent book on Hindi film music (Ranade 2006). I do not always adhere to his categorizations, but they could be useful at the beginning of a class.

41. Indian filmmakers today try to follow the classical Hollywood narrative structure on demand from filmmakers, critiques, and audiences. However, such attempts are invariably and intermittently punctured by the introduction of the *item* or cheez words used to include all kinds of dramatic-performative units Ashok Ranade explains *cheez* (thing, item) in Indian classical music. "Unlike like *bandish* (>) *cheez* as a concept, is less value-oriented. It refers to the ground plan of the musical idea, which a musician intends to explore further." So every performance becomes specific because of the types of cheez introduced. But cheez can never become more important than the bandish and the raga. In the case of many films, an item number comes to be synonymous with the film itself; everything else—form, content, style—is forgotten. The *cheez* or the *item* numbers in such cases is all about the popularity and glamour quotient of the film.

42. Rabindranath Tagore wrote several poems and songs on this topic. Similar thoughts resonate in the works of later social thinkers and activists like Vinoba Bhave. The "work is worship" dictum is also borrowed from Christian sources (notably the Unitarian Church).

43. There are thirty-three types or groups *(koti)* of gods and goddesses.

44. Female goddesses are important, but they are never the *nirgūna brahma,* who is always imagined as a man. One would think that not having form and quality would make "God" everything—male, female, and neuter. Naturally, this has not gone unexplained; the male principle can act only when energized by the feminine principle. However, this has been one way of suppressing the Great Mother cults and subsuming their worship under that of the male gods (a parallel history is that of the consolidation of patriarchal societies and monarchies). The figure of the woman in Indian films is often very important; she is the principle narrative agent and the bearer of the Look. Ultimately, however, she becomes the means of signification for the male discourse—in these films made by male directors.

45. A teacher could briefly mention the ancient atheist traditions of the past and the spread of atheism in the modern period—or fully develop it to showcase the number of Indian films—art and commercial—that completely ignore the fact of religion.

46. There is a rising obsession with the color saffron as signifying the growth of militant Hinduism in India and among nonresident Indians living in the United States. This study, however, helps one to look at other colors.

47. It is quite a fascinating history, and one needs to look at the Sufi saints, whose works influenced religion in India, and at the innumerable religious cults in India that are the interface of Hinduism and Sufism. In the nationalist period, religious preachers like Sri Aurovinda and Meher Baba or, in the postindependence period, J. Krishnamurty and Rajaneesh made important contributions. The writings and songs

of Rabindranath Tagore are another source for the full understanding of how love is connected with the formation of individuality and religion.

48. Human love as sacred, spiritual, and capable of causing total transformation in a person is at the base of many popular films. The theme lingers on, for example, in *Veer-Zara* (Yash Chopra 2004; in Hindi).

49. *Priyéré devatā kori; devatāré priyo.*

50. Anyone who studies the history of these or other languages in a linguistic group and designated as vernacular would be required to read these poets.

51. The Bengali versions of these two films use the poets' original compositions. In the Hindi *Vidyapati,* Kidar Sharma (the maker of *Jogan*) composed the lyrics.

52. The influence of the Western binary of agape and eros is evident here.

53. Actor Pahadi Sanyal again plays a liberal humanist capitalist; he has often played the Shiva-like husband in many Bengali and Hindi films.

54. This film is available in VCD format; a DVD format may soon be available.

55. These fossils are of twelve kinds and are found on the banks of the river Gandak in Nepal. The use of these stones as standing for the Supreme Being had a significant impact on religion in India. Ordinary Brahmans and non-Brahmans could keep them at home and not worry about temple hierarchy.

56. This film is available in the United Kingdom in DVD format and with English subtitles.

57. In several places various characters sing in praise of money and wealth. In fact, in the *śānti parva* it is said that "On wealth depends the rise of *dharma.*"

58. That religious institutes and churches served as banks in the medieval period might be a common knowledge, the way churches in the West have colluded with (or opposed) the ruling monarchy may be a widely studied phenomenon, but I do not believe the religious communities are vocal about their attachment to money and power. Hindus in India have been unequivocal about the importance of money.

59. Naturally one must imagine money not as paper currency or metal coins. One has to know about the economic system, including the role of the barter system and the constant, direct experience of the value of things).

60. *Mokṣa* is the cessation of all dealing and action, all desires, all need for values-in-things (all words and actions); all pleasure seeking and happiness. Those four technical terms forming the *caturbarga* in the Hindu, Jain, and Buddhist systems are pursuits primarily for men; women are not totally outside the pale of this, but they also not central to these matters.

61. Each interpretation demarcates the three *brothers* and determines the nature of each species they will one day represent.

62. We see *vratas* being conducted in early texts like the *Matsya Purāna.* A *brata* and a novena are conducted in much the same way: A devotee takes a vow with some desire in mind, undergoes an unbroken chain of acts and rituals, and at the completion performs a special *puja,* which is accompanied by a balladic narration about protagonists who have also completed the *brata* and benefited or else broken the chain and suffered. The desire is to be made productive at the completion of the *vrata,* which is a transaction between the devotee and the devotee's favorite god.

63. A detailed analysis of this film and references to other reading material can be found on the website of Philip Lutgendorf (http://www.uiowa.edu/~incinema/).

64. Vishnu Vardhan asks this about Telegu cinema, but the question is valid for the mythological and the *vrata* films in all languages.

65. Alternatively, one could make an abstract offering in the form of a fast or the sacrifice of a favorite object.

66. For example, *rupam dehi, jayam dehi, jaśo dehi* may be chanted during the durga puja in Bengal, or worshippers might use the call of *darśan mātre kāmanā pūrtī* during the Ganesh ārti in Maharashtra.

67. Films began to change appreciably in the mideighties, and the transformation in appearance and the finances involved could be attributed to several factors: (1) India was bursting out of its lethargic growth in GDP; (2) movies began to show changes that people desired and expected—not what was actually attained; (3) the need for change was felt in Bombay; movies made in this city began to look glitzier, resulting in the wide use of the term "Bollywood"; (4) this transformation was congruent with the rise of the underworld. In the eighties an enormous amount of money from the underworld poured into film production, and film content changed significantly (crime then replaced romantic love in a big way); (5) in the nineties, the Indian government began to amend the situation; filmmaking was accorded the status of "industry," and banks began to finance films; (6) in the nineties, India began to make tremendous progress in trade and finance, and per capita income increased from 293 in 1985 to 726 in 2005; (7) the Indian presence was felt in the United States and the United Kingdom, and films exaggerated the Indian reality in order for Indians at home and abroad to feel good about themselves; (8) community, poverty, rural reality, and poverty in the city were all *foreign* concepts to second-generation filmmakers, producers, and actors; (9) despite these issues, it is not at all clear how increased capitalism and the world market could impel people to suddenly change. I am grateful to Rohini Sahni for clarifying these matters and providing me with statistical figures.

68. Ramarao played Krishna twenty-two times.

69. In 1982 Ramarao founded the Telegu Desam party and served as the chief minister of the state until 1989.

70. How much of the phenomenon is cultural and how much political is something that calls for scholarly investigation. The actors (and others involved with the business of filmmaking) gained popularity and political importance this way, but each differs in the political changes, progress, or regression they mobilized after gaining power. The stars have not always been associated with the same political party.

71. Sundarambal became the first woman legislator of the state of Madras.

72. Ramachandran was the chief minister of the state for many years, and a temple was built with him as the deity. With this began the phenomenon of the temple with a star presiding as the deity; the trend spread to other states as well. The type of incident seems to be regional. Prem Nazir, the star from Kerala, appears in the *Guinness Book of World Records* for having acted in more than five hundred films. However, when he ran for public office, he lost even the deposit he was required to pay; the people of Kerala apparently did not want to mix cinema and politics. Stars from other states, too, join political parties or are appointed members of the regional and central parliament, but most of them leave after a couple of years.

73. Though much of the primitiveness is evident in real practice, Indian films rarely show that—for example in films about snake-people or people who were snakes in their previous lives. Interestingly, we regularly see it in American films like *The Exorcist* or *Damien*. It is argued that this is so because the concept of the demon or Satan exists in the West, and the Indian *asura* is not that. The discussion could continue in many directions.

REFERENCES

Altman, Rick. 1999. *Film/Genre*. London: BFI.

Anderson, Benedict. 1983. *Imagined Communities: Reflections on the Origin and Spread of Nationalism*. London: Verso.

Barnouw, Erik, and S. Krishnaswamy. 1980. *Indian Film*, 2d ed. New York: Oxford University Press.

Bhole, Keshavrao. 1964. *Mazhe Sangeet*. Bombay: Mauz Prakashan.

Briggs, George Weston. 1938. *Gorakhnath and the Kanphata Yogis*. New Delhi: Motilal Banarsidass.

Calasso, Roberto. 1999. *Ka*. London: Vintage.

Chabria, Suresh. 1994. *Light of Asia: Indian Silent Cinema 1912–1934*. New Delhi: Wiley Eastern.

Chatterjee, Gayatri. 2006. "Durga Khote: The Contour of a Life and Work." In *I, Durga Khote: An Autobiography*, trans. Shanta Gokhale (xvii–xxx). New Delhi: Oxford University Press.

———. 2004. "Icons and Events: Reinventing Visual Construction in Cinema in India." In *Bollyworld: Popular Indian Cinema through a Transnational Lens*, ed. Kaur Raminder and Ajay Sinha (90–117). New Delhi: Sage.

———. 2002. *Mother India*. London: BFI.

Chatterjee, Partho. 1993. *The Nation and Its Fragments: Colonial and Postcolonial Histories*. Delhi: Oxford University Press.

Cutler, Norman. 1987. *Songs of Experience: The Poetics of Tamil Devotion*. Chicago: Chicago University Press.

Dandekar, R. G. 1965. *Vaishnavism, Saivism, and Minor Religious Systems*. Varanasi, Uttar Pradesh, India: Indological Book House.

Das, Veena. 1981. "The Mythological Film and Its Framework of Meaning: An Analysis of *Jai Santoshi Ma*." *Indian International Quarterly* 8(1). Special issue.

Dasgupta, Shashibhushan. 1968. *Obscure Religious Cults*. Calcutta: University of Calcutta Press.

Dwyer, Rachel. 2007. *Filming the Gods: Religion and Indian Cinema*. New York: Routledge.

Eck, Diana L. 1998. *Darśan: Seeing the Divine Image in India*, 3d ed. New York: Columbia University Press.

Ghosh, Bishnupriya. 1992. "Satyajit Ray's *Devi*: A Third-world Feminist Critique." *Screen* 33(2) (Summer): 165–73.

Israel, Milton, and N. K. Wagle, eds. 1987. *Religion and Society in Maharashtra. South Asia paper* no. 1, University of Toronto.

Kapur, Anuradha. 1993. *Actors, Pilgrims, Kings, and Gods: The Ramlila of Ramnagar*. London: Seagull.

Kapur, Geeta. 1987. "Mythic Material in Indian Cinema." *Journal of Arts and Ideas* 14–15: 79–108. This article, revised and many illustrations added, appears as "Revelation and Doubt in Sant Tukaram and Devi," in *When Was Modernism: Essays on Contemporary Cultural Practice in India* (233–64). New Delhi: Tulika Book, 2000.

Lederle, Matthew. 1976. *Philosophical Trends in Modern Maharashtra*. Bombay: Popular Prakashan.

Lele, Jayant, ed. 1981. *Tradition and Modernity in Bhakti Movements*. Leiden, the Netherlands: Brill.

Lutgendorf, Philip. 2002. "A Superhit Goddess: *Jai Santhoshi Maa* and Caste Hierarchy in Indian Films." *Manushi* 131: 10–16, 24–37.

———. 2006. "Is there an Indian way of filmmaking?" *International Journal of Hindu Studies* 10(3): 227–56.

Mishra, Vijay. 2005. *Bollywood Cinema: Temple of Desire.* New York: Routledge.

Neal, Steve. 2000. *Genre and Hollywood.* New York: Routledge.

Pandian, M. S. 1992. *The Image Trap: M. G. Ramachandran in Films and Politics.* New Delhi: Sage.

Pathak, C. B. 1972. *Phirta Cinema.* Pune, India: Prapancha Prakashan.

Pinney, Christopher. 2004. *"Photos of the Gods": The Printed Image and Political Struggle in India.* New York: Oxford University Press.

Prasad, Madhav. 1998. *Ideology of the Hindi Film: A Historical Construction.* New York: Oxford University Press.

Rajadhyaksha, Ashish. 1987. "The Phalke Era: Conflict of Traditional Form and Modern Technology." *Journal of Arts and Ideas* 14/15: 47–78.

———, and Paul Willemen, eds. 1995. *Encyclopaedia of Indian Cinema.* New York: Oxford University.

Ranade, Ashok. 2006. *Hindi Film Song: Music Beyond Boundaries.* Chicago: Bibliophile South Asia.

Ranade, R. D. 1933/1983. *Mysticism in Maharashtra.* Albany, N.Y.: SUNY Press.

Richman, Paula. 1991. *Many Rāmāyanas: The Diversity of a Narrative Tradition in South Asia.* Berkeley: University of California Press.

Rotman, Andy, Christian Novetzke, and William Elison, eds. 2008. *Amar Akbar Anthony: Nation, City, and Family in a Landmark Hindi Film.* (In process.)

Schechner, Richard. 1983. *Performative Circumstances: From the Avant Garde to Ramlila.* Calcutta: Seagull.

Schomer, Karin, and W. H. McLeod. 1987. *The Sants: Studies in a Devotional Tradition of India.* Berkeley Religious series. New Delhi: Motilal Banarsidas.

Schulze, Brigitte. 2003. *Humanist and Emotional Beginnings of a Nationalist Indian Cinema in Bombay: With Kracauer in the Footsteps of Phalke.* Berlin: Avinus.

Shahani, Kumar. 1985. "The Saint Poets of Prabhat." In *Seventy Years of Indian Cinema, 1913–1983,* ed. T. M. Ramachandran (197–202). Bombay: Cinema India International.

Singer, Milton. 1972. *When a Great Tradition Modernizes: An Anthropological Approach to Indian Civilization.* Chicago: University of Chicago Press.

Taussig, Michael. 1993. *Mimesis and Alterity: A Particular History of the Senses.* New York: Routledge.

Tulpule, S. G. 1984. *Mysticism in Medieval India.* Wiesbaden: Harrassowitz.

Vardhan, Vishnu. 2005. "Has the Mythological Died?" Unpublished article in the archives of Sarai Media Collective.

Vasudevan, Ravi. 2000. "The Politics of Cultural Address in a 'Transitional' Cinema: A Case Study of Indian Popular Cinema." In *Reinventing Film Studies,* ed. Christine Gledhill and Linda Williams. London: Arnold.

———. 1993. "Shifting Code, Dissolving Identity: The Social Films of the 1950s as Popular Culture." *Journal of Arts and Ideas* 23–24.

Willeman, Paul. 2006. "Action Cinema, Labour Power and the Video Market." In *Hong Kong Connections: Transnational Imagination in Action Cinema,* ed. Meaghan Morris, Siu Leung, and Stephen Chan Ching-kiu (223–48). Durham, N.C.: Duke University Press.

5

Buddhism, Film, and Religious Knowing: Challenging the Literary Approach to Film

Francisca Cho

Academic knowledge is discursive and analytical by definition. If we want to learn about a great novel in the classroom, we study its themes, structure, and the historical context and process of its making. The conceptual categories that such analysis both employs and creates then produce meaning and our sense of knowledge. This is most often our approach to film as well—what might be called a literary approach, in which film is read like a text. In this literary practice, the visual images of the film cohere into a story that can be conceptually probed: Is *E.T. the Extra-terrestrial* a Christ narrative, for example? Movie images are replete with symbolism.

The aim of this chapter is to explore a nonliterary approach to film by seeing it as a form of religious practice. I use Buddhist principles and language in order to talk about this practice simply because Buddhism is the tradition with which I am most familiar. My point is not to argue that there is something inherently Buddhist about the medium of film. Rather, it is to demonstrate how film allows us to enact certain practices that we can readily recognize as religious in nature. Gregory Watkins has explored the idea that certain techniques in film can function religiously by erasing the distance we normally feel between ourselves and the worlds we view (1999). The effect of such erasure is to morally engage and implicate us by virtue of the ways in which films can configure our relationship to subjects seen—the protagonist of the film can look directly at us, for example, and involve us in the story, or we may be given access to a view of the story that demands a greater response from us than is possible for the film's own characters.

In this chapter I take up the theme of seeing the subjects of film in a different way. I am interested in how film can command our attention to the daily practice of seeing, with an emphasis on the ordinary rather than the extraordinary. Film can engage us in a real-time experience, in which the camera holds our attention on an object for a duration of its (rather than our) choosing. While many films seek to entertain us with a plethora of fast-moving and stylish images, some employ the opposite strategy, in which the camera slows and holds our gaze. This ability to control the pace at which the viewer sees is not shared by photography and other still images. Film, therefore, possesses a unique ability to address the religious phenomena of attention and contemplation. I first explore this religious/filmic experience and then discuss the Japanese film *Maboroshi* and my use of it in the classroom.

Seeing versus Thinking about Film

Buddhist tradition is full of vision metaphors—much like the English language itself—when it comes to talking about the acquisition of true knowledge. In the standard tale of the Buddha's enlightenment, it is said that he acquired the "divine eye," with which he could see the entire realm of death and rebirth and all of the beings within it. The Buddha's supernatural ability to see the past, present, and future of all beings is a way of saying that he knows the world and that he sees it deeply. This ability entails looking beyond the surface, or the present, to see the past and the future. Crossing temporal spaces in this manner leads the Buddha to a greater knowledge that liberates him from the conceptual and value structures that exercise their hold over us in the present.

It is safe to say that despite the variety of Buddhist texts and practices in Buddhism's twenty-five centuries of existence, a recurrent theme of the tradition is the danger of cognitive thinking to true religious seeing. This thinking comprises language, its conceptual categories, and its inevitable values—the mental doings and makings that Mādhyamika Buddhism deems *prapažca,* or "fabrication." This conventional "reality" in which we necessarily live can be renounced or embraced, depending on the variety of Buddhism, but either way, its power to seduce and deceive us is equally acknowledged.

Buddhist tradition recognizes that seeing is different from thinking and that knowing this difference is an significantly important act. It is interesting, then, that the same insight is made in the context of film theory, making the religious potential of film a viable proposition. According to David MacDougall, "the meaning we find in what we see is always both a necessity and an obstacle. Meaning guides our seeing. Meaning allows us to categorize objects. Meaning is what imbues the image of a person with all we know about them. But meaning, when we force it on things, can also blind us, causing us to see only what we expect to see or distracting us from seeing very much at all" (2006, 1).

MacDougall goes on to assert that it is therefore crucial to examine our patterns of observation and that this is especially so for filmmakers because they have restricted means of seeing and recording life. For example, the surveillance camera is quite blind, recording and looking with no intelligence behind it. The cameras of inexperienced filmmakers can be restless, anxiously moving from image to image but "constantly dissatisfied, as if nothing were worth looking at" (ibid., 7). Some filmmakers may possess intelligence but are so worried by what they should be thinking that the camera never gives itself over to an image, proffering judgments instead. Clearly, what a film shows us (or does not show us) is an extension of how we ourselves see and do not see.

What, then, might a religious film allow or even make us see? Because film is a sensory medium, it is innately nondiscursive in nature. "Seeing," of course, stands in for all of receptive experience, insofar as we can postulate a physical experience that is separate from the mental constructions that we use to give them meaning. This is not to impose a Cartesian dualism. The point simply is that we can conceptualize and give meaning to any phenomenal experience in a variety of ways, depending on context and culture. Some filmmakers use all of the techniques at their disposal—music, camera angles, mise-en-scène—to make their intent all too clear. Others, however, invite a complexity of inter-pretations that can vary according to the viewer or the values we hold. A certain way of seeing experience refuses certainty of meaning in favor of a meaningful uncertainty. MacDougall captures the essence of this religious practice:

> In films the complexity of people and objects implicitly resists the theories and explanations in which the film enlists them, sometimes suggesting other explanations or no explanation at all. In this sense, then, film is always a discourse of risk and indeterminacy. This puts it at odds with most academic writing, which, despite its caution and qualifications, is a discourse that advances always toward conclusions. (ibid., 6)

A literary approach to film enlists religion as a theory that moves the viewer toward clear conclusions. The nonliterary approach of interest here, on the other hand, focuses on the ability of film to fix our gaze on phenomena in a nondiscursive way—in a manner that advances us from meaning to seeing, which is a form of religious practice.

A discussion of Kore-eda Hirokazu's 1995 film, *Maboroshi*, will demon-strate how film can enable such seeing, as well as the reasons for using such a film in the classroom context. First, however, it is worth addressing the the-oretical question of *how* film can function religiously. We have already iden-tified the purpose of such a function; that is to say, one way in which film can function religiously is to help us see in a way that disorders and perhaps even transcends the vise grip of our usual conceptual fabrications. Buddhist and film theory converge, furthermore, in understanding how such a process can come about. They do this by attending to the nature of our phenomenal ex-periences, and by virtue of this, they provide a philosophical meditation on how we constitute "reality."

Early in the history of Buddhist tradition, the *Sabba Sutta* of the Pali Canon (*Samyutta Nikāya* 4.15–20) famously declares that the Buddha's teachings are concerned only with sensory experiences (which include the mind and mental experience) and the phenomenal world they create. Notably absent from the realm of Buddhist discourse is the question of what, if anything, phenomenal reality ultimately refers to. The Buddha rejects speculations about ultimate or transcendent reality because they cannot be confirmed by phenomenal experience and, more importantly, because they are the very conceptual fabrications that give rise to conflict and delusion.

The early tradition's privileging of embodied experience over abstract referents takes on pedagogical substance in Mahayana Buddhism, with its theory of the Buddha's three bodies. In large part, Buddha-body theory accounts for the many Buddhas and bodhisattvas that populate Mahayana texts and play an important role in popular Buddhist worship. Of greater interest for us, however, is the understanding of the historical Buddha Shakyamuni as a *nirmā-nakāya*, or illusory, "manifestation body" that appears to the world for the purpose of teaching and liberating all beings. Let us be clear about what has happened here: The real, historical Buddha is "demoted" into a sensory apparition that only appears to live and die like a mortal being. According to the sixteenth chapter of the *Lotus Sutra*, the reason for this trickery is to inspire people to follow the Buddhist path. This compassionate objective justifies all kinds of artifice in the Mahayana universe, including literary ones such as "similes, parables, and phrases" (Watson 1993, 226). All kinds of stories and literary inventions are allowed because of their pedagogical efficacy in spite of their lack of literal truth. This is how the diverse and even conflicting sets of Buddhist teachings are understood and justified in Mahayana tradition as well.

The implications of this "theology" in which the "savior" need be real only at the level of our sensory and emotional experience have been immense in the course of Buddhist history. They account for the reasons that Buddha images are treated as no different from the original living Buddha. They also explain why secular aesthetic practice and experience can merge so seamlessly with religious ones. According to Platonic theory, the senses trick us into mistaking the unreal for the real. In Buddhist theory, however, "Truth becomes fiction when the fiction's true; Real becomes not-real where the unreal's real" (as quoted in Cao 1973, 55). In other words, fiction and the artifice of all art are capable of making us experience the truth of things. If fiction can speak the truth, that is because the sensory and emotional experiences that art is capable of engendering are what really matters in the world. This couplet from the first chapter of the eighteenth-century Chinese classic novel *The Story of the Stone* encapsulates a literary theory that justifies the truth of fiction, based on a religious theory that sees the world itself as an artistic illusion.

A current premise of film theory fortifies the sentiment that the experiences precipitated by art are indistinguishable from those engendered by life itself. This theory recognizes that film is a medium in which the corporal body is very much present. Echoing the sentiments of the Chinese novel, Gilberto Pérez notes that "presence is not an illusion in the movies . . . [but rather a] hallucination that is true" (1998, 26–28). That is because the presence of bodies in film directly affects and engenders our own bodily experiences. Linda Williams refers to the film genres of horror, pornography, and "women's weepies" as "body genres" in their capacity to invoke "an almost involuntary mimicry of the emotion or sensation of the body on the screen," such as cries of pleasure, screams of terror, and sobs of anguish (1991, 4). The fact of this observation is masked when film criticism limits itself to the discursive—to the political, the psychoanalytic, and the feminist readings that "reduce film to signs, symbols, and other domesticated meanings" (MacDougall 2006, 14).

If we give ourselves over to the corporeal experience of film, the real becomes not-real because the unreal is real. That is to say, if the effect of such body genres is real pleasure, terror, and anguish, then the not-real nature of what we ordinarily take to be real becomes apparent. This is because all it takes to be "real" is the response of our bodies and emotions, as opposed to some Platonic standard. It is all too common in life, as well as in art, to be moved by stories and events that have no reality beyond themselves. In this, art and life itself become "significantly more about the body's vulnerability to sensations than they [are] about the reality of the referents causing these sensations" (Williams 1995, 9). We can go further and add that if film can make us see and feel as well as any real-life experience, then perhaps it can even surpass real life in training us to see. Like the sensory apparition of a Buddha, the illusion of film can lure us into a better practice of seeing.

The Seeing of *Maboroshi*

I screen the film *Maboroshi* in the context of a course I teach called Religion and Aesthetics. The course is a broad comparative look at Western and East Asian views of art and aesthetic experience in relation to religion. To cover the East Asian side, I focus primarily on Buddhist culture as displayed through fiction, poetry, and film. These sources—Lady Murasaki's *Tale of Genji* and the haiku of Bashō, for example—are nondiscursive by nature and cannot be read as a primer on Buddhist beliefs. And this is precisely the point. Rather than teach Buddhism as a discursive tradition, the aim of the course is to demonstrate how Buddhist beliefs have shaped East Asian artistic visions.

Maboroshi is set in contemporary Japan and never mentions Buddhism. The only link is provided by the title, "maboroshi," based on the Chinese character *huan*, meaning illusion, dream, or phantom—all common Buddhist epithets for life and phenomenal reality. The term is not used until the end of the film. The plot of the movie is relatively simple: A young married woman, Yumiko, experiences the inexplicable suicide of her husband. With the help of a matchmaker, Yumiko remarries a widower in a small seaside town. The transition is relatively smooth, and the marriage is happy. The dramatic tension of the film revolves around Yumiko's experiences of loss, beginning with her grandmother, who wanders off to die—an event recollected as a dream prologue to the film's main story. The dramatic climax consists of Yumiko's outburst of uncomprehending sorrow at her first husband's death, which is precipitated by a visit back home to Osaka, as well as a more recent incident— an anxious wait for an old fisherwoman whom she fears has been lost at sea. In response to Yumiko's anguish, her current husband offers that sometimes fishermen are enticed to their death by a strange or "phantom light" ("maboroshi no hikari," which is the actual Japanese title of the film) far out at sea. This suffices as an explanation and resolves Yumiko's grief over those she has lost.

Plot is not the central element of the film, however. Its most newsworthy event—the first husband's suicide—happens off camera, and any anticipation of surprise or dramatic revelations that make sense of the death is unfulfilled. The character and psychology of the protagonists are not highlights, either. The film favors long-range shots that establish a distance between the viewer and the bodies on screen. The movie neglects to offer a single close-up, and any shot that comes close tends to bathe the actors' faces in shadow. Thus it is difficult to discern facial expressions, and even the use of voice and inflection is highly subdued. By the end of the film, one has had no more than a glimpse of Yumiko's features.

The film spends much of its time in looking at things that advance neither plot nor psychology. This often entails filming peripheral objects, such as the row of shod shoes at the entrance of the house, where one can hear the ambient noise of the guests inside. The camera is often still, training itself on a shot well beyond the time necessary to establish the action. A bus stops and dislodges a passenger, for example, and we watch in distant stillness as the bus pulls slowly outside of the camera's frame. Only the next shot reveals that the passenger is Yumiko, almost fully enclosed in shadow inside the shelter of the bus stop. The film frequently captures children at play, staying just distant enough to replicate the experience of watching the naturalness of children who are unaware that they are being observed.

Maboroshi virtuously fulfills Donald Richie's observation that "if the American film is strongest in action, and if the European is strongest in character, then the Japanese film is richest in mood or atmosphere, in presenting characters in their own surroundings" (1971, xix). One can find this feature of Japanese films articulated in the literary theory of early China as well. The "Great Preface" to the *Book of Poetry,* a dominant work of poetic theory that goes back to the end of the Han dynasty (206 BCE–220 CE) articulates "affective image" *(xing)* as a function of poetry. According to Stephen Owen, affective image is "the stirring of a particular affection or mood" that is not referred to but actually generated. The priority of moods "follows from the conception of language as the manifestation of some integral state of mind, [in contrast to] the Western rhetoric of schemes and tropes [that] follows from a conception of language as sign and referent (Owen 1992, 46). What both poetry and film do is to *manifest* rather than discourse on an intention or a state of mind, and this manifestation is meant to affect our own bodies and minds.

Maboroshi uses its camera to depict its characters in relation to their environment through distant shots that frame their everyday actions, and the effect is a mixture of pure visual awe and cognitive silence. The prolonged and still camera trained on Yumiko bathing her infant gently but persistently pauses on the palpable contentment of this simple domestic act. The slowly panning camera follows the play of her son and his stepsister as they run along the textured rocks, water, snow, and fields that form the patterns of the coastal geography. An exquisite contemplation of light and shadow is offered in a darkened bedroom, when a window is opened to reveal the roaring morning sea, which forms a block of light and sound on the black screen. One of the most ethereal images is captured in a shot of Yumiko washing the wooden stairs. The trapdoor open at the top lets in a stream of tangible light like a thick daub of numinous paint that might, in another religious context, signify the appearance of angels or an annunciation.

All of this lingering to look in lieu of an advancing plotline produces a viewing experience that is indubitably slow. Trying to figure out what the scenes signify is a futile and frustrating viewing strategy. It is much better simply to give oneself over to the images. Richie explains:

> One looks long at the mountain or the flower, and what it is—its mood of existence, as it were—is slowly apprehended. *It* is apprehended because contemplation ensures that nothing else is. One either looks at [Yasujiro] Ozu's single, motionless figure, or is bored. It is presumed (and this is a presumption that Western art, to its loss, no longer makes) that there is something within you, the viewer, which can respond and comprehend. (1971, 112)

The possibility for boredom, of course, is quite real when using *Maboroshi* in the classroom. That risk also pertains to the films of Ozu, a Japanese director whose monumental *Tokyo Story* (1953) I regularly screen in the same class. To counteract the possibility, I find it helpful to provide conceptual aids, such as the medieval Japanese aesthetic terminology of *yūgen*, which describes a mysterious and profound depth that can be glimpsed in the ordinary world of sensory appearances. Such concepts help alert students to be attentive to moments that they might otherwise look past. Shortly after the bus-stop scene mentioned earlier, Yumiko encounters a funeral procession, which we view from above, in a clearing in late-autumn foliage. As the procession moves through the middle of the frame, a few flakes of snow fly above the leaves in the foreground of the camera. After a few whirls, there is a sudden burst of snow, like a heaven-sent shower of pale flower petals. To look and be moved in some indescribable way by such a vision is well worth some practice and prompting.

My primary purpose in showing *Maboroshi* to undergraduates is to introduce them to a different pace and style of seeing. One question this chapter raises is whether academic learning can incorporate more than discursive content and critical analysis to include aesthetic, or sense-based, learning. Can we teach and learn through our senses as well as with our cognitive faculties? Additionally, can aesthetic learning augment and perhaps even surpass cognitive knowledge? I have described the aim of suspending our conceptual schemes about the world as a religious practice that Buddhist traditions particularly embrace. But it is possible to translate this aim into more general pedagogical values.

Let us begin with the first question about the possibility of sense-based learning. Our modern emphasis on cognitive skills tends to ignore the degree to which somatic, performance-based learning has been prevalent in many societies. This is especially true of East Asian settings where Confucian learning, for example, was essential to the stability and continuity of society. Such learning was a matter of first imitating and then mastering the performance of rituals. Theoretical understanding of how and why the rituals worked or the entities to which they referred—such as the ancestors—were deemphasized: "More important to creating common understandings of the nature of ancestors were the rites themselves and thus indirectly the liturgies which described in matter-of-fact ways how they should be performed" (Ebrey 1991, 207). An "action-oriented pedagogy" is also evident in contemporary Buddhist monastic education in Sri Lanka (Samuels 2004, 2005), in which correct ritual performance is the means by which novice monks acquire ideal demeanor, behavior, and attitudes. Again somatic training plays a fundamental role prior to intellectual and textual learning.

To be sure, the inculcation of ritual performance in a Confucian or Buddhist setting perhaps fits better into the category of "molding" than formal "schooling." The former is more akin to the child rearing and socialization that are practiced with varying degrees of formality in all societies. However, as Ebrey points out, formal education systems usually attempt to mold, as well as to school (1989, 277), and learning through the body perhaps imparts a more intimate kind of knowing than the knowledge of the intellect: "Those who learn physically learn differently, and experience their knowledge differently as well. It becomes ingested, becomes, like food, part of one's cell structure" (quoted in Samuels 2005, 351).

If so much learning takes place through kinesthetic channels in the history of cultures, it is quite likely that it continues, no matter how much we underutilize it in our own educational institutions. It is worth considering what other contexts in our society pick up this slack and whether formal education should incorporate this kind of learning in a conscious way. This leads us to the second question: In what way is aesthetic knowledge an advantage over intellectual knowledge? One answer is that aesthetic knowledge is a training for action. The kind of ritual performances found in Confucianism and Buddhism is geared toward teaching young people how to act not just in a formal ceremony but in the context of life itself—to know instinctively when to bow, when to speak, how to speak, and what to do in various situations. Such religiously based training is obviously inappropriate for public and secular institutions. The absence of explicit religious training, however, does not mean that secular institutions forgo the task of molding students' behavior.

But in what way does our system of formal education, with its emphasis on the intellect, impinge on the broader social goal of learning how to act? We commonly aver that education exceeds mere acquisition of information and must include the development of critical skills. The purpose of critical skills is to learn how to think for oneself—to question and probe the assumptions that freight any intellectual assertion. There is the implication of performance in all of this—that the purpose of critical thinking is to *decide* about things and that such decision leads to action. However, in fact, the nexus between thought and action is very difficult to ascertain. We have faith that our actions are (or should be, at any rate) driven by intellect and reason, and yet there is much evidence to the contrary. Too often our actions contradict what we earnestly espouse, suggesting that our performances are driven by habits and assumptions that are much more unconscious and innate than reason.

Perhaps any system of education that emphasizes the intellect should also include some reflection on its limits. At a certain juncture, propositions and arguments reach a point of diminishing returns. Ultimately, acting requires the suspension of thought and relies instead on intuitive ways of seeing. Nonetheless, intuition does not automatically lead to good or fruitful results, for our intuition itself is trained in various ways. We act without awareness of these deep-seated structures and use reason to cobble together after-the-fact stories about why we do what we do. Still, these intuitions have a logic and a set of assumptions all their own. If meaning guides our seeing, as MacDougall says, it is quite likely the case that meaning structures from prior environments have become so ingrained that they form a part of our somatic and unconscious selves.

In this context, it is perhaps desirable to actively train our intuition to become free of its own embedded logic. The active practice of seeing might be useful here not because it fortifies the will to act in prescribed ways but because it enables us to free ourselves of all signifying and meaning systems. If such an aim seems baffling, it is worth considering that sometimes the situations we encounter, in and of themselves, force us to concede the inadequacy of how we see. Training is required if we are to be able to accept the limitations of our meaning systems without reprisal. Willingness to accept uncertainty may be a constructive act in its own right, and the ability to suspend judgment and conceptuality is itself a deeply learned response.

I have had my share of students who complain about being bored by the films I screen, but not as many as one might expect. In truth, twenty-year-olds are quite responsive to aesthetic stimuli—being less deformed by the habit of cognition—and the way they articulate what they experience can be downright breathtaking. But the most concrete and satisfying evidence of success was offered to me not too long ago when a former student paid a visit. Having graduated some years previously, he filled me in on his activities, and then the subject turned to movies. He had seen a recent film that had garnered good reviews. It was one of the more serious and substantial varieties. Nevertheless, he complained. It was overdone, he reported. The politics was too black and white and did not allow for complexity. The music, too, was manipulative, signifying when to emote and what to feel. The effect was overbearing and annoying. The films he saw in class, he stated, have changed the way he views other motion pictures. I would wager (or hope, at least) that they have changed more than the way he views other movies. The habit of rejecting obvious stories in favor of open-ended perception through the body as well as mind certainly makes for good art criticism, but it is a life skill as well.

Conclusion

To say that film can function religiously cannot help but engage ongoing discussions about the relationship between religion and art generally. In the contemporary art world, overtly religious art is a ghettoized subcategory, with the understanding that it is not truly serious art (Elkins 2004). Sincere piety has no place in contemporary art, and religious symbols must be clothed in postmodern ambiguity or irony in order to be acceptable at all. On the other hand, the frequency with which artists invoke the language of spirituality to describe the process and import of their work is quite notable (Wuthnow 2001). Many artists embrace a nontraditional and private spirituality over institutional religions, which in turn generates debate about appropriate labels— to wit, whether this is really "religion." Hence, while the art world rejects religious subject matter as inimical to "real art," scholars and other observers of religion are frequently dubious of the "spirituality" claims of modern artists.

What I mean by "religion" in the present case is the cultivation of a certain way of seeing that pursues noncognitive and sensory contemplation, which certain films can encourage. This practice can be deemed normative from a Buddhist religious, a secular aesthetic, or an educational perspective. That is to say, we need not get caught up in a debate about whether "religion" is being properly used in this instance. It is a fact, however, that in the context of one course that I teach, I convey the nature of Buddhist thought through aesthetic means both because it reveals something of East Asian history and culture and because it encompasses an educational good. This can hopefully contribute to any consideration of the relationship between religion and film.

REFERENCES

Cao Xueqin. 1973. *The Story of the Stone: A Chinese Novel in Five Volumes,* trans. David Hawkes. Vol. 1. Harmondsworth, Middlesex: Penguin.
Ebrey, Patricia Buckley. 1991. *Confucianism and Family Rituals in Imperial China.* Princeton, N.J.: Princeton University Press.
————. 1989. "Education through Ritual: Efforts to Formulate Family Rituals during the Sung Period." In *Neo-Confucian Education: The Formative Stage,* ed. Wm. Theodore de Bary and John Chafee, 277–306. Los Angeles: University of California Press.
Elkins, James. 2004. *On the Strange Place of Religion in Contemporary Art.* New York: Routledge.
MacDougall, David. 2006. *The Corporeal Image: Film, Ethnography, and the Senses.* Princeton, N.J.: Princeton University Press.
Owen, Stephen, ed. 1992. *Readings in Chinese Literary Thought.* Cambridge, Mass.: Council on East Asian Studies, Harvard University.

Pérez, Gilberto. 1998. *The Material Ghost: Films and Their Medium*. Baltimore: Johns Hopkins University Press.

Richie, Donald. 1971. *Japanese Cinema: Film Style and National Character*. Garden City, N.Y.: Doubleday.

Samuels, Jeffrey. 2005. "Texts Memorized, Texts Performed: A Reconsideration of the Role of *Paritta* in Sri Lankan Monastic Education." *Journal of the International Association of Buddhist Studies* 28(2): 339–67.

———. 2004. "Toward an Action-oriented Pedagogy: Buddhist Texts and Monastic Education in Contemporary Sri Lanka." *Journal of the American Academy of Religion* 72(4): 955–72.

Watkins, Greg. 1999. "Seeing and Being Seen: Distinctively Filmic and Religious Elements in Film." *Journal of Religion and Film* 3(2).

Watson, Burton, trans. 1993. *The Lotus Sutra*. New York: Columbia University Press.

Williams, Linda. 1995. "Corporealized Observers: Visual Pornographies and the 'Carnal Density of Vision.' " In *Fugitive Images: From Photography to Video*, ed. Patrice Petro, 3–41. Bloomington: University of Indiana Press.

———. 1991. "Film Bodies: Gender, Genre, and Excess." *Film Quarterly* 44(4): 2–13.

Wuthnow, Robert. 2001. *Creative Spirituality: The Way of the Artist*. Los Angeles: University of California Press.

6

The Pedagogical Challenges
of Finding Christ Figures
in Film

Christopher Deacy

When is theology an integral part *of* a film, and when is it brought *to* a film? To help answer these questions I offer a critique of the increasing tendency among a number of theologians and religious studies practitioners to examine the interface between religion and film by forging superficial correlations between the New Testament Jesus and so-called cinematic Christ figures. While acknowledging that such an approach has undoubted missiological or confessional value, its uncritical appropriation in the classroom is not only theologically unsophisticated but has limited pedagogical utility as well. After teaching an undergraduate course on religion and film for three consecutive years, I have learned that students tend to use the Christ-figure typology (Kozlovic 2004) in their work, not least when they are required to write a twenty-five-hundred-word theological interpretation of a film of their choice. Even though in such instances students may be able to discern parallels between, for example, Keanu Reeves's character Neo in *The Matrix* (1999) or John Coffey (Michael Clarke Duncan) in *The Green Mile* (1999) and Jesus of Nazareth, there is a degree to which Christian symbolism and values are being imposed on films. These movies are accordingly judged not qua film or for the quality of filmic properties such as mise-en-scène, cinematography, sound, editing, or direction but solely for their structural and (all-too-frequently) alleged narrative convergences with biblical passages. Such films are thus examined for the extent to which they either do or do not have the necessary definitional properties and, whether consciously or otherwise, students are categorizing them as manifestly "Christian" products. The assumption is that, in a gnostic-type scenario, these themes are present in the film—albeit hidden, disguised, or camouflaged to the uninitiated—and that it is the theologian's special prerogative to analyze the film in order to reveal its purported Christological core. Indeed, in Kozlovic's words, "innumerable Christ-figures and other holy subtexts are hidden within the popular cinema" (2004, ¶ 5), to the point that "secular films can engage in religious storytelling about biblical characters, ideas, and themes without appearing 'religious'" (ibid.).

It is my contention, however, that nobody functions in a cultural vacuum, and there is no such thing as a definitive, normative, or objective theological lens through which one may embark upon a theological conversation. There are a multiplicity of ways of "doing theology," depending on whether one is a liberal or an evangelical, Protestant or Catholic, believer or nonbeliever, atheist or agnostic, to name just some of the available options. Moreover, as Melanie Wright correctly discerns, "a consideration of a film's religious qualities, like that of its meanings more generally, is not something that an individual critic can determine once and for all" (2007, 78).

It can thus be somewhat disquieting when a student claims in an essay, to paraphrase an example from one of my own students, that a particular film—in this instance, the ostensibly satirical *Monty Python's The Life of Brian* (1979)—"could displease Christians" or that "Christians could see this film as insulting to their faith," as if there is something innately homogeneous about how anybody who subscribes to a particular faith affiliation will respond to a given text. Unless attention is accorded to wider questions such as the filmmaker's motivations in creating a film, whether a movie is indeed a satire (and, if so, what it satirizes), and how successful the filmmaker has been to this end, then there is clearly more work to be done.

Broader questions are also raised in any attempt to claw from a film a specific understanding of how it harmonizes (or not) with what we can glean from the New Testament record of Jesus. How do we really know who or what Jesus was? What sources are at our disposal? We can never really know whether characters that have been likened to Jesus were in fact intended that way, and this raises important questions about who is actually involved in the creation and dissemination of films. How paramount, for example, is the director's intentionality in creating a given film? The way Kozlovic sees it, a sole filmmaker is responsible for each individual filmic "text," and that person "consciously decides to make that heroic Christ-figure choice; the script almost writes itself" (2004, ¶ 11).

As Wright points out, however, contemporary emphases in cinema studies "query auteurism, foregrounding the collaborative, industrial nature of filmmaking and challenging the notion that any film has a single, intrinsic meaning" (2007, 60). The situation may not be so very different from the tendency (less common in academic circles but nonetheless prevalent in more evangelical contexts) to accord authorship of the Pentateuch to Moses or of the Gospels to four discrete but harmonious eyewitnesses rather than see the likes of Matthew, Mark, Luke, and John as "shorthand labels for the various contributors and processes" (ibid.) that are believed to stand behind a gospel text. Some see John's Gospel, for instance, as based on the Synoptics—to form what

Clement of Alexandria in the second century called a spiritual gospel—while the majority of scholars tend to see the Fourth Gospel as independent of the other three and resting on "its own complicated prehistory of many sources" (Barton 2004, 20).

There is thus no certainty in this debate, and, in John Barton's words, "In the last twenty years or so there has been a major shift in biblical studies," in which "Consensus even about method has broken down, and the field is now a battleground of conflicting approaches, with no agreed conclusions any longer" (ibid., 18). Within such a context, it appears somewhat obsolete, even precritical, to attempt to "read" Christological content into films without at least looking into whether alternative readings may also contain currency and whether these are expressly theological. As David Jasper suggests, for example, with respect to *Edward Scissorhands* (1990), in a savage indictment of this kind of approach, gospel comparisons may actually be a distraction from what is really a "rather slight modern fairy story that draws on a range of mythic antecedents from *Frankenstein* and *Peter Pan* to 'Beauty and the Beast' " (1997, 239). Attempts to bring the gospels and film together in this way do no more, according to Jasper, than underline "the universal nature of biblical texts" (ibid.). A mere illustration of theology is thus a somewhat phony endeavor, which prompts the inevitable retort: So what?

It is not surprising, therefore, that conversations between theologians and scholars who work in film and cinema studies are few and far between when film interpretations are predicated upon this kind of leap of faith in order to be efficacious. Even where points of affinity are discerned between film characters and the New Testament Jesus, the question must be raised as to whether this really resembles a theological activity. This is not of course to say that theology is an easily defined activity. Debates are manifold, for example, as to whether it comprises an academic discipline that can be practiced irrespective of one's personal beliefs or whether, as Gerald Loughlin sees it, "theology can only really be undertaken in faith, the communities and cultures of those who understand themselves to stand in relation to a transcendent source, and recognize and seek to understand such a relationship" (2005, 3). Theologians are also often unsure where, if at all, the line of demarcation exists between theology and secular culture, to the point that, when it comes to ethical issues such as stem cell research and debates over when human life begins and ends, there are sometimes closer connections "between Christians and their secular counterparts than there are between opposing Christians" (Gill 2004, 13). The idea that a clearly defined "theological" sphere of activity exists is thus a fallacy, and, when it comes to the Christ-figures debate, there can be no preset rules or norms as to what should or should not be construed as comprising a legitimate area of theological exploration.

Nevertheless, it remains a little too wide of the mark to look merely for points of convergence and correlation between "Christ" and "Christ figure" when there are, equally, occasions in which a point of *departure* exists between a film and a scriptural text. Productive though it may be forge a link between the figure at the heart of a two-thousand-year-old tradition and, to cite a familiar example, the alien at the heart of Steven Spielberg's *E.T.* (1982), as one of my students recently pointed out there is a notable discontinuity—for in the Christian story *Jesus* teaches the disciples (in the words of Jesus in Matthew 19:14, "Let the children come to me, and do not hinder them"), whereas in the film it is the *children* who teach E.T. This raises wider questions about whether an alleged Christ figure needs to bear witness to all of the facets of Christ's life in order to be properly designated a Christ figure. According to Kozlovic (2004, ¶ 66), "twenty-five structural characteristics of the cinematic Christ-figure" have been identified, ranging from the willingness of film characters to perform a sacrifice for the benefit of often unworthy and ungrateful individuals, to the presence of twelve associates or disciples, the existence of a betrayer or Judas figure, and a sexually identified woman (in the manner of Mary Magdalene), as well as all manner of cross and resurrection-type allusions. Yet, it is significant that Kozlovic is unable to identify any films that fulfill even half of the structural characteristics that he so painstakingly delineates, with most of the films he discusses bearing witness to, at most, just three or four.

One of the most cited films in Kozlovic's list is Nicolas Roeg's science fiction parable *The Man Who Fell to Earth* (1976), which conforms to just four of the twenty-five structural characteristics. For example, Kozlovic sees the protagonist, the alien visitor Thomas Jerome Newton (David Bowie), as an "Outsider Figure" (number three in his list) because he comes from a realm that is above, beyond, or "out there" and is thus, like Christ, *in* the world but not *of* it (cf. John 1:10). However, Kozlovic also distances himself from this reading, on the grounds that Jerome's pathetic lapse into a dissolute and drunken lifestyle such that he is no longer set apart from the rest of humankind as "holy" or "other," diminishes the Christ-figure attribution (¶ 30). Similarly, despite Kozlovic's noting that *The Man Who Fell to Earth* also corresponds to number twelve on his list of structural characteristics—"a decisive death and resurrection"—his connection to this facet of Christ's life is at best tenuous since, in place of a full-fledged resurrection motif, the film contains no more than a precursor to death and resurrection. In this regard Kozlovic quotes Loughlin, who says that "As Newton lies prostrate and naked on the bed, in a room suddenly grown dark, he has become the deposed Christ, lying in his tomb, awaiting his anointing for burial" (quoted in ibid., ¶ 48).

However, does this really *reinforce* Newton's Christic nature since, at the end of the film, his mission to rescue his dying planet from extinction has failed and he finds himself stuck on earth, powerless to effect change? Moreover, his agelessness and increasingly self-indulgent and disinterested existence seriously undermines any attempt to read into this film any notion of either a decisive death (Newton does not die) or resurrection (he has lost interest in any form of salvation or new life or even present life). To give another example, Carl Skrade wrote in 1970 that Paul Newman's protagonist, Lucas Jackson, in *Cool Hand Luke* (1967) was "the filmic Christ-figure par excellence" (1970, 21), yet it is curious that Kozlovic's article draws only three Christic parallels with this film. These links are made with regard to Luke's "alter ego" (number five in Kozlovic's list of structural characteristics) in that he is both a Christ figure and a prison inmate (admittedly not the most con-crete of correlations), the fact that he stands at one point in a "cruciform pose" (number seventeen), and that there is a "cross association" (number eighteen) at the end of the picture, where "the filmmakers artistically fuse an actual crossroad with a cross image as seen from a heavenly viewpoint, and link it with Luke, the Christ-figure, at the time of his undeserved death" (Kozlovic 2004, ¶ 57).

The pedagogical utility of this needs, however, to be questioned. The vast majority of my students have seen Peter Weir's *The Truman Show* (1998), for instance, and it is not uncommon for a seminar discussion to revolve around Kozlovic's claim that the scene at the end of the picture when Truman Burbank (Jim Carrey) "walks on water as he steps into the ocean" (ibid., ¶ 58) signals Truman's Christ-like status. But, since Kozlovic's own thesis is predicated on the claim that there are twenty-five structural characteristics that make up a Christ figure, it is hard to see how an overly literal reading of one small visual ingredient of a much larger film is sufficient to justify his unqualified claims that "religious themes should be pointed out in the secular pulpit of the cin-ema during traditional film appreciation classes" (ibid., ¶ 71) and that "feature films should be employed as part of a postmodern religious education" (ibid.). It seems difficult to rationalize the showing of a film for no better reason than that a visual motif within the last five minutes happens to coincide, in the eyes of one interpreter, with a passage contained in the Fourth Gospel, written some two thousand years ago, in which the disciples "saw Jesus walking on the sea and drawing near to [their] boat" (John 6:19).

Instead of a suggestion that Truman is a Christ figure, we need a critical, scholarly dissection of the properties that are being cited as functionally equivalent. I have read many student essays that take the line, for instance, that John Coffey in *The Green Mile* is omnipresent, omniscient, and omnipotent, but without a subsequent exploration of how these classic characteristics of God's identity impinge on the film, the idea is not as rewarding as it might be. According to Richard Swinburne, God is "present everywhere, the creator and sustainer of the universe, a free agent, able to do everything . . . knowing all things, perfectly good, a source of moral obligation, immutable, eternal, a necessary being, holy and worthy of worship" (1993, 2), but it is difficult to see how all of these qualities are interchangeable with this particular character in Darabont's film. Is Coffey really omniscient or just wise, astute, and sagacious? He may be able to cure Paul Edgcomb's (Tom Hanks) urinary infection, but does this make him omnipotent or a miracle worker? That he is a healer is not in question, but does he actually possess supernatural, transcendental powers? It may be that he is reputed, in the film, to have "fallen out of the sky," but this may say more about his mysterious origins than constitute a specific testimony to his divinity. When a film is not seen qua film but only for its affinity with scriptural accounts of Jesus's divinity, then limitations to the ensuing explo-ration are inevitable.

Similar deficiencies in developing a convincing or workable typology also arise in the case of other biblical prototypes. In the case of *Edward Scissorhands*, for example, it has been alleged that one of the characters is a Judas figure. In Peter Malone's words, "Jim, Kim's boyfriend, is the betrayer, even persuading Kim for some time to be part of his scheme" and offering "Edward his mock kiss" (1997, 83). But, unlike Judas in the Gospels, who, according to Matthew 27:5, "went and hanged himself," Jim does not take his own life after realizing the enormity of his crime. Indeed, there is not even a suggestion that Jim feels any sense of guilt about betraying Edward and implicating him in a crime (breaking and entering) that he did not commit. Clive Marsh has argued that "We would be unwise to try and conduct a theological conversation, however useful its subject matter may be, with a 'bad film': a film which people simply would not want to watch" (1997, 32). Turning this claim around, we could just as easily claim that we would be unwise to try to conduct a filmic conversation with "bad theology," that is, with a theology that relies solely on visual correlations in order to be instructive. The fact that a film is deemed to bear witness to certain Christ-like characteristics is not by itself theologically valuable, and we end up with the situation whereby there is no film in which one cannot forge a theological connection. The net result is that this will, in Lyden's words, "stretch the interpretation of such films to the breaking point and do an injustice both to Christianity and to the films in question" (2003, 24). Indeed, it becomes difficult for a film to be heard *in its own right,* and ultimately it becomes a dishonest—not to mention exasperating—enterprise if no consideration is given to the context within which the alleged Christ figure appears. Where, indeed, does one draw the line?

Furthermore, useful though it may be in a classroom context to compare, say, what a romantic comedy, such as *Love Actually* (2003), has to say on the subject of love with Saint Paul's treatise on the topic in 1 Corinthians 13, we must consider such an endeavor in the light of the work of Robert Jewett, for instance, who looks at a range of contemporary films through the lens of Paul's epistles and asks whether films actually do subscribe to a Pauline paradigm. Despite finding a number of pertinent parallels between *Forrest Gump* (1994) and the celebration of love in Paul's first letter to the church at Corinth—"Only Gump remains true to these simple virtues of belief in God, doing one's best with one's abilities, loving one's family and friends, and expecting the best of others" (Jewett 1999, 53)—Jewett readily highlights the differences between them: "Although unworthy misfits were given equal honor in [early Christian] love feasts, there is no presumption of a Forrest-Gump-type of innocence in 1 Corinthians 13 or anywhere else in Paul's writings" (ibid., 55). Films are undoubtedly capable of wrestling with ideals such as love, kindness, compassion, morality, and marriage, but we should also ask whether it is ever really possible to appropriate a Christian ideal through popular film. To what extent do the qualities of agape—unconditional love—shed light on the dynamics that lie at the core of any given motion picture? What sacrifices are involved? Is theology diluted in the process? Is the theologian expected to read the motivations and behavior of film characters through a specifically Christian lens so that, in the case of the racial drama *Crash* (2005), for instance, the film must be labeled as deficient because Jesus's commandment to "love your neighbor as yourself" in

Matthew 22:39 does not appear to have made any direct impression on the characters in this film? Do any films actually pose a challenge to the New Testament understanding of Jesus and initiate a conversation in which theologians need to participate? In other words, is it a one-way or a two-way street?

To give an example, the film *Sin City* (2005) is potentially theologically rich, at least from a cursory examination of its title, which one might think calls to mind, first, in its reference to sin, Saint Augustine's famous treatise on the fallenness, depravity, and sinful nature of the human race, from which "no one can escape without the toll of toils and tears and fears" (quoted in Deacy 2001, 38). Indeed, believing that Adam's sin and spiritual death had been inherited through concupiscence from generation to generation, Augustine claimed that "so great a sin was committed, that by it the human nature was altered for the worse, and was transmitted to their posterity, liable to sin and subject to death" (quoted in ibid.). Second, the title evokes the "city" in Augustine's *City of God*, which constituted the last and greatest apologetic work of the early Christian Church and gave rise to much political thought in the Middle Ages and beyond (including the publication in the mid-1960s of Harvey Cox's seminal *Secular City*) concerning the composition of the church as a mixed body of people.

Yet, whatever superficial links one may be inclined to forge, *Sin City* is an unapologetically misogynistic film, as one of my students pointed out, and the sexist behavior and violence that are meted out to women in any context do not lie outside the province of the theologian. In a classroom context, therefore, such a film should not be viewed through the lens of whether links may be forged with Augustine's own early fifth-century understanding of a "sin city." In his view, although the church is *in* the world, it is not *of* the inexorably sinful and fallen world, and only at the Last Day will this tension between the earthly and heavenly "cities" be resolved. Nor, indeed, is it appropriate to examine the film through the lens of whether any of its leading heroes and villains might constitute Christ figures (or, for that matter, in this context Eve figures).

Rather, the pressing matter concerns the way in which women are dehumanized and viewed as objects rather than subjects, which has a detrimental effect on women's humanity. The most obvious Christ-figure referent in the film is the Bruce Willis character, Hartigan, whose mission is, Travis Bickle–style, to save the life of a prostitute (whose life is being violated by a dangerous sadist) and who is beaten and punished for a crime he did not commit. Hartigan's forgiveness and self-sacrificial love provides one of the film's few grace notes. However, a more suitable classroom discussion would center on the efficacy of always having women being "redeemed" and rescued by men. What effect does this have on women's dignity, autonomy, and sense of personhood?

In a similar way, what is the point of looking at the likes of *One Flew over the Cuckoo's Nest* (1975) or *The Life of David Gale* (2002) for Christ-figure resonances if one is thereby overlooking wider theological positions these films advance about the dangers of nonconformity or institutionalization (in the former) or the adequacy of the death penalty as an instrument of justice (in the latter), which have enormous implications for the pursuit of theology? The same can be said of *The Godfather, Part Three* (1990), which raises many ideological questions about the sanctity of family, the glorification of criminality, and theology and economics in the light of Michael Corleone's (Al Pacino) attempt to "buy" his pardon through the purifying power of money, with the complicity of the Catholic Church. These are all more profitable portals into a theological discussion of the film than one that merely looks for biblical prototypes. To this end, one of my students generated a useful discussion on the tendency to find Christ-figure motifs in cinematic adaptations of comic book superheroes, to the point that the *X-Men* (2000–2006) franchise seemed more of a study of prejudice and social ostracism than a story about liberators and redeemers; in the same vein, *Batman Begins* (2005) is more about fear and the need to stand up for one's own beliefs than about Bruce Wayne (Christian Bale) being a modern-day Jesus.

The danger with simply forging superficial correlations is that such wider issues tend to go untreated and unnoticed, and it is hard to see how, as Kozlovic (2004) suggests, theology and religious studies benefit from the quest for cinematic Christ figures. In a classroom context it is easy to apply the syllogism that since religion and film are involved in related quests, such as that both "are about 'life' and its meaning," then, by definition, "all films are 'religious,' or are amenable to some kind of religious reading" (Wright 2007, 16). However, as Wright argues, this kind of hypothesis "is effectively meaningless—so broad that it can be neither proved nor disproved" (ibid.). The tendency is to fall into the trap of suggesting that religion and film are functionally equivalent agencies, so that, by watching a film with a Christ-figure referent, religion is in some way able to sneak past the back door unnoticed.

If this is so, we need to raise wider questions about what films are actually doing to audiences. Is it some kind of propaganda tool for making them "more religious"? This is the position Kozlovic appears to have adopted, as shown in his attestation that the Christ-figure typology "can be fruitfully employed in a prescriptive, cookbook fashion by filmmakers who want to engineer powerful Christ-figures into their productions" so that they can thereby "proverbially snowball their audiences into accepting their covert religious argument without the need for blatantly overt arguments" (2004, ¶ 19). There are serious implications here, however. Underlying Kozlovic's argument is the implicit suggestion that one of the filmmaker's roles is to hoodwink and manipulate an audience under the guise of presenting escapist entertainment. As Rob Johnston puts it, "All too frequently, movies are controlled by crass commercial interests. They merely provide escape or indulge our prejudices and fantasies, oversimplifying life in the process" (2000, 87). For bell hooks, similarly, "most of us, no matter how sophisticated our strategies of critique and intervention, are usually seduced, at least for a time, by the images we see on the screen. They have power over us and we have no power over them" (quoted in Lynch 2005, 83). Earlier in the twentieth century, Theodor Adorno, a leading figure from the Frankfurt School of social and cultural analysis, suggested that popular culture, at least the machinations of Hollywood, was a serious threat to human welfare because it provided people with, in Lynch's words, "a range of manufactured entertainments and distractions" whose ultimate goal was to "generate profit rather than promote human well-being" (ibid., 71). While Kozlovic's talk of "snowballing" an audience lacks the same ideological scaffold that is intrinsic to Adorno's talk of the way in which popular culture has the capacity to co-opt "the vast majority of society into an exploitative cultural system over which they had no control" and to "preserve the basic structures of global capitalism and to pacify any attempts to challenge the way in which this system operates" (ibid.), there is a similar underlying suggestion that viewers are pawns of—in this case—duplicitous, theologically minded filmmakers whose mission is to dupe "secular" audiences by overwhelming them with implicitly theological images and narratives.

Another problem that arises with the fixation on parallels is that sometimes a film is believed to contain either more than one Christ figure or an alleged Christ figure is found to bear a striking resemblance to other gospel (or extrascriptural) characters. In the words of John Fitch, "In many cases, on-screen characters take on the traits of Jesus, St. Paul, King David, Odysseus, and Judas all at once" (2005, ¶ 14). Larry Kreitzer falls into the trap of suggesting, in his analysis of the classic Western *High Noon* (1952), that "the storyline seems to parallel the biblical story of the life and ministry of Jesus Christ" (2002, 127), to the point that the protagonist, Will Kane (Gary Cooper), amounts to "a Christ-figure" who calls "others to face judgment by his example" (ibid., 129). At the same time he construes Kane as "the embodiment of Elijah, exhorting the people to face the judgment that is on the horizon" (ibid., 134) and thus as an "Elijah-figure" (ibid., 129). However, he does not suggest how a character can—or ought—to be seen as both a Christ figure and an Elijah figure, and, if anything, the efficacy of a Christ-figure typology is diminished if the exclusivity of Christ figures is compromised in this way.

Taken to extremes, one of the manifestations of this position occurs when students look at the etymology of a character's name. In the case of *The Truman Show* (1998), for example, one of my students looked up the meaning of the two names, Sylvia and Lauren, of the Natascha McElhone character, who both reveals to Truman the limitations of the fake, commodified environment of Seahaven, where he resides, and prompts him to leave this world behind in favor of the freedom of the "real" world, away from the constant glare of TV cameras. There his life will no longer be scripted and manufactured according to the designs of a reality TV program. Yet, while making some instructive points about how Sylvia stands for "tree" and Lauren means "guardian spirit," one could also say that, in tempting Truman to want to exit the self-contained Eden, Sylvia/Lauren is a serpent figure. In this sense, one needs to say something about the dangers of reading too much into superficial designations. The same could apply to *The Godfather*, for which one of my students made a strong case for seeing Michael Corleone as a Christ figure, an Adam figure, and an advocate of Satan.

In a similar way, one of the most popular films that my students choose to look at in their theological interpretation is *The Shawshank Redemption* (1994), in which the links between Andy Dufresne (Tim Robbins) and Jesus are often described as "undeniable." But are they? Does this analysis not depend on one's knowledge or understanding of the roles that both Jesus and Andy play? There are a number of different interpretations as to whether Jesus accepted his ignominious punishment and death stoically, with calmness and accep- tance, as reflected cinematically in Max von Sydow's performance in *The Greatest Story Ever Told* (1965), or whether, as Willem Dafoe's somewhat schizophrenic and tortured Jesus in *The Last Temptation of Christ* (1988) sug- gests, Jesus was unable to bear the sacrifice that was expected of him on behalf of a sinful humanity. Is any film therefore capable of bearing witness to easily identifiable facets of Christ's life, ministry, death, resurrection, and ascension when there are so many Christological positions in existence?

Perhaps there are even other figures besides Jesus Christ who would make a more fitting correlation with the nonviolent suffering Dufresne experiences in *The Shawshank Redemption* at the hands of a corrupt and sadistic prison warden. Might Mahatma Gandhi make a more suitable point of reference than Jesus in this regard, so that Andy could be said to be a "Gandhi figure"? The problem with making associations between Christ and Dufresne on the basis that both were innocent, wrongly convicted teachers and saviors and perfect role models (along the lines of Immanuel Kant's claim that Christ was a perfect moral exemplar) is that the floodgates are opened to allow for everyone who is wrongly accused of a crime (or indeed all teachers) to be categorized as Christ figures. Might non-Christian role models or exemplars thus function no less rigorously than Christian ones? Or must the film be deemed to have some kind of Christianizing agenda at work in order for the Christian correlations to succeed? If this is so, is such a film alienating to non-Christian audience members, or may they be able to derive something comparable from the film- viewing experience?

Pedagogically, it is important to ensure that students are encouraged to look at a film's entire range of interpretations rather than concentrate solely on narrative and textual points of convergence. As Wright sees it, some of this unsophistication has a pragmatic basis. For example, she suggests that courses "need to be attractive and intelligible to students with increasingly diverse educational and cultural backgrounds" (2007, 13). Within this marketplace, a course on religion and film could be an attempt "to appear legitimate in the eyes of university administrators and external agencies" (ibid.). Since film is perceived as being both popular and relevant (and more sellable than a course on, say, Sanskrit), then religion-film courses make good strategic sense. The problem, however, is that those teaching these classes are not sufficiently versed in the vocabulary of film studies, and it is easy to see how, if Wright's critique is correct, this can result in some rather naïve instances of theological interpretation. Indeed, despite the "growing bibliography and plethora of courses," it may be the case that "*film* is not really being studied at all" (ibid., 22). Her call for a "decent course on film within a theology and/or religious studies programme" to consist of "familiarising students with key areas of film-studies practice as one of its aims" (ibid., 23) is thus a serious one and may help to reduce the existing tendency to go through a film scene by scene, identify a number of possible biblical parallels, and provide the relevant scriptural references, the downside of which is that what ensues is not so much a theological critique or engagement as a list of surface allusions. When Kozlovic therefore claims that "One simply cinematically retells the Jesus story and mechanically connects the plot dots" (Kozlovic 2004, ¶ 11), it is apparent that this constitutes a misreading of the many complex processes at work in the creation of a cinematic product.

In its place, classroom discussions would be more productively spent looking at wider debates between theology and film than ones that see cinematic characters as little more than ciphers whose existence is predicated upon the existence of the New Testament Jesus and who are accordingly not instrumental in their own right. If there is anything theologically significant about the likes of E.T. and John Coffey, it is not because they are intrinsically efficacious—on Kozlovic's criteria, if they perform miracles, die, and are born again, any redemptive value that exists is necessarily credited to Jesus Christ, who alone supplies the point of connection. However, as Aichele and Walsh affirm, a film cannot "transfer the written, biblical text" into the medium of film without "otherwise affecting it" (2002, viii). Thus, to assume that something about Christ's activity is straightforwardly transferable to the realm of modern-day cinematic Christ figures is to necessitate an insupportable leap of faith. Rather than seeing Jesus as preeminent, students should be encouraged to investigate whether a more reciprocal relationship between Christ and any Christ figure is able to operate. If there is no monolithic or inviolable reading of any text, why should not all texts—scriptural as well as cinematic—be continually negotiated and renegotiated by the interpreter? As George Aichele sees it, no meaning is ever fixed but lies between texts and in "intertextual configurations of texts that intersect one another in a wide variety of ways" (Aichele in Kreitzer 2002, 9). It would therefore be absurd to suggest that the biblical text should be treated with a degree of reverence that no other text could possibly emulate. Unless both sides are treated with parity, it will be difficult to move beyond the superficial classification of religious themes and imagery and engage in more substantial theological reflection. This may take students to new and unexpected places, but on the grounds that the job of the theologian in a university is not to proselytize but to educate, teachers of theology should be welcoming the fresh and innovative ways of "doing theology" that freedom from the restrictions of conforming to a preestablished typology of twenty-five structural characteristics is able to engender.

REFERENCES

Aichele, George. 2002. "Foreword." In *Gospel Images in Fiction and Film: On Reversing the Hermeneutical Flow*, ed. Larry Kreitzer, 7–10. London: Sheffield Academic Press.
———, and Richard Walsh, eds. 2002. "Introduction: Scripture as Precursor." In *Screening Scripture: Intertextual Connections between Scripture and Film*, ed. George Aichele and Richard Walsh, vii–xvi. Harrisburg, Penn.: Trinity Press International.
Barton, John. 2004. "Biblical Studies." In *The Blackwell Companion to Modern Theology*, ed. Gareth Jones, 18–33. Malden, Mass.: Blackwell.

Cox, Harvey. 1966. *The Secular City*. New York: Macmillan.

Deacy, Christopher. 2001. *Screen Christologies: Redemption and the Medium of Film*. Cardiff: University of Wales Press.

Fitch, John, III. 2005. "Archetypes on Screen: Odysseus, St. Paul, Christ, and the American Cinematic Hero and Anti-Hero." *Journal of Religion and Film* 9(1) (April). http://www.unomaha.edu/jrf/Vol9No1/FitchArchetypes.htm.

Gill, Robin. 2004. "The Practice of Faith." In *The Blackwell Companion to Modern Theology*, ed. Gareth Jones, 3–17. Malden, Mass.: Blackwell.

Jasper, David. 1997. "On Systematizing the Unsystematic: A Response." In *Explorations in Theology and Film: Movies and Meaning*, ed. Clive Marsh and Gaye Ortiz, 235–44. Malden, Mass.: Blackwell.

Jewett, Robert. 1999. *Saint Paul Returns to the Movies: Triumph over Shame*. Grand Rapids, Mich.: Eerdmans.

Johnston, Robert. 2000. *Reel Spirituality: Theology and Film in Dialogue*. Grand Rapids, Mich.: Baker.

Kozlovic, Anton Karl. 2004. "The Structural Characteristics of the Cinematic Christ-figure." *Journal of Religion and Popular Culture* 8 (Fall). http://www.usask.ca/relst/jrpc/art8-cinematicchrist.html (accessed November 25, 2007).

Kreitzer, Larry. 2002. *Gospel Images in Fiction and Film: On Reversing the Hermeneutical Flow*. London: Sheffield Academic Press.

Loughlin, Gerard. 2005. "Cinéma Divinité: A Theological Introduction." In *Cinéma Divinité: Readings in Film and Theology*, ed. William Telford, Eric Christianson, and Peter Francis, 1–12. London: SCM.

Lyden, John C. 2003. *Film as Religion: Myths, Morals, and Rituals*. New York: New York University Press.

Lynch, Gordon. 2005. *Understanding Theology and Popular Culture*. Malden, Mass.: Blackwell.

Malone, Peter. 1997. "*Edward Scissorhands*: Christology from a Suburban Fairy-tale." In *Explorations in Theology and Film: Movies and Meaning*, ed. Clive Marsh and Gaye Ortiz, 73–86. Malden, Mass.: Blackwell.

Marsh, Clive. 1997. "Film and Theologies of Culture." In *Explorations in Theology and Film: Movies and Meaning*, ed. Clive Marsh and Gaye Ortiz, 21–34. Malden, Mass.: Blackwell.

Skrade, Carl. 1970. "Theology and Films." In *Celluloid and Symbols*, ed. John C. Cooper and C. Skrade, 1–24. Philadelphia: Fortress.

Swinburne, Richard. 1993. *The Coherence of Theism*. New York: Oxford University Press.

Wright, Melanie J. 2007. *Religion and Film: An Introduction*. London: Taurus.

7

Film and the Introduction to Islam Course

Amir Hussain

"They describe us," the other whispered solemnly.
"That's all. They have the power of description,
and we succumb to the pictures that they construct."
—Salman Rushdie, *The Satanic Verses*

Introduction

In the years before the terrorist attacks of 9/11, I would begin my courses on Islam with a standard historical introduction to the life of Muhammad and the beginnings of Islam.[1] I did this because my students—whether they were Muslim or not—often knew very little about Islam before they took my course. In the semester after 9/11 I found that this was no longer effective as the students came in with what they thought was a great deal of knowledge about Islam and the religious lives of Muslims. Unfortunately, most of their "knowledge" came from the popular media and was often at odds with the ways in which the majority of Muslims understand their own faith. As a result, I began to use a book that described how television news works.[2] I begin with this anecdote as it shows the power of the media in constructing our understandings of Muslims and Islam. In this chapter I discuss the use of film in the introductory course on Islam.[3] Since I have taught in both large public universities and smaller private ones, this chapter will be of interest to a wide range of instructors, including those who do not teach a separate course on Islam but instead teach about Islam as part of another course. However, I begin with a brief discussion of the role of the media in shaping perceptions of Islam.

The literature on religion and media is growing. One thinks, for example, of the fine work of Stewart Hoover, Debra Mason, Lynn Clark, Diane Winston, and Claire Badaracco.[4] Their work has shown both how religious groups use the media and how the media understand, misunderstand, and cover religion. The Religion Newswriters Association (RNA), which Debra Mason directs, as well as the religion and media workshops at the American Academy of Religion (arranged by S. Brent Plate) have been invaluable resources for both journalists and scholars. With respect to Muslims and the media, there have been good studies of how Muslims themselves are using the media.[5] One can also find excellent studies of the ways in which the media view and create representations of Islam.[6] These views are often negative. For example, according to an online poll of the members of the RNA, the top two religion news stories in 2006 were about Islam: reactions to the publication of cartoons about Muhammad in Denmark and Pope Benedict XVI's linking of Islam and violence in a speech in Germany.[7]

Moving from the media in general to television in particular, I also find that the images of Muslims are often negative. I have written elsewhere about Muslim characters on television.[8] A useful exercise in an introductory class is to ask students about Muslim images on television. At first they are stumped as no images come immediately to mind. After some time, a student usually comes up with the cartoon character of Apu from *The Simpsons* but is quickly corrected by other students who point out that Apu is a Hindu, not a Muslim. Dave Chappelle is perhaps the most famous Muslim on television, yet none of the major characters on *Chappelle's Show* are Muslim. Eventually students come up with the characters of Sayid on *Lost,* Imam Kareem Said and the Black Muslims in *Oz*, or terrorists such as Marwan or Abu Fayed in *24*. Some mention characters from Showtime's *Sleeper Cell*. A select few mention professional wrestlers such as the Sheikh, Abdullah the Butcher ("the madman from Sudan"), the Iron Sheikh, Sabu ("homicidal, suicidal, and genocidal"), and Muhammad Hassan. All of these characters are evil, violent men: The wrestlers are all villains ("heels"), Sayid is a former member of the Iraqi Republican Guard, and Kareem Said and the Black Muslims are all prisoners, while the terrorists in *24* and *Sleeper Cell* are, well, terrorists. Only one major character, Darwyn Al-Sayeed from *Sleeper Cell,* is a good guy, an undercover FBI agent. However, he too is heavily involved in violence. These portrayals do not of course reflect the realities of American Muslim life, where American Muslims are on average wealthier and better educated than non-Muslims. The situation is different in Canada, with the Canadian Broadcasting Corporation's sitcom *Little Mosque on the Prairie* (available on DVD). In this show, one sees the poetry of ordinary Canadian Muslim lives enacted with humor on the small screen. Ironically, one of the major characters in the show, Canadian actor Carlo Rota, also has a role in *24*.

These negative portrayals of American Muslims on television must have some correlation with the ways in which actual American Muslims are perceived. The violent actions of a tiny minority of Muslim terrorists are amplified when they are virtually the only images available on television. One sees this, for example, in a poll by the Pew Forum on Religion and Public Life following the terrorist attacks in London in July 2005. In that survey 36 percent of Americans felt that Islam was more likely to encourage violence in its followers (which was down from 44 percent in 2003), while those holding unfavorable opinions of Islam increased slightly (from 34 percent to 36 percent between 2003 and 2005).[9] In 2006 the Council on American Islamic Relations (CAIR) recorded 1,972 civil rights complaints from American Muslims, up almost 30 percent from 2005 and the most ever recorded by CAIR in its twelve-year history.[10] Also in 2006, a poll by the *Washington Post* and ABC News showed that 46 percent of Americans had negative views of Islam (up from 39 percent after the 9/11 attacks).[11] For an Islam class, this makes the instructor's task different from that in other religion courses, where students may come in ignorant but usually not with preconceived biases. It may be necessary to de-exoticize Buddhism, but one almost has to humanize Muslims.

Muslims in American Films

The situation I have just described for television portrayals of American Muslims is not markedly different from that in film. The classic study of Arabs in Hollywood films is *Reel Bad Arabs,* by Jack Shaheen.[12] In the book, Shaheen describes more than nine hundred films that portray Arabs. He describes Hollywood's portrayal of Arabs as the "systematic, pervasive and unapologetic degradation and dehumanization of a people."[13] In 2006 Sut Jhally directed a one-hour documentary on the book. The film is available from the Media Education Foundation (http://www.mediaed.org/) and is a good introduction to Shaheen's thesis about the misrepresentations of Arabs.[14]

Rubina Ramji has written an excellent article that expands the misrepresentation of Arabs to include Muslims.[15] The article pairs well with Jhally's documentary, and both can be discussed in two class periods. In the article Ramji notes that, after the 9/11 terrorist attacks, rentals of videos such as *True Lies* (1994), *Air Force One* (1997), and *The Siege* (1998), all of which feature Muslim terrorists, increased dramatically. In the case of *Air Force One,* whose plot revolves around Muslim terrorists hijacking the president's plane, rentals of the film were ten times higher in Canada than before the attacks. Clearly, people were turning to films in light of current events. Given both the negative portrayals of Muslims in films and the movies' popularity post-9/11, it is important for instructors to address this issue in their courses on Islam.

Diversity and Complexity in Courses on Islam

Instructors of courses on Islam must be aware of the complexities of Muslim lives and avoid the easy trap of presenting Islam as some sort of monolithic entity. When one shifts the focus to Muslims, it is easier to discuss variations in ethnicity, gender, sectarian differences, and so on. When teaching in a large university, one often has the advantage of having several Muslim students in any class on Islam. In certain locations, one may have a variety of Muslim traditions represented in the classroom. As a result, class discussions of films can be quite interesting as students may bring their personal experiences to the conversation. In smaller universities, this may not be possible, and there may be no Muslim students present in the class. As a result, it is even more important to select films that represent the diversity of Muslim lives.

In addition, whether we teach in a secular institution in a religious studies department or a more confessional department of theology will have an impact on our courses. I completed a PhD at the University of Toronto's Centre for the Study of Religion. To make it clear that what we did was the academic study of religion, the name was changed from the earlier Centre for Religious Studies, which might lead people to think that we were somehow being "religious" in our work. While there, I was taught by Donald Weibe and Neil McMullin about the academic study of religion and how it differed from the teaching (or doing, for that matter) of theology. As a result, I became an advocate of the religious studies paradigm of a secular, nonconfessional discipline. However, when I began to teach courses on Islam, I realized that there were no North American seminaries to which I could send students who wanted a more theological approach to their tradition. There was no Muslim equivalent of the Toronto School of Theology. Moreover, no matter how adamant I was that my courses on Islam were *about* this religious tradition, for some of my Muslim students, these classes presented the only opportunity for them to seriously engage with their own religious understandings. Moreover, for religious non-Muslim students, my classes also allowed them to add Islam to the list of traditions against which they had to define themselves.

This raises the issue of teaching Islam in the university. I use a deliberate ambiguity here: Although I strive to teach *about* Islam, I also *teach* Islam, mostly to Muslim students but to non-Muslim students as well. At the beginning of each course I ask students to say something about themselves and their reasons for taking that particular course. Usually a number of the students in my introduction to Islam course self-identify as Muslims, and many of them state that they are taking the course to learn more about their religion. With this, the easy dichotomy of religious studies versus theology becomes not so easy any more. The Muslim students are learning about Islam, but since it is their own tradition, it has a personal impact on many of them. They may have no other place to learn about their own tradition.

A second issue that is implicit here is the nature of the university in which one teaches. I taught courses on Islam at three public universities in Canada while I finished my dissertation. Two of them were large schools, the University of Waterloo and McMaster University, while the third, Wilfrid Laurier University, was of medium size. My first full-time position was at California State University–Northridge. This is again a large, public, state university with a diverse group of students. In all of these settings, the religious studies paradigm that I learned in graduate school was assumed. We were there to teach our students about religion. A number of our students, as well as our faculty, were, of course, religious.

I soon realized that, as a Muslim teaching Islam, I needed to learn more about theology. In 2005 the opportunity arose for me to move to Loyola Marymount University, the Jesuit university in Los Angeles. Prior to this, my only formal connection with the Catholic tradition was that I was born in a Catholic missionary hospital in Lahore. However, the move was an important one for me to make. Four decades earlier, my mentor, Wilfred Cantwell Smith, had gone from McGill University to Harvard University so that he could move from the particular study of Islam to the more general study of religion. For me, it was an opportunity to move from a department of religious studies into a department of theological studies. It was Smith's work that helped me to bridge the two worlds. He was also an ordained Presbyterian minister, and one of his most important books was 1981's *Towards a World Theology*. That same year he also published a collection of essays about Islam in which he wrote the following:

> I as an intellectual in the modern world have always as my primary obligation and final commitment my loyalty to truth—subject to test at the hands of my fellow intellectuals, who constitute, of course, the primary audience of every thesis proceeding out of a university. I have developed the view, however, and articulated it elsewhere at some length, that the arguments of a student of religion or of a particular religious or indeed any human community, should in principle be persuasive to other intellectuals, not only, but in addition also to intelligent and alert members of the group or groups about which he and she writes.[16]

Additionally, the move to Loyola Marymount allowed me to learn more about the Catholic tradition, the dominant religious tradition in Los Angeles. Of course, the Jesuit excellence in both education and social justice was also appealing.

The third issue transcends the religious studies versus theology dichotomy. What, if any, type of "Islam" is considered "normative"? Is the course taught from a Sunni perspective? How does one teach about groups that are marginalized (e.g., the Ahmadi community) or those that many other Muslims consider un-Islamic (e.g., the Nation of Islam)? Is there adequate discussion of the Shi'a, who form substantial minority communities in cities such as Toronto and Los Angeles? Sometimes a problem arises when some Muslim students do not consider other groups to be "Muslim enough" for them. Many colleagues report that some of their students were concerned when they were taught about the Nation of Islam, whom the students considered to be non-Muslim. Students have repeatedly posed the same question to me. When I mention to them that Louis Farrakhan has made the Hajj several times, an act reserved for Muslims, the students are required to rethink their position on the Nation of Islam.

A fourth issue is representation, especially that of Muslim interests in North America, for whom a wide variety of groups claim to speak. Some compete with one another in their claim to be an (or "the") authentic voice of Muslims. Consider, for example, the struggle between the Canadian Islamic Congress and the Muslim Canadian Congress. In November 2004 the Progressive Muslim Union of North America was launched, to the acclaim of many Muslims and the concern of many others. Those of us who teach about Islam have to talk about these issues of representation. On my web page, for example, I have the following disclaimer to a list of North American Muslim groups: "This list includes links to various groups who consider themselves to be Muslim. I make no judgment about their Islam, but I understand that others may be all too willing to do this."

Beginning the Introductory Course on Islam

Given the misinformation about Islam and Muslims created by the media, it is often necessary to provide corrective information about Islam and Muslim lives. Since most of our students get their information about Islam and Muslim lives from television, it is important to begin with how the television news works. I also use a videotape of Bill Moyers on *NOW* interviewing Jon Stewart and talking about *The Daily Show with Jon Stewart*. My students are admirers of Stewart's work and agree with me that the "fake" news that he presents is much better than the "real" news. I have also had guests from local television stations talk to my class about ratings and their importance to the local news. Bringing in someone from a local news station to discuss how the news "works" can be a helpful exercise.

In the introductory packet of readings for my Islam class I include Edward R. Murrow's famous 1958 speech to the Radio and Television News Directors Association. Among the most prophetic lines, more important a half century after they were first spoken, are these:

> We are currently wealthy, fat, comfortable and complacent. We have currently a built-in allergy to unpleasant or disturbing informa-
> tion. Our mass media reflect this. But unless we get up off our fat surpluses and recognize that television in the main is being used to distract, delude, amuse and insulate us, then television and those who finance it, those who look at it and those who work at it, may see a totally different picture too late.[17]

A version of this speech begins the 2005 film *Good Night, and Good Luck* (directed by George Clooney). The first scene of this film, with David Strathairn as Murrow, can be quite useful in the class.

Having discussed media constructions of Muslim lives, one can then move on to something of a case study (a possible, although controversial, strategy). In the United States, the news media construct Palestinians—whether they are Muslim, Christian, or secular—as "Muslims." This can of course create political tensions in the classroom as both the media and many university departments have taken a pro-Israel stance that is in direct conflict with the position taken by most Muslims around the world. To teach about Palestinians, therefore, and to question the pro-Zionist position is to take a daring political standpoint—made all the more challenging by the fact that some conservative Christian groups in the United States, who now wield significant political power, also hold a pro-Zionist position. To support Israel in university classrooms, therefore, can be seen as "neutral," while to support the Palestinian cause can be seen as "radical" and even anti-American after 9/11. To raise some of these issues I sometimes ask students to read a "graphic novel" (i.e., comic book) that describes something of the realities of Palestinian experience and contrast that presentation with the ways in which Palestinians are perceived in the United States.[18] There is a great advantage to using a comic book in class (aside from the reactions of students who are either delighted or appalled to have a comic book on the reading list).

Some students still think that a photograph is "objective" and that it "tells the truth." They do not consider how it is composed. It is much easier to show this with drawings, where it is obvious that someone has made the drawing and that someone else might do it differently. This allows us to begin talking about the beginnings of visual and film theory. Useful in this exercise, particularly when it comes to photographs, is the work of Susan Sontag. With regard to the Palestinian/Israeli conflict she writes:

> To an Israeli Jew, a photograph of a child torn apart in the attack on the Sbarro pizzeria in downtown Jerusalem is first of all a photograph of a Jewish child killed by a Palestinian suicide-bomber. To a Palestinian, a photograph of a child torn apart by a tank round in Gaza is first of all a photograph of a Palestinian child killed by Israeli ordnance. To the militant, identity is everything.[19]

This helps in a discussion of how various subjects are "positioned," to use Renato Rosaldo's term. Of position, Rosaldo writes that the ethnographer "occupies a position or structural location and observes with a particular angle of vision. Consider for example, how age, gender, being an outsider, and association with a neo-colonial regime influence what the ethnographer learns. The notion of position also refers to how life experiences both enable and inhibit particular kinds of insight."[20]

Documentary Films about Islam

Following the discussion of photographs and objective reality, it is often useful to turn to documentary films. Like photographs, documentaries are supposed to tell the truth and thus can be useful in differentiating between fact and fiction. For those who begin with a chronological introduction to Islam, a good resource is the 2002 PBS documentary *Muhammad: Legacy of a Prophet* (directed by Michael Schwarz). The film has an accompanying website that is very helpful for classroom discussions.[21] One can use the film to talk about how Muslims understand the life of Muhammad. It provides a standard hagiographical account with the use of prominent Muslims and scholars of Islam. This can be contrasted with more historical/critical accounts. Another way in which the film can be used is to talk about how contemporary Muslims draw on the life of Muhammad to make sense of their own lives. The segment with Kevin James, a Muslim fire marshal who helped out at the World Trade Center after it was attacked on 9/11, is particularly effective, as is the segment on Muslim American calligrapher Mohamed Zakariya.

Another helpful film about contemporary Muslim rituals is the 2007 PBS Wide Angle Special, *Pilgrimage to Karbala*.[22] The film covers Iranian Shi'a pilgrims who travel by bus to the shrine of Imam Hussein in Karbala, Iraq. The film ends with an interview with a noted scholar of Shi'a Islam, Vali Nasr. One of the points that Nasr raises in the documentary is that many of the Iranians who make the pilgrimage would otherwise be considered "secular": One family of a rug merchant has a Western-style apartment complete with dog and a mother who wears makeup and no hijab in front of strangers. Yet the son in the family desperately wants to make the pilgrimage. This problematizes the simple dichotomy between "secular" and "religious." The son is secular, but very much wants to make the pilgrimage. The film is also obviously important in discussions of images of Shi'a Islam.

With interest in mysticism at a high level, most courses on Islam have some coverage of Sufism, the mystical tradition within Islam. A dated (originally made in 1979) but nevertheless excellent documentary film is *Islamic Mysticism: The Sufi Way* (directed by Elda Hartley), narrated by noted world religions scholar Huston Smith. The thirty-minute film is available on a 2003 DVD compilation, *The Mystic's Journey* (available from Wellspring Media). The film is ideal for classes that meet for fifty-minute sessions as it can be viewed and discussed within one class period.

With respect to Muslims and the media, a good documentary film is *Control Room*, directed by Jehane Noujaim (2004; eighty-six minutes; available from Lions Gate Films). The film is about Al-Jazeera television and can be quite productively used in discussions about television in the Arab world. It also gives interesting perspectives on how differently Al-Jazeera and American media cover similar stories.

For courses that deal with contemporary Islam in the United States, an important topic is African American Muslims, who make up at least 25 percent of American Muslims. A worthwhile introduction is a 1992 CBS news video titled *The Real Malcolm X: An Intimate Portrait of the Man* (produced by Brett Alexander; sixty minutes). Students are still very much interested in Malcolm X and in his transition from the Nation of Islam to Sunni Islam. The film, narrated by Dan Rather, features interviews with Malcolm's contemporaries, including his running buddy, Malcolm "Shorty" Jarvis, and Malcom's widow, Betty Shabazz. For those not wishing to show the whole film, the last third talks about Malcolm's transition to Sunni Islam, as well as his legacy among African Americans. That last segment features interviews with Chuck D from Public Enemy and actors such as Wesley Snipes and Keenan Ivory Wayans.

An important issue among American Muslims relates to the tensions that sometimes occur between African American and immigrant Muslims. A wonderful film to illustrate this friction is Zareena Grewal's 2004 documentary, *By the Dawn's Early Light: Chris Jackson's Journey to Islam* (fifty-two minutes; available from cinemaguild.com). The film profiles Chris Jackson, the all-American point guard at Louisiana State University who changed his name to Mahmoud Abdul-Rauf when he converted to Islam. In 1996 Abdul-Rauf was suspended by his NBA team, the Denver Nuggets, for one game due to his refusal to stand for the national anthem due to his "Muslim conscience." This was seen as an important act of conscience by indigenous Muslims, but immigrant Muslims regarded it as an act of defiance that was somehow "un-American." The film ends with a discussion of Abdul-Rauf's work as a Muslim leader in his hometown of Gulfport, Mississippi.

Finally, any course on Islam usually has discussions about women's roles. A very helpful documentary is *Me and the Mosque,* directed by Zarqa Nawaz (fifty-two minutes). Nawaz has also made two short films, *BBQ Muslims* and *Death Threat.* In 2007 she was responsible for the Canadian Broadcasting Corporation's hit show called *Little Mosque on the Prairie.* Information about those films, as well as about Nawaz, can be found on her website, Fundamentalist Films.[23]

Distributed by the National Film Board of Canada, *Me and the Mosque* is Nawaz's first documentary. The film is directly related to her own concerns as a Muslim woman, namely as to space available to her in the mosque. The film begins on a lighthearted note with Muslim comic Azhar Usman joking about the lack of appropriate space in mosques for Muslim women.

The documentary covers mosques in Canada and the United States, including places such as Aurora, Illinois; Mississauga, Ontario; Winnipeg, Manitoba; Regina, Saskatchewan; Surrey, British Columbia; and Morgantown, West Virginia. It includes the voices of established scholars such as Asma Barlas, Umar Abd-Allah, and Aminah McCloud, alongside the newer scholarly voices of Aisha Geissinger, Jasmine Zine, and Itrath Syed. In addition, there are interviews with a wide range of people from the Muslim community, from activists such as Asra Nomani and Aminah Assilmi to scholars such as Abdullah Adhami and Tareq Suwaidan.

As mentioned earlier, the film begins on a humorous note with the comedy of Azhar Usman (of "Allah Made Me Funny" fame). However, what Usman jokes about (e.g., the nice "dungeons" that many people mention when they talk about the basements in which some mosques allot space to women) is no laughing matter. The film then moves to the mosque in Aurora, Illinois, to begin its discussion of these issues. I would like to think that this is Nawaz's subtle homage to another Canadian filmmaker, Mike Myers, who bases his fictional character Wayne Campbell in Aurora. Nawaz then mentions her upbringing in Toronto and contrasts the mosque that she attended there (the Jami' mosque) with the one her mother currently attends, the new Islamic

Centre of Canada in Mississauga (the Canadian headquarters of the Islamic Society of North America [ISNA]). Nawaz's discussions with her mother raise questions about differences based on generations and experiences in countries of origin. In Pakistan, for example, mosque space may be exclusively male space, but in Canada, the mosque may be the only Muslim space available to women. As such, women in Pakistan and Canada may have very dissimilar attitudes about the space open to them in mosques.

In addition to the number of mosques visited in the United States, Nawaz includes footage of a recent ISNA conference in Chicago. There she interviewed a number of African American Muslims about their views on women in the mosque. This is one of the most important segments in the video, as African American Muslims have had a much longer history than immigrant Muslims in trying to balance what it means to be "American" (or "Canadian," for that matter) with what it means to be "Muslim." The film also mentions converts to Islam, including one young woman who converted because she believed Islam to be a religion that honors women, only to have that impression changed when her local mosque erected a physical barrier between men and women.

The film is a gem. It is recommended and should perhaps even be required viewing for both Muslims and those interested in Islam. It can also be used with great success in courses about Islam or women in religion. My own students appreciate the humor (the cartoon segments are a particular favorite) used to illustrate situations that often are not very funny. Muslim women in North America are dealing with very serious issues around their participation in religious life at the mosque, and this film captures those matters with eloquence and poise.

Hollywood Films

With regard to issues of representation, one may use some of the Hollywood films that were described earlier. Given the current wars in Afghanistan and Iraq, two interesting films to screen in class are *Red Dawn* and *Rambo III*. *Red Dawn* (1984; directed by John Milius) was released at the end of the Cold War and tells the story of American teenagers who band together to defeat a Cuban/ Soviet alliance that has invaded the United States. *Rambo III* (1988; directed by Peter MacDonald), released almost a decade after the Soviet invasion of Afghanistan, completes the Rambo œuvre. In this film, Rambo (the Vietnam War vet played by Sylvester Stallone) goes to Afghanistan to rescue his mentor, who has been captured by the Soviets. In the course of the film he befriends and helps to train the Afghani mujahideen, who a decade later would become the Taliban. Here, in the last days of the Cold War, they are seen as noble heroes.

While not a "Hollywood" film, another commercial film that can be used effectively is *My Son, the Fanatic* (1999; directed by Udayan Prasad; available from Miramax Films; eighty-seven minutes). Set in England, the film tells a father-son story. The father, who is secular, wants to assimilate into English culture. The son, who learns through racism and discrimination that his skin color and religion will never allow him to be considered "English," becomes much more religiously conservative. In light of the London bombings of 2005, the film becomes even more important.

Films from the Muslim World

Another alternative is to use films from the Muslim world to illustrate the diversity of Muslim lives. While there are interesting movies from places such as Egypt, Pakistan, and Turkey, some of the best-known films from the Muslim world are from Iran. One can use any number of movies from Iranian directors. A personal favorite is *Children of Heaven* (1997; directed by Majid Majidi; available from Miramax Films in Persian with English subtitles; eighty-three minutes). *Children of Heaven* tells the story of two children in postrevolutionary Iran, Ali and his sister Zahara. Due to their family's financial difficulties, the children have to share a pair of shoes. Majidi is renowned for his ability to tell stories of children, and this film is magical with respect to the youngsters' lives. At the time of this writing, with tensions existing between the United States and Iran, the film serves to put a human face on Iranians.

NOTES

1. Peters, *Muhammad and the Origins of Islam.*
2. Postman and Powers, *How to Watch TV News.*
3. For an introduction to other issues in teaching about Islam see Wheeler, ed., *Teaching Islam.* Wheeler's book includes a chapter by Corrine Blake on using information technology in courses on Islam.
4. See, for example, Hoover, *Religion in the News;* Buddenbaum and Mason, eds., *Readings on Religion as News;* Hoover and Clark, eds., *Practicing Religion in the Age of Media;* Giggie and Winston, eds., *Faith in the Market;* Badaracco, ed., *Quoting God;* Hoover, *Religion in the Media Age.*
5. See, for example, Eickelman and Anderson, eds., *New Media in the Muslim World;* or cooke and Lawrence, eds., *Muslim Networks.*
6. See, for example, Shaheen, *TV Arab;* Said, *Covering Islam;* or Karim, *Islamic Peril.*
7. *Religious Studies News* 22(3) (May 2007): 11.
8. Hussain, "The Fire Next Time."
9. Poll available at http://pewforum.org/docs/index.php?DocID=89.
10. "The Struggle for Equality," available at http://www.cair.com/CivilRights/CivilRightsReports/2006Report.aspx.
11. As reported in the *Washington Post,* available at http://www.washingtonpost.com/wp-dyn/content/article/2006/03/08/AR2006030802221_pf.html.
12. Shaheen, *Reel Bad Arabs.*
13. Ibid., 1.
14. The film has the same name as the book and is available at http://www.mediaed.org/videos/MediaRaceAndRepresentation/ReelBadArabs.

15. Ramji, "From *Navy Seals* to *The Siege*"; available at http://www.unomaha.edu/jrf/Vol9No2/RamjiIslam.htm.

16. Smith, *On Understanding Islam*, 282.

17. Available at http://www.turnoffyourtv.com/commentary/hiddenagenda/murrow.html.

18. Sacco, *Palestine*. Sacco has also written about Bosnia in his comic, *Safe Area Gorazde*, and has pioneered a new form of "comics journalism." He has applied this approach to the Iraq war in "Down! Up!"

19. Sontag, *Regarding the Pain of Others*, 10.

20. Rosaldo, *Culture and Truth*, 19.

21. See http://www.pbs.org/muhammad/index.shtml.

22. Resources for the film are available at http://www.pbs.org/wnet/wideangle/shows/karbala/index.html.

23. Available at http://fundamentalistfilms.com/.

REFERENCES

Badaracco, Claire, ed. 2005. *Quoting God: How Media Shape Ideas about Religion*. Waco, Tex.: Baylor University Press.

Buddenbaum, Judith, and Debra Mason, eds. 2000. *Readings on Religion as News*. Ames: Iowa State University Press.

cooke, miriam, and Bruce Lawrence, eds. 2005. *Muslim Networks: From Hajj to Hip Hop*. Chapel Hill: University of North Carolina Press.

Eickelman, Dale, and Jon Anderson, eds. 2003. *New Media in the Muslim World: The Emerging Public Sphere*, 2d ed. Bloomington: Indiana University Press.

Giggie, John, and Diane Winston, eds. 2002. *Faith in the Market: Religion and the Rise of Urban Commercial Culture*. New Brunswick, N.J.: Rutgers University Press.

Hoover, Stewart. 2006. *Religion in the Media Age*. London: Routledge.

———. 1998. *Religion in the News: Faith and Journalism in American Public Discourse*. Thousand Oaks, Calif.: Sage.

———, and Lynn Clark, eds. 2002. *Practicing Religion in the Age of Media: Explorations in Media, Religion, and Culture*. New York: Columbia University Press.

Hussain, Amir. 2008. " 'The Fire Next Time': *Sleeper Cell* and Muslims on Television post-9/11." In *Faith in High Definition: Religion and the Television Drama after 9/11*, ed. Jane Iwamura and Diane Winston. Waco, Tex.: Baylor University Press.

Karim, Karim. 2003. *Islamic Peril: Media and Global Violence*, rev. ed. Montreal: Black Rose.

Peters, F. E. 1994. *Muhammad and the Origins of Islam*. Albany: SUNY Press.

Postman, Neil, and Steve Powers. 1992. *How to Watch TV News*. New York: Penguin.

Qureshi, Emran, and Michael A. Sells, eds. 2003. *The New Crusades: Constructing the Muslim Enemy*. New York: Columbia University Press.

Ramji, Rubina. 2005. "From *Navy Seals* to *The Siege*: Getting to Know the Muslim Terrorist, Hollywood Style." *Journal of Religion and Film* 9(2) (October).

Rosaldo, Renato. 1993. *Culture and Truth: The Remaking of Social Analysis*. Boston: Beacon.

Rushdie, Salman. 1988. *The Satanic Verses*. London: Penguin.

Sacco, Joe. 2007. "Down! Up!" *Harper's* (April), 47–62.

———. 2001. *Palestine*. Seattle: Fantagraphics.

———. 2000. *Safe Area Gorazde: The War in Eastern Bosnia 1992–1995*. Seattle: Fantagraphics.

Said, Edward. 1997. *Covering Islam: How the Media and the Experts Determine How We See the Rest of the World,* rev. ed. New York: Vintage.

Shaheen, Jack. 2001. *Reel Bad Arabs: How Hollywood Vilifies a People.* New York: Olive Branch.

———. 1984. *The TV Arab.* Bowling Green, Ohio: Bowling Green State University Press.

Smith, Wilfred Cantwell. 1981. *On Understanding Islam: Selected Studies.* The Hague: Mouton.

Sontag, Susan. 2003. *Regarding the Pain of Others.* New York: Farrar, Straus, and Giroux.

Wheeler, Brannon, ed. 2003. *Teaching Islam.* New York: Oxford University Press.

8

Is It All about *Love Actually?* Sentimentality as Problem and Opportunity in the Use of Film for Teaching Theology and Religion

Clive Marsh

The use of film in the teaching of theology and religion is now in its fifth decade. There is still no methodological unanimity in how film should be used, and perhaps complete agreement is not attainable. In this field, four questions are of importance. First, what is the impact of a teacher's institutional location (e.g., in religious studies or theology, in a university, college, or seminary) on the use of film? Second, how much or how little do teachers need to take account of what is going on in film studies? Third, does the term "use" itself indicate more than we might appreciate about the practice (and perhaps especially abuse), which is rife within examination of the interaction between film and religion in theology and religious studies? Fourth, what other disciplines (e.g., sociology, psychology, philosophy, cultural studies, social history) should inevitably be brought into the discussion when films are discussed? I touch on all of these questions in this chapter.

Melanie Wright's excellent *Religion and Film: An Introduction* has thrown down the gauntlet to all of us working in the field. Her work recognizes its limitations, however. It looks at films that address religion even while challenging others to attend more rigorously to film-critical, cultural studies, and contextual perspectives when interpreting movies. In this chapter my aim is likewise limited, and it is unlikely that I shall escape Wright's critical questions. There is much, much more to be asked about the films I use, but I begin in a number of very different places from Wright, and my contexts have shaped my methods. To put it simply, my job is to teach Christian theology. I do this in both a university and a seminary/theological college. In the case of the university context, I find myself teaching *about* theology and film for the purpose of clarifying aspects of theology and culture. However, I also try to teach theology *through* film, especially because my classes have many people who have no personal faith, for whom religion is simply fascinating, and yet who come to texts from the likes of Augustine, Calvin, Ruether, and Cone "dry." My pedagogical purpose therefore has to be to make such texts "live" (existentially) when many of the students do not themselves live within the traditions from which the texts come. Yet they all watch films.[1] This chapter reports on the pedagogical considerations that lie behind my use of a number of feel-good movies in the teaching of Christian theology. It is a case study in the use of critical exploration of the cognitive and affective interaction between students (as film viewers) and the content of a sample of such films in the context of theological education.[2]

My case study concerns the three films written (and in one case directed) by Richard Curtis: *Four Weddings and a Funeral, Notting Hill,* and *Love Actually,* three romantic comedies that in the eyes of some film critics become increasingly lightweight as the series progresses. *Love Actually* has thus been sometimes reviewed as schmaltzy, sickly sweet, and not in the same league as the much more critically successful *Four Weddings.* So these are three films within the same genre; they are of questionable critical acclaim but are nonetheless hugely popular. Their topic is love. The social background of all of the main characters is limited—wealthy twenty- or thirty-something North London life. As romantic comedies their central focus is by definition the meeting of a man and a woman and, despite whatever the plot throws in their way, a happy ending. As feel-good entertainment, they must make us laugh and leave us warm and satisfied.

Why use them in theology or religious studies? Some of us do so not, of course, to suggest that they simply convey the views about love (or about anything else) of any particular religious tradition. To express a rationale for their use at its methodological simplest, *we show such films because they are popular and because in Western culture they provoke viewers both to consider what they mean about love and to explore its multiple dimensions.* In showing these movies and offering them as material for cultural and theological analysis, a teacher is thus handling influential, cultural products that are varyingly received critically but are nevertheless examples of good-quality popular culture. We do so as a way of broaching topics with which theology and religion inevitably have to deal. My pedagogical strategy is to focus on how such films have been received, including their reception by students in the class. This approach is in keeping with one of the recent trends in film studies. It also invites students to become conscious of emotional aspects of their life experience and to see critical reflection upon them as a legitimate aspect of theological enquiry.

Evidence from the Classroom

In considering what the showing of films (or film clips) produces *at the point of reception*, the impact of genre identification and of film-critical assessment are especially important.[3] Films come labeled, as part of the marketing strategy, within a genre. The three movies I consider here are classed as "romantic comedy." They also come, for some viewers, with judgments attached. Especially in the case of *Love Actually*, the judgment of "sentimental" was quickly passed. In the classroom, however, this means that one further aspect to such films' reception becomes prominent. *Because* they are romantic comedies and *because* they are labeled as sentimental, students sometimes question their usefulness. In my experience, too, male students in their late teens or early twenties in particular feel uncomfortable about admitting to liking such films. They find it difficult to own up to enjoying going to see them or to finding them useful either for their personal development or theological exploration.[4] Nevertheless, group discussion can make reflection on the films work for theology. All I want to do here is to probe further the issues that arise in the pedagogical context of these films' reception with respect to what theology and religious studies as disciplines may learn.

I want to make and explore three observations. The exploration of all three, I contend, demonstrates how emotional literacy is inevitably a part of theological enquiry. First, the labeling—both in terms of genre and critical judgment—limits the potential of what the films can (and often do) achieve on the part of viewers. Second, the ease with which sentimental and sentimentality become terms of negative judgment runs the risk not only of preventing a film from working but also of devaluing the viewer's emotional life. Third, the failure to respect the way in which such films *are* actually working (and what they are achieving publicly) runs the risk of perpetuating a sense that theology is a solely cognitive discipline.

First, then, let us consider the problems and opportunities for theology and religious studies of films that are labeled sentimental romantic comedies. As noted, this appears to be more of a problem than an opportunity for many *male* students. Female students become much more attentive when I first reveal that we are going to be looking at romantic comedies as they relate to theology.[5] For one thing, films such as the three Curtis movies are often among women students' favorites anyway. For another, the thought that theological work can be done in relation to such samples of contemporary culture is an exciting prospect. But in a teaching context, some of the male students are in danger of losing interest at that point because they just do not *do* romantic comedy. Second, theology is regarded as a much more serious discipline than working with such films implies. In other words, the rationality of theology (and perhaps its standing as an academic discipline in the university) is being compromised by such an approach.[6]

Reception of the Curtis films in the classroom context, though, has taught me some interesting lessons. In one of the courses I taught, some of the women students challenged the view that Curtis's films had uncomplicated happy endings. With reference to *Love Actually* in particular, they pointed out that two of the interlocking stories remain tragically unresolved. One marriage is in danger of breaking down, and we witness the pain of the Emma Thompson character, who is trying to handle her husband's infidelity while keeping her family together. We also see the cost to Laura Linney's character, Sarah, who is supporting her mentally ill brother. Neither of these subplots has a happy ending. One student in particular maintained that, despite the fact that viewers do feel warm and happy at the end of the movie, the unresolved aspects of the plot as a whole are those that remain with the audience. They leave their emotional mark on viewers, who then go on working with them.

That insight led me to think further about the earlier two Curtis films. Hundreds of thousands of copies of Auden's poems—especially "Funeral Blues," used at the funeral scene in *Four Weddings*—were sold as a result of the film. The funeral, rather than the weddings, sticks in the mind. Furthermore, the funeral celebrates a gay relationship. In two ways, then, *Four Weddings* begins to challenge the genre of romantic comedy, which, as the textbooks remind us, "operates almost exclusively with respect to heterosexual relationships."[7] Though the ending is happy, the sad subplot lingers in the viewer's consciousness. And it is not simply man-woman relationships that are being celebrated here.

Notting Hill also has its own element of subversion, a point not lost on the current Archbishop of Canterbury. In a lecture in 2000, when he was Archbishop of Wales, Rowan Williams commented on the "clumsy courtship" between the Julia Roberts and Hugh Grant characters, drawing a stark contrast with the portrayal by Tim McInnerny and Gina McKee of the two successful lawyers, one of whom was paralyzed and unable to have children.[8] Williams commends the latter relationship as "far more erotic," given that "every word and gesture they come out with is full of absolute mutual joy," and he commends the watching and discussion of the film in the church's preparation of couples for marriage.

We are dealing here, then, with the subversion of the genre of romantic comedy from within. From the perspective of their reception, the Curtis films show that there is more to them than the feel-good factor alone—if viewers are willing to let the films go on working a bit with their experience and if some kind of reflective process is allowed to happen. Each of the films has a dimension that leaves the viewer challenged about various forms of love, the depth of love that occurs in many forms of human relationship, and the place of pain bearing and sacrifice. *How* these films work—as feel-good comedies—is important with respect to what they can achieve. However, *what* they achieve, as part of what cultural studies analysts recognize as patterns of "meaning making," goes beyond what the basic genre implies. Moreover, this is what makes them interesting for theology and religious studies. For as well as examining what religions are doing explicitly with respect to their ritual practices and belief systems, theologians and religion scholars cannot but be interested in similar kinds of meaning making that occur outside of religion.

As sociologists and media analysts have long begun to recognize, there are new, complex forms of interwovenness between religious and more general cultural patterns of meaning making.[9]

The Step to Theological Reflection

In terms of theological reflection in the light of such reception, of course, especially in seminary settings, it is easy to argue that such films present a set of issues, to which a religious tradition then supplies answers. Or religious traditions smugly imply that they know all there is to know about love. This has been the perennial problem of theology and film dialogue. I do not explore this point in detail here, but these brief references to the actual reception of Curtis's films reveal, among ordinary viewers, a desire to explore the topic of love more deeply or incisively than much public discussion of human relationships currently permits.

Here religious traditions have much to contribute. They can enter discussion about the meaning of love if they can move beyond the simple question-and-answer framework that a "correlationist method" implies.[10] In the case of Christianity, the contributions of Christian theologians will be informed by reflection on the narratives of the life, death and resurrection of Jesus Christ, and of the understandings of God and human being which relate to that reflection.[11] The Jesus narratives (Gospels) invite reflection on the complex costliness of what it means to love and to live *for* others. This is not simply to regard Jesus as a moral exemplar and Christology as thinly veiled moral philosophy, but it does highlight the fact that theological reflection on scriptural texts always has an ethical dimension.

Theological insights from reflection on tradition are brought alongside whatever "raw material" is brought—be it life experience or a cultural text (in this case a selection of films). That is how theology works—through open, communal, critical dialogue between life/art and tradition. Appropriately contemporary understandings of the meaning of the cross in Christianity are more likely to be gained from working with the underside, the loose ends, of Curtis's feel-good comedies in relation to the Jesus narratives than from beginning from a film such as *The Passion of the Christ*. This is simply because the meaning of the cross will be explored in relation to the experienced cost of what it means to love in the context of normal human affairs.

Now let us consider the ease with which "sentimental" and "sentimentality" become terms of negative judgment. As I mentioned earlier, such an opinion runs the risk not only of preventing a film from working but also of devaluing the viewer's emotional life. The reception of Curtis's films leads us to ask harder questions about the way in which the terms "sentimental" and "sentimentality" are used with regard to any film. Whether the label "sentimentality" as a term is in fact used more (and usually negatively) by male rather than female film critics is a moot point. Be that as it may, "sentimentality" and "poignancy" are distinguishable.[12] However, such a distinction, even if valid, is not always easy to make. Films labeled sentimental are often melodramatic and prone to exaggeration, excess, short-circuiting, and simplifying complex emotional processes. They risk the charge of manipulation of viewers even if some form of manipulation can be claimed to be occurring with any film (or indeed any work of art). But the charge of sentimentality can be leveled too glibly and a negative judgment made lazily within the dominant therapeutic paradigm of Western culture. First, though, it is important to acknowledge that there may be a problem for theology and religion here.

Discussions about salvation and redemption are actually easy to have because so much of our public life is about self-exposure (e.g., when we encounter stories of celebrities recovering from addictions). To declare publicly "where one is emotionally" is not unusual, regardless of whether one is famous. It has been widely suggested that this is an aspect of the so-called Diana phenomenon in Britain, which provided evidence that in a supposedly straitlaced culture, public outpourings of grief are indicating a new twist in the way that people express and deal with emotions. Such public grief is easy to label as mawkishness. "Redemption" can then be reduced to mere "moral improvement."

Concern about such public display of emotion is widespread. In the academy, in the world of sociology, Frank Furedi has written in *Therapy Culture* that such cultural developments should be a cause for alarm.[13] Moreover, in the arts, it is striking to find a British artist like Mark Wallinger critiquing the work of video artist Bill Viola for being prone to too much emoting in his art.[14] Opposition to films that tug at the heartstrings displays a hostility to the dominance of a therapeutic culture along similar lines. Showing the Curtis films in the context of theology and religious studies classes could easily be seen as merely buying in to a not-so-subtle combination of consumer satisfaction and therapy culture. It results in students leaving their classes with the clear impression that theology and religion have to do with talking about yourself, especially about what makes you cry.

In response to that undoubted possibility I argue that *resisting* the cultural importance of films such as Curtis's is more dangerous than engaging with them for one simple reason: theology certainly, but possibly religious studies too are not merely cognitive disciplines. What you do when you respond to these films is laugh and cry. This opens you up emotionally. You feel good once you have watched them. Nonetheless, the scenes and subplots that linger do more than leave you with the feel-good experience. You are invited to *think* by the way the film works, so long as there is space around the film-watching experience for the viewer to do so. So the actual reception of the film becomes *both* a cognitive and an affective matter. Even if this taps into therapy culture, the practice of reception of and interaction with the films will not allow the viewer to remain content with the feel-good factor. It is, however, also true that the cognitive encounter with the films' content is most effectively undertaken when the *affective* response to the movies is also taken into consideration.

Watching such films in the context of theology and religious studies classes thus runs the risk of suggesting that all theology might be talk about ourselves or that all theological inquiry is reducible to pastoral or practical theology (and not very good practical or pastoral theology at that).[15] However, it also holds out the possibility that students will be enabled to see that the theological task has many dimensions, and unless we find ways of exploring cognitive and affective aspects of theological inquiry, then theology continues to be more cognitive than it should be. The perennial Western problem of not knowing how to handle emotional elements in religion (recognized in Christian terms as having a weak doctrine of the Spirit) will persist.

This second observation is further confirmed by the third and final observation I want to make. This is an insight that has been prominent within film studies in recent years and which I first accessed when reading the work of Ed Tan and Nico Frijda, who have written on the value of cognitive psychology for understanding what happens when we watch films.[16] Especially helpful in the collection of essays in which their work appears is the fact that psychological insights are offered without being overly reductive about the film-watching experience. The essays unite in their opposition to the dominance of psychoanalytical approaches to film theory.[17] What they achieve from the perspective of psychology is the recognition of the interplay between emotional reactions to film and the cognitive worlds that viewers inhabit as they watch. Tan and Frijda's essay begins especially powerfully, given the way I have been exploring the reception of the Curtis films, as it cites the example of a father weeping at a showing of the Disney film *Pocahontas.* It begins to explore the significance of the tears and also of the safety of the environment within which the weeping occurs, but it does so knowing that emotion can be identified only within a cognitive context.

Tan and Frijda go on to explore three themes in all their emotional complexity in relation to the way in which the cinema arouses emotions. The themes are separation and reunion, justice in jeopardy, and awe. Their treatment of "sentiment" and "sentimentality" ends up much richer and more comprehensive than many of the usual references to sentimentality with regard to the cinema often are. What they show is that the experience of watching a film—perhaps more than many experiences—brings affective and cognitive aspects of human living together. They stress above all the experience of being "lost" in the cinema, of losing one's autonomy. This may have psychological roots—a desire to return to the womb or for the return of paradise-like childhood experiences. However, what the sentimental exposure of the viewer's emotion achieves is a range of responses that might not be at all addressed outside of the context of the film-watching experience.

In other words, the teaching context picks up on the fact of what is *already* happening in the form of responses to movies. In the context of current social experience in Western cultures one can argue that such basic religion-like experiences are occurring in the cinema.[18] To be consistent with my own starting point, I end by arguing that men who fail to respond well to romantic comedies might be in denial about their emotional responses. However, tearful fathers watching *Pocahontas* give me confirmation that there is nevertheless something in my pedagogical line of inquiry and that it is important to encourage men to explore emotion in theology classes.[19]

Concluding Comment

Sentimentality may not, then, be a bad thing. Or at least the term must be rescued from the merely negative sense in which film critics often use it. The processing of emotions in the context of so-called sentimental films in what may at first seem quite superficial ways may in fact be crucial social locations of where any kind of interplay of cognitive and affective treatments of what it means to love happens *at all*. If this is so, then psychologists, film studies lecturers, sociologists, and cultural studies lecturers will all want to have their say as to what is going on. However, in theology and religious studies we need to pay attention and contribute to the debates, too, for we cannot let the experiences happen without taking notice of the cognitive worlds within which they occur. And, as I have mentioned, even some psychologists agree with that.

Taking this pedagogical line is admittedly problematic in the present theological climate. On the one hand it looks like warmed-over Christian liberalism of the kind that celebrates Schleiermacher's "turn to the subject" theological methodology (now considered by many to be mistaken). On the other, it feeds the therapy-culture version of this subjective turn as it has taken form in the debates about "progressive spirituality" in the contemporary West.[20] Some contend that theology—actually talking about God as something more than human experience—gets left out altogether. Schleiermacher was, though, smarter than that, and his critics—or at least those who link him too readily with some versions of 1960s' Christian liberalism—clearly do not know his work well enough. How we use experience in theology *is* a crucial question, one that those who follow progressive spirituality will need to do much more work on. But at least we can all agree that the lecture/seminar room is an ideal place to start exploring this. Only those against whom progressive theologians rightly rail—those who speak from on high, claiming to be able to able to speak rather unproblematically from external authorities—may quibble. The rest of us know how significant experience (of life, art, media, and culture) actually is. Thus, beginning the excitement of theological exploration from what people are watching, how they feel in response, and what they think about what they feel even when responding to popular movies seems a very good place to start.

NOTES

1. Tyron Inbody makes this point in his pedagogical reflections at the start of *Faith of the Christian Church* (2005) (cf. Marsh 2007, 1–4).

2. The background for such use is explored more fully in my *Cinema and Sentiment* (Marsh 2004). In *Theology Goes to the Movies* (Marsh 2007) I explain how this exploration fits into the broader use of film in theological education.

3. There is, of course, a world of difference between showing whole films and just clips. The latter runs the risk of the teacher's "controlling" the responses but is required by time constraints. However, while I acknowledge the limitations of showing clips, even they can have surprising effects.

4. I suspect that the labels of "sentimental" and "sentimentality" in relation to these and similar films are much more readily applied by male film critics than female reviewers, but that needs to be explored.

5. I cannot here look into the question of *why* this might be so. I simply note that it *is*. The gendered aspects of students' personal relationships, family patterns, religious backgrounds (if they have them), and patterns of response to and consumption of art and culture all come into play.

6. That said, some of the chief doubters of this approach to theology have been women students. The gender dimension is thus not simple. At issue here is theology's academic credibility, the extent to which it can both maintain serious attention to its cognitive, rational dimension while acknowledging that it is handling material that is not simply rational.

7. Blandford, Grant, and Hillier (2001, 202).

8. This section draws on material in Marsh (2004, 79–80).

9. Some of the main works in this area that I have found helpful are Beaudoin (1998), Partridge (2004), Lynch (2004), Cobb (2005), and Hoover (2006). Interestingly, there seems to have been a move away from making claims for the use of popular culture as "implicit religion." It is more a matter of mapping what is happening and clarifying how people are making meaning rather than finding the right labels.

10. The correlationist method was prominent in the work of Paul Tillich (Clayton 1980). Important in its day, it arguably now looks too apologetic a form of theology. It remains valuable nevertheless, even if Tillich's use of the arts is rather highbrow.

11. In Marsh (2007, 60–78) I consider the films in the chapter on "Human Being."

12. Film critic Ryan Gilbey's review of the film *Titanic* distinguishes between sentimentality and poignancy. *Titanic* was, in his judgment, guilty of the former (Marsh 2004, 61–65).

13. Furedi (2004).

14. Cited in Marsh (2004, 111).

15. We must be careful here: There is a fine tradition of theology (one that I support) that sees practical theology as the pinnacle of theological inquiry. The difficulty is that too much practical and pastoral theology still does not do enough with biblical study and systematic theology, even though it has made great strides (in a way that systematic theology often does not) in engaging with, say, sociology and psychology.

16. See Tan and Frijda (1999) (cf. Plantinga 1997).

17. I have been criticized on many fronts (for example, in Kraemer [2006] and Brintnall [2006]) for failing to do justice to psychoanalytical approaches to film. I accept the charge. I have simply linked up with cognitive psychologists and audience response work in film studies because their work is more conducive to the findings of empirical studies of actual movie goers. This is not to deny that we could say much more about what films are doing, but theological exploration has to start somewhere. It is not superficial to be working theologically with what actual viewers think is happening, and it is not necessarily more theological to be working at a level that only the psychoanalytically trained claim to be able to see.

18. This is where my work is tied very closely to that of John Lyden (2003), even though I develop it somewhat differently. In my own book *Cinema and Sentiment* I show that, even though it may not be right to call film watching "worship," there can be something religion-like in the experience of watching films (Marsh 2004, chapter 2).

19. Bear in mind that critical exploration of emotion is not the same as turning our classes into therapy sessions, but we should nevertheless recognize that this is risky territory.

20. See Lynch (2007, esp. 55–60).

REFERENCES

Beaudoin, T. 1998. *Virtual Faith: The Irreverent Spiritual Quest of Generation X.* San Francisco: Jossey-Bass.

Blandford, S., B. G. Grant, and J. Hillier. 2001. *The Film Studies Dictionary.* London: Arnold.

Brintnall, K. 2006. "What Hath Vienna to Do with Jerusalem? The Value of Psychoanalytic Film Theory for Religion and Film Scholarship." Paper delivered to the Religion, Film, and Visual Culture Group of the American Academy of Religion, Washington, D.C., November 19.

Clayton, J. 1980. *The Concept of Correlation: Paul Tillich and the Possibility of a Mediating Theology.* New York: De Gruyter.

Cobb, K. 2005. *The Blackwell Guide to Theology and Popular Culture.* Malden, Mass.: Blackwell.

Furedi, F. 2004. *Therapy Culture: Cultivating Vulnerability in an Uncertain Age.* New York: Routledge.

Hoover, S. 2006. *Religion in the Media Age.* New York: Routledge.

Inbody, T. 2005. *The Faith of the Christian Church: An Introduction to Theology.* Grand Rapids, Mich.: Eerdmans.

Kraemer, C. H. 2006. Review of *Cinema and Sentiment. Religious Studies Review* 32(3) (July): 187.

Lyden, J. 2003. *Film as Religion: Myths, Morals, and Rituals.* New York: New York University Press.

Lynch, G. 2004. *Understanding Theology and Popular Culture.* Malden, Mass.: Blackwell.

———. 2007. *The New Spirituality: An Introduction to Progressive Belief in the Twenty-first Century.* New York: Tauris.

Marsh, C. 2004. *Cinema and Sentiment: Film's Challenge to Theology.* Waynesboro, Ga.: Paternoster Press.

———. 2007. *Theology Goes to the Movies: An Introduction to Critical Christian Thinking.* New York: Routledge.

Partridge, C. 2004. *The Re-enchantment of the West: Alternative Spiritualities, Sacralization, Popular Culture, and Occulture.* New York: T. & T. Clark International.

Plantinga, C. 1997. "Notes on Spectator Emotion and Ideological Film Criticism." In *Film Theory and Philosophy,* ed. R. Allen and M. Smith, 372–93. New York: Oxford University Press.

———, and G. M. Smith, eds. 1999. *Passionate Views: Film, Cognition, and Emotion.* Baltimore: Johns Hopkins University Press.

Tan, E., and N. Frijda. 1999. "Sentiment in Film Viewing." In *Passionate Views,* ed. C. Plantinga and M. Smith, 48–64. Baltimore: Johns Hopkins University Press.

9

Women, Theology, and Film: Approaching the Challenge of Interdisciplinary Teaching

Gaye Williams Ortiz

The Theology, Religious, and Cultural Studies Department of the College of Ripon and York Saint John (now York Saint John University) has for many years offered a sound pedagogical tradition of theological dialogue with contemporary culture. Its innovative practice since the 1970s of offering an undergraduate course in theology and film was augmented in the 1990s with the creation of an interdisciplinary upper-level undergraduate course titled Women, Theology, and Film. It was designed to synthesize a variety of theological, feminist, and film criticism perspectives in exploring the representation of women in film. This chapter addresses the rationale and delivery of the course and also discusses some of the opportunities and challenges for its delivery that were created by its interdisciplinary approach.

From 1994 until 2002 I was senior lecturer in theology and religious studies at the college and was the film enthusiast responsible for creating the course titled Women, Theology, and Film. Since the 1970s Theology through Film and Literature has been a signature course offered by the department, and it has become so popular that it is offered at every level, from the first year of undergraduate studies through the Master of Theology degree program (with corresponding complexity at each level). As expertise and the publication of original research on theology and film increased among our faculty, the course was seen as a natural next step, integrating film and theology with another of the department's specialties, feminist theology. It was developed within the departmental context of interdisciplinary study, in which students drew from disciplines such as sociology, psychology, philosophy, theology and religious studies, media and film studies, and literature studies. The Theology and Religious Studies and Cultural Studies BA degrees offered by the department created a matrix of courses that enhanced the development of generic, transferable skills, along with the acquisition of academic knowledge. In six semesters the degree program developed coherence, both conceptual and intellectual, in its learning outcomes for students through a series of core and specialist elective courses. The teaching and learning strategies included traditional methods such as lectures and seminars and also introduced others such as learning journals, small group discussions, and presentations.

In the fifth semester, when independent learning ended, students had an opportunity to integrate a combination of independent learning modules (e.g., academic exchange, community placement, career or academic research in dissertation form) and structured learning with courses such as Women, Theology, and Film. This approach had three objectives: subject knowledge and understanding; cognitive skill development; and key transferable skills. During this semester a student could choose electives offered by other interdisciplinary programs. Because upper-level students in other BA disciplines such as history or English could also select electives in their fifth semester, these students, besides theology majors, were able to take the Women, Theology, and Film course as well.

Course Structure and Resources

The rationale for the Women, Theology, and Film course was as follows: Both feminist theology and feminist film theory have helped to tell stories that might otherwise have remained hidden or lost. It is important to realize that these stories help us to better understand the cultural, social, and religious factors that have affected women's lives. The images of women we see on the screen today are affected by and replete with religious and theological meanings of sexual identity and difference; some are more explicit than others. When we apply feminist film theory and feminist theology to these images, we can create a rich intertextual analysis.

As this was an original course not derived from specialist texts dedicated to the subject, the creator of the course compiled an extensive reading and viewing list and encouraged students to apply their skills of critical interpretation and objective analysis to the material. And, within the context of a philosophy of interdisciplinary study, the course was enriched by the participation of all students, regardless of their major.

The instructor's challenge, then, was twofold: how to integrate feminist theology with feminist film theory in a way that retained the integrity and rigor of both disciplines, and how to make the course accessible to a group of students who might display a varied range of theological knowledge (from none to advanced). This consideration was especially important since the grades students received for third-level level work impacted significantly upon the final degree classification. It also had implications for the future of Saint John's pedagogical philosophy of interdisciplinarity if students found they could not perform well in such a degree program.

The strategy for circumventing these challenges lay in the way learning outcomes were linked to assessment strategies. Upon successful completion of the course students would be able to do the following:

1. devise methods for collecting information related to extended research on theology and film
2. apply skills of critical interpretation and analysis to women's complex social and religious problems, experiences, and ideas as presented in selected films
3. demonstrate an understanding of a range of contemporary theological and feminist perspectives in order to reflect upon theological issues that have an impact on and deepen our understanding of women

The department's expectation was that upper-level students, whatever their area of study, would have attained competence in the transferable skills needed to fulfill the course requirements. The corresponding coursework included critical essays and a research file. Students drew upon an extensive and varied body of resources, not the least of which were films they viewed within a structured course schedule; required and recommended texts; journals, periodicals, and online resources. Lectures covered the course content; in addition, following each screening, students participated in a seminar discussion of the movie. Regular tutorials with the course leader were also built into the schedule, in which student progress was reviewed and academic support or advice was offered.

As I have already mentioned, implicit in the structure and resources of the Women, Theology, and Film course was the assumption that third-level students had by now developed the generic academic skills articulated in the learning objectives stated earlier: They should be able to collect information while engaging in research and be capable of completing a lengthy review, in this case a research file (which was a common type of assessment tool in BA courses). They should also be able, with the application of appropriate criteria on watching films, to interpret and analyze filmic representations of women. The acquisition of specialist knowledge, through directed reading and insights gained through seminar discussions, should help students to reflect upon the theological and feminist issues identified in the course. The integration of perspectives and knowledge, while challenging because of the differing academic profiles of students in the class, nonetheless offered exciting opportunities for students to articulate and exhibit the standpoints and opinions they had formed by diverse types of academic knowledge and pedagogical formation.

Women's Voices

The introductory session of the course featured a lecture titled "Women's Voices." This topic was meant to provide a generic reflection on women's stories, as well as the historical and linguistic boundaries that have constrained women during their attempt to tell their stories. The absence of women's voices and accomplishments in history is summed up by Rosalind Miles: "The lives of unsung heroines have the fascination of the greatest story never told."[1] In the Christian tradition this is also the case, but simply because it is not told does not mean that the history does not exist. Amy Oden writes in her introduction to *In Her Words:*

> The corpus of extant women's writings within the history of Christianity is vast, rich and diverse. This comes as a surprise to many in the light of the historical resistance within Christianity and its resident cultures to the education, speech and writing of women. We have too easily accepted history's *dicta* against women's speech, convinced that indeed there is no record left by women.[2]

Feminist theology and feminist film theory have helped to tell and to explain stories that might otherwise remain hidden or lost, but the language we use to tell those stories is often not gender neutral, and another function of the first class is to increase awareness of the etymological existence of women in the history of the English language. Using Jane Mills's *Womanwords* (1989) to trace the shifts in meaning of words such as "woman" or "hysteria" helps students to see the bias against and stereotyping of women in the English language. Old dictionaries offer definitions that list the qualities of women, such as gentle, intuitive, submissive, and fickle, whose connotations contribute to the essentialist theory of woman. Once those are discussed in class, students are asked to reflect upon the ways in which women are culturally stereotyped in both language and history.

A third area of defining women through essential qualities is religion; a wealth of quotes and writings by church fathers, religious leaders, and theologians attests to that fact. A picture of the domination of women's lives by patriarchal forces begins to develop, corresponding with an appreciation of the difficulty that women have had in making their voices heard. The women's movement, from the first wave of suffrage in the nineteenth century to today, has been committed to giving women a voice in society. This lecture develops the idea that films—some fictional, some based on both fact and real women's experiences—tell stories that help us to understand more fully the cultural, social, and religious factors that have affected women's lives. Once this general perspective is established through the examples of history, language, and religion in the introductory lecture, students are ready to tackle material more specific to film theory and theology.

A tutorial on how to "read" a film is another important course component; just as competence in literacy is vital for students of literature, so competence in viewing films enables students to use and understand the specific cinematic vocabulary crucial to the discussion of films viewed by the class. A basic grasp of vocabulary, defining elements such as mise-en-scène, editing, soundtrack, and cinematography, along with a rubric for recording reactions to a film during the actual screening, helps all students, no matter what their major program of study, to articulate their film-watching experience more accurately.

Feminist Film Theory and Feminist Theology: Parallels

The following lecture introduces concepts in feminist film theory, specifically, the major areas of female spectatorship, identification, the "male gaze" theory, and film as cultural text. The third lecture covers the feminist critique of religion and focuses on the systematic method of analysis of the practice and rationale, assumptions, and preconceptions that underpin Christian teaching and doctrine. A major aspect of critiquing tradition that is inherently male centered and male authored is the developmental nature of feminist thought: Feminist theologians are engaged in recovering the biblical and historical legacy of women and reclaiming tradition by theological reconstruction and the incorporation of newly understood historical material and contemporary feminist insights into theology.

A key session of the course then identifies parallels in the feminist critiques of both theology and film theory. Although these two disciplines are very different, they have both been affected by the women's movement of the past fifty years in many similar ways. Ursula King says that if we take all of the different voices of women together, "one can discern a certain connection between the different themes, an overall pattern and dynamic, and an acute sense of responsibility and concern."[3]

In addition to being products of the women's liberation movement, scholars within both feminist theology and feminist film theory are aware of the male authorship of narratives and control of structures: Just as Mary Daly points out that "when God is male, the male is God,"[4] Ally Acker, one of the foremost researchers into the early era of filmmaking, bemoans the absence of writing about women in the film industry: "He who has access to major publishers gets to make history."[5]

Other parallels exist in the process of reclaiming women's voices in both theology and film: A profusion of material aimed at women follows an increase in women's involvement in critiquing and interpreting the products of theology and film, and a subsequent upsurge in women's influence and agenda setting sometimes fools recent observers into assuming that women have been in control the whole time! The organic pluralism that exists within both feminist theology and feminist film theory and filmmaking is a cultural characteristic of the feminist movement: Women of diverse ethnic, religious, and ideological backgrounds are making their voices heard. However, the ethic of solidarity is a strong imperative in feminist intercultural discourse: Kwok Pui-Lan remarks, "As the world is becoming much more linked together because of the global market, women cannot afford to be divided because of their identity politics."[6] Moreover, women are not choosing to work solely within "malestream" culture: Just as Mary Daly, Carol Christ, and Daphne Hampson rejected the standpoint within Christianity and chose to write and think outside organized religion, so too have many feminist filmmakers decided that the film industry is inherently and hopelessly flawed and worked outside the system as independent filmmakers in order to create their unique cinematic vision.

The session on parallels concludes by asking where feminism will go from here. The images of women we see on the screen today are affected by misreadings of sexuality and gender throughout Western history, what Rachel Muers might term "theological 'scripting' of people's lives through the symbols of gender."[7] Applying feminist film theory and feminist theology to these images can create a rich intertextual analysis. By presenting these possibilities to students, they in turn feel empowered to interpret and challenge what they see on screen.

Stereotypes and Archetypes

The three images of virgin, temptress, and mother are enduring and powerful archetypes that affect our notions of women in Western culture. In many ways the images of women as presented in contemporary media are ambiguous, which perhaps reflects the enormous changes in gender roles in our society that have taken place in the past century. Exploring the stereotypes of women in film roles, which either reinforce or subvert the function of the ancient archetypes of virgin, temptress, and mother, students gain an insight into the cinematic production and representation of women. The resources used in this section of the course include authors as varied as Susan Brownmiller (*Against Our Will*, 1975), Marina Warner (*From the Beast to the Blonde*, 1995), and Salman Rushdie (*The Wizard of Oz*, 1992). Students view films such as *La belle et la bête* (1945), *Carrie* (1976), and *Elizabeth* (1998) in their exploration of the virgin archetype; *The Maltese Falcon* (1941), *Fatal Attraction* (1987), and *The Postman Always Rings Twice* (1946) for the temptress archetype; and *Steel Magnolias* (1989), *Alien 3* (1992), and *The Terminator* and *Terminator II: Judgment Day* (1984, 1991) for the mother archetype. They articulate their understanding of these films and their portrayals of women with the help of feminist film theorists such as Carol Clover, Annette Kuhn, and Claire Johnston, whose perspectives on the ideology and iconography of female representation have been vital to the discipline.

In the final part of this section of the course, the often problematic topic of female Christ figures is an appropriate focus of study. Academic discourse in the past few years has seen a lively exchange of views (particularly in the American Academy of Religion conference rooms) about films such as *Babette's Feast* (1987), *Breaking the Waves* (1996), and *The Spitfire Grill* (1996). A Christ figure, in my own definition of the term, experiences the kinds of things Jesus Christ did or personifies the righteous, loving, self-sacrificing Christ of the Christian tradition. When we watch a film in which this figure is female, there are many incongruous messages from within the Christian theological and iconographical traditions alone that assail us. When compounding the interpretation of such an image with the feminist critique, students can be introduced to an entirely new and often personally challenging way of seeing how film and theology can affect one another.

This is one example of how feminist tools of criticism and questioning can disturb and thrill, to use students' own words. Giving students the space and support necessary to confront their own preconceptions and symbolic constructions is a crucial part of pedagogy: Lectures establish a base for students, who process new information, but the synthesis of this information with their own interpretations and prior beliefs and attitudes is what makes for authentic learning. It is a privilege and a challenge to the theologian who cares enough to provide the ingredients for this to occur. A quote from Susan Frank Parsons is appropriate to this process: "Is it not the theologian's burden to be the place wherein truth comes to dwell, and thus to be always vulnerable to the havoc caused by its arrival, and yet to be always and astonishingly made ready to bear it?"[8]

Conclusion

It is a hallmark of feminist pedagogy that academic and personal development are inseparable learning objectives. The "doing" of theology, so vital to the ethos of the Department of Theology and Religious Studies at York Saint John, balances the often impersonal, theoretical analysis of theological issues. Traditional theology, as taught for so long in the academy, devalued the experience of women, which usually did not reflect the dominant values of our society. Traditional theology, following the millennia-old patriarchal underpinnings of religious thought, linked abstract, conceptual thought with the male and embodiment with nature and women. Women's experience is essential to the feminist perspective, including personal transformative experience, also known as consciousness raising.

Something I often observed during my time at York Saint John was the transformation undergone predominantly by female students who, after recognizing the pervasiveness of gender in culture and reflecting upon the ethical and political implications of their feminist studies, made subsequent life-changing decisions about their own personal faith perspectives and even their lifestyles and relationships. King affirms the holistic nature of women's experience as it touches and transforms all areas of life: "Authentically lived experience, rooted and grounded in wholeness and greater reality, radiates power, the power of spiritual energy and strength, of a large, continuous life web and rhythm of which the individual person forms an integral part."[9] What teacher would not want to engage students in a learning process that has, as its ultimate aim, not simply the acquisition of knowledge nor even theological expertise but authentic living, where knowledge and spirituality are embodied and energized for the greater good of the planet?

Dry, abstract pedagogy that allows for compartmentalized thinking is now mainly a long-outdated concept in higher education, and the experience of teaching interdisciplinary material, with its potential for students to combine insights and challenge status-quo teaching and learning strategies, has been an enriching and fulfilling one. Students, even those without previous theology courses, invariably rose to the challenge of grasping upper-level theological concepts through film. At the end of the semester many of them said that they would never be able to look at a film the same way again—they were not complaining but rather implying a filmic literacy that would stand them in good stead in the future. It is important to the person who developed the Women, Theology, and Film course at York Saint John that it has played a part in encouraging and enabling students to find their own voice by examining those of women in theology and film.

NOTES

1. Miles (1989), preface.
2. Oden (1995), 11.
3. King (1993), 3.
4. Daly (1973), 19.
5. Acker (1991), xix.
6. Pui-Lan (2002), 33.
7. Ford (2005), 447.
8. Parsons (2002), 130–31.
9. King (1993), 86.

REFERENCES

Acker, Ally. 1991. *Reel Women: Pioneers of the Cinema, 1896 to the Present.* New York: Continuum.
Axel, Gabriel. 1987. *Babette's Feast.*
Brownmiller, Susan. 1975. *Against Our Will: Men, Women, and Rape.* New York: Simon and Schuster.
Cameron, James. 1984. *The Terminator.*
———. 1991. *Terminator II: Judgment Day.*
Cocteau, Jean. 1945. *La belle et la bête.*
Daly, Mary. 1973. *Beyond God the Father: Toward a Philosophy of Women's Liberation.* Boston: Beacon.
Fincher, David. 1992. *Alien 3.*
Ford, David F., ed. 2005. *The Modern Theologians: An Introduction to Christian Theology since 1918.* Malden, Mass.: Blackwell.
Garnett, Tay. 1946. *The Postman Always Rings Twice.*
Huston, John. 1941. *The Maltese Falcon.*
Kapur, Shekar. 1998. *Elizabeth.*
King, Ursula. 1993. *Women and Spirituality: Voices of Protest and Promise.* London: Macmillan.
LaPalma, Brian. 1976. *Carrie.*
Lyne, Adrian. 1987. *Fatal Attraction.*
Miles, Rosalind. 1989. *The Women's History of the World.* London: Paladin.
Mills, Jane. 1989. *Womanwords: A Vocabulary of Culture and Patriarchal Society.* London: Longman.

Muers, Rachel. 2005. "Feminism, Gender and Theology." In *Modern Theologians*, ed. Ford, 431–50.

Oden, Amy, ed. 1995. *In Her Words: Women's Writings in the History of Christian Thought*. London: SPCK.

Parsons, Susan Frank, ed. 2002. "Feminist Theology as Dogmatic Theology." In *Cambridge Companion to Feminist Theology*, ed. Susan Frank Parsons, 114–32. New York: Cambridge University Press.

Pui-Lan, Kwok. 2002. "Feminist Theology as Intercultural Discourse." In *Cambridge Companion to Feminist Theology*, ed. Parsons, 23–39.

Ross, Herbert. 1989. *Steel Magnolias*.

Rushdie, Salman. 1992. *The Wizard of Oz*. London: BFI.

Von Trier, Lars. 1996. *Breaking the Waves*.

Warner, Marina. 1995. *From the Beast to the Blonde: On Fairy Tales and Their Tellers*. London: Vintage.

Zlotoff, Lee David. 1996. *The Spitfire Grill*.

PART III

The Religious Studies Approach

IO

Seeing Is Believing, but Touching's the Truth: Religion, Film, and the Anthropology of the Senses

Richard M. Carp

Film can help us teach about religion in many ways. In this chapter I consider ethnographic and documentary films (and videos) that provide students with views of religion: Rituals, daily practices, architecture, pilgrimages, and even the sweep of religious history all appear in living color in these vivid and impressive displays.[1] I concentrate on undergraduate, especially introductory, classes since these are by far the most commonly taught and the only religion classes many students take.

Documentary and ethnographic films are wonderful classroom enhancements. Students like movies, and they are already familiar with documentaries and ethnographies through their experience with, for example, the Discovery, National Geographic, and History television channels.[2] In class, these films extend the information we can present about religion, and they often engage students and motivate them to conversation more effectively than readings. Most contemporary textbooks come with CD-ROMs that include documentary film.

As seductive as these materials are, they obfuscate religion and the religions even as they present them with impressive realism. This realism, though in one way an obstacle to understanding, can offer students an opening onto a sophisticated consideration of religion and to the limitations and potentials of the means by which we study it. In order for ethnographic film to function in this way, we need to set it in two contexts for students. The first is sensorial anthropology, and the second is film theory as it relates to the anthropology of perception.[3] The first demonstrates that the world disclosed by "our" senses is not necessarily the one revealed by "theirs." The second links ethnographic and documentary film to Western sensory acculturation and shows how cinematic techniques create the illusion that "as a scientific instrument of representation, ethnographic film assumes that the camera recorded a truthful reality, 'out there'—a reality distinct from that of the viewer and filmmaker" (Russell 1999, 12).[4]

The Enculturation of Perception

Since 1991, when David Howes first published *The Varieties of Sensory Experience*, it has become increasingly evident that perception varies significantly from culture to culture and within an individual culture from social location to social location and from time to time. As the senses vary, so does the seemingly immediate experiential world they present and the store of knowledge built up about it (Carp 1997; Howes 1991, 2005; Classen 1993, 1998, 2005; Classen, Howes, and Synnott 1994; Korsmeyer 2005; Bull and Back 2003; Drobnick 2006; Seremetakis 1994; Ingold 2000).

One implication is that the cultural components of our own sensory engagements are part of our knowledge apparatus, both a condition and a limit of what we can know. In that vein C. Nadia Seremetakis asks, how "can perceiving subjects from [the modern Western] context perceive the senses of the cultural other?" (1994, 125). This is the question we must put to our students as they investigate religion. We need to help them develop a critical approach to their perception in the study of religion, just as we do with their language and their religious commitments.

Though rooted in inherent capacities, human perceiving is a skilled act, "cultivated, like any skill, through practice and training in an environment" (Ingold 2000, 283). These skills are learned through *"systems of apprenticeship"* (italics in the original) in which less experienced practitioners (infants and children) learn from more experienced ones (older children and adults) (ibid., 37). As a result, people from different backgrounds do not interpret the same sensory information differently. Rather, "due to their previous bodily training, their senses are differentially attuned to the environment" (ibid., 162). Human landscapes are largely cultural ones, though they are embedded in ecologies; human skills are largely determined by culture, although the range of cultural possibilities is limited by ecological necessities. Experienced practitioners are almost exclusively human and therefore cultured. Thus bodily training is largely cultural training, and differential perception largely reflects cultural difference.

Bodies, cultures, sensing and perceiving, and knowing and believing are woven together in a net of interconnections that cannot be cut. To paraphrase Ingold, religious people do not interpret the same world differently; because they participate in networks of bodies, cultures, sensing and perceiving, and knowing and believing, they experience different worlds that they interpret. For scholars of religion this points to an inescapable tension between their senses and the senses of those whose religions we study. What is important to scholars may be insignificant or even imperceptible to those we study, while we are likely not to notice matters of prime concern to them.

If there is anything about which scholars of sensation agree, it is this: "Modern Western culture is a culture of the eye" (Classen 1998, 1). This visualist bias shows itself in our search to understand others' worldviews, to which Constance Classen counterposes the notion of "worlds of sense" (1993, 138 and passim). Bull and Back propose "thinking within a 'democracy of the senses' [in which] no sense is privileged in relation to its counterparts" (2003, 2). They challenge us to discover a kind of deep listening that enables "thinking with our ears" (ibid., 3). A sensitive study of religion encounters people thinking with noses, tastes, movement, touch, and various simultaneous or rhythmically structured combinations. This thinking cannot be rendered visually, which is to say, filmically. However, film, when placed in appropriate contexts or used in appropriate ways, can open students to an awareness of religious thought and experience in all sensory modalities.

It is important to point out that the critique of visualism applies to a particular mode of vision, not "sight itself." Ingold (2000) notes that "the reduction *to* vision, in the West, has been accompanied by a second reduction, namely the reduction *of* vision" (282), a fact that is important when considering the visuality of others who look at the world quite differently from the way in which we do, especially as visuality affects religion (e.g., Shipibo-Conibo shamanism or Hindu *darśan*).

These twin reductions of Western visuality are evident throughout the post-Renaissance development of the Euro-American ecumene. Kant, for example, believed wrote that scent had no intellectual or aesthetic value and was therefore not worth cultivating. Darwin claimed that evolutionary advance was marked by reduction in the capacity to smell, whereas others have found this reduction to be a sign of cultural sophistication and even mental health (Classen, Howes, and Synnott 1994, 89). However, visualism is not limited to the domain of thought or to metaphors of knowledge. It is embodied in our practices of vision and reflected in our creation of the cultural landscape.

Take olfaction, for example. As Edward Hall writes, our cultural landscape exhibits "olfactory blandness and sameness that would be difficult to duplicate anywhere else in the world" (1969, 45). This process of deodorization has gone hand in hand with one of enhanced visualization. An excellent example is the domestic rose. For a long time, European gardens were valued more for the variety and delight of their scents than their sights, and the rose held a place of honor because of its fragrances. Thus Shakespeare writes, "A rose by any other name would smell as sweet." Odor had other uses besides pleasure; for example, scent was once a primary means of medical diagnosis. Beginning in the eighteenth century, olfaction declined in value as reliance on sight increased. Modern roses have been bred in a bewildering variety of colors and forms, but many have little, if any, odor (Classen 1993, 15–36). Today there is a reodorization of specific sites (such as shopping malls) in an explicit attempt to manipulate mood and behavior. However, this reodorization is restricted in area, focused in application, and extremely simple in comparison to the olfactory richness of many cultural landscapes. In fact, it depends on the blank olfactory slate produced by modernity as the backdrop on which single (usually artificially produced) scents can be made evident (Classen, Howes, and Synnott 2005, 341).[5] Deodorization directly affects the practice of religion: In the early church priests were held to give off a special odor, while later Christians experience an "odor of sanctity" associated with the Holy Spirit and clinging to saints even after death (Drobnick 2006, 375–90).

It would be possible to write a similar history of other senses, or, better, of the transforming engagement of bodies with the world in the West and the corresponding transformation of bodily skills of sensing associated with it since, as we have seen, sensing is a whole-body activity, not the summation or integration of some number of senses operating independently. Such a sensory history would reveal a hidden tradition of sensory thought hovering just outside our current experience of Christianity. Classen states the following:

> Christianity would seem to have escaped the visualizing tendencies of modernity and remained a stronghold (or perhaps a museum?) of multisensory iconology. Many churches . . . are still fragrant with incense. Religious services are still held in the time-honored oral fashion. However, if the traditional sensory signs of worship remain . . . much of the symbolism which once integrated them into a larger sensory and sacred reality has been forgotten. (1998, 2)

Classen devotes the first section of *The Color of Angels* (1998) to "this vanished multisensory cosmic order" (ibid.). When students read all or part of this text, they begin to discover what it might mean to think haptically, to inhabit sensory theology.

A certain visuality, then, is a hallmark of Western culture, doubly so since it is also the primary source of our metaphors for knowing. The title of this chapter is a folk saying about the relationship between sensing and knowing. It articulates skepticism about the apparent lucidity of visual evidence and a preference for direct, tactile experience with the material in question. I have chosen it, though, because most of us are likely to be unfamiliar with the second component of the saying, which today is mostly truncated to "seeing is believing," a very different proposition indeed (Howes 1991, 169).

Film emerges from and responds to our preference for visuality as a cognitive medium. This visualism is often traced to the Renaissance and Alberti's codification of how to create the illusion of depth in two dimensions through linear perspective. Even at this early state, perspectival painting was linked to photography; many Renaissance painters used versions of the camera obscura to create images they then drew over on their canvases.

By placing a window between seer and world, perspective breaks the bond between them. Seer becomes spectator; world becomes spectacle. Self sits, detached and observing, over against what lies "on the other side" of the window (Romanyshyn 1989, 31). This particular mode of vision (soon reproduced in the cultural landscape, as well as in visual art) affects not just sight but the whole sensorium as well, "deemphasizing the other senses as ways of knowing and communicating" (Howes 1991, 5).

Western visuality developed in tandem with (and many scholars believe as the result of) our increasing reliance on text. "Literacy," writes Constance Classen, "and particularly print, is generally recognized as the major cause of this visualism" (1993, 6). Paradoxically, showing students films to break the hegemony of the text in some ways simply reinforces it. "Harnessing . . . vision to a project of objectification . . . has reduced [vision] to an instrument of disinterested observation" (Ingold 2000, 273; see also 287).[6]

The development of film is part of this project of objectification. Although films, like perspectival painting, can convey powerful emotions, the filmic medium intensifies the separation of seer and seen initiated in the Renaissance.[7] Ordinary vision is a whole-body affair intimately linked to all aspects of perception. Turning the eyes to focus on something, for example, also moves the ears and alters the auditory field, while the kinesthesia involved in the movement subtly changes proprioception (ibid., 261). Film changes this, for the filmic image is not open to further acts of exploratory perception, as is the world at large. One cannot act in such a way as to alter the filmic image. Any exploratory movements on my part will, in fact, lessen my focus on the film and bring to awareness the environment within which the film is being shown. The screen is as Susan Buck-Morss would have it, a "prosthetic organ [that] does not merely duplicate human cognitive perception, but changes it" (Seremetakis 1994, 48). "The techniques of cinema," writes Buck-Morss, separate perception from the world at large in order to "hold it suspended, floating in a seemingly autonomous set of dimensions" (ibid., 49).

Film has become such a powerful metaphor of experience that cognitive scientist Antonio Damascio's explanation of consciousness as "a movie in the brain" seems self-evidently correct to my students—until they read "Consciousness as 'Feeling in the Body' " (Howes 2005, 164–78), in which Kathryn Lynn Guerts critiques Damascio's metaphor, which is, she claims, anthropologically naïve and bound by "technological individualism" (ibid., 177). Students are flabbergasted to learn that the Anlo-Ewe of West Africa articulate consciousness as *sesalelame,* a kind of feeling in the body that is "inherently intersubjective and rooted in shared feelings" (ibid.). Consciousness, or self, is a key experience and concept in religion. Once students grasp that others experience consciousness in quite a different way, they are ready to examine their own metaphors of consciousness. They quickly realize that "movie in the brain" as a metaphor for awareness could make sense only in a highly technologized and mediated culture.

Without a critical approach, showing students ethnographic and documentary films captures religion within the visuality that is the hallmark of modern experience and thought, corresponding to what Russell calls the "regime of veracity . . . in which social observation is presented as a form of cultural knowledge [while overlooking] the ways in which this 'knowledge' is bound to the hierarchies of race, ethnicity, and mastery" (1999, 10). As

MacDougall notes, this concern "increasingly applies to ethnographic films made *within* Western society, since the subjects are almost always from a class or subculture different from that of the filmmaker" (2006, 218).

Teaching with and against Film

Reading

Although we show films partly to escape the domination of texts, texts can help us come out from under the domination of the visual since there is a growing literature about sensory religion. I have already noted some of the texts I use in teaching religion to undergraduates in classes where I also show films. Other texts lend themselves to this task as well.

For example, many of us use Diana Eck's *Darśan* (1998) to help students understand religious seeing among India's Hindus. This is helpful because it highlights the fact that many ways of seeing vary cross-culturally. There are at least two ways to extend this investigation. One is to look more deeply into Hindu religious seeing (for example, by reading Phillip Lutgendorf's study of how watching the televised version of the *Ramayana* became itself a religious practice, turning televisions into decorated and venerated home shrines, or John Stratton Hawley's description of the creation of a new goddess as the result of a Bollywood film; both excerpted in Plate 2002). This helps students understand not only that seeing is not just seeing but also that media have alternate histories and culturally differing presences. Film and television in India are evidently not the same as in the United States.

In "A Taste of India" (in Howes 1991), Sylvain Pinard takes us farther, challenging Eck's central premise that sight is the key to Indian religious experience and to Western scholarly understanding of it. In particular, Pinard criticizes Eck's contention that photographic images provide special entrée into Indian religion, noting "the fact that photographs have no taste or smell or sound" (ibid., 223; see also 230). Citing Appadurai's statement that for Hindus "food, in its physical and moral forms is the cosmos" (ibid., 226), reminding us that Hindu thought understands the universe to be composed of flavors (ibid., 227), and pointing out that the Upanishads call both *atman* and *Brahman* "food" (ibid., 226), Pinard makes a compelling case for eating, including the various stages of digestion, as key to the practice, self-understanding, and scholarly investigation of Hinduism.

Whether a religious studies class centers around a single tradition, a survey of traditions, comparison, a theme, or a period of time, there are appropriate readings that present the topic's sensual dimensions in their intellectual, spiritual, and bodily significance. I make a special effort to have students read these before I show films. Then, in class discussion and written assignments, we alternate between what we have seen and what we have not tasted, smelled, touched, heard, or moved. Whenever possible, I assign students field experiments designed to encourage them to engage the full-body reality of religious meaning in situ and to compare it to the cinematic experience.

Several sources of appropriate short readings for undergraduates are readily available. "Part VII: Sublime Essences" of *The Smell Culture Reader* (Drobnik 2006) offers five short, accessible essays about religion and scent, addressing European Christian, Arab Muslim, South Indian Hindu, and Umeda (West Sepik, New Zealand) cultures, along with an essay about scents associated with one who is recently deceased (371–430). Alain Corbin's "Auditory Markers of the Village" describes how church bells in nineteenth-century Europe (and earlier?) shaped time, space, and community and served to sanctify the space where they were heard; they were even believed to have the power to dispel demons and summon angels (Bull and Back 2003, 123). "Section IV: Body and Soul" of *The Taste Culture Reader* (Korsmeyer 2005) provides six essays appropriate for undergraduate students; they address food and healing in Arabic Islam, mind-cleansing foods used by Hindu saints, the tea ceremony in Japanese Buddhism, fasting and feasting in Moroccan Ramadan, the meaning of foods, tastes, and textures in the Seder meal, and the feast of *el día de los muertes* [day of the dead] in Mexico.

In addition to thinking about what texts can tell us about sensual religion and contrasting these sensory domains with the visuality of film, students must develop a critical awareness of the ways movies create an impression of reality.

Looking

Ethnographic films give us a privileged view of religious practices, persons, spaces, buildings, costumes, and so forth. They make us voyeurs and the religions we view spectacles, while "for the participants, neither African ritual, nor Hindu architecture, nor Chinese funeral practices, nor the Hajj are primarily visual, nor, for that matter, are Eucharist, Baptism, or the procession of the Torah Scroll" (Carp 2007, 8).

Documentary film distances us from what we see ("those others, over there") even as it clarifies. Sharp images, crisp editing, and authoritative voiceovers help us to feel that "this is the way it is." "Knowledge is presented as readily apparent—all one has to do is look" (Classen 2005, 5). In contrast, terms for knowledge based in other senses reveal tensions inherent in coming to know (ibid.; Bull and Back 2003, 3). The "self-evident" quality of visual knowledge, further reified in film, tends to strengthen the seemingly self-evident, largely visual, categories of race and gender (see Poole 2005; Rony 1996; Feng 2002; Shohat 1991). This is especially troubling when, as is often the case in religious documentaries, those depicted have darker complexions than many students and articulate gender in forms that seem strange and exotic. "The history of ethnographic film is thus a history of the production of Otherness" (Russell 1999, 10).

There is a substantial and growing literature about the pitfalls of visual anthropology and strategies to overcome them, and a number of ethnographic films intentionally work to subvert modernist visuality. There are, for example, Jean Rouch's ethnographic and "ethnofiction" films, which Paul Stoller has likened to Artaud's theater of cruelty, compelling us "to reflect on our latent racism, our repressed sexuality, the taken-for-granted assumptions of our intellectual heritage" (1997, 131). These films are required watching for in-depth study of West African religion or African religion in the New World, but they are of little use for most undergraduate classrooms because of their restricted subject matter and how unsettling they are to watch. Some of Rouch's "descendents," however, make more accessible work (Ginsburg, Abu-Lughod, and Larkin 2002; MacDougall 2006; Russell 1999; Feng 2002; Rony 1996).[8]

Theorists and filmmakers agree that films that challenge modernist visuality make us conscious of "cinematic conventions (designed to assure [sic] legibility, veracity, and authority) . . . [and] work against ethnic commodification, and movies that aspire to transparency of technique promote the conception of ethnic difference" (Feng 2002, 207). Films that help us see our own seeing effect "the displacement of the reader/spectator from the margins of the work toward its center" (MacDougall 2006, 246).

Trinh T. Minh-ha's "Film as Translation: A Net with No Fisherman" (1992) is a wonderful exploration of many of these issues and is accessible to undergraduate students. I like to show her short film, "Reassemblage" (1982), which runs about forty minutes, when we discuss her article.

Trinh is an artist and a filmmaker. Born in Vietnam, she learned English in school and came to the United States in 1970. In "Film as Translation," she meditates on the ambiguities of representation obscured by the filmic conventions of ethnographic and educational films. Trinh believes that in film, as in texts, we are better served by revelations of the creator's point of view and biases and of the limits and conventions of the expressive medium than by the pretense that the camera is neutral and has is no framing eye (and mind) behind it. She insists that making film is doing theory (1992, 122).

"Reassemblage" is a film about women's culture in three adjacent Senegalese societies. Refusing common filmic conventions, including auditory ones of music and voiceover, "Reassemblage" makes us aware of how those conventions are used and hidden in other films. "There is nothing," Trinh writes, "objective in filmmaking. . . . What you often have is a mere abidance by the conventions of documentary practice, which is put forward as the 'objective' way to document other cultures" (ibid., 119).

An undergraduate student recently wrote, "Watching 'Reassemblage' was the most challenging thing we did this semester. [We also read Derrida and Foucault.] It made me uncomfortable because it did not look or sound at all like the films I am used to seeing on the Discovery Channel. I realized how much I take for granted when I watch them, and how easily I believe what they show and say." Watching Trinh's film sensitized this student to the illusion of "empiricism and objectivity conventionally linked to ethnography," engaging her in "the critique of authenticity" (Russell 1999, xi–xii).

"Reassemblage" is explicitly not about religion "in the narrow sense of the term." Trinh shows "people's daily lives," not "the usual focal points of observation for anthropology's fetishistic approach to culture, such as the so-called objects of rites, figures of worship and artifacts, or . . . the ritualistic events and religious practices" (Trinh 1992, 116). This does not mean, however, that "Reassemblage" is devoid of Senegalese religion. Rather, it helps students to consider the oft-repeated comment that for many people religion is primarily a matter of daily life rather than something separate from it.

Once students have read and watched Trinh's work, I ask them to identify the conventions used in the films we watch in class and to write both about the films in their own terms and how their conventions affect their meaning. Students demonstrate surprising sophistication about how media are constructed, once asked to reflect on it. This exercise, sustained throughout a course, produces a growing visual sophistication and a critical visual awareness that complements the critical thinking about written texts most teachers demand (Carp 2007, 8).

Sensing

Finally, of course, we have an opportunity to engage students' whole bodies in the study of religion. Sensual religion is not religion devoid of intellect, removed from theology, separated from ethics, or distinct from spirituality. Rather, engaging in what Stoller (1997) calls sensuous scholarship brings students face to face with the ways in which people think in and through materials and material forms. The readings I suggested earlier reinforce what Larry Sullivan points out: The religion we want to understand is "often transmitted through culturally shaped experiences of the body" (1990, 87). It is not that people have sensory experience on the one side and understandings of it on another; rather, understanding (theology, ethics, spirituality, and so forth) are part and parcel of sensory experience.

Such sensory experiences can be made available in the classroom to some extent, although site visits are more effective. In the classroom, sacred objects, sacred music, and sacred acts are three means of getting outside the visual study of religion to include other sensory realms. For example, I may bring to class a selection from Bach's *Mass in B Minor,* or Vivaldi's *Magnificat,* or a Saivite chant, or a Kuranic hymn and ask students to listen carefully, perhaps with their eyes closed. Alternatively, I may provide a small, sculptural representation of Jesus, or Ganeśa or Guan Yin and ask students to look at and handle them. It is important to remind students that these objects are seldom intended to be used in isolation from special environments, actions, liturgies, or other contexts. There is, of course, the added problem of blasphemy: To the extent that they are sacred, the artifacts and music are defiled by our less-than-sacred use of them. In addition to making students aware of the ambiguities involved in the exercise, it is important to remind them (as well as ourselves) that the same ambiguities apply when we read sacred texts in order to understand the religions to which they belong. Within their religious contexts, sacred texts are holy realities, and reading them is a sacred and devotional activity, not a dispassionate or scholarly one.

In my introduction to world religions class, I require students to visit a religious site (e.g., attend a ritual or ceremony or go to a worship space or visit some other sacred architectural structure), a collection of sacred objects and/or images, or something else dedicated to the conduct (not the study) of religion) and spend at least an hour there. I tell them to observe carefully, using all of their senses and noting how their bodies and their imaginations (including their understandings) are affected, what their experience is, how the site uses their bodies, and anything else that seems significant. I point out that space is olfactory, auditory, and kinesthetic, as well as visual, and I remind them to notice how their experience changes over time. They write up the field experience in a five-page paper and compare it to religion as we have seen it on film. For extra credit, they can return to the site to make a video and then compare and contrast what the video shows with their field observations.

In another class, students spend a week engaging in some form of silent attentiveness (not necessarily "prayer" or "meditation" since we do not enforce religious practice), spaced throughout the day in a manner resembling *salat* (Muslims' obligation to pray five times daily at specified intervals). They consider the effects of this experience on their daily routine and everyday awareness in a daily journal kept for a week, and they compose a summary journal entry at the end of the week. Part of the assignment is to consider how this investigation of Islam compares with textual and filmic investigations we also pursue. After this exercise, we often discuss "how body postures and motor behavior affect attitudes, social perception, and higher-order cognitive operations" (Fuller 2007, 46). We then come full circle, remarking on the body postures and motor behavior that characterize academic pursuits, including watching film, and imagining how they affect academic "higher-order cognitive operations."

Conclusion

Scholars' senses, like every other aspect of our knowledge practices, are inflected by culture. This is doubly a concern in studying religion. First, we altogether miss aspects of religion that fall outside our enculturated sensorium. Second, the people we study often sense the world quite differently from the ways in which we do. This, again, has two implications. First, their experiential worlds and ours are incommensurable; some of what they sense we cannot, and vice versa. Second, their knowledge practices, implicated in their religion and part of our subject of study, rest on and include their enculturated sensorium. Both their worlds of sense and the sense they make of them diverge from ours.

Conventional ethnographic and documentary film participates in the peculiar visuality that characterizes the modernist project by overlooking the worlds of sense they seem to present so vividly. If shown without a critical context, these films obscure as much as they clarify religion and the religions. These films can, however, be an important part of the study of religion when we set them in the dual context of sensorial anthropology and of film as a medium.

NOTES

1. For simplicity, I use either "documentary" or "ethnographic" in this chapter to refer to both genres; at times I simply use "film." I also use "film" as a generic term to refer both to films proper and to videos, which in most classrooms function analogically, though as media they have significant differences (see, e.g., Russell 1999, 313–14).

2. In fact, the techniques used to create authenticity and a sense of reality in documentary film are the same as those used to create realism in fiction films and even in science fiction or fantasy. Thus *King Kong, Lawrence of Arabia, Dances with Wolves,* and *Star Wars,* as well as, for instance, John Ford's Westerns, the Indiana Jones movies, the *Matrix* trilogy, and the *Pirates of the Caribbean* films all participate in "ethnographic" tropes (see Rony 1996; Anderson 2003; Shohat 1996). These same techniques permeate the news as well. (After reading a draft of this chapter, a colleague remarked, "Sounds like PowerPoint, too.") Many of the concerns this chapter raises, then, apply with equal force to the use of fictional film and news in teaching about religion.

3. I use sensation and perception interchangeably in this chapter. There are, of course, numerous out-of-awareness processes that underlie even the simplest acts of noticing anything whatsoever. This, however, is not the place to address the coming-to-awareness of the world. Suffice it to say that culture is evidently involved at every step.

4. I use "we," "the West," and "the Euro-American ecumene" interchangeably. I am of course aware of the problems involved in the use of these concepts, as well as their seeming inescapability. For a concise discussion see Ingold (2000, 6–7).

5. Selective reintroduction of other senses also relies on previous desensualization to provide context and control for the "new" sensory experiences (Howes 2005, 281–303).

6. This visuality has a gendered aspect, and its appearance is connected to familiar dyads such as male/female, mind/body, and seeing/feeling, but there is more to it as well. Elucidating these many strands is beyond the scope of this chapter.

7. The question of film's effect on other cultures is a complex and interesting question that is beyond the scope of this chapter.

8. This includes indigenous filmmakers. Some of their films reveal alternate visualities, some are propaganda, and some mimic the West, demonstrating what Seremetakis calls "the eye of the Other" (1994, 8).

REFERENCES

Anderson, Kevin Taylor. 2003. "Toward an Anarchy of Imagery: Questioning the Categorization of Films as 'Ethnographic.'" *Journal of Film and Video* 55(2–3): 73–87.

Bull, Michael, and Les Back, eds. 2003. *The Auditory Culture Reader.* New York: Berg.

Carp, Richard. 1997. "Perception and Material Culture: Historical and Cross-cultural Perspectives." *Historical Reflections/Réflexions Historiques* 23(3): 269–300.

———. 2007. "Teaching Religion and Material Culture." *Teaching Theology and Religion* 10(1): 2–12.

Classen, Constance, ed. 2005. *The Book of Touch.* New York: Berg.

———. 1998. *The Color of Angels: Cosmology, Gender, and the Aesthetic Imagination.* New York: Routledge.

————. 1993. *Worlds of Sense: Exploring the Senses in History and across Cultures.* New York: Routledge.

————, David Howes, and Anthony Synnott. 1994. *Aroma: The Cultural History of Smell.* New York: Routledge.

Drobnick, Jim, ed. 2006. *The Smell Culture Reader.* New York: Berg.

Eck, Diana L. 1998. *Darśan: Seeing the Divine Image in India,* 3d ed. New York: Columbia University Press.

Feng, Peter X. 2002. *Identities in Motion: Asian American Film and Video.* Durham, N.C.: Duke University Press.

Fuller, Robert C. 2007. "Spirituality in the Flesh: The Role of Discrete Emotions in Religious Life." *Journal of the American Academy of Religion* 75(1): 25–51.

Ginsberg, Faye D., Lila Abu-Lughod, and Brian Larkin. 2002. *Media Worlds: Anthropology on New Terrain.* Berkeley: University of California Press.

Hall, Edward T. 1969. *The Hidden Dimension.* New York: Doubleday.

Howes, David, ed. 2005. *Empire of the Senses: The Sensual Culture Reader.* New York: Berg.

————, ed. 1991. *The Varieties of Sensory Experience: A Sourcebook in the Anthropology of the Senses.* Toronto: University of Toronto Press.

Ingold, Tim. *The Perception of the Environment: Essays in Livelihood, Dwelling and Skill.* New York: Routledge.

Korsmeyer, Caroline, ed. 2005. *The Taste Culture Reader.* New York: Berg.

MacDougall, David. 2006. *Film, Ethnography, and the Senses: The Corporeal Image.* Princeton, N.J.: Princeton University Press.

Plate, S. Brent. 2002. *Religion, Art, and Visual Culture: A Cross-cultural Reader.* New York: Palgrave.

Poole, Deborah. 2005. "An Excess of Description: Ethnography, Race, and Visual Technologies." *Annual Review of Anthropology* 34: 159–79.

Romanyshyn, Robert. 1989. *Technology as Symptom and Dream.* London: Routledge.

Rony, Fatimah Tobing. 1996. *The Third Eye: Race, Cinema, and Ethnographic Spectacle.* Durham, N.C.: Duke University Press.

Russell, Catherine. 1999. *Experimental Ethnography.* Durham, N.C.: Duke University Press.

Seremetakis, C. Nadia, ed. 1994. *The Senses Still: Perception and Memory as Material Culture.* Chicago: University of Chicago Press.

Shohat, Ella. 1996. "Gender and Culture of Empire: Toward a Feminist Ethnography of Cinema." *Quarterly Review of Film and Video* 12(1–3): 45–84.

Stoller, Paul. 1997. *Sensuous Scholarship.* Philadelphia: University of Pennsylvania Press.

Sullivan, Lawrence E. 1990. "Body Works: Knowledge of the Body in the Study of Religion." *History of Religions* 30(1): 86–99.

Trinh, T. Minh-ha. 1992. "Film as Translation: A Net with No Fisherman." In *Framer Framed,* by Trinh T. Minh-ha, 111–33. New York: Routledge.

II

There Is No Spoon? Teaching *The Matrix*, Postperennialism, and the Spiritual Logic of Late Capitalism

Gregory Grieve

Do not try to bend the spoon. That is impossible.
Instead, only try to realize the truth . . . that there is
no spoon. Then you will see that it is not the spoon
that bends but only yourself.
— Spoon Boy (01:11:23–01:12:23 [70])

Written and directed by Larry Wachowski and Andy Wachowski, *The Matrix* (1999)[1] welcomes us to "the desert of the real": a dystopic future in which (for most of humanity) the perceived world is the "matrix"—a simulated hyperreality created by sentient machines who control the human population.[2] For those select few who have been freed by the "red pill," the real world is a postapocalyptic wasteland of ruined cities and sunless skies. It has been argued that the film alludes to many philosophical and religious systems: Advaita Hinduism, Buddhism, gnosticism, Judaism, Kantianism, Dostoevsky's nihilism, Sartre's existentialism, and Platonic idealism.[3] The case has also been made that the film's foregrounding of awakening is a treatise on empiricist skeptic ontology and an example of the Buddhist concept of emptiness and even indicates a Christian gnostic cosmology.[4] Yet there is little in the film to raise Bishop Berkeley's ghost; the *Matrix*'s epistemology is closer to Platonism than it is to the Buddhist concept of *sunyata,* and the gnosis achieved has more to do with Emersonian voluntarism than with the *pleroma.*[5]

Because no direct relationship exists between traditional religious systems and *The Matrix,* it would be easy to dismiss the film's spiritual elements as shallow quackery used only to legitimize extreme wire-fu martial arts action and digital eye candy. As film critic Todd McCarthy writes, "It's Special Effects 10, Screenplay 0 for 'The Matrix,' an eye-opening but incoherent extravaganza of morphing and superhuman martial arts" (*Daily Variety*, March 29, 1999). In such a case, one could argue that the film does not *discuss* religion but rather *uses* religious imagery to create a "popular metaphysics" to support "the best action scenes and the coolest computer graphics ever."[6] However, as *The Matrix*'s editor, Zach Staenberg, maintains, the film's visual effects are not "razzle-dazzle . . . but conceptual tools, which the [Wachowski] brothers use to move ahead the story."[7] As the Wachowskis themselves point out, *The Matrix* is about "mythology, theology, and to a lesser extent, higher-level mathematics. . . . All are ways human beings try to answer bigger questions, as well as the Big Question."[8]

Yet, what is the film's big question? In the "Oracle's apartment" scene the protagonist, Neo (Keanu Reaves), goes to learn his spiritual fate. Is he the One? Or is he just another human battery? Before he can consult with the Oracle (Gloria Foster), however, Neo is left in a waiting room with a half-dozen children with paranormal powers (1:10:57–1:12:23 [69–70]).[9] Two girls levitate alphabet blocks as they watch a television program about giant white rabbits. A second boy reads from an ancient Chinese book. Another child, a skinny boy with a shaved head and dressed in Gandiesque clothing, meditates in front of a pile of twisted spoons. Neo walks across the room and sits next to him. The boy holds a spoon in his hand and uses his telekinetic power to cause it to sway back and forth like a blade of grass. The boy hands Neo the spoon and calmly states: "Do not try to bend the spoon. That is impossible. Instead, only try to realize the truth . . . that there is no spoon. Then you will see that it is not the spoon that bends but only yourself" (01:11:23–01:12:23 [70]).

Many have interpreted *The Matrix*'s "no spoon" message as an updated version of Descartes' epistemological skeptical conundrum (the brain-in-the-vat question: "How do you know that you are not dreaming?"[10]) or an onto-logical investigation into "what is really real." As the Spoon Boy's statement indicates, however, *The Matrix* is less about epistemological or ontological questions and more about spiritual emancipation.[11] For instance, in the film, after Neo opens his door and hands the cyperpunk character, Choi, a com-puter program, he exclaims, "Hallelujah! You are my Savior, man! My own personal Jesus Christ!" (8:33–8:44 [10]). Precisely from what, however, is the audience being saved? Many have contended that *The Matrix*'s message is about salvation from the ideology of the simulated reality of late capitalism. As Read Mercer Schuchardt writes in "What Is the Matrix?" it is "a new testament for a new millennium, a religious parable of the second coming of mankind's messiah in an age that needs salvation as desperately as any ever has."[12]

What spiritual logic is employed here? Unlike films such as Mel Gibson's *The Passion of the Christ* (2004), which reach back to premodern religious logics for emancipation from contemporary society, *The Matrix* relies on the religious logic of "postperennialism." I coin this term to cover that broad spectrum of alternative spiritualities "from Jungian-based paganism to eco-logically sound yuppie entrepreneurship"[13] that have been called postmodern religions and, more specifically, consumer religions.[14] What postperennialists have in common is that their religious practice is based on the logic of late capitalism, which, as Fredric Jameson writes in *Postmodernism, or, the Cultural Logic of Late Capitalism*, is "a new depthlessness . . . a consequent weakening of historicity . . . a return to older theories of the sublime . . . which is itself a figure for a whole new economic world system . . . in the bewildering new world space of late or multinational capital."[15] In action, postperennialists pursue their spirituality through the consumption of consumer goods—from angel cards to Wiccan craft supplies.[16] In theory, postperennialists approach salvation through the postmodern skeptical ethic that "there is no spoon." That is, since all systems are ideological cages, one cannot change the cage, and one can therefore spiritually develop only oneself. Structurally, postperennialism has three chief beliefs: (1) that the universe is integrated and monistic; (2) that the purpose of life is personal spiritual growth; and (3) that because authentic spirituality is not limited to any one tradition: one's personal religious practice should be assembled from all of the planet's faiths.

This chapter aims to help students understand the ideology of *The Matrix*, in particular the ideological relation between postperennialism and late capi-talism. I pursue this goal through three main lines of analysis. First is for the student to analyze how *The Matrix* is a product of and a response to the culture of late capitalism. Second is to use the film to decode postperennialism's skeptical ideology of the self and to illustrate for students how a "no-spoon" ethic naturalizes the individual. Third is to describe the late capitalistic eco-nomic conditions that brought about the need for postperennialism. What I am particularly interested in is fostering in students an understanding that while many might argue that postperennialism is "constructed," "inauthentic," and a form of colonialism, it is still a real expression of particular material realities. That is, as Karl Marx writes, because religion stems from economic and social injustices, "*Religious* suffering is, at one and the same time, the *expression* of real suffering and a *protest* against real suffering."[17]

Goal 1—What Is the Matrix? The Culture Industry as the System of Late-Capitalistic Ideology

It's the question that drives us, the question that brought you here. You know the question just as I did.
        —Trinity (Carrie-Anne Moss; 11:26–11:39 [13])

The question that drives *The Matrix* is, what happens when alienated, medi-ated existence completely replaces an "unplugged" existence? When, in our globalized technological age, are we no longer even able to discern that we have lost touch with reality? The idea of media as a form of social control is epitomized by Guy Debord and the Situationist International. For Debord, the world we live in is unreal because "the spectacle *holds up to view* the world of the commodity dominating all lived experience."[18] What has occurred in contemporary society, he argues, is that consumer capitalism has taken away authentic human experience and transformed all of life into a commodity that it then sells back to us: "Reality emerges within the spectacle, and the spectacle is real. This reciprocal alienation is the essence and support of the existing society."[19]

What is the relationship between the spectacle and *The Matrix*? The word "matrix" can refer to a womb, a tubular representation of data, or a mold.[20] In the language of the Internet, the matrix is "a superset of the Internet that includes all networks and computers that can exchange email."[21] In the film, the matrix is depicted as a downward "digital rain" of fuzzy neon-green CRT character code.[22] The matrix is also represented audibly by a "modem mantra," the squeal of the carrier signal used on early modems.[23] Both the visual and audio representations of the matrix are used throughout the film. Visually, for instance, when Neo first goes to meet Apoc, Switch, and Trinity, he sees rain pouring on the window like cascading code (22:40–25:15 [23–26]). Also, throughout the film, the scenes inside the matrix have a predominately money-green tinge, the "real" world—or "meatspace"—of humans is emphasized by blue, while the world of the machines, such as the city 01 and the power plants, is overwhelmingly red. Audibly, as we move closer and closer to the matrix's cascading green characters, the hum turns into an ominous roar.

In the film, the matrix is a simulated virtual environment created by a malevolent Artificial Intelligence to enchain the human race. As Morpheus (Laurence Fishburne) explains, "The Matrix is a system, Neo, and that system is our enemy" (57:03–57:11 [53]). As Morpheus tells Neo earlier, it hides the truth, "that you are a slave ... [and that] like everyone else, you were born into bondage, kept inside a prison that you cannot smell, taste, or touch. A prison for your mind" (28:14–28:30 [30]). In the film, the matrix is ubiquitous and nearly undetectable. As Morpheus states earlier, "The Matrix is everywhere. It's all around us, here even in this room. You can see it out your window or on your television. You feel it when you go to work or go to church or pay your taxes. It is the world that has been pulled over your eyes to blind you from the truth" (27:46–28:13 [29]).

This plugged-in existence is malevolent because it keeps humans from being free. As Morpheus bluntly puts it, "What is the Matrix? Control." The matrix is even more dangerous because it is so comfortable and familiar that people will fight to maintain it. As Cypher (Joe Pantoliano) declares through a virtual piece of scrumptious steak, "Ignorance is bliss" (1:04:16 [61]). Accordingly, as Morpheus explains to Neo in the "training program," "until we [free people], these people are still a part of the system and that makes them our enemy" (57:13–57:23 [53]). But what is the system? As many scholars have shown, *The Matrix* is a metaphor for the system of technological globalized society come to full and horrifying but prosaic fruition.[24] In this light, we can understand the film's constant reference to mediated existence: the Internet, television, and telephones. As Cornel West states in "the philosophers'" commentary of *The Matrix* DVD in the "Ultimate Matrix Collection," the film depicts "a global information system, surveillance" (1:52.00). What is at stake for the directors, according to Larry Wachowski, is that "so much of our reality is our [own] construction based on communication."[25]

The Matrix is alluding to the "culture industry," the alienated-reified social substance of capital—"a computer-generated dream-world built to keep us under control" (43:37–43:44 [42]). The "culture industry" is a term coined by two key members of the Frankfurt School, Theodor Adorno and Max Horkheimer, to describe how the entertainment industry produces popular culture through commodified cultural goods.[26] As critical cultural theorists, these two scholars argue for a shift from nineteenth-century "base structure" capitalism organized around production to a later form of "superstructure" capitalism organized around consumption, media, information, and technology. In this media-driven society new forms of domination and abstraction appear. Through gradual bureaucratization, rationalization, and commodification of all social life, the "culture industry" defuses critical consciousness through distraction and stupefaction. According to Adorno and Horkheimer, the culture industry produces a shallow, homogenous, but safe product and "pollutes" the high arts but is most dangerous because its easily consumable nuggets of entertainment ensnare the masses into the capitalistic system through the creation of "false needs." Like Cypher's steak, which "doesn't exist [but which is] mmmm so goddamn good," the culture industry's "media systems," like imperial Rome's bread and circuses, fill leisure time with amusements to distract consumers from the truth of their real situations.

The Frankfurt School operates from within a modernist critique that attempts to emancipate the masses through the demystification of capitalism's ideological systems. *The Matrix,* however, has a postmodern "no spoon" ethic, which operates as if all systems are ideological, and thus does not agitate for demystification but rather is suspicious of all metanarratives. The film's skeptical postmodern stance is clear, for instance, in the irony of being saved from the control of the matrix only to be awakened as a "battery" in the apocalyptic, ruined real world. This is Neo's fate, when, after taking a red pill, which leads him to the truth, he spasms awake inside a glowing pod. Naked, bald, his body slick with gelatin, Neo is floating in a magenta amnion with tentacle-like tubes the diameter of lawn hoses hooked up to every part of his body. Outside his pod, level after level of identical pods stretch out to the horizon. From above, a machine sizes him up, seizes hold of him, and then violently unhooks the cables. Suddenly, like the opening of a jet's door, Neo is sucked out of his pod and slides down a waste line into the main sewer. Neo struggles in the thick waste and then is plucked up into the belly of a futuristic hovercraft. He finds himself aboard the cramped, cold, submarine-like space of the hovercraft, the *Nebuchadnezzar*. Neo blurrily awakes, and Morpheus whispers, "Welcome to the real world" (35:23 [33]).

Goal II—Postperennialism: A Strategy for Survival in the Desert of the Real

[Y]ou cannot change your cage. You have to change yourself.
                    —Neo (2:08.41 [125])

What is this real world? In *The Matrix*'s "construct" scene, Morpheus asks Neo, "What is real? How do you define real? If you're talking about what you feel, taste, smell, or see, then real is simply electrical signals interpreted by your brain." He goes on to explain to Neo that he has "been living inside a dream world. . . . This is the world as it exists today." Morpheus turns and points off into the distance, where we see the long dead ruins of a city, and he says to Neo, "Welcome to the desert of the real" (40:15–41:16 [39]). Viewers seemed to be offered a dilemma. One can either be blissfully ignorant, a slave to illusionary, Matrix-like master narratives of late capitalism, or one can live skeptically in the ruined posthumanist world.[27] However, *The Matrix* offers the viewer a third path, a guide for spiritual emancipation in the desert of the real. The film ends with a scene that mirrors the opening sequence. The screen is filled with a pulsating cursor. A phone begins to ring, and the screen fills with the trace program. Over the image of the running program, Neo's voice tells us that "to be free, you cannot change your cage. You have to change yourself" (2:08.31–2:08:39 [125]). We dive through the numbers of the trace program and are sucked toward a tight constellation of stars. Neo tells us that "a different world is possible. A world of hope and peace." The stars transition into the holes of a phone's mouthpiece. Neo hangs up the phone, slides on a pair of sunglasses, and then blasts into the sky like a speeding bullet (2:08:41–2:09:17 [124–26]).

What kind of spiritual emancipation does this scene suggest? To articulate the Wachowskis' conception of salvation, we need to return to the "no-spoon" scene in particular, with its multiple, conflicting allusions.[28] On one level, the "no-spoon" statement denotes a famous saying by Zen Buddhist sixth patriarch, Hui Neng. Two monks are arguing about a flag. One says, "The flag is moving." The other says, "The wind is moving." The sixth patriarch happens to be passing by and states: "Not the wind, not the flag; mind is moving."[29]

At the same time, however, the replacement of the flag with a spoon undercuts the implicit authority of this reference to Buddhist koans because the spoon alludes to the trickery of spoon bending, which has become, due to the publicity in the 1970s surrounding magician Uri Geller, a common visual symbol for fraudulent paranormal ability.[30] A similarly playful skeptical "no-spoon" ethic is evident in the packaging of the "director's" commentaries for the DVDs of the "The Ultimate Matrix Collection." The Wachowskis feel that that the best way for fans "to find an answer" to the film's meaning is to offer them two opposing tracks of commentary. The first track is by "the critics," Todd McCarthy and David Thomson, both of whom "kill the film for six hours." The second is by "the philosophers," Cornel West and Ken Wilber, "who enjoyed the film."[31]

As the Wachowskis maintain, "[t]he point," of the juxtaposition between the two tracks, "was not to suggest that one was right and was not." Like the "no-spoon" statement, the juxtaposed tracks are attempts to show that all metanarratives lie and that the curious can "make up their own damn mind."[32] The Wachowskis' position is similar to the postmodern nominalist stance toward any metanarrative: those "global totalizing cultural narrative schemes that order and explain knowledge and experience."[33] In postmodernism, metanarratives depict "master" stories such as Christianity, the Enlightenment, Freudian theories, and Marxism, which are typically characterized by some form of legitimizing transcendent or universal truth. These master stories organize and have authority and thus subordinate petits récits, the multitude of small local narratives. As theorist Jean-François Lyotard argues, the defining condition of postmodernism is in fact "incredulity towards metanarratives."[34] In a similar fashion, the Wachowskis believe that since all systems are, in the end, simply another bad choice, one must change oneself.[35] In The Matrix they demonstrate this postmodern skepticism by making the "meatspace" of Zion not a spiritual Shangri-La but a dystopic, ruined, postapocalyptic world. As Sarah Worth writes in "The Paradox of Real Response to Neo-Fiction," "The Matrix suggests the 'real' reality is much worse than the illusion we live in."[36]

The most developed version of such postmodern religions is the "integral thought movement," which seeks to go beyond the dogmas of both science and religion in order to form a spiritual understanding of the evolving relationship between humans and the universe.[37] That the Wachowskis are knowledgeable of at least the basics of integral thought is clear because they invited Ken Wilber, a prominent spokesperson for the integral thought movement, to be on "the philosophers'" commentary of The Matrix DVD in the "Ultimate Matrix Collection." Moreover, Larry Wachowski has read Wilber's Sex, Ecology, Spirituality.[38] Wilber follows what he calls neoperennial philosophy, which argues for a type of cosmic evolution through the unfolding of the "great chain of being."[39] He argues that individuals play a direct part in this process of spiritual growth and that all authentic religions are ultimately the same and can be mapped out through an "Integral post-metaphysics."[40]

At first blush, it may seem that the emancipation that The Matrix advocates consists of this: If you cleanse your mind of all metanarratives, you will be set free. In perennial liberation strategies, if one wipes the mind clean of all culturally constructed systems, what remains is a perception of the true underlying reality. In The Matrix, the spiritual notion of "cleansing" can be traced to Aldous Huxley's short book The Doors of Perception. The book's title stems from a quote from William Blake's A Marriage of Heaven and Hell: "If the doors of perception were cleansed every thing would appear to man as it is, infinite."[41] The Doors of Perception is a detailed theorizing of Huxley's experience of mescaline, in which he argues that reality can be perceived only when we disintegrate the "cosy [sic] world of symbols." That the Wachowskis are familiar with The Doors of Perception is clear. In the scene in Neo's apartment, after the protagonist opens the door for the cyperpunk Choi, Neo asks, "You ever have the feeling that you're not sure if you're awake or still dreaming?" Choi answers, "All the time. It's called mescaline and it's is the only way to fly" (9:00–9:09 [11]).

The notion that, if one "cleansed one's perception" of all metanarratives, what would remain would be the ultimate truth stems from Huxley's "perennial philosophy," a term Huxley uses to designate a common, eternal set of beliefs—especially in contemplative and esoteric mystical practices—underlying all religions. While the term was used as early as the sixteenth century, perennial philosophy was not popularized until 1944 by Huxley's book *The Perennial Philosophy*. Huxley argues that all humans possess a capacity for intuitive perceptions of ultimate or absolute truth and that this perception is the final goal of human beings; in addition, its pursuit marks the core of all authentic religious practice. Accordingly, Huxley argues that if one jettisons religions' external trappings—what Max Müller has dismissed as "genuflections and candlesticks"—all religions are ultimately the same.

The difference between Huxley's perennialism and what I am calling postperennialism, however, is that Huxley still mystically argues for an ultimate reality beyond all humanly constructed cultures. Structurally, this is a stance similar to that of the Frankfurt School, which argues for a nonalienated level of cultural production. Following Vedantic Hinduism, Huxley argues that "that art thou," that our individual Atman is in reality the greater world soul of the Brahman.[42] He writes, "Divining the One within and beyond the many, we find an intrinsic plausibility in any explanation of the diverse in terms of a single principle."[43] On the other hand, *The Matrix*'s "red pill" stance is actually closer to the liquefying logic of capitalism, especially late capitalism. As Marx writes, "all fixed, fast frozen relations, with their train of ancient and venerable prejudices and opinions, are swept away, all new-formed ones become antiquated before they can ossify. All that is solid melts into air, all that is holy is profaned."[44] As in late-capitalistic society, in postperennialism, since all social structures are leveled, all that is left is the lone reified individual—no longer trapped in Weber's iron cage but quagmired in an infinite swamp of convenient but empty commodities, all available at the click of a mouse. As Larry Wachowski comments in a conversation with Ken Wilber, "This is very complicated, but essentially the Hegelian idea that the development of everything is leading towards the singularity of the individual, right?"[45]

While an almost infinite number of groups fit under the category of postperennialists—from the joke religion of discordianism to the ultraorthodox Gardnerian Wiccans—all share three basic elements.[46] First is the notion that the universe is integrated and monistic. That is, as integral philosopher Ken Wilber argues, everything in the universe is part of the "Great Holarchy of Being," and the core of the great contemplative religious traditions is the spiritual quest to become conscious of this fact.[47] Much like Wilber's vision of the universe, in the film the monistic nature of reality is demonstrated by the matrix's code itself—the neon-green alphanumeric data cascading down the screen. In the matrix everything is a code, all reality is merely the arrangement of computer instructions, and one of the powers that Neo receives as he proceeds along his spiritual journey is the ability to see the underlying grid of reality. For instance, after Neo has been brought back to life by Trinity's kiss, he is able to see through the curtain of the matrix: "For a moment, the walls, the floor, even the agents become a rushing stream of code" (2:05:26–2:05:38 [122]).

Second, for postperennialists, because all systems are cages, what remains constant across all traditions is the individual self, which is held to be the perfect, natural source of all things that are good. This is similar to capitalism's "elementary ideological effect," which reduces all social relations to the individual in order to make it appear obvious that people are autonomous selves who are possessed of a unique subjectivity that is the source of their actions and beliefs.[48] Much like perennialism, integral thought maintains that contemplative mystical practices are at the heart of all religions. As the authors of *God and the Evolving Universe* maintain, "[s]uch devotion, called *bhakti yoga* by Hindus is fundamental to Christian contemplative life, as well as to Jewish and Islamic mysticism."

Yet, unlike perennial practices, integral thought does not want to wipe away our everyday habits but "give us more command of habitual behaviors, promote access to our spiritual depths, and begin to reveal our deepest self within all mental and physical events."[49] Historically, one can see the relation between postperennialism and the ideology of late capitalism. As Paul Heelas maintains, "[i]n tandem with the triumphalist capitalism, which developed during the 1980s, increasing numbers of avowed New Agers have become active in the world of business."[50] Or from an emic perspective, Phil Laut, author of *Money Is My Friend,* argues, "the more spiritual you are, the more you deserve prosperity."[51] As such, the postperennialist practices that naturalize the individual self are radically different from traditional Asian wisdom traditions, whose practices are meant to overcome an attachment to the self, not to reify it.[52]

Reflecting the ideology of the self, the purpose of postperennialism is to pursue personal growth. In *The Matrix,* that spirituality is about personal growth is seen through Neo's transformation into the One. As the Oracle says to Neo, after he has decided that he is not the One, "Sorry, kid. You got the gift, but it looks like you're waiting for something" (1:15:10–1:15:18 [73]). What Neo is waiting for is to believe in himself. For example, when Neo finally starts to overcome the agents, Morpheus says, "He's beginning to believe" (1:51:32 [112]). Such emphasis on personal growth leads to what Paul Heelas calls "self-religiosity," the belief that authentic religion is the language of the heart; furthermore, what a particular religious tradition says is neither orthodox nor the academic "exact truth."[53] Instead, for postperennialists, authentic religious practice is what makes your self feel "integrated."[54] That is, in what Steven Tipton calls the "expressive ethic," all dogmas and other encoded moralities of traditional religiosity count for nothing, and one should accept as genuine only what rings true to one's own inner self.[55] As Trinity says to Neo before he sees the Oracle, "the Matrix cannot tell you who you are" (1:08:43 [65]).

The third basic postperennialist belief is that authentic spirituality is not limited to any one tradition. Instead, each individual's personal religious practice should be assembled—like a trip through the supermarket—from those religious myths, practices, and symbols that work best for oneself. Ken Wilber calls the reliance on one tradition the "monological mode" and compares it disfavorably to the "translogical," which seeks a nondual gnosis in the authentic core of all traditions.[56] As Adam Possamai argues, this leads to religious bricolage à la carte, "in which people no longer accept religious 'set menus' offered by traditional religions" but are more interested in constructing personal subjective mythologies.[57] The cultural buffet is clear in how the Wachowski brothers borrow from many religious traditions. In an interactive Internet chat, on November 6, 1999, a participant asked the Wachowskis, "Your movie has many and varied connections to myths and philosophies, Judeo-Christian, Egyptian, Arthurian, and Platonic, just to name those I've noticed. How much of that was intentional?" The Wachowskis answered, "All of it."[58]

Goal III—Postperennialism and the Late-Capitalistic Mode of Production

The handmill gives you society with the feudal lord; the steam mill, society with the industrial capitalist.
               —Karl Marx, The Poverty of Philosophy

If the question *The Matrix* asks is what happens when alienated, mediated existence completely replaces an "unplugged" existence and the reality that the film illustrates is a ruined world of technological domination, then the historical condition that makes this possible is late capitalism. Fredrick Jameson argues in *Postmodernism, or, the Cultural Logic of Late Capitalism* that we are living in an age of simulacrum in which "the very memory of use value is effaced."[59] Jameson's description of contemporary society is similar to that of Jean Baudrillard, who maintains that in our late-capitalist society, reality has been replaced with symbols and signs—we live in a postmodern world in which the real territory has eroded and been replaced by a map of simulated images. According to Baudrillard (and not unlike Debord's Society of the Spectacle), in contemporary life, the signs that the media system controls are all one can know, and therefore all we think and feel is actually a simulation of reality. This prison of virtual reality is what the Wachowskis have in mind for the matrix. When Neo is visited at his apartment by cyberpunks in need of digitized information, he reaches inside a hollowed-out copy of Baudrillard's *Simulations and Simulacra*.[60] The phrase "desert of the real" (discussed earlier) was also inspired by Baudrillard.[61] The reference to *Simulations* is even clearer if we look at the 1997 draft of the screenplay. As in the earlier citation, the Wachowskis had inserted the following into Morpheus's monologue: "As in Baudrillard's vision, your whole life has been spent inside the map, not the territory."[62]

Our simulated lives, however, are neither something that appeared magically nor something that humanity consciously willed into existence. Instead, as Karl Marx writes in *A Contribution to the Critique of Political Economy:*

> In the social production which men carry on they enter into definite relations that are indispensable and independent of their will ... [t]he mode of production of material life conditions the general character of the social, political and spiritual processes of life. It is not the consciousness of men that determines their existence, but, on the contrary, their social existence determines their consciousness.[63]

How did we enter into this condition of postmodernity? When did it start?[64] In his work *Late Capitalism,* Ernest Mandel argues for three "long waves" in the development of capitalism.[65] First is market capitalism, which occurred from 1700 to 1850 and is characterized largely by the growth of industrial capital in domestic markets. Second is monopoly capitalism, which lasted until approximately the late 1960s and is characterized by the imperialistic development of international markets, as well as the exploitation of colonial territories. Third is late capitalism, which displays features such as Western deindustrialization, suburbanization, and a dramatic increase in flexible capital accumulation that leads to multinational corporations, globalized markets, and labor.[66] Fredric Jameson argues that the postmodern turn toward the ultimate reality of pessimism stems from the conditions of intellectual labor imposed by the late-capitalist mode of production.[67] He maintains that postmodernism's merging of all discourses into an undifferentiated whole is the result of globalized corporate capital's colonization of the entire cultural sphere.[68] As in the matrix, from almost any point on the planet and through a network of constantly changing liquid nodes, each of us is a human battery whose very life powers the late-capitalistic system of shifting, increasingly flexible corporate structures of accumulation and modes of consumption.

Taking Marx's argument that religious practice, along with other aspects of culture, reflects the historical mode of production, each of these periods of capital produces a different characteristic dominant religious form. As Max Weber has argued, market capitalism stemmed from the iron cage of Protestant, rule-based, rational control of the world, which tore individuals away from the premodern enchanted world.[69] In *The Protestant Ethic and the Spirit of Capitalism,* Weber writes that, for the Puritans, "no trust in the effects of magical and sacramental forces on salvation should creep in."[70] With the dominance of capital and the consequent increase in imperial British power, perennialism—as the Protestanization of other religions from colonized regions—became the dominant religious mode. As Georg Simmel argues, this period witnessed the emergence of a "post-Christian religiosity."[71] However, in the same way that European culture was used to structure the content of non-Western cultures, it was an idealized Protestantism that provided the underlying organizational structure of the world's religions.

With the shift to late capitalism, the most obvious aspect is that the logic of the marketplace has been extended into all facets of culture. Like Debord's Society of the Spectacle, all life has been repackaged for sale. Comparing such consumption to Max Weber's concept of bureaucratization, George Ritzer has described it as McDonaldization, "the process by which the principles of the fast-food restaurant are coming to dominate more and more sectors of American society as well as the world."[72] In this hypercapitalistic McWorld, there is a general loss of faith in any grand narrative, and people suffer intense feelings of fragmentation, pluralism, and dissolving that mirrors the bewildering diversification in the liquid modernity of contemporary consumer society itself. As Zygmunt Bauman writes, the " 'Liquid modern' is a society in which the conditions under which its members act change faster than it takes the ways of acting to consolidate into habits and routines."[73] The "no-spoon" ethic that *The Matrix* and other postperennialist texts profess is a hyper-Protestantized strategy for allowing the "individual" to survive in this desert of the real. The symptom that postperennialism alleviates is the late-capitalist alienation created by the totalizing global system that melts any permanent social identity. As Jean Baudrillard writes in *America*, "you are delivered from all depth . . . a brilliant, mobile, superficial neutrality . . . an outer hyperspace, with no origin, no reference-points."[74]

Conclusion: The Red Pill as Poison or Cure?

There is no spoon.
—Neo *(1:45:36 [102])*

Near the conclusion of *The Matrix*, in order for the machines to learn the encrypted codes to the mainframe of Zion and thereby destroy the last remaining free human city, Agent Smith (Hugo Weaving) attempts to break Morpheus's mind. To save their leader, Neo and Trinity return to the matrix and storm the military-controlled government building in which Morpheus is imprisoned. After an intense fight scene, Neo and Trinity are precariously suspended above an elevator shaft. Neo looks down the long, dark throat of the shaft, takes a deep breath, and says, "There is no spoon." He whips out his gun and shoots the cable. The counterweight plummets, yanking them upward. The elevator falls away beneath them and hits the bottom, spreading out a massive wave of flame (1:41:05–1:45:36 [101–102]).

Read Mercher Schuchardt writes, "many people watching *The Matrix* see only the 'content' . . . while missing the serious sermon."[75] What is the film's sermon? What is the big question the Wachowski brothers are asking? They are infamously silent about this and refuse to comment on the film's ultimate meanings. As Larry Wachowski states, "you don't want [the audience] to rely on somebody to tell them what it is, or . . . it's like, the whole nature of the movie is exactly that . . . inspect it and pursue it yourself."[76] Yet, just because the Wachowskis are reticent about the meaning of their film does not mean that *The Matrix* does not have an ideology. As Louis Giannetti writes, "every film has a slant, a given ideological perspective that privileges certain characters, institutions, behaviors and motives."[77]

In this chapter I have demonstrated that *The Matrix* is a sermon in postperennialism, that wide spectrum of alternative spiritualities that displays the religious logic of late capitalism. As I have shown, postperennialists pursue their spirituality through the consumption of consumer goods, believe that the universe is integrated and monistic, have faith that the purpose of life is personal spiritual growth, and act as if authentic spirituality should be assembled from all possible religious traditions. Pedagogically, an instructor of religion and film can use *The Matrix* to illustrate the culture of late capitalism and its relation to postperennialism's skeptical "no-spoon" ethic, which justifies the colonization of others' traditions through the naturalization of the "individual." However, the most important question to pose to the students is whether the Wachowskis' sermon, the ideological stance of postperennialism, should be considered a cure or poison. Does swallowing the red pill heal the liquid life of late capitalistic existence? To compare and continue the pharmaceutical metaphors, is *The Matrix* a cinematic dose of Huxley's mescaline, which awakens the viewers by cleansing our doors of perception, or is it Marx's opium, which relieves the symptoms of suffering but only deepens the actual causes?[78]

For Neo, dangling perilously from the elevator's cable, the pondering of the late capitalistic koan, "there is no spoon," gives him the courage to excel within the world of the matrix. What the "no-spoon" religious logic creates is faith in oneself, which is necessary because the modern liquid-life logic of late capitalism has all but dissolved all other social forms. As such, one could argue that postperennialism is the ideal salve or, to continue the pharmaceutical metaphor, the perfect OxyContin for a late-capitalistic, postmodern society. Yet, because its practices consist of the consumption of commodities in the form of products, services, and experiences, postperennialism is not opposed to late capitalism but rather hides a liquid-modern wolf in the sheep's clothing of other traditions.[79] Such spiritual repackaging might take the form of the appropriation of indigenous cultures, historical periods, or popular culture.[80] Using this spiritual logic, practitioners describe their spirituality as a unique, personalized collage that consists of bits and pieces of a seemingly infinite number of religious traditions.[81]

Yet, as one of my students skeptically asked the last time I taught Marx, "If you are in pain, what is wrong with opium?" If we take a step back and reflect meaningfully on this question, we see that, although opium relieves pain, it causes hallucinations, stupor, addiction, and ultimately acceptance of suffering. Accordingly, in Marx's use of the metaphor, religious practices relieve the symptoms but do not eliminate the cause. Still, just as the pain that opiates relieve is real, the distress that postperennialism relieves is also real. Like Neo, dangling precariously from a disintegrating lifeline, the inhabitants of late capitalism need all of the resources they can muster so as not to be crushed under the cresting wave of liquid modernity. Nevertheless, postperennialism is not an alternative to, or even an escape from, late capitalism but rather a strategy to manage its alienating effects. That is, postperennialism does not clear culture away so as to free perception; instead, through cultural strip-mining, consumes cultures and repackages them into bite-sized nuggets of personal mythology. Postperennialism is not an alternative to late capitalism but a reification of the globalized, consuming self. In fact, *The Matrix* leaves unquestioned the very thing that is most in need of problemitizing in late-capitalistic society. That is, it reifies an individual bounded Self and the illusion of freedom that it entails. Rather than being liberated, postperennialism makes the commodification of life and the corporate colonization of life just a little less painful.

Acknowledgments

I would like to thank Jane Iwamura for the chapter's original inspiration, Ben Ramsey for advice along the way, and the National University of Singapore Asia Research Centre Globalized Religion Cluster for the fellowship that allowed the time to write the final version. I would also like to acknowledge Sarah Krive for her crucial suggestions.

NOTES

1. My interpretation is based upon the original *The Matrix* (1999), DVD (Warner Bros., 2001); the section of the film referred to is indicated by the time signature (e.g., 1:10:57–1:12:23). Along with the DVD I employ *The Matrix*'s "numbered shooting script," dated Mar. 29, 1998; the page number of the script follows the time signature (e.g., [69–70]). I also utilize the "Ultimate *Matrix* Collection" (Warner Bros., 2004), which includes *The Matrix Reload* (2003), *The Matrix Revolutions* (2003), *The Animatrix* (2003), and other supplemental discs. In addition to the 1998 script, I refer to the 1996 and 1997 drafts. All of these can be downloaded from http://www.horrorlair.com/movies/the_matrix.html (accessed Nov. 27, 2007). The scripts for *The Matrix Reloaded* and *The Matrix Revolution* are also available on this site.

2. Coproduced by Warner Brothers and the Australian Village Roadshow Pictures, *The Matrix* earned more than $456 million in worldwide sales. The film is the jewel of the *Matrix* franchise, a group of entertainment vehicles that includes the other two films of the trilogy, *The Matrix Reloaded* (2003; 138 min.) and *The Matrix Revolution* (2003; 129 min.), as well as the collection of animated shorts known as *The Animatrix* (2003; 89 min.). Along with the films appeared a number of video games, *Enter the Matrix* (2003), the two MMORPGs (Massively Multiplayer Online Role-playing Games), *The Matrix Online* (2005), and *The Matrix: The Path of Neo* (2005).

3. On Plato see Stephen Faller, *Beyond the Matrix: Revolutions and Revelations* (St. Louis: Chalice Press, 2004), 19. The following works can all be found in *The Matrix and Philosophy: Welcome to the Desert of the Real,* ed. William Erwin (Chicago: Open Court, 2002): On Kant see James Lawler, "We Are (the) One! Kant Explains How to Manipulate the Matrix," 138–52. On Dostoyevsky see Thomas S. Hibbs, "Notes from the Underground: Nihilism and the Matrix," 155–68. On Sartre see Jennifer L. McMahon, "Popping a Bitter Pill: Existential Authenticity in *The Matrix* and *Nausea,*" 166–77. See

Jorge Gracia and Jonathan J. Sanford, "The Metaphysics of *The Matrix*," 55–65. On Socrates see William Irwin, "Computers, Caves, and Oracles: Neo and Socrates," 5–15.

4. For Buddhism see James L. Ford, "Buddhism, Christianity, and *The Matrix*: The Dialectic of Myth-making in Contemporary Cinema," *Journal of Religion and Film* 4(2) (2000) (http://www.unomaha.edu/jrf/thematrix.htm [accessed Nov. 27, 2007]). Ford argues that the film embodies the Yogacara school of Buddhism, which asserts that all things are only mind. Ford also has a later article, "Buddhism, Mythology, and the *Matrix*," in *Taking the Red Pill: Science, Philosophy, and Religion in* The Matrix, ed. David Gerrold (Dallas: Benbella, 2002), 125–44. The problem with Ford's work, however, is that the matrix maintains a duality between the real world and the simulated world, which Yogacara does not. Cf. Hattori Masaaki, "Yogacara," in *The Encyclopedia of Religion* (New York: Macmillan, 1987), vol. 15. Also for Buddhism cf. Read Mercer Schuchardt, "What Is the Matrix?" in *Taking the Red Pill*, ed. Gerrold, 9, 1–21. Michael Brannigan, "There Is No Spoon: A Buddhist Mirror," in *Matrix and Philosophy*, ed. Erwin, 101–10 (Chicago: Open Court, 2002). For Christianity see Chris Seay and Greg Garrett, *The Gospel Reloaded: Exploring Spirituality and Faith in* The Matrix (Colorado Springs: Piñon Press, 2003).

5. See Kelley L. Ross, "There Is No Spoon: *The Matrix*" (http://www.friesian.com/matrix.htm [accessed Nov. 27, 2007]).

6. Richard Corliss, "Popular Metaphysics," *Time* (April 19, 1999) (http://www.time.com/time/magazine/article/0,9171,990761,00.html [accessed Nov. 27, 2007]).

7. Commentary by Carrie-Anne Moss (Trinity), visual effects supervisor John Gaeta, and editor Zach Staenberg. *The Matrix* (original DVD, 1999) (31:23–31:50).

8. See note 6.

9. See note 7.

10. See Lyle Zynda, "Was Cypher Right? Part II. The Nature of Reality and Why It Matters." In *Taking the Red Pill*, ed. Gerrold, 33–43. Gerald Erion and Barry Smith, "Skepticism, Morality, and *The Matrix*," in *Matrix and Philosophy*, ed. Erwin, 16–27.

11. Joseph Heath and Andrew Potter, *The Rebel Sell: Why the Culture Can't Be Jammed* (Toronto: Harper and Collins, 2004).

12. *Taking the Red Pill*, ed. Gerrold, 5.

13. See Daphne Francis, "Crystal Balls," *Trouble and Strife* 22 (Winter): 45–47, cited in Paul Heelas, "The New Age in Cultural Context: The Premodern, the Modern, and the Postmodern," *Religion* 23 (1993): 103.

14. I developed this term from the work of Adam Possamai, especially his article "Alternative Spiritualities and the Cultural Logic of Late Capitalism," *Culture and Religion* 4(1) (2003): 33. Possamai uses the term *Perennism* to differentiate this postmodern religiosity from the perennial philosophy of Aldous Huxley. I use the term *postperennialism* because I do not see a difference so much as a telescoping of perennial philosophy's religious logic. In short, if perennial philosophy is the religious logic of modern capitalism, postperennialism is the religious logic of late capitalism.

15. Fredric Jameson, *Postmodernism, or, the Cultural Logic of Late Capitalism* (Durham, N.C.: Duke University Press, 1991).

16. See Magical Gifts New Age and Metaphysical Shop! (http://www.magical-gifts.com/ [accessed Nov. 27, 2007]).

17. Karl Marx, "Introduction to A Contribution to the Critique of Hegel's Philosophy of Right." In *Deutsch-Französische Jahrbücher* (1844) (http://www.marxists.org/archive/marx/works/1843/critique-hpr/index.htm [accessed Nov. 27, 2007]).

18. Guy Debord, *Society of the Spectacle* (Canberra: Treason Press, 2002), 11 (italics in original).

19. Ibid., 7.

20. Gregory Price Grieve, *Retheorizing Religion in Nepal* (New York: Palgrave Macmillan, 2006), 20.

21. "Matrix" in the *Net Dictionary* (http://www.netdictionary.com/m.html [accessed Nov. 27, 2007]).

22. The cascade includes mirror images of Japanese half-width Katakana characters and Latin letters and numerals. Katakana, used mainly for writing foreign words, is one of the three Japanese writing scripts. In the film, this cascade of data is an homage to the 1995 Japanese anime *Ghost in the Shell* (1995).

23. "Ennnnnnnnnnnnnnnnn ... beepboopbeepbopboopbeepbopboop ... brrrrrr-brrrrrrrrrring ... <click> Screeeeeeeeeeeeeeeeee! SCREEEEEEEEEEEEEEE! Chrunch-BeCrackleBeChrunch." "Modem," in the *Net Dictionary* (http://www.netdictionary.com/m.html [accessed Nov. 27, 2007]).

24. Mercer Schuchardt, "What Is the Matrix?" 13.

25. "The Many Meanings of *The Matrix*—Larry Wachowski and Ken Wilber" (http://www.kenwilber.com/blog/show/230 [accessed Nov. 27, 2007]).

26. Theodor Adorno and Max Horkheimer, *Dialectic of Enlightenment* (Stanford, Calif.: Stanford University Press, 2002).

27. See Slavoj Žižek, *Welcome to the Desert of the Real!: Five Essays on September 11 and Related Dates* (New York: Verso, 2002).

28. On a critique of the idea that films such as *The Matrix* are liberating see Heath and Potter, *Rebel Sell*.

29. "Case 29: Not the Wind, Not the Flag," in *Mumonkan*. The *Mumonkan* is a collection of forty-eight koans, compiled and provided with commentaries and verses by Mumon Ekai. It was first published in 1228 (http://perso.ens-lyon.fr/eric.boix/Koan/Mumonkan/index.html [accessed Dec. 5, 2007]).

30. H. M. Collins, "Editorial: Uri Geller," *Philosophy* 49(188) (1974): 121. T. J. Pinch, "Private Science and Public Knowledge: The Committee for the Scientific Investigation of the Claims of the Paranormal and Its Use of the Literature," *Social Studies of Science* 14(4) (1984): 521–46. To view a film of Geller's technique see http://www.skepticreport.com/psychicpowers/urispoon.htm (accessed May 14, 2007).

31. Wachowski brothers, "An Introduction from the Wachowski Brothers," in *The Ultimate Matrix Collection* (booklet; Warner Bros. Entertainment Inc., 2004).

32. Ibid.

33. John Stephens and Robyn McCallum, *Retelling Stories, Framing Culture: Traditional Story and Metanarratives in Children's Literature* (New York: Garland, 1998), 17.

34. Jean-François Lyotard, *The Postmodern Condition: A Report on Knowledge* (Minneapolis: University of Minnesota Press, 1984), xxiv.

35. Gregory Bassham approaches the film's religious neopluralism. However, he misses the point because he simply gives up trying to understand it. As he writes, "while fashionable [the film's religion stance] is very difficult to make sense of, or to defend." Gregory Bassham, "The Religion of the Matrix and the Problems of Pluralism," in *Matrix and Philosophy*, ed. Erwin, 125.

36. In *Matrix and Philosophy*, ed. Erwin, 178.

37. See James Redfield, Michael Murphy, and Sylvia Timbers, *God and the Evolving Universe: The Next Step in Human Evolution* (New York: Tarcher, 2003).

38. Ken Wilber, *Sex, Ecology, Spirituality: The Spirit of Evolution* (New York: Shambhala, 1995). Larry Wachowski's reading of the book is mentioned in "The Many

Meanings of the Matrix—Larry Wachowski and Ken Wilber" (http://www.kenwilber .com/blog/show/230 [accessed Nov. 27, 2007]).

39. "The Kosmos according to Ken Wilber: A Dialogue with Robin Kornman" (http://www.shambhalasun.com/index.php?option=com_content&task=view&id= 2059 [accessed Nov. 27, 2007]).

40. Ken Wilber online (http://wilber.shambhala.com/index.cfm/ [accessed Nov. 27, 2007]).

41. Aldous Huxley, *The Perennial Philosophy* (New York: Harper and Brothers, 1945).

42. Ibid., 1–21.

43. Ibid., 5.

44. *Manifesto of the Communist Party* (1848) (http://www.anu.edu.au/polsci/ marx/classics/manifesto.html [accessed May 17, 2007]).

45. See note 25.

46. Gregory Price Grieve, "Imagining a Virtual Religious Community: Neo-pagans on the Internet," *Chicago Anthropology Exchange* 7 (1995): 98–132.

47. Ken Wilber, "The Integral Agenda," in *The Marriage of Sense and Soul: Integrating Science and Religion* (New York: Random House, 1999), 202–14. In the conclusion to *Sex, Ecology, Spirituality* (1995) Wilber writes: "See the Kosmos dance in Emptiness; see the play of light in all creatures great and small; see finite worlds sing and rejoice in the play of the very Divine, floating on a Glory that renders each transparent, flooded by a Joy that refuses time or terror, that undoes the madness of the loveless self and buries it in splendor. Indeed, indeed: Let the self-contraction relax into the empty ground of its own awareness, and let it there quietly die." Ken Wilber online (http://wilber.shambhala.com/index.cfm/ [accessed May 21, 2007]).

48. Louis Althusser, *Lenin and Philosophy and Other Essays* (London: New Left Books, 1971), 161.

49. "Basic Principles of Transformative Practice," on Beliefnet.com (http:// www.beliefnet.com/story/101/story_10100_1.html [accessed Nov. 27, 2007]).

50. "The New Age in Cultural Context: The Premodern, the Modern, and the Postmodern," *Religion* 23 (1993): 106.

51. Paul Laut, *Money Is My Friend* (Cincinnati: Vivation, 1989), 14.

52. Jeremy Carrette and Richard King, *Selling Spirituality: The Silent Takeover of Religion* (London: Routledge, 2004).

53. Paul Heelas, "The New Age in Cultural Context: The Premodern, the Modern, and the Postmodern," *Religion* 23 (1993): 104. See also "Californian Self Religions and Socializing the Subject," in *New Religious Movements: A Perspective for Understanding Society,* ed. Eileen Barker, 69–85 (New York: Mellen Press, 1982); "The Limits of Consumption and Post-modern 'Religion' of the New Age," in *The Authority of the Consumer,* ed. Nicholas Abercrombie and Nigel Whitely, 102–18 (London: Routledge, 1993); "The Sacralization of the Self in New Age Capitalism," in *Social Change in Contemporary Britain,* ed. Nicholas Ambercrombie and Alan Warde, 139–66 (Cambridge, Mass.: Polity, 1992).

54. Marion Bowman, "Reinventing the Celts," *Religion* 23 (1993): 147–56.

55. Steven M. Tipton, *Getting Saved from the Sixties: Moral Meaning in Conversation and Cultural Change* (Berkeley: University of California Press, 1982).

56. Wilber, *Marriage of Sense and Soul,* 36–39.

57. Adam Possamai, "Alternative Spiritualities and the Cultural Logic of Late Capitalism," *Culture and Religion* 4(1) (2003): 35.

58. Matrix Virtual Theater, Wachowski brothers transcript, Nov. 6, 1999 (http://www.warnervideo.com/matrixevents/wachowski.html [accessed May 15, 2007]).

59. Jameson, *Postmodernism*, 18.

60. Originally published as *Simulacres et simulation* (Paris: Galilée, 1981). Available in English as *Simulations* (New York: Semiotext(e), 1983).

61. Baudrillard himself discounts the connection between his philosophy and *The Matrix*. As he states in an interview for *Le Nouvel Observateur*:

> There is a misunderstanding of course, that is the reason why I previously hesitated to talk about *The Matrix*. The Wachowski staff did contact me after the first episode to involve me in the following ones, but that really was not conceivable! [Laugh] What we have here is essentially the same misunderstanding as with the simulationist artists in New York in the '80s. These people take the hypothesis of the virtual as a fact and carry it over to visible fantasms. But the primary characteristic of this universe lies precisely in the inability to use categories of the real to speak about it. (http://www.empyree.org/divers/Matrix-Baudrillard_english.html [accessed Dec. 5, 2007])

62. In the film's 1997 draft the statement continues: "This is Chicago as it exists today . . . The desert of the real. The average temperature in Chicago these days is minus eighty degrees Celsius. Of course, the wind chill makes it feel like minus one-twenty."

63. Karl Marx, *A Contribution to the Critique of Political Economy* (New York: International Publishers, 1970), 389.

64. David Harvey, in *The Condition of Postmodernity: An Enquiry into the Origins of Cultural Change*, argues that the precise space-time for the end of modernity was 3:32 P.M. CST on July 15, 1972, in Saint Louis, Missouri, with the dynamiting of the modernist Pruitt-Igoe housing development (Cambridge, Mass.: Blackwell, 1990, 39). For a sociological study of Pruitt-Igoe see Lee Rainwater, *Behind Ghetto Walls: Black Families in a Federal Slum* (Chicago: Aldine, 1970).

65. Ernest Mandel, *Late Capitalism*, trans. Joris De Bres (London: Humanities Press, 1975).

66. Harvey, *Condition of Postmodernity*.

67. Jameson, *Postmodernism*.

68. Fredric Jameson, "Fear and Loathing in Globalization," *New Left Review* 23 (2003); http://newleftreview.org/A2472 (accessed Dec. 5, 2007).

69. Max Weber, *The Protestant Ethic and the Spirit of Capitalism* (New York: Scribner's, 1958).

70. As Marx writes in *The German Ideology*, "The fact is that social structure and the State are continually evolving out of the life-process of definite individuals as they really are, as they operate and produce materially. The same applies to mental productions like politics, laws, morality, religion, metaphysics, etc. of a people. It is real active men who are the producers of their conceptions" (chap. 4.a.1) (http://marxists.org/archive/marx/works/1845/german-ideology/ch01a.htm [accessed May 15, 2007]).

71. Georg Simmel, "The Crisis of Culture," in *Georg Simmel: Sociologist and European*, trans. Peter Lawrence (New York: Barnes and Noble, 1976), 259.

72. George Ritzer, *The McDonaldization of Society* (New York: Pine Forge, 1993), 1 (cf. "McDonaldization," http://www.mcdonaldization.com/ [accessed Dec. 5, 2007]).

73. Zygmunt Bauman, *Liquid Life* (Malden, Mass.: Polity, 2006), 1.

74. Jean Baudrillard, *America* (London: Verso, 1988), 124. See also pages 1–13, 66–71, and 123–126. Also see *The Gulf War Did Not Take Place* (Bloomington: Indiana University Press, 1995).

75. "What Is the Matrix?" In *Taking the Red Pill*, ed. Gerrold, 10.

76. "The Many Meanings of the Matrix" (http://www.matrixfans.net/symbolism/meanings.php [accessed May 15, 2007]).

77. Louis Giannetti, *Understanding Movies* (Englewood Cliffs, N.J.: Prentice-Hall, 2001).

78. My thoughts on this spring from the essay "Plato's Pharmacy," in which Jacques Derrida argues that the *Phaedrus* hinges on the translation of a single word, *pharmakon*, which in Greek can mean *both* "poison" *and* "cure." In *La dissémination*, trans. Barbara Johnson in *Dissemination* (Chicago: University of Chicago Press, 1981), 63–171.

79. Zygmunt Bauman, "Postmodern Religion?" in *Religion, Modernity, and Postmodernity*, 55–78.

80. D. Cuthbert and M. Grossman, "Trading Places: Locating the Indigenous in the New Age," *Thamyris* 3(1) 1996: 18–36. Anne-Marie Gallager, "Weaving a Tangled Web? Pagan Ethics and Issues of History, 'Race,' and Ethnicity in Pagan Identity," *Diskus* 6 (http://web.uni-marburg.de/religionswissenschaft/journal/diskus/gallagher.html [accessed Dec. 5, 2007]). James Lewis, "Approaches to the Study of the New Age Movement," in *Perspectives on the New Age*, ed. J. Lewis and J. Gordon Melton, 1–13 (New York: State University of New York Press, 1993).

81. Jon Block, *New Spirituality, Self, and Belonging: How New Agers and Neo-pagans Talk* (Westport, Conn.: Praeger, 1998).

12

Teaching *Film as Religion*

John C. Lyden

The insight that led me to write *Film as Religion: Myths, Morals, and Rituals*—that films can be viewed as functioning like religions in culture—was born out of my efforts to teach religion and film courses. I was unhappy with the approaches that simply read Christian theological content into films or set up a simplistic dialogue designed to show the emptiness of the values of popular culture in comparison with historic religious traditions such as Christianity. I found such approaches unable to take the films seriously enough to assess how they were working on audiences, apart from whether they cohere with Christian doctrine. Even as a Christian theologian and professor of religion, I was annoyed at what I perceived as a largely defensive posture in regard to popular culture that failed to see it on its own terms. Certainly, not all theological scholarship on film can be stereotyped in this way, but I have found that when students register for a course on religion and film, they assume that I will take such an approach—in short, that I will simply compare Christianity and popular films. In part this is because of the homogeneous culture of Nebraska, which leaves most of my students, whether religious or not, without any real experience of religious or cultural diversity. "Religion," to them, means conservative Christianity because this is usually all that they have known under that rubric. And although there are Jews, Muslims, and Hindus in cities like Omaha (as well as liberal Christians), they remain invisible to many Nebraskans due to their smaller numbers and a culture that does not encourage interreligious dialogue.

Facing this paucity of religious experience in my students, I sought to enlarge their perspective by pointing out that many of the influences in their lives—such as those of popular culture—have an effect on them that is analogous to the impact of religion. They could better understand what religion is and how it functions by looking at these filmic impressions and learning how to analyze them as religious influences. Doing so would in turn give them a better grasp of film and popular culture. However, I found no books that took this approach; hence, I wrote *Film as Religion*. Having used it as a text for a few years now, I can assess how well it has served my intended purpose and what insights this approach provides.

Interpretation Does Not Live by Audience Reception Theory Alone

In developing my own method I have made extensive use of audience reception approaches because these indicate how actual filmgoers are understanding films rather than imposing interpretations on a movie that may have little to do with most filmgoers' reading of it. If one is to comprehend how films function religiously for viewers, it will not be very helpful simply to know how the film theorist understands the film. Admittedly, ideological film analysis may uncover meanings that audiences are perhaps receiving unknowingly, but such analysis remains speculative to the extent that it cannot verify this. I have never recommended that ideological analysis cease, but it needs to be supplemented by studies of what audiences believe they are understanding as this is also a relevant consideration in uncovering how films function for audiences.

In *Film as Religion* I admitted that I have not done extensive audience studies (Lyden 2003, 137). This work is in its infancy even within film studies proper, although some good audience reception studies have been done, and more are being carried out every year. I have dealt with that lack by utilizing some of these studies, as well as by doing ethnographic study within my classes. This creates a curious situation for me as teacher; I am interested in students' raw reactions to a film as data for my research, but I also want to teach them how to better understand their own responses and take a critical stance toward them. If they are only objects of study, they will never become subjects who can interpret films themselves, even while admitting that they are affected as any audience members are. However, to the extent that I teach them how to view films, I interfere with the experiment of discovering how films function for them prior to my interference. I realize that the observer's presence changes data in all ethnography and that this need not mean the data are useless, but it is necessary to admit that one's presence may be having an effect.

However, aside from the question of what the researcher can learn from students' reactions to films, we still have the issue of whether the focus on audience reception helps viewers to become better interpreters of film or religion. One problem is the tendency toward banality. If students are asked to study their own reactions to a film as a way of discovering what it means to them, they may simply record random impressions or feelings with no real analysis, and if audience reception theory assumes that any and all interpretations are valid, there is no basis on which to challenge the students to go beyond whatever superficial observations they have made. As a corrective to this, I insist that, although meaning is defined by individual viewers, it is shaped by an encounter with the film itself, as well as with other viewers in the same culture. I take it as axiomatic that there is, in fact, a film "out there" that we are watching together, even though we see different things in it. I see no point in denying that the object of study exists in spite of some postmodernist theories that seem to advance this sort of conclusion.[1]

On the contrary, the assumption that a film exists apart from us allows us to have conflicting interpretations and to argue about "what it really means." The fact that we can never find the uninterpreted film does not require us to deny that we are arguing about something. And in that argument we can perhaps agree about its meaning even while allowing some diversity of opinion. On the other hand, if there is no object of study but only interpretations, we have no basis on which to critique other views but also no basis on which to agree with them. In this case we exist in our private viewing worlds, and nothing anyone else says about the film has any relevance to me whatsoever. This would make any discussion of film pointless, which certainly includes the academic study of film.

In order to avoid this sort of subjectivity, we need to introduce students to other hermeneutical approaches even while recognizing their limits. For example, I believe it is still relevant to ask about the "authorial intention" of a film. What the filmmakers say they are trying to show in a film is not the final level of meaning and may be irrelevant to the viewers in some ways, but it is not totally immaterial to evaluating how a film affects audiences or what meanings it contains. Some filmmakers even foreground the meanings they intend to put across in a film, as when a film is marketed as a "message" film that speaks to a particular contemporary issue—as *Brokeback Mountain* did to homosexual rights or as *Munich* did to the post-9/11 "war on terror." Moreover, even in movies that are clearly not marketed as message films but are meant as entertainment, the filmmakers' intentions are still important to understand as they hope to have a particular effect on viewers in order to encourage box-office sales.

The meanings "intended" by the film may also be distinct from what the filmmakers articulate as their objectives. For example, they may not deliberately recognize or admit the extent to which their films inscribe traditional views of race, class, or gender, but these may still be meanings that viewers perceive. For instance, D. W. Griffith was baffled by the accusation that *Birth of a Nation* was racist—he did not intend it to be. Today, however, we can clearly see that the film expresses the racist attitudes of its time, which many viewers also failed to recognize. Ideological criticism is still required to uncover such meanings so that students can better understand how a film functions and the messages it sends. But ideological criticism must also be responsive to the text it analyzes (the film); it has the burden of showing how the film intends the ideological values the analysis identifies.

I have combined all of these approaches in my classes. Students need to be able to identify and analyze their own reactions and those of others, including *why* they felt a certain way about a film. In this manner they begin to understand the values they bring to it. It is also important for them to consider what the film seems to be saying to audiences and what meanings the filmmakers either consciously or unconsciously intended. They should also question these deliberate meanings and decide whether they are valid for themselves or others.

In all of this, one may ask to what extent religion is involved. Much of what I have said about finding the meaning of films might be said without reference to religious meaning. Yet, I have found it helpful to view films through religious categories because these may illuminate levels of meaning that would otherwise remain obscure. Here I would like to examine how some of those concepts have proved useful in the classroom, both to introduce students to the study of religion and to better comprehend films and their messages. In particular, I highlight the role of four key ideas: myths and literalism; the relation of real to ideal; sacrifice; and liminality and catharsis.

Myths and Literalism

I follow Clifford Geertz in defining religion functionally as a symbol system that provides meaning in the midst of chaos and suffering through "conceptions of a general order of existence," namely, myths (Lyden 2003, 42). Utilizing such a broad definition precludes defining religion narrowly as comprising certain beliefs (e.g., in a transcendent protector God or a path to eternal salvation). Religion scholars know that these Western beliefs are not found in all religions, but students are often unaware of this fact. They are frequently reluctant to give up their standard concepts of religion simply because they are in the habit of thinking of religion in terms of their own experience.

Getting them to see religion in a wider sense requires them to see myths in a different way as well. Usually they begin with the assumption that a myth is something that is not true; therefore, myths are the stories of other religions but not of their own. I suggest to them that a "myth," as we are defining it, can be any story that functions symbolically for a community to provide it with meaning and identity; therefore, the stories of Christianity, as well as those of other religions and even films, can function as myths. Perhaps because they are not used to thinking of myths in this way, they tend to literalize the meaning of myths. They know the stories of their own religion, which they may take to be both literally and symbolically true, but for that reason they are not aware of the differences between literal and symbolic truth and that a story may have one kind of truth without the other. In particular, when one studies the stories of other traditions, which one may not believe to be literally true, it is important to be able to unpack their meanings in order to understand their point. However, it is difficult for many students to move beyond the literal meaning of a myth to establish its symbolic content, the value of which may make the question of whether it is literally true almost irrelevant.

For example, I showed *Big Fish* to one of my classes because I thought it was an excellent example of how films can function mythically and a fine reflection on the concept of myth in general. The story concerns a young man who has not spoken with his father for several years. When he hears that his father is dying, he and his pregnant wife go home. His father tells tall tales, which everyone enjoys—everyone, that is, except his son, who feels that his father has never told him the truth about anything. The plot involves the son's making sense of his father's life, finding the meaning and truth in his stories, and finally accepting his father as he is. To do this, the son has to become a mythmaker himself and finish his father's own story before the old man can die. Part of what the son learns is that there is in fact more literal truth to his father's stories than he had thought, but this is not the most relevant piece of information. Instead, the son learns that his father is also a better man than he had thought, that his devotion to his mother is real, and that he loves his son even though he has had to express this indirectly. As father and son are reconciled, the myths are not abolished, but the son comes to understand why his father felt compelled to express things mythically. All in all, there is more to truth than the literal.

I was disappointed, however, with the reaction of my class because they attached too much importance to the literal details of the story and so seemed to miss what I considered to be the point of the film. They interpreted the father's stories as simply exaggerated versions of the truth and thus missed the reason he had to tell them as he did. His storytelling was not only to boast about his abilities, as it at first seemed to the son; it was also a way in which to view his life as a meaningful struggle with "the big fish," a metaphor for his efforts to accomplish something in the world. His stories of all of the people he befriended give substance to his myth, which was connected with actual events, but these incidents are knowable only in the mythical form in which the father presents them. There is no getting behind the myth to a historical core, yet this does not stop the myth from being meaningfully linked to reality—both in the film's plot and in the viewers' reality.

In order to see how myth functions apart from the literal level of the narrative, students need to read more about myths and also think of examples of stories that have affected them personally without being literally true. If they can then link this insight to films and see how films are thus functioning religiously, they may also begin to grasp how myths work in the context of traditional religions, even their own.

The Real and the Ideal

Religious myths provide a model both of how the world is believed to be (the real), as well as a conception of how it could be (the ideal)—in Clifford Geertz's terms, a model *of* and *for* reality. These are linked to the extent that the empirical world does not exactly correspond with the visions of reality held by religions, and so it is claimed both that a "deeper" reality exists, beyond the visible world, and also that a future reality exists in which the empirical world will correspond more closely to the ideal world of myth. Thus Christians can speak of how the world is already redeemed in its structure although it does not always seem so and also claim that at the end of time the process of redemption will be fully actualized in the world as we know it. All religions have ideals present in their worldviews that they hope to see progressively realized, and even if they cannot literally realize them, these ideal visions can still have an effect on how they perceive the world and act in it—for example, in moral behavior (Lyden 2003, 48–55).

For students to comprehend this concept in a film, they must look for the messages in it (e.g., they need to see both the explicit and implicit meanings, which can be found in various interpretations, as well as in close textual analysis of a film's design and possible ideological content). Many students have never imagined that a film can be anything but entertainment or that it might have a message or values to express. Looking at movies as modern myths, they begin to see that their entertainment value is linked to the fact that they tell us what we want to hear, thereby reinforcing our values or suggesting new ones that may be comforting, compelling, or even confrontational. They can also begin to understand why we do not prefer confrontational myths even though they may be salutary, as we usually choose to hear religious stories that make us feel better—not worse. At the same time, they perceive that we may choose to be confronted or comforted, depending on the context, and that this duality runs through popular films, as well as what we normally call religions. It will not do to judge all popular culture as simply supplying comfortable myths, just as it will not do to suggest that "real" religions are superior because they are always more confrontational and hence deeper. There are superficial church services just as there are superficial films, and there are compelling church services and films as well.

Sacrifice

Concepts of sacrifice form a central part of both religion and films. Here again I insist that some understanding of how the concept of sacrifice has functioned in religion is crucial if one is to comprehend its adaptation to film. When characters sacrifice themselves for some higher cause in an action film, a Western, or a war movie, the plot tends to involve violence that the audience views as meaningful and even sacred not only because it accomplishes the objective of saving the innocent but also because the one who makes the sacrifice appears heroic and moral in intention. Such role models reinforce the value of violent sacrifice by drawing on a history of how the concept has been used religiously, which most American viewers are familiar with from Christianity but which goes unexamined in its essential structure.

Christians know the story of Jesus's sacrifice for their sins, but they do not recognize how the concept of sanctified sacrifice may be used to legitimate violence both in film and in political reality. Evidence of this can be seen in how easily most Christian viewers accept the ethics of action movies that promote violence as a way to deal with evil. Although Jesus prayed for his persecutors and refused to respond to them with violence, most American Christians have not become pacifists as a result of their familiarity with this story. One would think that a recognition that Jesus died to end all violence would provide a critique of violent sacrifice itself, as Réne Girard (1977) has argued. Nevertheless, the paradox is that this "end of sacrifice" in Christian terms is accomplished only by the greatest sacrifice of all, which is replayed by Christians over and over again, and thus may perpetuate and legitimize violence rather than abolishing it. As evidence of this, consider the fact that the conservative Christians who approved of the ultraviolent portrayal of Jesus's crucifixion in Mel Gibson's *Passion of the Christ* also tended to be extremely supportive of the U.S. attacks on Afghanistan and Iraq.[2]

In *Film as Religion* I argued for a concept of sacrifice that does not sanction violence but ritualistically expresses repentance and a desire for forgiveness (Lyden 2003, 83–87). This can occur if the sacrifice is considered representative of our own repentance rather than a mere substitute for it. In such a case, Jesus's passive response to his brutal slaying becomes a model for our own responses to cruelty, so that we too are called to the way of nonviolence rather than to a celebration of merciless killing. However, if my own participation in Jesus's submissive denunciation of violence is not required and if his act is so unlike any other acts of sacrifice that no comparison can be made (as tends to be the case in conservative Christianity), then his nonviolence is no longer a model for my actions but simply the means whereby my own sins (violent or otherwise) are erased.

In fact, we may even sanctify war by rationalizing that the sacrifice of our soldiers' lives makes legitimate and holy the cause for which they are fighting. Therefore, the killings they perform not only go uncritiqued but are actually celebrated as righteous. Since September 11, 2001, it seems that the latter understanding of sacrifice has been the dominant one in the United States. Soon after U.S. military intervention in Iraq began in 2003, many people called for unqualified support of U.S. troops, which essentially meant that the cause of the war could not be critiqued because the deaths of our soldiers could be interpreted only as purposeful and even sacred sacrifices. Even the decreasing support of the war as it entered its fourth year were largely due not to an ethical critique (or even a recognition) of this notion but rather to pragmatic concerns that our presence might make it impossible for the United States to achieve its stated "noble" purpose of "establishing democracy." There has been little criticism of the underlying logic that legitimates this sort of intervention, which is tied up with assumptions that violence is best answered by violence, that the United States has the right to interfere with other countries' governments for their own good, and that we can accept both violence done by and to Americans when it is performed for the holy purposes of "defending the nation" or "establishing democracy."[3]

In teaching about movies in such a context, I find it important to help students understand and critique the ways in which films often portray violence as a legitimate sacrifice for some higher purpose. They thus discover how both religions and films have condoned hostility and perhaps learn to reflect on their own values in the process. This is not an easy thing to do; these issues create a tremendous amount of emotional tension since classes may contain both students who protest the Iraq war and those who support it, including members of the military who may have been in Iraq. Nonetheless, we need to learn to discuss these difficult topics, and the college classroom is a fairly safe environment in which students can begin to confront these questions. I also hope that even in peacetime such conversations will continue as we reflect on how our culture and our religions have sanctified violence and whether we can support those values or need to create new ones. As this example certainly shows, the task of analyzing films and religion together is hardly an innocuous exercise; indeed, it may cause us to challenge our ethical, political, and religious values in significant ways.

Liminality and Catharsis

I have perhaps spent more time in my film and religion classes dealing with liminality and catharsis than any other religious concept. This may be because it is relatively easy for students to see how films function as an escape from the everyday world to a fantasyland where characters can engage in all kinds of socially unacceptable behaviors and get away with it. Particularly as adolescents, they enjoy films that feature characters who question authority figures or break society's rules, especially regarding sexuality. They also accept the idea that this involves a cathartic release for viewers because they can experience the emotional rush of these behaviors without entailing the consequences.

Sometimes, however, students stop at this point and fail to connect this cathartic experience to any larger religious concept, thereby missing the point that religions have used liminal catharsis as a transformative and not merely a recreational experience. When characters step outside their ordinary social roles in a religious ritual and experience liminality, they are afterward better equipped to understand and accept their normal social roles. These responsibilities are sometimes temporarily questioned and even equalized in a brief reference to a utopian *communitas* that includes no social differences, but after the ritual the ordinary world reasserts itself (Lyden 2003, 95–97; Turner 1969). Still, the utopian ideal may linger as a transformative hope as it inspires the community to reflect on its ultimate transformation to a liberated society (e.g., African American slaves who practiced Christianity and hoped for an end to slavery).

I have found it helpful to point out to students that liminality exists even in the rituals of Christianity, in which the sacrament of communion invokes forbidden images of cannibalism in order to suggest a world order in which the community is "one in Christ" and thus devoid of social differences. Sometimes the most familiar religious rituals need to be made strange to students so that they can see the shock value such rituals would have had when they were first instituted; the Romans, after all, accused the early Christians of cannibalism because they were horrified at the language Christians used to describe the Eucharist.

The liminality present in films, of course, does not often rise to such levels of utopian hope; it may involve only something as prosaic as the "ideal" of teenagers freed from parental control of their sexual lives. However, it is still important to analyze the myths and values present in such films because they reflect and influence our attitudes on a range of issues. Students are often unwilling to admit the extent to which popular culture may affect or even reflect either their own attitudes and beliefs or those of society. Nonetheless, if they begin to consider why they like certain films or why particular movies are box-office successes, they can start to recognize the reasons for these choices.

By itself, marketing does not determine the success of a film; in particular, although an extensive advertising campaign may ensure a good opening weekend, it will not determine whether the film has legs—that is, whether it will continue to keep viewers coming. No one could have predicted the success of the original *Star Wars,* which remained in some theaters for six months after its release, or the success of films like *Titanic* or *The Sixth Sense.* The latter film had a rather small production and advertising budget, and the former a large one, but both far exceeded their producers' expectations. It is also not clear that a film that invests a great deal in production values will always be the most successful; a lavish film like *Heaven's Gate* can flop, and a low-budget film like *The Blair Witch Project* can succeed. I point out to students that the success or failure of a film largely correlates with whether it connects with viewers, that is, whether it is a "live" myth that can speak to the worldview and values of a particular audience. In this way films can operate like religions for them.

Through attention to all of these aspects, students come away from class with a better understanding of both religion and films. In spite of the frustrations I have sometimes experienced in getting them to accept the idea of film as religion, they have also often surprised me by the depth of their analyses when they begin to discern the ways in which films affect them and thereby parallel the influence of religion. It is rewarding to approach the study of religion and film by helping students to move beyond simple dichotomies to a greater appreciation of the difficulty of distinguishing between religion and popular culture inasmuch as they are interpenetrating realities in our complex and endlessly fascinating world.

NOTES

1. In religious studies this tendency is demonstrated in works such as McCutcheon's *Manufacturing Religion* (1997).

2. It is only fair to admit that Mel Gibson himself voiced his opposition to the Iraq war, although the media did not cover this as much as some of his remarks on other issues.

3. See Stout, *Upon the Altar of the Nation* (2006), for a theory of how this idea developed as a result of the experience of the American Civil War.

REFERENCES

Girard, Réne. 1977. *Violence and the Sacred*, trans. Patrick Gregory. Baltimore: John Hopkins University Press.

Lyden, John. 2003. *Film as Religion: Myths, Morals, and Rituals.* New York: New York University Press.

McCutcheon, Russell. 1997. *Manufacturing Religion.* New York: Oxford University Press.

Stout, Harry. 2006. *Upon the Altar of the Nation: A Moral History of the Civil War.* New York: Viking.

Turner, Victor. 1969. *The Ritual Process: Structure and Anti-structure.* Ithaca, N.Y.: Cornell University Press.

13

Filmmaking and World Making: Re-Creating Time and Space in Myth and Film

S. Brent Plate

The lights dim in the movie theater, the crowd goes quiet, and viewers begin to leave their worries behind, anticipating instead a new and mysterious alternative world that will soon capture their imagination. Even before viewers get to the feature presentation they are already being gently inducted into the world-making dimensions of cinema. Previews of coming attractions begin the process by introducing some forthcoming film with phrases such as "In a world where . . ." And just before the main event, viewers sit through a few seconds' worth of production companies' moving logos, which portray a predominant theme through their scenarios: The heavens and earth are connected through the productions of cinema.

The logo for Universal Pictures depicts a spinning earth, with a thousand points of light appearing across the continents (presumably movie theaters) as the view zooms out to show the whole globe; the name "Universal" whirls into place as a belt around the planet. The Dreamworks logo begins with an image of still water into which a fishing line is dropped; then the camera pans upward to spot a boy cradled in the curve of the "D" of "Dreamworks" as the name hangs suspended in midair and surrounded by clouds, evoking a lunar look on the world below. Elsewhere, Warner Brothers displays the "WB" shield floating among the clouds; the now-defunct Orion showed its eponymous star sign; and Paramount and Columbia both set their icons so high up on a pedestal that only the clouds and a few mountain peaks can join them in their pantheon of world imagining.

Film production companies are fully cognizant of the other worlds and ethereal perspectives they provide for their viewers and gleefully promote them as they reaffirm a cosmology that evokes a "looking up" to where the wondrous things are. In this way, cinema offers a glimpse of the heavens—of other worlds beyond Earth. Transcendent of earthly concerns, the cinema enables a god's-eye view of the world even if we have long ago given up the "heaven above/earth below" cosmic separation.

In this chapter I expand on the parallel world-making activities of both film and religion, stretching beyond trailers and production-company logos to formal aspects of filmmaking and focusing specifically on what critical-theoretical studies on film label mise-en-scène. I propose that we can learn about the formal structures of religion, especially in the guise of myth and ritual, by investigating the formal structures of film. (If space permitted and if it were the focus of this volume, I would also suggest the opposite—that we can learn about film by looking at religion—but here I focus on the first half of the relation.) Herein I play the role of editor, juxtaposing film theory and religious theory in order to develop the ways both religion and film are engaged in the practice of world making. They both start with the raw materials of *space* and *time* and manipulate them in ever-new ways to produce the desired result: promises of a blissful afterlife, a utopian society, the threat of a dystopian nightmare, or just a world in which semicute guy meets up with semicute girl. I do not cover all of these topics, but such themes are what film production can produce, with or without verbal narrative structures.

The chapter begins by briefly examining the concept of world making and re-creation, drawing from the work of Peter Berger in particular. Then I turn to the ways films participate in world-making activities through the filmic aspect of mise-en-scène. The films *Star Wars* and *The Matrix* are both discussed through attention to a single scene inasmuch as the props, characters, lighting, and overall scenario of these scenes offer clues to the mythological structures given in the films as a whole. Mythological references operate in film not simply by narrative trajectories but also by creating a scenario in which carefully placed objects and carefully chosen characters are shown in various relations to each other on screen and then offered to viewers for a further relation. My aim is to encourage religious studies scholars and students to think through the specificities of film. General narrative structures can be guidelines, but here I draw attention to the specifics of the audiovisual components of filmmaking, which offer inroads into the religious enterprise of world making.

World Making and Re-Creation

In the background of my argument are the world-building and world-maintaining processes of religion brought out in Peter Berger's now-canonic work, *The Sacred Canopy*. We humans, Berger suggests, collectively create ordered worlds around us to provide us with a sense of stability and security "in the never completed enterprise of building a humanly meaningful world."[1] This is the role of culture, society, and all of their products. And if culture staves off meaninglessness at the societal level, religion does so at the cosmic level as it keeps the forces of chaos at bay. Ever important is the grounding of human laws and regulations in cosmic structures. The *nomos* (the meaningful societal order) must be in synch with the *cosmos* (the universal, metaphysical order). There is a dialectical, ongoing process between the two realms, and it is religion that serves as the link: "Religion implies the farthest reach of man's self-externalization, of his infusion of reality with his own meanings. Religion implies that human order is projected into the totality of being. Put differently, religion is the audacious attempt to conceive of the entire universe as being humanly significant."[2] Recall here the Hollywood production-company logos with their (quite literally) *projected* views of the cosmos, and we come some distance toward understanding the analogy between cinema and religion.

Indeed, Berger himself states that, while most of history has seen religion as key to creating such a meaningful totality, in modern times "there have been thoroughly secular attempts at cosmization."[3] Science has most importantly made the attempt, but I suggest that we think about cinema as another audacious attempt. Cinema may be part of the symbol-creating apparatus of culture, yet it also aspires to more—to world-encompassing, lunar-looking visions of the nomos and the cosmos.

Philosopher Nelson Goodman similarly understands the culturally constructed nature of the world, particularly as discussed in his book *Ways of Worldmaking*. Approaching the topic from an epistemological standpoint rather than Berger's sociological one, Goodman nonetheless draws an analogy between philosophy and the arts to understand how we humans go about creating worlds around us:

> Much but by no means all worldmaking consists of taking apart
> and putting together, often conjointly: on the one hand, of dividing
> wholes into parts and partitioning kinds into subspecies, analyzing
> complexes into component features, drawing distinctions; on the
> other hand, of composing wholes and kinds out of parts and members
> and subclasses, combining features into complexes, and making
> connections.[4]

The activity of creation is one of taking things apart and putting them back together, of reassembling the raw materials available to us, of dissection and analysis, and of mending broken components. Such philosophical activity is easily translatable in terms of filmmaking, with its partitioning of time through edited cuts and the recombining done in the editing room, or the dividing and framing of space through cinematography. World making, like filmmaking, is an active intervention into the space and time of the universe. It is the performative drama in which we humans partake when we attempt to make meaning of the spaces, times, and people that make up our lives. And it is what filmmakers and artists offer to this human drama.

World making is deeply bound to what Berger (1967) calls "world-maintenance." Because there is a dialectical process between the projected societal views of the cosmos and individual creativity, the world must be re-created on a continual basis. For reasons that I hope to make clear, I am transposing this term as "re-creation" in order to get at the dynamic dialectics that Berger and Goodman (1978) highlight. The world is not simply "built" but is constantly being maintained through rebuilding, reconstruction, and re-combining. An intrinsic link exists between religion and film when it comes to the act of re-creation. The hyphen is injected into "re-creation" to remind us how to pronounce this word in a way that resonates with its true meaning. Modern English has transformed the term into "recreation"—as in "recreational vehicle" or departments of "parks and recreation"—it is something we do to get away from the world. Yet at the heart of the idea, even if we forget it, is the activity of creation. Recreation is a way to re-create the world, which often means taking a step back from it to see how it is put together, if only to figure out how it can be rearranged. On those days of recreation, the world looks different; we see what we should have seen all along.

That recreation, including moviegoing, occurs on the weekends in the modern world is not accidental. These two days coincide with the Jewish and Christian holy days, when the good folk of the world attend religious services, participate in their "true" communities, and take time to be in touch with their Creator. At least, that is the idea. As the Western world has grown restless with its religiosity, new forms of re-creation have emerged, one of which is of course the world of cinema. Indeed, what preacher's sermon can compete with multimillion-dollar special effects? What Sabbath meal can steer us away from the possibility that beautiful people such as Julia Roberts and Richard Gere might fall in love?

The Jewish tradition of the Sabbath is particularly insightful as a way to approach the re-creation of the world as it relates to film. "On the seventh day, God rested," we are told in the beginning of Genesis. However, in the next chapter we read that the Creator was not so passive at this time. If religions, in contemporary religious studies language, are centered around that which is "sacred," then the Jewish and Christian traditions would be first and foremost centered around the Sabbath day, for that is the first thing that God blesses and makes holy (Hebrew *kadosh*), according to the scriptures: "God blessed the seventh day and made it holy" (Gen. 2:3). As Abraham Heschel puts it in his classic little book on the Sabbath, "It is a day on which we are called upon to share in what is eternal in time, to turn from the results of creation to the mystery of creation; from the world of creation to the creation of the world."[5] Contrary to public opinion, the idea of the Sabbath is not one hollowed out by a list of rules and regulations that leave a community in a state of passivity but rather is an active, vital time. Judaism has a strong tradition of understanding the Sabbath as the *completion* of creation, that on the seventh day God did not refrain from creating as much as God created the Sabbath. The Sabbath, in this view, is the "real world," the rest of the week a necessary other world. "The Sabbath is not for the sake of the weekdays; the weekdays are for the sake of the Sabbath."[6]

If the Sabbath is the day we turn "to the mystery of creation" and "from the world of creation to the creation of the world," then film mimics this very process. It makes us wonder about the world again and say "wow!" by presenting images that allow us to see things in a new way. This is not to say all film accomplishes this, for there seems to be somewhat of an inverse relation between the spectacular images of film and the capacity of the viewer's imagination—the more dazzling the image, the more depressed the imagination—but then again, the challah bread, the candles, and the recitation of prayers are not foolproof ways to stir our minds either. At its best, the Sabbath puts people in touch with their Creator, their family, and the created world. And at its best, film puts people in touch with the world again in new ways. In both of these, one is connected with one's world only by experiencing another world. The attraction and indeed promise of cinema is the way it offers a window into another world, even if only for ninety minutes at a time, which is as much as can be said for the promise of myths and rituals in religious traditions.

To be active consumers and participants in front of the film screen or altar or at the Sabbath table—in order to maintain the hyphen in re-creation—it is necessary at times to dissect and analyze, to take things apart and then recombine them, as Goodman (1978) suggests. As students of film and religion, we must see, hear, feel, and think our way through the ways these worlds are made and re-created. Such are the goals of religious studies and film studies programs across the world. In the following I provide analyses of two film scenes and note the ways world making and re-creation take place through the formal components of filmmaking and describe how such creative action parallels the activity of religious structures.

Myth and Mise-en-Scène

A careful look at two scenes from the beginnings of two masterfully mythical films sheds light on the ways mythologies are depicted in nonnarrative, nonverbal ways. *Mise-en-scène* is a term commonly used in film studies and, simply put, it refers to everything that is seen inside the frame of the film: decoration, props, lighting, costume, colors, and characters, as well as how the framed image is set up through camera angles.[7] Film sets are created spaces, and every object and visual orientation, every costume and color that the viewer sees on screen is the result of a highly thought-out process on the part of directors, cinematographers, production designers, and others. Props have meanings as much as the words spoken by the main characters, and camera angles can express cosmic significance.

Star Wars (i.e., the original, also known as "Episode IV," written and directed by George Lucas, 1977) and *The Matrix* (written and directed by the Wachowski brothers, 1999) are arguably two of the greatest mythological films of all time. The writers and directors of each one self-consciously incorporate the myths of multiple religious traditions into their re-created worlds. While plenty of people have commented on the narrative similarities between the films and the older verbal myths from Buddhist, Taoist, Christian, and other traditions, the following sections focus on the ways the audiovisual components of film also re-construct those myths by offering re-created worlds for their viewing, listening audiences.[8] My arguments here only touch on the larger narrative of each film and home in on one scene each, demonstrating just how much two or three minutes of film can contain audiovisually.

Star Wars: Cosmos versus Chaos

After the production company credits—a computer-generated view of the logo "20th Century Fox" rising like a megaskyscraper above the Hollywood skyline—Star Wars shows a black screen with the simple and now well-known phrase "A long time ago, in a galaxy far, far away..." Immediately we are ushered into the realm of myth. Compare this introduction with Genesis 1.1: "In the beginning, God created the heavens and the earth." In each rendering we are given the standard deployments of narrative introductions: At the start of a story one should provide the setting. The audience has to know the time and place of the world they are observing.

Yet, what initially sets Star Wars apart from films about more everyday life and begins to set myths apart from regular stories is the ambiguity of the setting. The time and place are given, and yet they are not specific. There is no "April 14, 1832" stated here. Instead, it is "A long time ago." But how long is "long"? To a paleontologist, two million years might be a long time. To my two year-old daughter, five minutes seems an eternity. In Genesis, "In the beginning" is likewise vague. When exactly was the beginning? Beginning of what? And the same is true for the spatial setting—"a galaxy far, far away"—or in Genesis it is essentially "space" that is in process of being created when "God was creating the heavens and earth." In other words, myths provide a built-in ambiguity that makes them applicable to a variety of people in diverse times and places. George Lucas understands this and inscribes it in the beginning of his film, turning a science fiction story (most of which begin with precise dates sometime in the future) into something mythical. Lucas's "time" is further confounded by the fact that most science fiction films take place in the future and deal with technology beyond our present day, but here he is setting it in the past. Star Wars looks futuristic, but we are told this has already occurred.

So, like all stories, myths begin with a setting in time and space. Films achieve a similar effect in audiovisual ways through what are known as "establishing shots," usually long (or extreme long) shots that show the viewer the most general setting possible. Standard Hollywood films might show a large image of a city (the Manhattan skyline shot from across the East River; Chicago with its John Hancock Tower; London with the houses of Parliament) and then slowly move in to more and more local places until they reach the main character's location within the city. In addition, visual clues along the way (e.g., vehicles, clothing, hairstyles) give the audience hints of the temporal setting.

In Star Wars, the establishing shot that follows the verbal beginning provides a further introduction to the mythic structures of the movie and indicates why it is not just another boy-meets-girl film or another tale about good guys versus bad guys. The shot is set in outer space, with nothing but stars dotting an otherwise black sky—there are no planets or anything else to give us an initial grounding. Then the title "STAR WARS" immediately appears on screen, accompanied by a bang of orchestral music (by John Williams). The audience is jolted and excited by what is to come. As the triumphant, heavy-percussion music continues, a prologue scrolls up the screen, setting out verbal details of what has happened and what is to come. Viewers are caught up in the narrative and thrust into the middle of the action through these words and the music.

Then the grander mythical cues come just as the words scroll up the screen and disappear into the ether. At that precise instant, the jubilant music also all but disappears, leaving only a solo flute playing alongside chimes. For five seconds there is utter calm: The heavens are in their place, the music plays softly, soothingly; there is a cosmic order to the universe. But all we are allowed is five seconds, for then the camera, which has been stationary until now, tilts down to reveal an orange-hued planet below, with other planets visible in the distance. As the camera tilts downward, violins frantically rise up, and the percussion crashes as two spaceships are caught in battle, firing laser guns at one another. Chaos erupts into the cosmos; wars emerge in the midst of stars.

By setting up the establishing shot in outer space, suggesting an ordered calm to a universe, and then introducing chaotic elements, Lucas triggers many elements common in cosmogonies: In the beginning, chaos and cosmos are in conflict. In myths as diverse as the Hebrew, Iroquois, Babylonian, and Greek creation stories, the grand struggle, the establishing shot, is that of cosmos versus chaos. Throughout history, such myths indicate, this battle perpetually remains just below the surface of things as humans (or other volitional, sentient creatures) enter into this struggle, creating their own *nomic* order. *Star Wars,* writ large, is about stars and wars, cosmos and chaos, and then about relating the human social order to the cosmic order.

The six episodes of *Star Wars* are rife with conflicts, political wagers, and power struggles as protagonists and antagonists fight to retain authority over the social order, continually rooting claims in the cosmic structures around them: Republicans, democrats, federalists, and monarchists can all be found, just as can the "other" spiritual realm of the Jedi Knights. (Another key visual clue that relates the cosmos to the nomos appears halfway through the original film, when Luke returns to his home to find his family slaughtered. He stares off at the dual suns about to set over his home planet of Tatooine and makes his decision to accept what George Lucas's intellectual mentor, Joseph Campbell, called the "hero's adventure.")

In the beginning, visually and mythologically, all of the remaining ten-plus hours of the *Star Wars* films are set up within the few seconds of the initial shot in the first film. The film announces itself as far more than a space-age story and instead tells us that these wars are those of all humankind, which is to say that it is no less ambitious than a myth.

The Matrix: Mythical Postmodern Pastiche

Scene two of the sci-fi masterpiece *The Matrix* introduces us to a strange hermit-prophet-hero called "Neo" (also known as Thomas Anderson; played by Keanu Reaves). Much has been written on the film's connections with Buddhism and Christianity (especially in its gnostic guise), and although these theological/doctrinal analyses are interesting, I again point out the visual portrayal of the differing mythical worlds that are created on screen, all of which takes place within the first three minutes.

Introduced in the first scene of *The Matrix* is the character Trinity (Carrie-Anne Moss), who is clad in a tight, black, shiny outfit and performing martial arts feats that leave a trail of police officers down. There is much to be said here about the mise-en-scène, including her clothing and the fact that she is introduced, sitting at her computer terminal in a ramshackle hotel room, number 303. The action-packed scene is accompanied by fast-paced music, stunning special effects, gunfights, and superhero-like hand-to-hand combat. Trinity runs vertically up walls and leaps from rooftop to rooftop across a city street twenty floors below. The viewer is left amazed but confused as to how all of this can happen in the "real world," especially since the first shot of the film is of Trinity's computer screen with green display characters that tell us the date: "2-19-1998." Not long into the film we realize again the ambiguous settings of myths, whereby the actual date is an illusion and the "real date" is unknown; it is probably one hundred years later than people perceive, but no one really knows. This is an apocalyptic myth that foretells the potential end of the world. Just as the beginnings of worlds are ambiguous, so are the ends.

The action of scene one, centered on Trinity in room 303, gives way to scene two, which introduces viewers to Neo, who is sprawled sedately across his desk in his apartment, room 101. (At the climax of the film Neo will reenter the original room 303, where fate seems to get the better of him, and Trinity will bring him back to life.) Neo's apartment is nothing short of a "cave"— dark, dank, and dreary. As with Trinity in scene one, we initially meet Neo through his green-tinted computer screen. (The entire film, including the "Warner Brothers" logo at the beginning, is bathed in green tones, suggesting a fecund or possibly fetid worldview.) Neo sleeps as his computer performs a search for one "Morpheus," and international news bulletins flash across the screen, illuminating Neo's face. The searching abruptly stops to show a blank screen, while the words "Wake up, Neo" crawl across the screen. And Neo does so. As if in Instant Messenger mode, Neo's computer screen tells him to "Follow the white rabbit" and then predicts a real knock at his real door. All of this time Neo is shot from behind his computer as he faces the screen in front, and the screen provides his only lighting. The effect is a standard filmic trick of lighting and character development: Half of his face is lit, the other half obscured in the dark. He is two people, divided within himself.

The door opens to reveal several people obviously looking to have a good time. They also wear black leather and rubber clothing, similar to Trinity's outfit in the previous scene. After they pay Neo some money through the slightly opened door, he goes and finds a special computer disk. What is on it, we never find out but are led to believe the computer program is not strikingly different in effect from hallucinatory drugs. Taking the disk from Neo, the lead male exclaims, "Hallelujah! You're my savior, man! My own personal Jesus Christ!" He looks at Neo's pale complexion and dour face and suggests that Neo needs to get out a bit more, get a little "R & R." He turns to his companion "Dujour," who happens to have a white rabbit tattooed on her shoulder. Recognizing the tattoo as the sign given through his computer, Neo follows, Alice-like, down the rabbit hole. As the film continues, the hole becomes grander and more upside down.

Neo walks around his dark apartment in this early scene, and the viewer continues to find clues to the myriad myths that are strewn across the film. The chiaroscuro lighting effect reveals several stations of a windowless space. The place where the computer disk is found is a book titled *Simulacra and Simulation*. Those who are familiar with postmodern theory will recognize this as a collection of essays by the late French sociologist Jean Baudrillard. Neo opens this "book," which turns out to be a simulated book with a carved-out, hidden storage space, much like we see in other movies with a gun or bottle of scotch in the center. The cavity that contains the special stash comes in the middle of an essay titled "On Nihilism," which is Baudrillard's essay on Nietzsche and his atheism. In the late nineteenth century Nietzsche told us God was dead, but in the new world of "simulated transparency," Baudrillard suggests, "God is not dead, he has become hyperreal."[9]

Relatedly, in a single essay titled "Simulacra and Simulation," Baudrillard offers his postmodern inversion of Plato's allegory of the cave, in which there are successive stages of the image. In the beginning, an image, as a referent, is a reflection of a basic reality (this is what religious icons around the world are based upon). Eventually, however, that grounding reality disappears and is swallowed up by the ubiquity of the image itself in a mass-mediated society, leading to the final stage, in which the image "bears no relation to any reality whatever: it is its own pure simulacrum."[10] Due to the prominence of mass media in our lives, we can no longer claim that anything is more real than anything else, including the gods and goddesses. (Later in the film, Morpheus even quotes Baudrillard as he introduces Neo to the matrix by saying, "Welcome to the desert of the Real."[11]) As a whole *The Matrix* is premised on a two-worlds view, in which the simulated world appears to be the real one but is in fact a computer program. As the Hindu sages and the Buddha claimed millennia ago, our perceived world is an illusion—maya.

Thus, in approximately three minutes of edited time at the start of *The Matrix* we find reference to myriad mythologies, both religious and secular, ancient and postmodern: from ancient philosophy (Plato's allegory of the cave) to postmodern inversions of it (Baudrillard's simulacra), from nineteenth-century fantastical tales (Lewis Carroll's *Through the Looking Glass* [the white rabbit]) to the larger prophetic figures of Jesus Christ and the Buddha. Neo as

Jesus Christ the Savior is invoked through not only the conversation at the door but also his continually referenced anagram as the "One." In the third installment of *The Matrix* Neo sacrifices himself, with arms in cruciform, as a "deus ex machina" intones "It is done," referencing the last words of Jesus Christ in the Christian gospels. The Christic-redemptive dimensions are fairly obvious to anyone who has grown up in Western, Christian cultures.

The additional suggestion of Neo as the Buddha comes in the first words addressed to him: "Wake up, Neo." The literal translation of the "Buddha" is "one who has awoken" ("enlightenment" is an abstraction of a more primary metaphor of waking from sleep). Further, Neo comments to the partygoers at his apartment door: "You ever have the feeling that you're not sure if you're awake or still dreaming?" Meanwhile, the final song of the film is titled "Wake Up" (by Rage against the Machine), and dreaming references abound in the movie. Indeed, Neo, Morpheus, Trinity, and others function as bodhisattvas, those who have achieved enlightenment but postpone entering nirvana in order to help others to see through this illusory life.

This is where the leather/rubber clothing worn by people who exist in the matrix is more than a fashion statement. Throughout the film, when characters enter the "false" world of the matrix, they usually wear leather. Such clothing is "second skin" that, while providing a surface coating to one's actual body, both reveals the body's contours and simultaneously hides the body. Its existence functions on a secondary level.

What we find is that *The Matrix*, like *Star Wars*, is a contemporary mythological story that combines multiple myths from several traditions. While this may be construed as a critique of the postmodern age, with its predilection toward pastiche, it is also concomitant with myths throughout the world and the ages. All myths are pastiches. They borrow from previous myths in order to construct something new. As James Ford suggests in a survey of the film, "Myths are constantly adapted to new cultural contexts and worldly realities."[12] Originality is not the key to mythic tellings; rather, what is important is a unique way of combining old forms in a new manner. Films such as *Star Wars* and *The Matrix* have reintroduced the power of myth for our contemporary lives, and they succeed precisely because they have borrowed from the powerful themes, ideas, symbols, and narratives of myths through the ages. They do this in verbal dialogue, as well as through a careful use of visual symbols, including props, clothing, and camera angles.

World Making and Filmmaking: A Warning

There is much more to say about *Star Wars* and *The Matrix* in relation to mythology, and many have done so. For *Star Wars* this includes the hero's journey undertaken by Luke Skywalker or the grand Tao-like energy of "the Force" used by the black-clothed Darth Vader and the white-clothed Skywalker. For *The Matrix* the further mythic connections include commentary on "Zion" as the longed-for place of return from exile, the role of "Thomas" Anderson (in

Syriac, "Thomas" means "twin," and the gnostic gospel of Thomas plays on the relationship between Jesus and Thomas), and Morpheus in the role of the pagan lord of the dreamworld. However, before suggesting that mythologies are simply good things to let into our lives, I end with an ideological critique of the mythology presented in the mise-en-scène of *The Matrix*.

In scene three of *The Matrix*, Neo and Trinity meet in a leather- and rubber-clad nightclub and make a connection that lasts throughout the remaining three films. This initial meeting begins the journey of "waking up" for Neo, as Trinity helps to clue him in to the way the world actually works. Because I have described the introduction of these two characters in the opening scenes, I want to turn to a later framing of them. At the beginning of the film we find a strong, white, female character (Trinity) and a strong, black, male character (Morpheus). They are both insiders to the matrix, with a good deal of knowledge about the reality of the two worlds. We can say that they are enlightened. Neo, the good-looking white male, is not enlightened, at least not initially, and the first half of the movie demonstrates his profound ignorance. Eventually he is edified when he comes to understand and experience the truth of the two worlds created by the matrix, but it takes some time. Throughout most of the film he is far behind other characters like Morpheus and Trinity in knowledge and understanding.

Nonetheless, the climactic scene, in which Agent Smith seemingly kills Neo, demonstrates another prominent mythology: the Hollywood myth of white-supremacist romantic relationships. Just as the Wachowski brothers draw from a variety of myths to create a new, hybrid telling of myth, Hollywood as a whole has become a serious contender for creating the most prominent mythologies of the contemporary age. Thus, what we see through *The Matrix* is a hybridizing of mythologies, most prominently Christian and Buddhist. Yet, what prevails over both in the end is the Hollywood myth of white, heterosexual relations between good-looking people.

As Neo is killed in the matrix, his "real" body also undergoes a death. The camera frames his body, which is lying back in his chair with his brain linked to the matrix, as Trinity gazes lovingly at him. He dies in both worlds, but Trinity comes down upon him like a spirit and kisses him. Their kiss is framed with what appear to be fireworks behind them (actually the evil sentinels, who are trying to break in with laser weapons). After all of the special effects and the original ways of telling old stories, *The Matrix* falls back on the same tired scenario to end with good-looking white male and good-looking white female kissing in the rain, under fireworks, and in the midst of generalized chaos. Just when we were sure that a strong white woman or a strong black male might take the lead, in the end they are simply props for the attractive white male who plays the role of the Savior, the Buddha, the One. This does not deny the strength of Trinity or Morpheus, but as the three films progress, it becomes increasingly clear that all of the other characters are there primarily to make way for Neo.

So, this blending of mythologies is part and parcel of what religious myths are all about: begging, borrowing, and stealing. This is what gives them such great power to affect people's lives. Contemporary films have tapped into this potent influence and will continue to do so. (Why write a new story when South Asian mythologies provide thousands of pages of wonderful tales to bring into play?) Students of religious studies have to carefully walk that line between praising the great imaginative stories of old and paying attention to the subtle ways they might maintain oppressive systems of power.

Conclusion

The deeper implication for a religious study of cinema is that films are not simply verbal narratives. They create and re-create the world through color, form, design, symbols, movement, and music. My suggestions here, while brief, can be used in a variety of ways in the religious studies classroom. By taking the human body, with all of its sensual perceptions, as a basis for interaction with persons and a central conduit for religious life, religious studies might take a cue from film studies by observing the visual and acoustic (and bodily in general) ways humans participate in the process of world making.

The general argument I am making is that films formally function like religions.[13] They are structured in similar ways through their mutual re-creations of space and time. This re-creation is then projected outward (externalized), making it appear, as Clifford Geertz might say, "uniquely realistic." In this way these audiovisual experiential stories impact human lives, offering models for living, not just cerebrally but through the body as well. This means that religious studies students need to pay attention to what is uniquely filmic about film and, by extension, that our lives as humans are constructed through the sights and sounds and smells that surround us. Meanwhile, some smells and sights are more persuasive then others, challenging us to live differently, which might have both positive and negative effects.

NOTES

1. Peter Berger, *The Sacred Canopy* (Garden City, N.Y.: Doubleday, 1967), 27.

2. Ibid., 27–28.

3. Ibid., 27.

4. Nelson Goodman, *Ways of Worldmaking* (Indianapolis: Hackett, 1978), 7.

5. Abraham Heschel, *The Sabbath: Its Meaning for Modern Man* (New York: Farrar, Straus, Giroux, 1951), 10.

6. Ibid., 14. Here Heschel is paraphrasing the *Zohar*.

7. "Mise-en-scène" began as a theater term but was quickly adapted to early cinema. Literally meaning "to put onto stage," mise-en-scène has been a serious topic for scholars and film critics almost since the beginnings of film theory. Good introductions include David Bordwell and Kristin Thompson's chapter titled "The Shot: Mise-en-scène," in *Film Art: An Introduction,* 8th ed. (Boston: McGraw-Hill, 2008) and the short book by John Gibbs, *Mise-en-scène* (London: Wallflower Press, 2002).

8. See George Lucas's interview by Bill Moyers, "The Mythology of Star Wars," available on video from PBS and excerpted in *The Religion and Film Reader,* ed. Jolyon

Mitchell and S. Brent Plate (London: Routledge, 2007). For the Wachowski brothers see *Time* magazine 153(15) (Apr. 19, 1999), 75. A number of religious studies scholars have written on both films. I especially recommend John Lyden, "The Apocalyptic Cosmology of *Star Wars*," *Journal of Religion and Film* 4(1) (Apr. 2000) at http://www.unomaha.edu/jrf/LydenStWars.htm; Andrew Gordon, "A Myth for Our Time" (on *Star Wars*) in *Screening the Sacred*, ed. Joel W. Martin and Conrad Ostwalt (Boulder, Colo.: Westview, 1995), 73–82; and Frances Flannery-Dailey and Rachel Wagner, "Wake Up! Gnosticism and Buddhism in *The Matrix*," *Journal of Religion and Film* 5(2) (Oct. 2001) at http://www.unomaha.edu/jrf/gnostic.htm.

9. Jean Baudrillard, "On Nihilism," in *Simulacra and Simulations*, trans. Sheila Glaser (Ann Arbor: University of Michigan Press, 1994), 159.

10. Jean Baudrillard, "Simulacra and Simulations," in *Jean Baudrillard: Selected Writings*, ed. Mark Poster (Stanford, Calif.: Stanford University Press, 1988), 170. Baudrillard argued against the use of his book in *The Matrix*, claiming the filmmakers got it wrong. This would be a much deeper philosophical argument than is possible to discuss here. See a translated interview with Baudrillard on the topic at http://www.empyree.org/divers/Matrix-Baudrillard_english.html (accessed Nov. 28, 2007).

11. Baudrillard, "Simulacra and Simulations," 166.

12. James Ford, "Buddhism, Christianity, and *The Matrix*: The Dialectic of Myth-making in Contemporary Cinema," *Journal of Religion and Film* 4(2) (Oct. 2000) at http://www.unomaha.edu/jrf/thematrix.htm (accessed Nov. 28, 2007).

13. I discuss this general concept further in my book *Religion and Film: Cinema and the Recreation of the World* (London: Wallflower Press, 2008). The aspects of bodily sense reception in relation to religion are addressed further in my books *Walter Benjamin, Religion, and Aesthetics: Rethinking Religion through the Arts* (London: Routledge, 2005) and *Religion, Art, and Visual Culture: A Cross-cultural Reader* (New York: Palgrave, 2002).

14

Introducing Theories
of Religion through Film:
A Sample Syllabus

Gregory J. Watkins

Origins of the Course

Despite having a background in film production, I did not immediately think about making film the subject of my academic work while a graduate student in a religious studies department. It was not until I attended my first panel of the Religion, Film, and Visual Culture Group of the American Academy of Religion (AAR) that my interest was piqued, driven mostly by a sense that the kind of work I heard about in the panel presentations was falling far short of capturing the depth and uniqueness of the film medium. To my mind, the connections being drawn between religion and film were too broad and mechanical. My attempt to describe both the kind of work I was seeing in this field and what I thought was possible led to my article "Seeing and Being Seen: Distinctively Filmic and Religious Elements in Film" (1999). Specifically, I wanted to tackle the following question: If film is a distinctive medium of art (i.e., if some elements of film are unique in artistic media), then might film also contain distinctive forms of religious expression and experience? Clearly, movies could be *about* religion, and one could expect theologies and theories of religion to facilitate discussions about movies and the movie culture just as much as any other cultural product or practice.

However, my particular interest centered on that specific terrain (if it existed) that represented a synergistic union of religion and film—where something new had been created. Furthermore, and as a corollary to this initial orientation, I knew that several brilliant filmmakers had taken the time to write about their understanding of film art and the religious dimensions of their own work (I immediately thought of Ingmar Bergman, Robert Bresson, and Andrei Tarkovsky). What might a scholar of religion make of their attempts to express religious visions in film, and would that investigation answer the question about the possibility of unique forms of religious expression and/or experience in film?

As scholars are wont to do, I drew upon this particular research interest when I had the opportunity to teach a course on religion and film. The course I describe here was designed around the investigation of this same question: Do films make possible distinctive forms of religious expression and/or experience? To answer that question, the class would have to consider both what to identify as fundamentally religious and what, if anything, is particular to film as an artistic medium. What is religion, anyway? And just what is film? Of course, the *process* of answering these "preliminary" questions is the main work and value of the course. While students might, by the end of the class, decide to dismiss these inquiries as unanswerable or ultimately unimportant, they would have investigated some of the many ways of thinking about religion and become much more skilled viewers of film along the way.

Pedagogy: The Value of Creative Confusion

My pedagogical style is to do my best to create intellectual confusion in my students—to challenge the understanding they have of a subject when first coming into the class. At the same time I give them the tools to think differently about it, even if the new thinking is short lived. I feel I have succeeded as a teacher if I manage to create wonder in my students—in this case, wonder about religion (which they often think they know from their own traditions or assume they understand on the basis of old convictions) and wonder about film (which means challenging the expert training they have as viewers of popular movies, an expertise that often brings with it narrow conceptions of art in general). Furthermore, I utilize something of a film editor's approach to creating this productive, intellectual confusion by bringing elements of the class into provocative juxtaposition.

In a sense, my goal for readers of this chapter is the same. Because readers of this volume will have much more knowledge of religion than the students of the course I describe here, I am hoping that a sketch of the syllabus will be enough to indicate my method or, even better, to spark a reaction in readers that will be productively suggestive on its own. As with film editing, even slight adjustments in the ordering of the elements (not to mention substitution of new parts) can create significantly different but equally effective results. What follows is a snapshot of the logic and design of the course, without a lot of detail, in the hope that it will prove useful. I invite you to contact me directly if you have questions about any particular element or would like to discuss the course further (filmgreg@gmail.com).

Guiding Principles and Course Constraints

The course described here has been taught to small classes of undergraduates at Stanford University and to medium-sized classes (about thirty students) of Stanford Continuing Studies students and Santa Clara University undergraduates. I mention this in part because of some of the practical challenges of studying film in the classroom. This course is likely less suitable for large lecture classes (especially because of the role I give to discussion), but teachers of large classes might find other elements worth borrowing.

Viewing Films

I find it invaluable to be able to discuss at least some movies immediately after viewing them as a class, but the sheer length of many movies makes this impossible. I tend to mix classroom screenings with homework viewing assignments, dictated in part by the length of the movies in question. To avoid competition for viewing when films are put on reserve, I typically set up one or two opportunities for group screenings outside of normal class meeting times; in this way, students are guaranteed a chance to see the movies, and they can decide exactly when and how they see them (sometimes students act on their own initiative to rent assigned movies, especially when they already use a rental service). At Santa Clara University I had the luxury of arranging group screenings that were run by the media library staff. When films are seen outside of class, it is important to show and discuss clips from those movies during class time; be prepared to recall certain scenes to mind when the class gets together (specifically as a recall exercise) and then to look at clips that are worth discussing. Many great discussions have been generated by the simple fact that students remember important scenes differently; being able to then watch the scene in question can be particularly instructive. This kind of classroom follow-up also trains them to be more attentive viewers.

Viewing movies together in class has its own challenges, of course. The syllabus I present here had the admittedly unusual format of being taught once a week: one and a half hours for class lecture and discussion, a one-hour break (in this case, for dinner), and then a two-hour time slot for film viewing and discussion. Though not a typical class schedule, this syllabus could be adapted to other class schedules; the important point is to have a time slot that allows for the full viewing of a feature film together, with time for discussion afterward.

Art House Films

Especially when the very nature of film as an artistic medium is the subject of investigation, it is imperative to include not only various kinds of films but also to expose students somewhat to the history of this remarkably young art form and to its reputed classics. No doubt many readers of this volume have already experienced the problems brought about by screening films that do not fit comfortably with students' Hollywood-trained viewing habits, but, especially in a course like this, those habits need to be challenged. In my classes, these viewing routines are constantly under discussion. If students are bored or annoyed by a movie, they know they need to tell me exactly what created that reaction. At the same time, I push throughout the entire class to get them to see what it is about *them,* as viewers, that makes certain movies hard to watch. In other words, it is important to get them to pay attention to the things they notice and why they are especially aware of them.

One of my pedagogical goals is for students to develop the habit of asking about a film they find unusual: What would the filmmaker's view of the world (and/or of film as a form of art) have to be for the movie to be made as it was? What would have to change about *me* as a viewer to have a different experience of this movie than the one I had? (And just why do I expect movies to work in a certain way in the first place?) I consider this aspect of the class a success if students are willing to entertain the ideas that movies that work in unexpected or unfamiliar ways might be worth some effort on their part and that they might change as viewers in the process.

When this issue is on the table in the classroom, discussion invariably leads to two questions: Is art great only when it comes to you (i.e., when it can succeed without your having to do a lot of work or even knowing that work has been done)? Or might great art require, at least in part, that we come to it (i.e., that we undertake some measure of work to see it for what it is)? It is good to address these issues as early as possible; I announce loudly and clearly at the start of the class that their viewing habits will be challenged. Finally, given the virtual disappearance of art house cinema, a course like this is the last opportunity most of these students will have for seeing some of these great works of art.

Reaction Papers

I find reaction papers particularly helpful in two important ways: (1) by putting their reactions to movies in writing, students start thinking about the movie critically while developing a vocabulary for doing so; and 2) getting some indication of their reactions helps me know what to address in class or even what to stir up if reactions are mixed (it can also be a nice way to invite participation from typically quiet students when their reaction papers reveal something interesting going on). I collect these assignments via email, making sure the deadline gives me time to review them before the next class meeting.

Laying the Groundwork

What Is Religion? What Is Film?

In the first class meeting I break students up into groups of three or four people to come up with preliminary answers to the question, what is religion?

I give them ten or fifteen minutes to talk about it as a small group and tell them that someone from the group will report on their findings when the class comes together again. To encourage them to approach this exercise as a brainstorming activity, I describe both how they might already think about religion and how others might view it. In the whole-class discussion I write elements of their reports on the board, prompt discussion as we go, and finally organize their answers into three general approaches to religion: functional theories, substantive theories, and "family resemblance" theories. Then I make it clear that we are developing a vocabulary that I expect them to use in their reaction papers, class discussions, exams, and papers.

I then ask them to do the same with the film side of the equation: What is a movie? Though it seems simpler on the face of it, students tend to have more trouble answering this question in a satisfying manner, and I am less inclined to lead this discussion to any definitive conclusions. Indeed, what is essential to this thing called a movie? Is narrative necessary? Is there a specific setting and/ or ritual for watching a movie? What features does it have in common with other art forms, and which ones are different? One way of describing film is as a sequence of photographs, but exactly what is photography? What does it mean to take a picture of something, and what is the experience of viewing it? (I find it especially valuable to leave the question about photography open, as the readings from Stanley Cavell probe that question systematically.) During this open conversation about film as a medium, I often ask for volunteers to describe their favorite images from movies. This question sometimes stumps students, as favorite movies are usually dictated by the story. When students start offering memorable images, they are usually of the "spectacle" variety— some image or sequence that amazes with its virtuosity or pyrotechnics. But invariably we arrive at a suggested image, the meaning of which is tied in a complicated way to story and style. In the course of this particular conversation I like to suggest that film art might be about the creation of meaningful images.

I end the discussion of these two preliminary questions by introducing the central topic of the class: Assuming we can figure out what religion and film are, will we then discover some distinctive realm of human expression and experience? In movie terms, this question is the MacGuffin in the class; it is the plot device around which the story and the drama of the class advance, regardless of whether our plot comes to a satisfactory conclusion. (For those new to this term, the classic example of a MacGuffin is the Maltese falcon statuette in *The Maltese Falcon* [1941, directed by John Huston]).

Elements of Film

Another goal of the class is teaching basic film language. Several entire sessions can be devoted to this purpose, though I sometimes focus on particular aspects of film language as the course proceeds, linking such discussions to the specific films of the week. Whether or not one uses it as assigned reading (I do not), I highly recommend David Bordwell and Kristin Thompson's *Film Art:*

An Introduction, 8th ed. (2008). As with the discussions about religion, an introduction to film language (both of filmmaking and of talking about movies) is part of the process of developing the students' technical vocabulary. I start by asking students to consider film as a language and then introduce them to Bordwell and Thompson's general approach, which breaks film language into what they refer to as four sets of cinematic technique. Two of these sets relate specifically to any single shot of a film: (1) mise-en-scène (essentially everything in the frame: actors, sets, costumes, staging, lighting strategies, the effects they create, etc.); and (2) cinematography (the photographic element of how things look, including discussion of lenses, depth of field, filters, film stocks, types of shots, camera movement, etc.). The third set focuses on the relationship between shots (examining technical aspects of editing, as well as the idea of creating meaning through the juxtaposition of images). The fourth set considers the relationship between sound and image. Bordwell and Thompson discuss the way in which these sets of technical elements are part of a general way of talking about the overall style of a film. I often also use this focus on film language to introduce students to three major styles of film language—realism, classical cinema (Hollywood narratives), and expressionism—which help them compare the films in the course.

Film Theory—Stanley Cavell

I do not assign any readings from the classics of film theory. For the purposes of this class, it is enough to teach film language and style and then explore connections to the films we are seeing and to our consideration of religion. Of course, discussion of cinematic language and style *is* theorizing about film, but I have found no need to supplement this approach with readings from canonical works of film theory. (For introductions to film theory I recommend *Film Theory and Criticism: Introductory Readings,* 6th ed., ed. Braudy and Cohen [2004] and Dudley's *Major Film Theories: An Introduction* [1976].) Though not generally considered a major work of film theory, Cavell's *The World Viewed: Reflections on the Ontology of Film* (1979) is the only reading I assign expressly about the nature of film. I find Cavell's plain-language approach to thinking about the distinctive nature of film to be perfect for the course.

Focusing especially on Cavell's first six chapters, I take time in class to work through his questioning of the film medium, which starts with an inquiry into photography (e.g., Is a photograph a record of something in the same way a sound recording is? Is it a kind of memory?). Put briefly, Cavell's remarkable conclusion to this part of his argument is that a photograph is an indication of a world that extends beyond the borders of the image. Moreover, we then function as viewers of a world that cannot see us and thereby create a unique set of ontological relationships within the world of art. Working through Cavell's argument in class has proven rewarding (partly due to the pleasure of making clear philosophical progress in Socratic fashion) and often transformational for how students are thinking about what movies do and how we relate to them. The Cavell reading is not integral to any particular week in the course, but I try to discuss his argument during the first couple of weeks. (Cavell's work plays an important role in the argument in my article "Seeing and Being Seen").

The Film and Reading Units

In this section I list thumbnail sketches of the reading and film elements of specific units. Again, I am brief, hoping a sense of the general approach proves suggestive.

Bible and Film: Crimes and Misdemeanors, David and Bathsheba, and A Short Film about Killing

Crimes and Misdemeanors (1989; directed by Woody Allen) is a great first film for classroom viewing. As a simultaneously funny, mainstream, and intelligent movie, it successfully engages students in talking about religion and film by raising explicit questions about the role of philosophy, religious tradition (Judaism), and even movie culture itself in modern moral life. The story is brilliantly crafted and warrants in-depth discussions of theme, characterizations, and the director's viewpoint. The texture of the story usually comes out by asking where "the good" can be found in the movie. I am also careful to tie discussions of the movie to our theoretical questions about the substantive versus functional definitions of religion. In the world of this movie, is there a moral order inherent in the universe, or is religion just a means of social control? Students assume it is the latter, but I think Woody Allen is trying to make a case for the former.

From here I move to *David and Bathsheba* (1951; directed by Henry King) and issues of the adaptation of biblical stories. If time allows, it is a helpful and fun exercise to discuss how the David and Bathsheba story (2 Sam. 11, 12) could be turned into a movie. What do we *not* know about the story that we would have to fill in? What about casting? (Students are always happy to play at casting a movie.) How will casting decisions affect the adaptation? It is a good idea to engage the students' creative imaginations with regard to a particular story before seeing a movie version because they gain a better sense of the obstacles the filmmakers faced and the decisions they made.

The bigger issue here, of course, has to do with the process of adapting sacred text to the medium of movies. How does a text work differently from a movie, and is anything important at stake in those differences? If, for example, it is in the very nature of biblical text to leave important elements of a story open to interpretation (thereby fostering an interpretive community), what is the effect of firmly deciding many of the story elements in a movie version? Furthermore, what are we to make of movies that contradict or distort the stories they adapt? In contrast to 2 Samuel, for instance, this adaptation opens with David on the front lines of a battle, fighting alongside his men, including Uriah. Students could consider why the writer (Philip Dunne) would make that choice. (This movie, incidentally, was nominated for an Oscar for best screenplay.) Also, what about the sheer power of images versus text? Will we ever picture King David again as anybody but Gregory Peck? What happens to "religions of the book" in an increasingly visual culture? And a final suggestion: Is the theology of the movie (the image of God and God's relationship to society) the same in the movie as in the text? Much can be accomplished with discussion alone, but I usually supplement this unit with readings from Alice Bach, "'Throw Them to the Lions, Sire': Transforming Biblical Narratives into Hollywood Spectaculars" (1996).

A Short Film about Killing (1988; directed by Krzysztof Kieslowski) works in sobering contrast to many of the themes in Crimes and Misdemeanors (note that part of Kieslowski's Decalogue project shows another version of this movie; either one is useful). On the face of it, both movies are about the biblical commandment against killing, but they are so different in style that they produce a great deal of comparative discussion about film language and thematic impact. Kieslowski's movie tells interweaving stories of a young man who commits a premeditated but essentially random murder and of the lawyer who unsuccessfully defends him against the death penalty. Depicting both the murder and the state-sanctioned capital punishment, the movie is powerfully textured and makes a great companion piece to Crimes and Misdemeanors both thematically and stylistically.

Religion as Feeling: Friedrich Schleiermacher and The Green Pastures

Attempting to move into a new way of thinking about religion while also sticking with issues of biblical adaptation, this unit pairs reading from Friedrich Schleiermacher's On Religion: Speeches to Its Cultured Despisers (1988) and the movie The Green Pastures (1936; directed by Marc Connelly and William Keighley). After reading text from Schleiermacher's first two speeches, we consider Romantic theories of religion, with their emphasis on the emotional component of religious experience (and even, for Schleiermacher, their express rejection of the prevailing view at the time that religion is fundamentally about metaphysics or morals). The reading is always harder for the students than I expect, especially in light of the fact that many of them are very receptive to the theory once they understand it (my sense is that the modern phenomenon of "spiritual but not religious" is related to an implicit effort to emphasize a dimension of feeling over convictions about metaphysics or morality).

The Green Pastures is not a completely natural fit with a Romantic theory of religion, but it manages to further the discussion of biblical adaptation while making just enough connection with Schleiermacher's argument. A film version of a wildly popular Broadway show, The Green Pastures presents a series of Old Testament stories told from the perspective of African Americans in the rural South. Working out the contrasts in style between David and Bathsheba and The Green Pastures is always productive, and the discussion of The Green Pastures eventually focuses on the idea that biblical stories are meant to serve a kind of native and fundamentally emotional piety. Additionally, the

Schleiermacher readings introduce the idea of the artist-as-prophet and argues for a deep and abiding link between the role of the prophet and that of the artist in connecting with the divine. As such, this issue of the status of the artist is revisited throughout the course.

Auteur Theory and the Search for Meaning: Bergman's
The Seventh Seal *and* Wild Strawberries

Working almost entirely from lecture and the discussion of these two movies, the class then moves into a construal of religion as that which gives meaning to life. Students have little trouble digging into Bergman's provocative mix of Protestant religiosity and philosophical existentialism in an essentially Catholic universe. In Bergman's *Seventh Seal* (1957), the knight's spiritual crisis after a crusade to the Holy Land serves primarily as a pretext for the modern crisis of meaning. At the same time, the movie shows a world in which God categorically exists (Jof's visions and the absence of the most pious characters from the famous "dance of death" make this clear). This movie rewards both a close analysis of each character's view of the Christian universe in which they live and a discussion of how to determine what the *director* thinks in the midst of these many voices. Given Bergman's cinematic genius, the film also deserves discussion of its techniques (touching on all of the Bordwell and Thompson sets of techniques).

Adding *Wild Strawberries* allows several strands to develop. First, it puts Bergman's search-for-meaning theme in a less explicitly religious setting (though there are still many references to religion). It tells the story of an aging professor's road trip to accept an honorary degree and the spiritual crisis he experiences along the way, which is provoked by disturbing memories, nightmares, and strained family relationships. Because of all the psychodrama, there is a potential for introducing psychoanalytic approaches to religion, but I tend to focus on the personal search for meaning, tying that in turn to auteur theory—namely, the idea that the films of a single director represent an artist's (or "author's") unique creative vision. I emphasize this filmmaker-as-artist idea because American students are utterly unfamiliar with it. If students know any directors by name, it is usually for their technical brilliance (or perhaps their skill in storytelling) and not for the personal vision they express in their work. Does *Wild Strawberries* help us understand *The Seventh Seal* and vice versa? Is there development in the artist's thinking? Will learning more about the director help us understand what is going on in the movies?

It is hard to find discrete pieces of writing by Bergman or single interviews that are good on this front, but it is important to lecture on relevant aspects of his biography, tortured as he was by his religious background and by fundamentally religious questions. Finally, this discussion allows the introduction of the idea that art itself might play a role in the creation of meaning. What is filmmaking doing for Bergman personally? If religion serves a meaning-making function for essentially existential predicaments, can art (and movies) do the same for filmmakers and their audiences? (If *The Seventh Seal* and *Wild*

Strawberries are both shown in class, I highly recommend a screening of the short film that spoofs Bergman's œuvre, *De Düva* [1968; directed by George Coe and Anthony Lover].)

Surrealism and the Critique of Religion: Breton, Un chien andalou, *and* Exterminating Angel

This unit explores the surrealist movement and two of the films of Luis Buñuel. It is good to show the brilliant and historic *Un chien andalou* (1929; directed by Luis Buñuel and Salvador Dali) without much of an introduction, especially as it consistently provokes gasps, groans, and averting of the eyes! Running about sixteen minutes, this surrealist classic has many shocking elements even by the standards of today's students. Indeed, one can ask in class how *Chien*'s images can be so troubling when our visual culture is awash in movie and television media images of sex and violence. Of course, shock is part of the original intention of *Un chien andalou,* so it may be best to do the historical contextualizing after the first viewing.

Moreover, with such a short movie, I recommend adding a second viewing after a fair amount of discussion. As part of the conversation, I emphasize how radically new this film art is. *Un chien andalou* demonstrates that something in this medium cannot be found in any other form of art, and students should talk about that fact. Of course, this film also has students wondering fairly early on what exactly this could have to do with religion. The connection to religion is developed with the Breton reading, the general discussion of surrealism, additional information about Buñuel as an artist, and discussions of Buñuel's *Exterminating Angel* after watching the movie. (To be clear, I believe *Un chien andalou* has a great deal to do with religion, when considered in the way this unit suggests; it is just that the case for seeing it in that light needs to be constructed more carefully than with the films viewed up to this point.)

The reading for this unit is taken from the opening sections of André Breton's "Manifesto of Surrealism" (1924). My argument in this unit has to do in part with the religious zeal of surrealism and its conviction that bourgeois culture and mentality (especially the tyranny of logic) have blinded us to the freedom that is our human birthright. Even a cursory reading of the manifesto makes this clear—Breton's contention, for example, is that dreams can be used "to solve the fundamental problems of life" (ibid., 12). A page later he puts the process in terms of atonement and later on sums up his line of reasoning with these words: "Surrealism is based on the belief in the superior reality of certain forms of previously neglected associations, in the omnipotence of dream, in the disinterested play of thought. It tends to ruin once and for all all other psychic mechanisms and to substitute itself for them in solving all the principal problems of life" (ibid., 26). Salvation, indeed.

For Buñuel, the Catholic Church plays a particularly noxious role in our spiritual oppression, and many of his films attack Catholicism (though often with great humor; "Thank God, I'm an atheist," Buñuel was reportedly fond of saying). Through the combination of Breton and Buñuel, these films can be seen as critical of institutional religion while claiming for themselves a kind of religious salvation by freeing people from the bourgeois rationality and morality that blind them to the truth (with, once again, the artist functioning as prophet). It is precisely this twofold surrealist project of institutional critique and human liberation that makes Buñuel's *Exterminating Angel* so powerful and interesting. It tells the strangely compelling story of Mexican aristocrats who become inexplicably trapped at a formal dinner party. Here the titular exterminating angel invisibly does its work of breaking down the thin veneer of social convention and uncovering expressions of raw religiosity beneath the surface. Although it is a good enough movie to warrant the screening of relatively poor VHS versions, this movie has been remastered for DVD release.

Horror and the Holy: Rudolf Otto and Jacob's Ladder

The idea for this unit came from a syllabus I found online for a course taught by Francisca Cho (a contributor to this volume). As I remember, she was combining Rudolf Otto's *Idea of the Holy* (1957) with a screening of *Carrie*. Although I had no other information to go on, I could see the potential (I have yet to be able to compare notes with Cho). Reading from Otto (chapters 1–7) allows a return to pure theory of religion—in this case, of the substantive variety. The assignment can be tough going for students, so covering the material carefully in class is especially important. Briefly, Otto emphasizes the nonrational dimensions of religious experience, the role of evocation (versus argumentation) in religious experience, and indeed the methodological emphasis that theory requires experience (advising readers who lack experience of the numinous not to bother reading his book). However, it is in connection to the horror genre that this theoretical model takes hold with students. Because of Otto's emphasis on the *mysterium tremendum* and experiences of dread and awe in the encounter with the "wholly other," a link to horror films is easily drawn. As Otto states:

> The ghost's real attraction rather consists in this, that of itself and in an uncommon degree it entices the imagination, awakening strong interest and curiosity . . . and it does this because it is a thing that "doesn't really exist at all," the "wholly other," something which has no place in our scheme of reality but belongs to an absolutely different one, and which at the same time arouses an irrepressible interest in the mind. (ibid., 29)

Otto's argument linking fear, awe, and dread to the Holy has a powerful effect on students once they start to relate it to their own visceral experiences of the same (whether in their own lives or at the movies); at a minimum, they get a good sense of how a nonpropositional, nonrational understanding of religion might work.

My pairing of this text with *Jacob's Ladder* (1990; directed by Adrian Lyne) is not a perfect fit with Otto; something more firmly in the horror genre would probably work better. Nevertheless, the movie allows for a number of connections to the course as a whole (including retrospectively, when we get to Buddhism) while working with these religious claims about the horror genre. Indeed, one of the movie's themes deals directly with the idea that fear is integral to spiritual progress and that the demonic becomes angelic when we come to a deeper understanding of ourselves.

Buddhism and Film: Why Has Bodhi-Dharma Left for the East? and the Documentaries The Tibetan Book of the Dead I and II

This unit takes a leap to a frame of reference that is significantly different from the Jewish and Christian material that precedes it. Continuing the survey approach, however, I let the films teach the Buddhism that is necessary for the purposes of the class (I have significant experience teaching Buddhism but am not a specialist). I start with the two-part documentary titled *The Tibetan Book of the Dead: A Way of Life* and *The Great Liberation* (1994; directed by Barrie McLean), which focuses on the Bardo Thodol and the funerary ceremonies intended to help the deceased to a good rebirth. While introducing students to a different religious worldview, the film also creates an opportunity to talk about the documentary genre (in contrast to all of the fiction films to this point) and raises the special problem of the representation of spiritual states.

The documentary uses only moderately successful animation sequences to represent spirit states and spiritual progress. In a fundamentally visual medium, how might a filmmaker capture what otherwise cannot be seen? I do not mean this just in respect to *documenting* (though I joke with the students that these films contain documentary footage of the afterlife). As part of the challenge of thinking about the intersection of religion and film, one has to carefully consider what images can and cannot communicate and what can and cannot be shown. Indeed—as several chapters in this volume ask—can film show us these things? If so, what does that actually mean, and how does it work? This line of thinking is in part a preparation for a later discussion of the "transcendental style" (the argument that cinematic style can communicate the nonvisual through a visual medium or, better, that it can enable us to see in an image what the image itself does not show).

Although from an entirely different tradition of Buddhism, *Why Has Bodhi-Dharma Left for the East?* (1989; directed by Bae Yong-Kyun) is also screened in this unit. It tells the story of a young man who comes to a Buddhist hermitage searching for enlightenment and of his relationship to the old meditation master and the orphan boy who live there. Slowly paced and quite long by today's norms (137 minutes), *Bodhi-Dharma* can be difficult for students to watch. Like the documentary, though, one can teach the film without a lot of introduction to Buddhism in the class. It is much better to build to the Buddhist insights the movie presents from a class discussion. The director himself claimed he wanted audiences to see the film without preconceived notions and added that it was his goal to provide the audience with a vision of reality rather than the assertion of doctrines (for supporting materials, in-

cluding director statements, visit the distributor's website at http://www
.milestonefilms.com).

This point is central to my use of the film, namely, the proposition that a
film can be a kind of cultivation of a certain way of seeing (see also Cho's
chapter in this volume for a detailed discussion of a similar idea). So, when
students describe the difficulties they have watching this movie, they can then
discuss their own "habits of seeing" and how the film might be "seeing"
differently. Specifically, what might the film's message be, and in what ways do
the cinematic techniques further it? Additionally, working backward, what
might we conclude about Buddhism knowing this movie is in some sense a
Buddhist movie? Is this movie "seeing" reality differently? Might it be possible
that watching this movie actually cultivates a spiritual state? This last question
often leads to comparisons of "consumable" and nonconsumable art. Other
discussion topics include whether or not the process of filmmaking can have
religious dimensions (can a film be "meditatively" made, as I believe this one
was?). Indeed, might there also be a meditative mode of film viewing? Though
too sophisticated to assign as reading in an introductory class of this kind,
I highly recommend Cho's article "Imagining Nothing and Imagining Otherness in Buddhist Film" (1999) for a remarkable analysis of this movie and its
relationship to a more general theory of Buddhist film.

Filmmaker as Religious Thinker: Tarkovsky's The Sacrifice and Sculpting in Time

This unit is guided (too much, perhaps) by my admiration for Tarkovsky and
his films. Though he is considered one of the true geniuses of cinema, he is not
nearly as popular as even some of the art-house film directors discussed in this
chapter. Still, by this point in the course, students have often developed the
patience to pay somewhat careful attention to *The Sacrifice* (1986), Tarkovsky's
last film, which he completed while dying of cancer. It tells the story of an aging
intellectual, Alexander, who is troubled by the spiritual state of the modern
world, a world that his young son will inherit. During Alexander's sedate birth-
day celebration at a remote summer home, World War III breaks out, marking
the beginning of a nuclear holocaust. In the eerie aftermath, Alexander learns
he might have the power to turn back the clock and redeem the world through
personal sacrifice.

This movie, like so many of those I have mentioned, could stand on its own
in this kind of course. Religious tropes in this movie are abundant, and it is
clear that the filmmaker is an artist who is trying to directly address modern
spiritual questions. However, what makes Tarkovsky especially worth including are the meditations on cinema and spirituality in his book *Sculpting in Time*
(1986). I typically assign passages from chapters 2, 4, 7, and 9, as well as the
conclusion, emphasizing Tarkovsky's discussion of art in general: "The allotted function of art is not, as is often assumed, to put across ideas, to propagate
thoughts, to serve as example. The aim of art is to prepare a person for death, to

plough and harrow his soul, rendering it capable of turning good" (ibid., 43). In a sense this is also the deepest layer of my pedagogy: for students to see that art can have profound purposes. Using the artist-as-prophet formulation we came across in Schleiermacher, Tarkovsky puts it this way: "Touched by a masterpiece, a person begins to hear in himself that same call of truth which prompted the artist to his creative act. When a link is established between the work and its beholder, the latter experiences a sublime, purging trauma" (ibid.). By no means do I expect students to find this kind of experience in the Tarkovsky movie, but my sense is they have resonant experiences in their own lives (usually with music) that enable them to understand and appreciate the argument. For Tarkovsky, the mass appeal of cinema demonstrates that modern people are seeking to fill the spiritual vacuum that comes from constant activity, the curtailment of human contact, and the culture of materialism and consumerism. This unit, at a minimum, encourages students to ask whether the movies they watch exaggerate modern alienation, conceal it, or provide a nourishing, if traumatic, alternative.

Mythic Time/Secular Time: Eliade, The Last Wave, and La jetée

For this unit I focus on a few specific features of Mircea Eliade's theories of religion by assigning the foreword, preface, and first chapter ("The Myths of the Modern World") from the collection *Myths, Dreams, and Mysteries* (1957). First, the general theme of this collection of essays is that there is a fundamental difference between modern and traditional (or archaic) societies and that it affects our understanding of religion. After describing the mythic world of traditional society—a world circumscribed by sacred history—Eliade asks what has happened to these myths in the modern world. The second element is thus the historical one, the idea that our understanding of religion may need to consider profound historical shifts. For Eliade, we have not, as human beings, lost complete touch with our archaic selves, and it is precisely the uncomfortable fit between modern society and archaic consciousness that allows his theory to function as description and criticism. The third feature has to do with our very sense of time: "It is by analyzing the attitude of the modern man towards Time that we can penetrate the disguises of his mythological behaviour" (ibid., 34). This method yields two lines of inquiry for the class. First, is it possible to understand the religious value of at least some movies in terms of their appeal to archaic consciousness and mythic modes of thinking? Of course, there are numerous movie possibilities here (and Plate's chapter in this volume addresses certain formal aspects of this mythic function of film), but I like that *The Last Wave* (1977; directed by Peter Weir) builds its story around this exact theme. It tells the story of an Australian tax attorney who falls into defending five Aboriginals in a murder case. Through dreams and visions, the lawyer is pulled into the "archaic" worldview of his clients to the point of discovering the mythic role he has to play in their drama. The story makes great connections with the Eliade material, and the way in which Weir gives a cinematic sense of mythic versus secular time (Weir is also typically brilliant in his use of sound editing) provides ample material for discussion. The movie feels a bit dated in style, but students find it engaging overall.

The second line of inquiry has to do with Eliade's arguments about *concentrated time* and *distractions* as the modern accommodation to sacred time. These concepts are useful for thinking about the cultural practices of movie-going, seeing them as both practices of concentrated time and distraction from the rigors of secular time. This discussion often leads to wider observations about the modern obsessions with sports (concentrated time) and activities like video games (the need for distraction). Furthermore, many contemporary movies have turned to thinking about time itself, in the mode of eternal return or time travel, for example, as a way into considering fundamental questions of human meaning (see *Groundhog Day, Twelve Monkeys,* etc.). It is as if the contemporary impotence of mythic stories and sacred history has forced the human drama onto the stage of mechanical time, of the ticking of the clock and the ceaseless progression of days. *La jetée* (1962; directed by Chris Marker) is one of the great films in all of cinema, and it connects well with Eliade's arguments about time. Running just twenty-eight minutes, it tells the story (using almost exclusively a still-photo montage) of an apocalyptic future and experimental attempts in an underground camp to travel back in time as a means of saving the human race (*Twelve Monkeys* is the Hollywood adaptation of this Chris Marker original story). What is remarkable about this story is its attempt to use historical time to address issues of human meaning—I maintain that the movie is an effort to make historical time sacred without appealing to traditional mythic stories. As cinema, *La jetée* is also a powerful reminder to students that cinema need not be spectacular in the usual ways in order to hold their attention; even today's students tend to be deeply engaged in this story told with little more than black-and-white photos and voiceover narration.

Transcendental Style: Paul Schrader, Tokyo Story, The Passion of Joan of Arc, *and* Pickpocket

In one sense this unit is at the heart of the class if only because Paul Schrader's argument in *Transcendental Style in Film* (1972) is in itself a kind of answer to the main topic of the course. Through his analyses of the style of Ozu, Bresson, and Dreyer films, Schrader argues for a particular link between the uniform filmic technique found in these separate analyses and an expression of the "transcendent" (Schrader works with a substantive theory, and references to Otto can help explain Schrader's argument). Through the interplay of *the everyday, disparity,* and *stasis,* each filmmaker expresses the transcendent (not *feelings about* it but the transcendent itself). As Schrader puts it in one of his summary formulations:

> If a viewer accepts that scene [of decisive action amid disparity]—if he finds it credible and meaningful—he accepts a good deal more. He accepts a philosophical construct which permits total disparity—deep, illogical, suprahuman feeling within a cold, unfeeling environment.

> In effect, he accepts a construct such as this: there exists a deep
> ground of compassion and awareness which man and nature
> can touch intermittently. This, of course, is the Transcendent.
> (ibid., 48)

It is a remarkable argument and worth careful study.

I show a film from each of Schrader's three filmmakers: Ozu's *Tokyo Story* (1953) (though it is long and slow, students are often moved by this film), Dreyer's *Passion of Joan of Arc* (1928), and Bresson's *Pickpocket* (1959). There are many films to choose from, but these three are generally considered to be among the greatest movies ever made. They are amazing movies in their own right and richly suggestive in the context of this course even without Schrader's theory. This unit, then, presents the most sustained single argument of the course and works through a particular theory of religion and film by analyzing three of the films used in its development.

Sacred Canopy: Peter Berger and Baraka

At least one or two students always come into the class as fans of *Baraka* (1992; directed by Ron Fricke). However, I often wonder whether the classes as a whole would like the movie as much as they usually do if it were not for everything they had learned up to this point. In any event, this movie always works very well. Difficult to describe, *Baraka* is in the mold of *Koyaanisqatsi* (1982; directed by Godfrey Reggio), for which Fricke served as a writer, and *Powaqqatsi* (1988; directed by Godfrey Reggio). It consists of sequences of stunning cinematography that show a mix of the power and beauty of nature, the effects of industry, the destruction of war, and the practice of religion (people in prayer, chanting monks, pilgrims). Again, the movie invites discussion, and, given the weeks students now have behind them in the course, the conversation can head in many different directions (it is also a great movie for discussing the cinematic technique of sound). The reading for this unit includes selections from Peter Berger's *Sacred Canopy* (1967).

Berger's theory of religion is worth working through in its own right, and I usually focus on the argument he makes about the human need to tie *nomos*, or the social order, to *cosmos*, or the order of the universe as a whole. Religion, he argues, is an attempt to project the human order onto the totality of being. Once students get a good sense of Berger's argument, it is fun to think through films from the entire course using this perspective, all the way back to the central question of *Crimes and Misdemeanors*: Is the proscription against killing a reflection of a moral order written into the very fabric of the universe, or is it only an attempt to give a social utility a "sacred canopy"? With respect to *Baraka* specifically, Berger gives students a language for critically evaluating the apparent impact of the movie, namely, the sense of a sacred order, which can in part be found in nature and to which we seem to be trying to relate. But does the film's emphasis on a kind of unifying sensibility run roughshod over the importance of difference in thinking about the many provocative images it shows? Can a kind of generalized sacred canopy work, or do sacred canopies have to run deep in a way that puts them at odds with each other?

Summing Up

By way of concluding the class, I ask students to consider the same question that is at the core of this volume: What are the many ways in which religion and film can intersect? Recalling our initial consideration of the concepts of religion and film, we explore the many different points of contact we have experienced and considered along the way. This discussion eventually settles into four different categories: (1) film as both vehicle and subject of particular theological perspectives (that is to say, both film as expressly incorporating theological perspectives and theological perspectives that take film as their subject matter); (2) theories of religion as tools for understanding certain films and vice versa; (3) film as a vehicle of modern cultural values and therefore religious in the sense of creating meaning and guiding the conduct of life; (4) and finally, the thesis proposition of the class, that film is a distinctive medium and must therefore make possible unique forms of religious expression and experience.

A Note on Testing

Finally, a quick note on testing if only because I tried something unusual for this course that seems to work well. In addition to reaction papers and a possible analysis paper (depending on the class), I usually include an in-class midterm and a final exam. The exam consists of showing a brief clip from four or five different movies. Students have to identify the movie and write a bit about its significance for the class (with reference to readings): What important issues did this movie help us consider? Good answers also mention how the specific scenes relate to the issues discussed in the course. Telling students about this kind of exam in advance also helps them become attentive viewers. The exact clips used sometimes depend on how particular discussions go each time the course is taught. Cuing the clips can be a chore, but with changing rules about copyright and the use of movies in the classroom, it should soon be possible to save them to a single "exam" DVD for screening in class.

REFERENCES

Bach, Alice. 1996. " 'Throw Them to the Lions, Sire': Transforming Biblical Narratives into Hollywood Spectaculars." In *Semeia 74: Biblical Glamour and Hollywood Glitz*, ed. Alice Bach, 103–26. Atlanta: Scholars Press.

Berger, Peter. 1967. *The Sacred Canopy: Elements of a Sociological Theory of Religion*. Garden City, N.Y.: Anchor.

Bordwell, David, and Kristin Thompson. 2003. *Film Art: An Introduction*. Boston: McGraw-Hill.

Braudy, Leo, and Marshall Cohen, eds. 2004. *Film Theory and Criticism: Introductory Readings*. New York: Oxford University Press.

Breton, André. 1924. "Manifesto of Surrealism." In *Manifestoes of Surrealism*, trans. Richard Seaver and Helen R. Lane, 1–47. Repr., Ann Arbor: University of Michigan Press, 1972.

Cavell, Stanley. 1979. *The World Viewed: Reflections on the Ontology of Film*. Cambridge, Mass.: Harvard University Press.

Cho, Francisca. 1999. "Imagining Nothing and Imagining Otherness in Buddhist Film." In *Imag(in)ing Otherness: Filmic Visions of Living Together*, ed. S. Brent Plate, 169–96. Atlanta: Scholars Press.

Dudley, Andrew. 1976. *The Major Film Theories: An Introduction*. New York: Oxford University Press.

Eliade, Mircea. 1957. "Myths of the Modern World." In *Myths, Dreams, and Mysteries*, trans. Philip Mairet, 23–38. New York: Harper and Row.

Otto, Rudolf. 1957. *The Idea of the Holy: An Inquiry into the Non-rational Factor in the Idea of the Divine and Its Relation to the Rational*, trans. John W. Harvey. New York: Oxford University Press.

Schleiermacher, Friedrich. 1988. *On Religion: Speeches to Its Cultured Despisers*. New York: Cambridge University Press.

Schrader, Paul. 1972. *Transcendental Style in Film: Ozu, Bresson, Dreyer*. Berkeley: University of California Press.

Tarkovsky, Andrey. 1986. *Sculpting in Time: Reflections on the Cinema*, trans. Kitty Hunter-Blair. London: Bodley Head.

Watkins, Gregory J. 1999. "Seeing and Being Seen: Distinctively Filmic and Religious Elements in Film." *Journal of Religion and Film* 3(2).

PART IV

The Values Approach

15

Touching Evil, Touching Good

Irena S. M. Makarushka

> Why is it that the good that I would do, I do not do;
> and the evil I would not do, I do...?
> —Saint Paul, Letter to the Romans 7:15

Evil is a vexed and contested concept. Like pornography, people claim
to know it when they see it; although they may not be able to define it.
Many undergraduates approach the concept of evil from an uncritical or a dualistic perspective in which they rely on received knowledge
and seek simple answers.[1] This generation of college students, the
millennials,[2] as they are called, has grown up during the presidency
of George W. Bush. Their values and attitudes have been shaped by
the tragedy of 9/11, the war on terror, the ascendancy of conservative
values, the polarization of the country into blue and red states,[3] Hur-
ricane Katrina and its aftermath, a widening racial and economic
divide, and the threat of global warming. They have seen the concept
of evil become increasingly politicized, as Richard Bernstein writes
in *The Abuse of Evil: The Corruption of Politics and Religion since 9/11.*[4]

A course that introduces students to evil as a complex dimension
of human experience has the potential to serve them on several levels.
To my mind, a course on religion, film, and the problem of evil is
particularly important at a time of political and social extremes. Many
students tend to see films primarily as entertainment. They watch
movies or play video games that reduce evil to a two-dimensional
"good guy/bad guy" battle, valorize violence, and celebrate horror. If
they have not been alerted to the subtleties of the text, they may fail
to see the cultural values embedded in iconic images. Although students have a high degree of visual literacy, they need to develop their
capacity for thinking critically about and interpreting visual texts.

Seeing films through a wider and more complex critical lens invites deeper reflection. By learning to interrogate visual texts, students develop the capacity to engage cultural values in a more intentional way. New interpretative frameworks can expand students' ability to identify the underlying assumptions that inform texts. Therefore, they may become more keenly aware of how, for example, the representation of gender, race, and sexuality in films reflects cultural values. Reading films critically increases the likelihood that students will move beyond either/or, black/white dichotomies toward a more integrated understanding of the problem of evil.

In this chapter I propose a reading of *Crash* as a myth of evil for our time.[5] The film, which was cowritten and directed by Paul Heggis, explores life in Los Angeles, a city that mirrors the crazy-quilt world of the American melting pot circa 2004. Los Angeles—LA, the land of Hollywood and make-believe—is the backdrop for Heggis's complex, often poignant, and always challenging visual narrative. With its racism, violence, wealth, and power, LA is a microcosm of both the American Dream and the American nightmare. My analysis of *Crash* focuses on evil experienced as racism and considers alienation, confession, and redemption as three core responses.

The perspective I bring to the analysis of *Crash* is consistent with the attitudes and values I described in "A Picture's Worth: Teaching Religion and Film."[6] Although the essay was written nearly a decade ago, the values that informed my thinking then still hold true today. I remain committed to offering students competing interpretative strategies that challenge them to think outside the narrow confines of received knowledge. I invite them to explore prejudices that lend a degree of safety and security to their lives but at the same time limit their perspectives, their self-understanding and their ability to relate to others. My critical perspective on religion, culture, and the craft of teaching is informed by postmodern interpretative theories, particularly feminist theories.

With regard to evil, I look to Paul Ricoeur's *The Symbolism of Evil*, which, in my view, provides a compelling analytical approach to the depiction of evil at the heart of this film.[7] Ricoeur's understanding of evil as a dimension of human finitude narrated in myths is a persuasive alternative to traditional theodicies, simplistic dichotomies, and objectifications. Ricoeur locates our consciousness of finitude and thereby the acknowledgement of the capacity for evil in the confession of fault. He addresses both our culpability and the sense of alienation that we suffer. Recalling Saint Paul's words in Romans ("Why is it that the good that I would do, I do not do; and the evil I would not do, I do . . . ?"), Ricoeur describes the experience of evil as both suffered and willed. In essence, the fact that we cannot avoid the experience of evil defines the human condition. How we respond to its inevitability signifies our freedom. The dialectic of the experience of evil as suffered and willed is reenacted in the confession of fault. Fault speaks of our culpability and of the breach or rupture that results. In the case of *Crash*, Ricoeur's schema of the symbolism of evil illuminates the human cost of evil as suffered and willed.

In the opening sequence of *Crash,* sitting in his rear-ended car in the midst of a chain collision, Detective Graham Waters reflects, "It's the sense of touch. In any real city, you walk, you know? You brush past people, people bump into you. In LA, nobody touches you. We're always behind this metal and glass. I think we miss that touch so much that we crash into each other just so we can feel something." With characters like Detective Waters, Heggis strives for complexity rather then two-dimensional stereotypes. For the most part, no matter how venal, racist, or unsympathetic the characters may be, through one small act of kindness, their fundamental humanity shines through. Guided by Waters's meditation on his sense of alienation and the desire for touch, my analysis falls into two parts: touching evil and touching good. I explore how Heggis's characters deal with alienation as they search for meaning between desire and resistance, hope and despair, good and evil.

Many recent films explore the problem of evil. The choice of *Crash* reflects my interest in the structural and thematic complexity of its approach to evil. Owing to the film's circular and asynchronous narrative structure, any attempt at a brief summary will inevitably fall short. My description of the myriad characters will, at the very least, introduce how their disparate lives are connected. My intention here is to present the bare bones of some of their stories revealed during a thirty-six-hour period when the characters "crash" into one another, both literally and figuratively. Their ethnic and racial differences are projected against the backdrop of LA as snowflakes drift over the cityscape at Christmastime. The film ends where it begins—with a chain collision on an LA highway. Between the beginning and the end, the story unfolds through multiple narrative strands that Heggis weaves together to form a rich tapestry depicting life in LA.

A black police detective, Graham Waters, and his detective partner and lover, Ria, who is a Latina, find themselves in the middle of a chain collision on their way to investigate a murder. As noted earlier, the detective's words about alienation and his intense desire for touch are the first ones spoken and establish the film's central theme. His feelings of alienation are visually reinforced by the drifting snowflakes, which are out of place in LA. The slick roads that the snowflakes create cause the chain collision. At the crash scene, Ria and Kim Lee, a Korean woman, argue about who was responsible for the accident. Each uses racial and ethnic slurs to make her point. As Ria deals with the accident, Detective Waters goes to the crime scene at the edge of the crash. When he picks up a sneaker with his pen, a look of recognition crosses his face as the scene fades out. At the end of the film, we discover that the victim is his brother, Peter. Their mother, a drug addict, had asked Waters to find Peter and keep him off the streets, but he had failed to do so.

Peter and his friend Anthony carjack the SUV belonging to the LA district attorney, Rick Cabot, and his wife, Jean. In the process, they threaten Jean with a gun. Since Rick is up for reelection, he wants to limit the political damage that he believes could result from the racial overtones of the crime. Concerned more about his career than his wife, at a debriefing with his staff in his living room he tells them, "I need a picture of me pinning a medal on a fucking black man." He remembers a heroic fireman who may suit his needs. When his assistant tells him that the hero in question is an Iraqi man named Osama, Rick becomes abusive. Jean suspects that her husband is having an affair with the black assistant DA, Karen. Angry and in shock after the attack, she projects her fears onto the Hispanic locksmith, Daniel, whom she and Rick have hired to change the locks on their house. Convinced that he is a gangbanger because of his shaved head and tattoos, within Daniel's hearing Jean asks her husband to hire someone who is not Hispanic to change the locks again. When Daniel returns home, he finds that Lara, his young daughter, is frightened by the gunshots she hears in the neighborhood. To help her feel safe, Daniel tells her a story about a cloak whose magical powers had protected him from gunshots in the past. He "gives" her his imaginary cloak to protect her.

Officer Ryan, a white LA cop, is frustrated and angry after a conversation with Shaniqua Johnson, the black woman administrator at his father's HMO. He is abusive and makes racist comments. When he hears on the police radio that the DA's SUV has been carjacked, he sees an opportunity to vent his anger. Over his partner's objections, he pulls over a different black SUV despite the fact that the plates do not match. He forces Cameron Thayer, a black movie director, and his wife, Christine, out of their car. Ryan is abusive toward Cameron and then sexually molests Christine as Cameron watches. Ryan's partner, Officer Hansen, tries unsuccessfully to intervene. Ryan encounters Christine again later in the film under very different circumstances.

An Iranian immigrant, Farhad, whose store has been vandalized several times, insists that Dorri, his physician daughter, go with him to buy a gun for protection. Dirk, the gun-shop owner, makes disparaging remarks because he assumes that Farhad is an Arab. Farhad gets angry and is removed from the store by a security guard, but Dorri stays to buy the gun. Dirk makes lewd, sexist comments about the bullets that fit the gun. Back in his store, Farhad hires Daniel, the Hispanic locksmith, to put a new lock on the back door. Daniel tells him to replace the broken door or the lock will not work. After the store is vandalized again, Farhad blames Daniel and goes to his house with his loaded gun. Insisting that Daniel pay for the damages, he threatens Daniel with the weapon. Lara watches from the window. Afraid that her father will be killed because he gave her his magic cloak, she runs out to protect him. As she jumps into his arms, Farhad fires, and the bullet appears to hit her. Miraculously, she is not harmed.

Speeding in the stolen SUV on their way to the chop shop, Anthony and Peter hit a Korean man who walks out from behind his panel truck parked on a desolate street in LA. His wife, it is later revealed, is the woman who argues with Ria at the crash site. The carjackers extricate the injured man from under the SUV, take his wallet, and leave him bleeding outside a hospital emergency room. Lucien, the chop shop owner, takes the SUV but refuses to pay Peter and Anthony because it is stained with blood.

Walking away from the chop shop, Anthony and Peter find themselves at a quiet intersection, where Cameron sits alone in his Navigator, feeling angry and humiliated. As he contemplates his encounter with Officer Ryan, he turns his wedding band. Pointing a gun, Anthony and Peter open the door to the SUV and are shocked to see a black man sitting inside. With the carjackers in the SUV, Cameron careens down the side streets while being followed by two police cars that are called to the crime scene. He pulls into someone's driveway, where a life-sized crèche is painted on the garage door and a very large inflated Santa stands in the front yard, waving. Peace to men of good will is not happening in this neighborhood. In the altercation that follows, Peter flees, and Anthony hides in the front seat of the Navigator as several cops, including Officer Hansen, try to arrest Cameron, who remains standing in the street. Assuming that Cameron is a car thief, the other cops threaten to shoot him. Understanding why Cameron is enraged, Hansen vouches for Cameron and persuades the cops to let him go.

Driving home that night, Hansen picks up a hitchhiker, who turns out to be Peter. As Peter reaches inside his jacket to fish out the Saint Christopher statuette that he places on every dashboard, Hansen, thinking that Peter is reaching for a gun, shoots and kills him. He pulls off the road, throws the body into the brush, and sets his car on fire just a few hundred yards from the crash site. He watches police lights in the distance approaching the scene.

As Anthony walks away from Cameron's Navigator, he finds himself alone on the street where he and Peter ran over the Korean man. He sees the panel truck and notices that the keys are still in the door. Thinking that he can at least make some money by selling the panel truck, he takes it to the chop shop. When Lucien opens the back of the van, he and Peter discover children, women, and men—trafficking victims from Thailand and Cambodia—chained inside. Lucien does not want the van but offers to buy the immigrants for five hundred dollars per person, expecting to profit when he resells them. As the film draws to the end, Anthony drives into Chinatown, releases all of the trafficked people, and gives them money to buy chop suey for dinner.

Christmas in LA may include a few snowflakes and a life-sized crèche in front of the hospital emergency entrance but little joy, peace, and good will. Ironically, what joy there is comes from the magic cloak that saves Lara's life. For the most part, alienation, miscommunication, and resentment plague the characters in *Crash*. They experience life behind the "metal and glass," whether they are literally encased in a car on the verge of exploding or figuratively enmeshed in the racism that defines their attitudes toward one another. How they respond to their experience of alienation is the concern of the following two sections.

Touching Evil

The experience of evil touches the lives of all of the characters in *Crash* from Detective Graham to Lara to the victims of human trafficking. Racism is the thread that weaves their stories together. They are connected to and isolated from one another by their inability to see beyond or beneath the surface. Skin color, names, accents, and other signifiers of diversity are experienced as bar-riers to human interaction. Heggis's choice of racism as a core element of the experience of evil forefronts its significance in American culture. In effect, if *Crash* is read as a myth of evil, the stories not only speak of the racism that currently plagues our cities but also remind us of our racist past and our potential for racism in the future.

When Ricoeur looks at the experience of evil through the metaphor of fault narrated in myths, he makes a claim about the religious imagination: "On the moral side of evil, first, the experience of guilt entails, as its dark side, the feeling of having been seduced by overwhelming powers and, consequently, our feeling of belonging to a history of evil, which is always already there for everyone."[8] The "already there-ness" of the experience of evil haunts us. The specter of death is already there from the beginning. We experience ourselves as already flawed—victims of the human condition and as the cause of others' suffering despite our best efforts. With the blend of cultures, races, and eth-nicities that characterize LA, Heggis reminds us that racism is already there—we are born into a racist culture. We are a country of immigrants who have not yet learned to get along. *Crash* is a confession of our failure to be an open society that treats all of its citizens justly. In other words, we are not in the habit of practicing the democratic ideals we preach, which makes our efforts to ex-port democracy somewhat suspect.[9]

For Ricoeur, myths of evil are both retrospective and prospective in their exploration of the two fundamentally religious questions: Where did we come from? Where are we going? They draw our attention to questions of origins and ends. As a repository of our collective memory, myths reenact the drama of human finitude. Insofar as myths speak of the origins and ends of evil, they address the human desire for wholeness or oneness with the sacred and the fear of rupture or loss of wholeness. Under the conditions of finitude, the human desire for meaning confronts the dread of meaninglessness (Ricoeur 1967, 4). In the language of *Crash*, the desire for touch is confounded by the ineluctable truth of its ambiguity—touch is both good and evil. The hope for connection bumps against the limitations of the human heart. Each of the multiple narrative strands Heggis creates is a reminder of our collec-tive failure to do the right thing. Each story recounts the tension between inside and outside—between who are we and how are we known. Similarly, each story explores the polarities of touch and crash, life and death, and good and evil.

My interest in *Crash* extends beyond its narrative and structural complexity. I see the film as a microcosm of life in the United States. A close study of *Crash* is an opportunity for students to reflect on the problem of evil within context of the American experience. It is all too easy to see evil as part of someone else's cultural, political, or religious experience. In *Crash*, as well as in films such as *House of Sand and Fog, Beautiful Country, Babel,* and *The Three Burials of Mel-quiades Estrada,* evil permeates the very fabric of our American life in the ex-perience of racism. In very different ways, these films focus on how Americans perceive themselves in relation to the "other," regardless of how the "other" is constructed. In all of these films, the deeply embedded ambiguity that informs American attitudes toward the "other" is a constant.[10] By choosing to see an individual as the "other," as a commodity rather than as a person worthy of respect, we permit ourselves to change the parameters of socially acceptable behaviors. In the case of *Crash*, racism, violence, and abuse of power are common across the spectrum of humanity. Ethnic and racial minorities are as intolerant of one another as are whites of minorities in general. Racial slurs are as much part of the vocabulary of Officer Ryan as they are of Shaniqua Johnson or Christine Thayer, of Ria as of Kim Lee or Farhad. In *Crash*, racism is a pervasive reality that cuts across all ethnicities, touches the life of every character, and defines the experience of evil.

The degree to which the stories in *Crash* function as a collective confession of cultural racism brings the film into closer alignment with Ricoeur's interpretation of the experience of evil. As I mentioned earlier, Ricoeur's analysis of the symbolism of evil begins with a commentary on the roles that confession and myth play in deepening our understanding of evil. Confession is an important trope for several reasons. "Through confession," Ricoeur writes, "the consciousness of fault is brought into the light of speech; through confession man remains speech, even in the experience of his own absurdity, suffering, and anguish" (1967, 7). Speech locates the individual confession within history and mediates between the particular and the imagined absolute. The dialectic of the confession of fault is reflected in the opening lines of *Crash*. Enclosed in metal and glass, Detective Waters confesses his deep sense of alienation and his desire to touch and be touched, as well as his desire to be connected to something beyond himself—to something that would make him feel whole. Heggis, however, sees all too clearly that touch, like all human experience, is ambiguous—it is both good and evil.

Furthermore, Ricoeur argues, confession of fault is powerfully present in myths, which are prior to explanations of evil proposed by philosophy or theology. Rejecting those traditional approaches, he offers an exploration of evil narrated in myths:

> In losing its explanatory pretensions the myth reveals its exploratory significance and its contribution to understanding, which we shall later call its symbolic function—that is to say, its power of discovering and revealing the bond between man and what he considers the sacred. Paradoxical as it may seem, the myth, when it is thus demythologized through contact with scientific history and elevated to the dignity of a symbol, is a dimension of modern thought. (ibid., 5)

Myths tell of both the origins and ends of evil. They narrate human experience as reminiscence and expectation (ibid., 6) and speak of an imagined time when humanity was at one with the sacred and of the hope for a return to oneness. In *Crash*, Heggis is not trying to explain racism, violence, or other ways in which evil is experienced. Rather, the stories he tells explore the nature of human nature. They range from the human capacity to inflict suffering through the violence of touch and the gift of healing through touch.

Officer Ryan's sexual molestation of Christine speaks most powerfully of violent touch. In this case, the violence is both racist and sexist. He punishes her for being a black woman. Ryan inflicts upon Christine the rage and impotence he felt dealing with Shaniqua Johnson, who refused to sign the form that would authorize his father's treatment for an enlarged prostate. Ryan stopped the Thayer's car because he suspected that Christine was performing fellatio on her husband while he was driving. By sexually assaulting Christine, Ryan transforms good sex into bad sex—good touch into bad touch. Heggis is not subtle about Ryan's feelings of impotence. Both the gun that he points and Christine's accusation that he finger-fucked her symbolize his dysfunction. The slow pace of the camera's movement over Christine's silk-clad body as Ryan is violating her paradoxically increases the viewer's level of discomfort. However reluctantly, the viewer becomes complicit in the act of violence, as do Cameron and Officer Hansen, who observe from the sidelines. The violence of Ryan's act has profound repercussions. Cameron's self-hatred reaches new heights, and his rage spills over when the white cops mistake him for a car-jacker and try to arrest him. No longer capable of playing the role of the compliant upper-middle-class black man, Cameron takes on the persona of a violent criminal, which nearly gets him killed.

Touch that inflicts suffering can be explicitly violent, as in the case of Officer Ryan, or it can be implicitly violent. Suffering is also caused by the absence of touch, as announced by Detective Waters in the opening scene. When Rick withholds touch from his wife, Jean, after their SUV is carjacked, her feelings of rejection impel her to hurt others. Both her maid, Maria, and Daniel are hurt by Jean's racist comments. Furthermore, Ria is wounded and angered when Waters takes a phone call from his mother during their love-making. To make matters worse, he tells his mother that he is having sex with a white woman. When Ria objects to his behavior, Waters tells her that he would have said "Mexican" but that would not have upset his mother as much as saying Ria is white. Since Ria is of Puerto Rican and El Salvadoran heritage, she feels even more insulted by Waters's racial and ethnic insensitivity. She accuses him of privileging his career over his personal life, in much the same way that Jean accused Rick of having time only for his career. By withholding his love, attention, and care from Ria, Waters perpetuates the aloneness he claims to suffer and refuses to accept the healing touch that he craves.

Insensitivity to racial and ethnic differences also touches the lives of other characters and causes them to suffer. The old adage "sticks and stones may break my bones, but names will never hurt me" could not be further from the truth. As Ricoeur states emphatically with regard to confession, speech—our ability to articulate who we are—is the single most significant aspect of our humanity. It connects us to the historical past through memory and propels us toward the future through hope. When we use speech to injure others, our words can wound deeply. When Dorri takes her father, Farhad, to buy a gun, Dirk, the shop owner, is offended that they communicate in Farsi. Assuming they are Arab, he says, "Yo, Osama, plan the Jihad on your own time." Farhad, whose English is not perfect, protests that he is an American citizen and has the same rights as anyone else. The assumption that everyone from the Middle East is an Arab comes up again when Shereen, Farhad's wife, tries to remove anti–Arab slurs spray-painted on the doors of their vandalized store. The insults and vandalism that Farhad and his family endure push him over the edge. Since he does not understand English perfectly, he misunderstands what Daniel is trying to tell him about the lock and the door. Enraged that he is unable to make himself understood and feeling betrayed by the country where he sought refuge, Farhad projects his anger onto Daniel. Having taken advantage of his right as a citizen to bear arms, Farhad takes his new gun and fires at Daniel.

Touching Good

Of all of the characters in *Crash,* Daniel is the most enigmatic. He is the only one to survive the violence and chaos relatively unscathed. Although Jean misjudges him by assuming that he is a gangbanger and Farhad verbally abuses him, Daniel does not allow his hurt feelings to control him. He appears to focus on the things that matter most to him, his daughter, Lara, and her safety. Heggis accords Daniel a narrative that is more tied to redemption than to alienation. We do not know much about him. We know that he works as a locksmith, lives with his wife and daughter in a marginally safe neighborhood, and has a gift for storytelling and pantomime and that his stories dispel Lara's fears. He also believes in magic. We can speculate whether Heggis chose the name Daniel for its biblical overtones. Does Heggis's Daniel survive the proverbial lion's den of LA's racially driven violence because he is a good man? With the name Daniel, which means "God is my judge," is Heggis suggesting that judging others by their appearance may not serve us well?

If Ryan's assault of Christine is paradigmatic of violent touch, then Daniel's story of the magic cloak is a parable of healing touch. In each story, Heggis explores the recesses of the human heart and the ways in which we choose to respond to the experience of evil. Ryan and Farhad, among others, allow their pain to drive them to physical violence. Daniel, however, does not allow hurtful words to penetrate too deeply. In a sense, his love for his daughter becomes the invisible cloak that protects him from verbal assaults. When he shares the story of the magic cloak that once saved his life, he is, in effect, confessing to violence he once experienced. We wonder whether this cruelty is narrated in the tattoos inscribed on his body. Tattoos, as Jean reminds us, are cultural signifiers of gangbangers.

The magic cloak extends its power to Farhad. Stunned that he did not kill Lara, he later explains to Dorri that Lara is his "firishita"—his angel, who in this case saved him from himself. Redeemed by his renewed faith in angels and relieved of his rage, Farhad sits smiling in a corner of his store and tells Dorri that things will be all right. Dorri puts the gun in her bag and reaches for the box of bullets. For a split second, the camera rests on the side of the red box, which is labeled "blanks."

Being saved and saving others are themes that Heggis threads through other stories as well. The day after Ryan assaults Christine, he is called to the scene of a multiple car collision. Several cars are overturned, and one is already ablaze. Ryan approaches an overturned Jeep with gas leaking out of the tank. Finding Christine trapped inside, he crawls into the vehicle to save her. Terrified, she screams and tries to push Ryan away, warning him not to touch her. Once he recognizes her and understands why she is afraid, he agrees not to touch her while continuing his efforts to save them both. With their faces inches away from one another, Ryan cuts the seat belt to release her. As the flames begin to engulf the Jeep, the police pull him out. He crawls back into the burning vehicle, however, and pulls Christine out as it explodes. As he puts a blanket around her shoulders, Christine allows herself to be enfolded in his arms. Contrary to their first encounter, in this instance touch was by mutual consent and saved them both. Chastened, Ryan redeems himself in her eyes. Later that evening, his rage depleted, he embraces his ailing father as he had not been able to do before. That same evening Christine calls Cameron, who is standing by the side of Hansen's burning car while snow settles on his shoulders. Her fury dissipated, she tells him that she loves him.

Not all acts of kindness turn out well: Hansen does save Cameron, but his encounter with Peter ends badly. The deep-seated mistrust and ambivalence that Hansen feels toward blacks surfaces when he picks up Peter, who is hitching after escaping from the attempted carjacking. Peter tells Hansen that he enjoys the country and western music playing on the radio and that he even wrote a country and western song. He also confesses that he likes to ice skate and had once dreamed of being a goalie. Mistrusting Peter's stories and convinced that Peter is mocking him, Hansen becomes scared and angry. Their failure to communicate leads to Peter's death. Hansen assumes Peter is a gang member and, therefore, would be carrying a gun, not a Saint Christopher figure. He shoots Peter, whose faith in the statuette's salvific powers is not rewarded. Magic cloaks, Heggis implies, are more reliable than saints. In one of the scenes that make up the ensemble of vignettes with which Crash ends, we see Waters crouching on the ground at the scene of Peter's murder. Something catches his eye. He uncovers the Saint Christopher figure, holds it in his hands, and grieves.

Despite Waters's resistance to Ria's affection, he has a deep and abiding love for his mother and tries to take care of her. Dropping by her house, he finds her slumped over a chair while high on drugs. He puts her to bed and holds her hand. When she sees him sitting by her side, she asks only about his brother. Noticing that the refrigerator is empty, he buys groceries for her. We are then reminded that no good deed goes unpunished. When Waters and Ria take his mother to the morgue to identify Peter's body, his mother blames him for Peter's death. She believes that Waters could have saved Peter but was too involved with his career to really care. Praising Peter as her good son, she recounts that, when she was asleep, Peter had brought her groceries. As Waters walks away from both his mother and Ria, Heggis brings us full circle, we come to a deeper understanding of Waters's desire for touch.

Conclusion

Crash ends in Chinatown, where Anthony releases the people imprisoned in the van, and Shaniqua Johnson's car gets rear-ended by a car full of Asian men. Shouted racial and ethnic slurs are absorbed into the music that fills the air. Just another day in LA! What can students learn from a close reading of *Crash?* As Heggis suggests, nothing is simple. The complexity of the experiences of evil recounted in the stories, as we have seen, is integrated seamlessly into the film's narrative structure. Heggis pays close attention to how scenes fade in and out, blending characters' lives into one another. Their lives may differ with regard to specifics, but they share the exigencies and vicissitudes common to the human condition, including the experience of evil. The power of the stories and images is enhanced by the musical score. Ranging from sounds reminiscent of medieval chants to country and western and hip hop, the music echoes the timelessness of the themes. The setting may be LA at the beginning of the twenty-first century, but the stories are as old as humankind.[11]

NOTES

1. See Perry's classic study on the stages of intellectual and moral development of college students. William G. Perry Jr., *Forms of Intellectual and Ethical Development in the College Years: A Scheme* (New York: Holt, Rinehart, and Winston, 1970), and his "Cognitive and Ethical Growth: The Making of Meaning," in Arthur W. Chickering and associates, *The Modern American College* (San Francisco: Jossey-Bass, 1981), 76–116.

2. Neil Howe and William Strauss, *Millennials Rising: The Next Great Generation* (New York: Vintage, 2000).

3. Polarization is perhaps the most powerful signifier in current politics and religion, both nationally and internationally. The rhetoric of the axis of evil, the rise of global religious fundamentalism, debates about immigration, and the politics of preemption have created an ever-widening gap between "us" and "them." Although it is beyond the scope of this chapter to provide a detailed analysis of this cultural shift, it is fair to observe that the "other" continues to be the signifier of the outsider—the alien.

4. Richard J. Bernstein, *The Abuse of Evil: The Corruption of Politics and Religion since 9/11* (Malden, Mass.: Polity Press, 2005).

5. *Crash,* directed by Paul Heggis, cowritten by Paul Heggis and Bobby Moresco; DVD, Lion's Gate Entertainment, 2004.

6. Irena S. M. Makarushka, "A Picture's Worth: Teaching Religion and Film," in *Religious Studies News, Spotlight on Teaching* 6(1) (May 1998).

7. Paul Ricoeur, *The Symbolism of Evil*, trans. Emerson Buchanan (Boston: Beacon, 1967).

8. Paul Ricoeur, "Evil: A Challenge to Philosophy and Theology," in *Journal of the American Academy of Religion* 53(3): 635–48. The quote appears on page 636.

9. For an excellent analysis of attitudes on immigration, see Ali Behdad, *A Forgetful Nation: On Immigration and Cultural Identity in the United States* (Durham, N.C.: Duke University Press, 2005).

10. The February 18, 2007, editorial in the *New York Times* titled "They Are America" offers a succinct analysis of the ambivalent attitudes we hold with regard to immigrants and immigration. Recent congressional debates have also demonstrated just how divided we are over these issues.

11. I would like to thank Dr. Laurie Kaplan of George Washington University for her impeccable editing and wise counsel.

16

Teaching Ethics with Film: A Course on the Moral Agency of Women

Ellen Ott Marshall

Introduction to and Objectives of the Course

The Moral Agency of Women is the name of a course in feminist ethics that asks what difference gender makes in our understanding and analysis of moral agency. In Seyla Benhabib's language, this course poses "the women's question," meaning that it refers to "women as objects of inquiry and as subjects carrying out such inquiry" (1992, 179). The starting point for the course is the observation that the dominant tradition of Western moral philosophy has assumed a male moral agent. What happens, then, when we study the moral agency of women? What happens when those conducting the study are women themselves?[1] Benhabib describes the experience this way:

> Women discover difference where previously sameness had
> prevailed; they sense dissonance and contradiction where
> formerly uniformity had reigned; they note the double
> meaning of words where formerly the signification of terms
> had been taken for granted; and they establish the persis-
> tence of injustice, inequality and regression in processes that
> were formerly characterized as just, egalitarian and pro-
> gressive. (ibid.)

To varying degrees, such things happen in this course when we study Aristotle's description of voluntary acts in the *Nicomachean Ethics*, Immanuel Kant's argument for adherence to duty and test for universalizability in *Foundations of the Metaphysics of Morals*, and John Rawls's description of the rational process in *A Theory of Justice*. But it is also important to note that many of the students have similar experiences when we read from feminist ethicists as well. That is, debate in the classroom does not stop after the critique of the "unencumbered self" that adheres only to duty and rigidly follows the rational process. The descriptions of women following an ethic of care, in which one values relationality over autonomy and deliberates with the use of emotion, also raise a host of critical questions. Moreover, the questions students raise are as fundamental as "is this *moral* agency?" and "is this the behavior of *all* women?"

Thus, like many courses, this one begins with an observation that becomes increasingly problematic as the semester proceeds. That is, the observation that traditional descriptions of moral agency assume a male moral agent initiates a "process of pertinent and constant questioning" (Testaferri 1995, xi). What does women's moral agency look like? Does it in fact differ from that which has been described traditionally? Additionally, given the plurality within women's experience, can we even speak in a monolithic way about their moral agency? By the end of the semester, it becomes clear that a more appropriate title for the course is The Moral Agency of Women?

We make our way through these questions with the help of literature and films that present a variety of women and expressions of moral agency. Students spend the first part of the term reading novels and viewing films so that we begin the more theoretical reading with a shared collection of female protagonists to consider. The interaction of theory and narrative is organized around features of moral agency such as autonomy and relationality, choice and voluntariness, epistemology and deliberation, and values and virtues. Along with the week's readings in ethics and feminist philosophy, students are asked to review a novel or film that carries particular relevance for that session. However, students are never precluded from bringing other characters and their own experiences into the conversation. Indeed, one of the course requirements is an analysis of a "moral moment" from one's own life.

Making narratives a central part of this course was natural, given that I regularly define the "moral agent" metaphorically as the protagonist of the story. Moreover, my own thinking on moral agency has been profoundly shaped by Katie Cannon and Sharon Welch, both of whom draw on literature to present models of moral agency not recognized by the dominant tradition of moral philosophy. My initial impulse was to use women's narratives as a proving ground for the theory, thus subverting the practice of measuring women's moral maturity according to theoretical norms. We would use narratives, ours and those of others, to test the theories. Here I was following the work of Carol Gilligan by suggesting that these narratives offer different expressions of moral agency—not necessarily lesser ones—than those mapped out in theory.

However, when the course design was actually implemented, the movement between theory, narrative, and student inquiry was different and more fruitful than I had anticipated. We found ourselves responding to the narratives critically as well, such that they entered into the mix rather than serving as an anchor for assessment of other material. It became apparent (and appropriate) that the syllabus contains no proving ground, whether it be theory, narrative, or personal experience. Rather, the varied material became a mix of representations of moral agency, and our discussions became part of an on-going effort to authentically describe a moral experience, to critically evaluate apparently constitutive features of moral agency and their embodiment or absence in the characters' lives, and to accomplish all of these things while avoiding essentialism.

I have written elsewhere about the power of film to engage students and generate discussion (Marshall 2003). I continue to find film a particularly effective pedagogical tool mainly because students readily engage this medium, although it is up to faculty members to make sure that we make the most of that engagement. In the context of this particular course I found that film worked well for two additional reasons. To explain the first one, I need to take a slight detour through Nancy Hartsock's description of feminist theory: "The role of theory, then, is to articulate for us what we know from our practical activity, to bring out and make conscious the philosophy embedded in our lives" (Hartsock 1979, 65). Some of the most exciting moments in the class-room happen when students come to understand their lives, culture, or world differently in light of a reading or discussion.

Sometimes, however, theory simply does not come alive in this way. De-tailed descriptions of a deliberative process often bore and frustrate students because they seem excessively analytical. This is where films can be very help-ful if they convey a theory and prompt students to interact with it more fully and critically. It is as though the theory takes on relevance when they see it embodied in the life of a character. Students attack and defend the "rational process" much more vigorously when it is embodied or missing in a character than when it remains in its theoretical form in the text. Thus, something that might seem an esoteric distinction only of interest to ethicists takes on life on the screen, and students find themselves enthusiastically debating voluntary and involuntary actions. In addition, even though Aristotle's painstaking dis-tinction of these acts rarely sparks debate, his text suddenly assumes new meaning and relevance. Quite simply, it gets on the field of discussion in a way that it does not usually do on its own. This is what comes to mind when I read Ada Testaferri's description of the cross-disciplinary aspect of film: "Cinema is an art form which more than any other crosses disciplinary boundaries and ties together the rather exclusive tendencies of creative discourses, such as art and philosophy, and the more inclusive tendencies of large technological phenomena, such as contemporary mass media and socio-political discourse" (1995, x). Film can make accessible otherwise exclusive discourses of moral theory and provide means and momentum for wrestling with them.

The films used in this course not only prompt debate over the theories of moral agency coming from the dominant tradition but also spark discussion of contending claims within feminist ethics itself. This second type of debate was particularly interesting to me in part because it captured the problems of constructive feminism. However, it was also striking because most of the students wrestled with the female protagonists in the films more vigorously than they did with those in the novels. It is entirely possible that the difference rests with the characters themselves rather than the media that depict them.

However, I believe that film prompts a stronger reaction because it is a more powerful medium. The stakes seem higher because films reach a larger audience and "are held to be particularly effective modern conveyers and even sources of cultural values and ideology" (Rosenberg 1983, 1). In this course, which is fundamentally concerned with the ways in which women's moral experiences are described and assessed, we found ourselves particularly vigilant about the representation of those experiences on the screen.

Given the influence of films and also their role as conveyers of culture, it can be particularly helpful pedagogically to examine problematic films. For the purpose of this chapter, therefore, I focus on one film and the screen adaptation of a play that proved particularly problematic and thus generated rich learning moments for students and for me. *The Deep End* features an affluent white woman who makes a series of questionable choices in an effort to protect her son. When students watch this film in the context of a course titled "the moral agency of women," the problem of essentialism breaks in as soon as the credits roll. Essentialism reifies aspects of the human body and human experience such that they appear to determine our identity and behavior. Any attempt, therefore, to speak monolithically about a group (e.g., the moral agency *of women*) raises the specter of essentialism.

August Wilson's *Piano Lesson* centers around the struggle between a brother, who wants to sell the family piano, and his sister, who holds onto it as testament to their family's pain. This narrative is less immediately provocative than *The Deep End,* but Delores Williams's essay on "August Wilson's women" prompts a more critical look at the problem of representation. Representation is the practice of ordering another's experience without granting that person subjectivity. The "represented other" remains a passive object in the narrative of a controlling subject. When this course engages female characters, it often engages representations (rather than subjective expressions) of moral agency. This poses a fundamental challenge to the course design and also a rich pedagogical opportunity.

I focus on essentialism and representation not only because they are central features of this course but also because they surface with every description and analysis of human experience. They therefore provide challenge and opportunity for all of us who teach religious studies, which is fundamentally the analysis of human experiences of the sacred. What claims do we make about these experiences and those people who become the objects of our study? How do we represent them through our stories, theories, and teaching? The following pages include description of the film and teleplay that pushed these issues most forcefully in our class, but I intend for the constructive comments pertaining to essentialism and representation to transcend "the Moral Agency of Women."

The Deep End: Synopsis and Analysis

After spending time with man-the-fashioner, man-the-citizen,[2] and the rational agent occupying the original position, one might turn to any number of

female protagonists to shake things up. I turn regularly to Margaret Hall from
The Deep End (Fox Searchlight 2002) because she causes as much trouble
among feminists as she does for the dominant tradition. In the first thirty
minutes of this film, the protagonist, played by Tilda Swinton, visits a nightclub owner named Darby Reese to tell him to stay away from her seventeen-
year-old son, Beau. The next morning she finds Reese impaled on an anchor on
her beachfront property at Lake Tahoe. First she pulls a piece of fabric from his
clenched fist and recognizes it as a scrap of her son's shirt. Then she pries the
anchor from his rib cage, heaves the body into a skiff, steers the boat to a quiet
cove, weights the body with an anchor, and shoves it overboard.

This story covers one week, from a Friday to the next Saturday. In the
course of this week Margaret is remarkably busy. On Monday she drives to
Reno to tell Darby Reese to stay away from her son. On Tuesday she finds
Darby's body and dumps it into the cove. On Wednesday her son reads about
Darby's death in the newspaper and accuses her of being glad he is gone. She is
then visited by the first blackmailer, a man who knows more than she did about
Beau's relationship with Darby and shows her a videotape to prove it. He then
demands $50,000 in exchange for the tape. She spends Thursday and Friday
trying to get the money together but fails to meet the deadline, and receives
more visits from the blackmailer. On Saturday she takes a cab to Reno (because
her car will not start), hocks her jewelry, and offers $12,000 to the blackmailer,
whom we now know as Alek and whom her son suspects is his mother's lover.
Feeling sympathy for Margaret, Alek tells her that someone has been arrested
for Darby's murder, which means that Alek's more evil partner, Nagle, has lost
his advantage. He will have to accept the $12,000 and leave her alone. Nagle,
however, does not see it that way. Instead, he follows Margaret home and slaps
her around in the boathouse before Alek arrives and strangles him, loads his
body into the car, and crashes. Margaret's week ends by retrieving the tape and
the money from the overturned car and saying a tearful good-bye to the man
who both added to her troubles and protected her from them.

What makes this story particularly intense and fun is that the action described so far represents only a part of Margaret's week. In between all of those
activities, she responds to her father-in-law's questions about the broken remote control and the insufficient dry cleaning service, reminds her youngest
son to put his sneakers on so he will not catch cold, comforts him when he
loses his baseball mitt, fulfills her carpool duties, attends her daughter's dance
recital, does the laundry, reassures her navy husband that all is well on the
home front, tries to reestablish communication with Beau, and supports his
efforts to secure a music scholarship for college. In other words, throughout
the week Margaret attempts to protect her family from danger itself, as well as
the knowledge of it. Thus the turning point between Margaret and Alek occurs
when he scolds her for not really trying to get the money. She responds:

> Oh really? Well, maybe you should explain "really trying" to me, Mr.
> Spera. How would you be really trying if you were me? You're not me,
> are you? You don't have my petty concerns to clutter your life or keep

you from trying. You don't have three kids to feed. Or to worry about the future of a seventeen-year-old boy who nearly got himself killed driving back from some kind of a *nightclub* with his thirty-year-old friend sitting drunk in the seat beside him. No, these are not your concerns. I see that. But perhaps you're right, Mr. Spera. Perhaps I could be trying a little harder. Maybe some time tomorrow, between dropping Dylan at baseball practice and picking up my father-in-law from the hospital I might find a way to try a little harder. Maybe I should take a page from your book. Go to the track. Find a card game. Maybe I should blackmail someone. Or maybe you have another idea. Maybe you have a better idea of how I might try a little harder to find this $50,000 you've come here to steal from me.

There are many ways in which a feminist analysis of this film might proceed, but our focus on moral agency directs attention toward Margaret's decisions and motivations. We begin by engaging her actions directly rather than critiquing the film's portrayal of them. That is, our first layer of discussion considers the story and characters rather than "film as medium" (Kamir 2006, xvi). We usually spend most of our time on Margaret's decisions to confront Darby Reese and then to dump his body into the lake. Her motivation behind each one is the same. She wants to keep Darby away from her family, in life and death. Reese is a thirty-year-old man who sexually exploits a confused and vulnerable seventeen-year-old boy. Indeed, he seems to relish his role as a corrupter of youth. He happily describes himself as Beau's "dirty little secret" and capitalizes on Margaret's concern by demanding $5,000 to leave Beau alone. If others knew of Beau's connection to this person, they would think differently of him. From Margaret's point of view, such knowledge would negatively affect Beau's relationship with his father and grandfather, jeopardize the family's reputation as a whole (including the younger siblings), and even block Beau's movement toward the future. Denying any connection between their lives and Darby Reese thus becomes Margaret's main motivation. It is the reason for confronting him, dumping the body, not coming forward when the police arrest someone for his murder, and leaving the scene of the second accident without acknowledging her relationship to the men killed there.

We have, in Margaret Hall, someone who thwarts the judicial process in order to protect her family. For the purposes of our course, therefore, this character offers a site for debating an ethic of care.[3] She does not completely capture this ethic (nor does she give it its best face), but she does embody some of its core features and shortcomings. For example, she responds to a particular need (her son's protection) rather than adhering to a more general principle. She is portrayed therefore not as a moral agent who stands "against a ground of social relationships, judging the conflicting claims of self and others." Rather, for Margaret the relationship defines self and others. "Within the context of the relationship, [she] . . . perceives and responds to perceptions of need" (Gilligan 1995, 34–35). However, Margaret determines the needs of others without consulting them and thus addresses a situation that affects them without involving them in it. She protects her family from danger by keeping them out of it. Her care, therefore, has a paternalistic quality. Moreover, her relationship with Beau and, by extension, the rest of her family takes on the "unidirectional" character that Sarah Hoagland has criticized (1991, 253). For much of the story, all of the care flows in one direction in large part because Margaret keeps everyone else in the dark.

This film, then, makes a substantive contribution to our course in women's moral agency because its main character embodies aspects and limitations of an ethic of care. Thus, she gives expression to a "different voice" and illustrates some of its flaws. But more than this, Margaret Hall makes a great pedagogical contribution to our course because she is an affluent, white housewife apparently driven by "maternal instinct" to protect her son. The minute that we consider her as somehow representing women's moral agency, the room erupts with concerns about essentialism, as well it should. Students criticize Margaret's concerns as bourgeois. She puts herself through this hellish week in order to save reputations, maintain a happy household, and enable her son to study music in college. Students also charge her with homophobia, arguing that her primary motivation is to hide her son's homosexuality. At some point in these debates, students shift from focusing on the character to thinking about the film's construction of Margaret, and this is where the next layer of critical engagement begins. Students stop taking the character at face value and begin examining her as an element in a dominant narrative that presents the experience of affluent, white, married women with children as normative.

Critique: Essentialism

The first nonliterary and noncinematic assignment in the course comes from Elizabeth Spelman's 1988 text, *Inessential Woman: Problems of Exclusion in Feminist Thought*, in which she argues "that the notion of generic 'woman' functions in feminist thought much the way that the notion of generic 'man' has functioned in Western philosophy: it obscures the heterogeneity of women and cuts off examination of the significance of such heterogeneity for feminist theory and political activity" (ix). She continues, "I have come to think even of the phrase 'as a woman' as the Trojan horse of feminist ethnocentrism" (ibid., x). Spelman's criticism appropriately complicates the constructive task of this course. In order to rectify the tradition's neglect of women's experiences, we must talk about them. However, how do we discuss the moral experiences and the moral agency of women without essentialism?

One way is to include as many different kinds of women in the course as possible. So, in addition to *The Deep End*, we read and/or watch *Like Water for Chocolate*, *The Woman Warrior: Memoirs of a Girlhood among Ghosts*, *The Women of Brewster Place*, *The Piano Lesson*, and *Babette's Feast*. Students are also asked to make their own autobiographies a part of the course by writing about a "moral moment" early in the term and then deepening their analysis of that moment as the semester progresses. We then embark on a task of looking for differences and similarities—differences from descriptions of moral agency extended from dominant voices in Western moral theory and similarities among women's stories.

Yet, Spelman challenges us here as well. Looking for the gender-related similarities that connect women of different ethnicities and social circumstances assumes what Spelman brilliantly terms "pop-bed" metaphysics, wherein "each part of my identity is separable from every other part, and the significance of each part is unaffected by the other parts" (ibid., 136). Thinking that we can talk about gender as something separate from ethnicity or culture or religion assumes that these aspects of our identity do not affect one another. Given these dangers, Spelman makes the following recommendations for those who would explore questions like the moral agency *of women:* "We have to investigate different women's lives and see what they have in common *other* than being female and being called 'women'" (ibid., 137).

One commonality that emerged in the course of our study in moral agency is that of constraint. All of the protagonists we studied seemed to be constrained in some way not mentioned by the dominant tradition that, in Katie Cannon's words, "take[s] for granted freedom and a wide range of choices" (1996, 60–61). Now, the type and severity of constraint ranged tremendously, from the kind of self-imposed limitations of Margaret Hall mentioned earlier to severe socioeconomic restrictions of structural oppression. But still there existed this common feature among our protagonists, such that a central question for our class became not *whether* one is acting under constraint but *how* she does so.

This seemingly simple observation is significant because the dominant tradition names freedom from constraint as one of the constitutive features of moral agency—and for good reason. In the *Nicomachean Ethics* Aristotle teaches his students to distinguish between voluntary and involuntary acts because one must not be held accountable for something that one does not do voluntarily. The agent can neither be praised nor blamed for an action performed "under constraint or due to ignorance." Aristotle explains that "An act is done under constraint when the initiative or source of motion comes from without" (1962, 3.1). What do we do, then, with all of those actions performed under some form of constraint? It seems that they are removed from consideration as moral acts. If so, what does this removal do to those who perform these actions and to those agents who live their lives under some form of limitation? It seems to discount their moral agency.

Fortunately, there is a rich collection of more recent writing in ethics that considers moral agency under constraint. In our course we relied heavily on Katie Cannon for articulating this line of inquiry, which has been central to her own work. For more than twenty years now Cannon has drawn attention to the "differences between ethics of life under oppression and [these] established moral approaches that take for granted freedom and a wide range of choices" (1996, 60–61):

> I discovered that the assumptions of the dominant ethical systems implied that the doing of Christian ethics in the Black community was either immoral or amoral. The cherished ethical ideas predicated upon the existence of freedom and a wide range of choices proved null and void in situations of oppression. The real-lived texture of Black life requires moral agency that may run contrary to the ethical boundaries of mainline Protestantism. . . . [T]he salient point here is that the ethical values that the Black community has fashioned for itself are not identical with the body of obligations and duties that Anglo-Protestant American society requires of its members. (ibid., 58–59)

Cannon mines her own family history for these expressions of agency under oppression. Moreover, she focuses on the work and life of Zora Neale Hurston and celebrates the virtue of "unctuousness" exhibited in Hurston's protagonist, Janie, from *Their Eyes Were Watching God.*

Toinette Eugene practices a similar method in her essay titled "Moral Values and Black Womanists." There she reflects on African American history as a "legacy of perseverance and self-reliance, a legacy of tenacity, resistance, and insistence on sexual equality—in short, a legacy of love spelling out standards for a new womanhood" (1994, 165). In these essays Cannon and Eugene illustrate a central feature of womanist ethics by turning to "the moral wisdom of African American women" (Townes 1995, 11).

These scholars have taught me to pair readings in womanist ethics to novels and films, such as *Their Eyes Were Watching God, Beloved, The Color Purple,* and *Daughters of the Dust,* narratives that help us to explore this wisdom and the lives that give rise to it. For the purpose of this chapter, however, I offer the following discussion of a play by August Wilson because it effectively raises the second problem that I want to address, namely, that of representation. *The Piano Lesson* takes its title and central image from a painting by Romare Beardon, in which a woman rests her hand on the shoulder of a girl who is playing the piano. Wilson brings this woman and girl to life in his play and uses the piano to represent the family's heritage. With this central image of a mother teaching her daughter about heritage, Wilson's play seems to be a fruitful site for reflection on moral agency and constraint. And it is this, but it also provokes a study in representation and thus further advances our process of continued questioning.

The Piano Lesson: Synopsis and Analysis

The Piano Lesson came to the stage in 1987 and to Broadway in 1990, when it also received the New York Drama Critics' Circle Award for best new play and the Pulitzer prize for drama. In February 1995 Wilson assembled the Broadway director, Lloyd Richards, and most of the Broadway cast to produce a screen adaptation for television. In "The Making of *The Piano Lesson,*" the narrator notes that more people saw this August Wilson play on that one night in February 1995 than have seen all of his plays on Broadway and in regional theater combined (Richards 1995). Thus, the teleplay assumes some of the power of film in terms of its larger audience and impressive claim to capture "the black experience."

Like all of August Wilson's plays, *The Piano Lesson* takes place in Pittsburgh and examines an African American family's efforts to wrestle with its legacy and the challenges of the future. The protagonist of the story is Boy Willie, who comes to Pittsburgh with a friend, a truck full of watermelons, and a plan to buy back the land that his family worked for generations as slaves and sharecroppers. This financial plan also requires the sale of the family's piano, which literally and metaphorically bears the family's legacy. Sutter, the man who owned Boy Willie's family, traded his great-grandmother Berniece and his grandfather Boy Willie in exchange for the piano as a gift to his wife, Miss Ophelia. Doaker, Boy Willie's uncle, continues the story this way: "Time go along. Miss Ophelia got to missing my grandmother... the way she would cook and clean the house and talk to her and what not. And she missed having my daddy around the house to fetch things for her. So she asked to see if maybe she could trade back that piano and get her niggers back" (Wilson 1990, 43). The man who traded the piano to them would not undo the trade, however, and Miss Ophelia "took sick to bed." Because Doaker's grandfather (Berniece's husband) was "a worker of wood":

> Sutter called him up to the house and told him to carve my grandmother and my daddy's picture on the piano for Miss Ophelia. And he took and carved this.... See that right there? That's my grandmother, Berniece. She looked just like that. And he put a picture of my daddy when he wasn't nothing but a little boy the way he remembered him. He made them up out of his memory. Only thing... he didn't stop there. He carved all this. He got a picture of his mama... Mama Esther... and his daddy, Boy Charles. Then he put on the side here all kinds of things. See that? That's when him and Mama Berniece got married. They called it jumping the broom. That's how you got married in them days. Then he got here when my daddy was born... and here he got Mama Esther's funeral.... Down here he got Mr. Nolander taking Mama Berniece and my daddy away down to his place in Georgia. He got all kinds of things what happened with our family. (ibid., 44)

Years later, Doaker's older brother, Boy Charles, determine to steal that piano from the Sutter family house, saying that "it was the story of our whole family and as long as Sutter had it... he had us" (ibid., 45). Doaker and his two brothers successfully abscond with the piano and take it to relatives in a neighboring county, but Boy Charles is caught and killed.

Twenty-five years after Boy Charles's death, the piano is in Pittsburgh in the home that Doaker shares with his niece (Boy Charles's daughter), Berniece, and her daughter Maretha. This is where Boy Willie comes knocking at 5:00 in the morning after driving into Pittsburgh. Right from the start, Berniece is suspicious of his visit because she knows that trouble always follows Boy Willie. Indeed, he is not in the house long before he starts eyeing the piano and explaining his plan to Doaker. Berniece is adamant throughout the play: Boy Willie will not sell that piano. Doaker refuses to take sides, but he does state Berniece's position whenever she is absent.

This, then, is the play's central question: What do you do with legacy? Boy Willie's opinion is that you build on it. He argues that the piano is not worth anything just sitting in the parlor: "[T]he only thing that make [sic] that piano worth something is them carvings Papa Willie Boy put on there. That's what make it worth something. That was my great-grandaddy. Papa Boy Charles brought that piano into the house. Now, I'm supposed to build on what they left me" (ibid., 51). In an interview August Wilson says that he agrees with Boy Willie's position. That is, he sees Boy Willie as someone who carries his legacy within him and does not need this external relic to remind him of it. Better, then, to "trade the piano in for the independence that land can bring" (Richards 1995).

Berniece sees things differently, however:

Look at this piano. Look at it. Mama Ola polished this piano with her tears for seventeen years. For seventeen years she rubbed on it till her hands bled. Then she rubbed the blood in . . . mixed it up with the rest of the blood on it. Every day that God breathed life into her body she rubbed and cleaned and polished and prayed over it. "Play something for me, Berniece. Play something for me, Berniece." Every day. "I cleaned it up for you, play something for me, Berniece." You always talking about your daddy but you ain't never stopped to look at what his foolishness cost your mama. (Wilson 1990, 52)

From Berniece's perspective, we see the piano differently. It is not an asset at all, it seems. Rather, it represents the family's loss and pain. It tells the story of slavery, human lives traded for an instrument, "thieving and killing," "foolishness," and "years" worth of cold nights in an empty bed" (ibid.). She seems to hold on to the piano as a material connection to her relatives and ancestors and also as a physical representation of their suffering. However, she does not play the piano, or at least she hasn't since her mother died seven years ago. In the climactic final scene Sutter's ghost appears, and Boy Willie fights with him. Berniece plays forcefully on the piano and appeals to her relatives and ancestors for help. It is as though she turns to the piano in this moment of crisis not as a source of pain but as one of strength, something that embodies the family's resilience and its ability to withstand tremendous pain, endure deep suffering, and survive.

Berniece enables us to engage a character grappling not only with her past but also with a brother who wants to "use" that past in a different way. We are able to talk about the value of heritage, what "value" it has, and what "value" actually means in the context of a story like this. However, we also pan out from the character herself to consider the play more generally and its play-wright with the help of a critical essay by Delores Williams. Williams begins and ends her essay with high praise for August Wilson and appreciation of his life's work, which has brought the black experience to the stage. However, her point is that the experience that Wilson really brings to the stage is that of black men. In these plays, Williams argues, women are not the subjects but the objects of men's experience: "[T]he women are 'props' on which the men lean or 'rail,' depending on their emotional needs at the time" (1990, 332). Frequently they feature in the plays as obstacles to men's ambition (ibid., 331). This is the case in *The Piano Lesson*, where Berniece is the obstacle to Boy Willie's financial plan. In Williams's words, "Boy Willie would be able to get the money he needs to buy a farm if his sister Bernice [*sic*] did not try to stop him from selling the family heirloom" (ibid.). Williams's critique raises the issue of representation.

Critique: Representation

"Representation" refers to a tangle of problems stemming from the argument that films arrange the story and position their characters as objects of the "male gaze." Although the practice was initially gender specific (i.e., men objectify women through this process), most theorists now recognize this as an issue of authority more broadly such that the more powerful represent the less powerful. However, the larger point remains intact: The storytellers order the experiences of the others such that they become objects of the narrative rather than subjects of their own experience. This practice becomes insidious when the narrative is crafted to maintain an order or perpetuate stereotypes that serve the interests of the more powerful storyteller. Feminist film criticism captures the danger this practice poses for women in a patriarchal society. For example, speaking of film and opera from the 1940s, Irena Makarushka writes of "offending representations of women [that] . . . reflect a perception of gender and the representation of that experience as determined by a male symbolic order" (1995, 143). She then quotes Raymond Bellour's description of classical films as a "system of representation in which the woman occupies a central place only to the extent that it's a place assigned to her by the logic of masculine desire" (ibid.). In these films, therefore, we do not find women as moral agents but rather the representation of their moral agency according to an order that renders them objects rather than subjects.

The practice of representation becomes particularly insidious when women identify with their representatives on screen and thus internalize various forms of patriarchal oppression. In her book, *Framed: Women in Law and Film* (2006), Orit Kamir offers a helpful summary of this point:

> Following [Laura] Mulvey's lead, feminist film scholars developed this critique of mainstream film theory and its social implications, expanding the feminist analyses to better scrutinize the film-viewing experience of female viewers. These viewers, they showed, were

manipulated into identifying with the "to-be-looked-at" women on-screen, uncritically accepting their passive role as the object of men's gaze and the source of male erotic, controlling, sadistic, pleasure. *Narrative film seduced women into accepting the construction of feminine sexuality as masochistic and submissive.* (23, my italics)

The theory of representation challenges this course design with the argument that seriously engaging such objects perpetuates women's identification with these male-created characters.

Nevertheless, as we have seen with essentialism, representation provides not only a challenge but also a method for analysis, teaching, and learning. For example, instead of steering clear of such representations, we can take them head on and pose Makarushka's question: "Is women's experience adequately represented... or is women's experience distorted?" (1995, 144). In other words, we use those feelings of dissonance as a starting point for discussion and critical engagement. We take up Teresa de Lauretis's argument that film is a "technology of gender" and expand it to consider film also as a technology of race and class, a mechanism through which patriarchy, racism, and classism renew themselves, to borrow language from Janet Thumin (1992, 3).

Sometimes it helps to pair a representation with a different kind of film, one that purposefully places marginalized persons in control of the narrative. For example, *Daughters of the Dust* (1991) was written and directed by Julie Dash, an African American woman, who set out to tell the story of African American women. In an interview with bell hooks, Dash explains that the film "is all from the point of view of a woman—about the women—and the men are kind of just on the periphery" (1992, 33). Then hooks describes the film's approach as "de-center[ing] the white patriarchal gaze," and she continues, "the film takes up that group that is truly on the bottom of the society's race-sex hierarchy. Black women tend not to be seen, or to be seen solely as stereotypes. And part of what *Daughters* does is de-center the usual subject—and that includes white women—and place at the center of our gaze a group that has not been at the center" (ibid., 40).[4]

Thus we can use the problem of representation constructively in at least these two ways: by making the feel and the mechanics of representation part of our discussion of the film and by pairing a representation with another kind of film that purposefully places the marginalized characters in the center as subjects of their own experience. Highlighting representation in film can also be pedagogically helpful because it alerts us to representation everywhere else. How does theory, for example, represent the other? How do I represent others in my course design, assignments, and lectures? Most importantly, why do we craft the representations that we do?

Consider the various representations at work in this chapter, including the representation of the class itself. Of course, the teaching and learning process was messier than this representation of it. We dealt much more intentionally and thoroughly with the issue of essentialism than that of representation, truthfully only scratching the surface of this complex theory and its meaning for our class. We shuffled between engaging characters and engaging the medium that brings them to us more often than we moved neatly from one layer of analysis to another. Some students never seemed too troubled by essentialism and representation, whereas others seemed paralyzed by them. However, my chapter on this course has moved more methodically from film to problem to proposal in an effort to provide an ordered reflection that might be more helpful to other teachers.

Sometimes, however, the order we maintain is less benign. Consider here my representation of August Wilson. In this chapter I began with a narrative about a white woman to raise the issue of essentialism; I then moved to womanist scholarship, which has not only voiced the essentialist critique very effectively but also highlighted other models of moral agency through history and literature; finally I focused on the representation of an African American woman to raise the second issue. I could have written about Steven Spielberg's version of Alice Walker's *The Color Purple* or Jonathan Demme's version of Toni Morrison's *Beloved*, but instead I chose August Wilson.

I have taught Wilson's plays in a few different courses because I believe that he is a great American playwright and that more students should be exposed to him. However, I frame Wilson in the syllabus of this course and in the context of this chapter as an architect of the male gaze and as the one who rendered Berniece a prop in her brother's story. Thus, I find myself implicated by bell hooks's essay titled "Representations: Feminism and Black Masculinity," in which she considers "whether or not feminist focus on black male chauvinism is harsher and more brutal than critiques of patriarchy in general" (1990, 68). That is, I find myself fairly criticized by the very theory I am teaching. When I, a white feminist teacher, assign a black male playwright the role of "sexist" in my syllabus, I perpetuate a practice that is deeply painful to women of color. That is, I use this representation to order oppressions, prioritizing sexism and suggesting that racism, classism, and heterosexism are ancillary. To be clear, I do not think oppression can or should be ordered this way. However, the narrative of white feminism relies on a structure that makes sexism the primary concern. If we think then about this class as a film and we interrogate my representation of Wilson, it is conceivable that a white feminist preoccupation with sex over race shaped that casting decision.

Conclusion

The pedagogical value of such inquiry is that it forces us to examine the order that we employ representations to maintain. We all have ideologies and commitments that shape the way we order material for a class, represent a viewpoint during a lecture, or frame a text or film with secondary material. The best of these intentions, I assume, is to provide a positive learning experience for our students, one that offers them the information they need when they need it, as well as the tools to engage that information critically and work with it constructively. There is, then, an instructive analogy to be drawn between faculty with our course designs and filmmakers with their productions. The syllabus is our script, the mechanism by which we try to order our students' learning experience. We aim to design a learning process that provides foundational material, introduces formative figures, and creates sites for critical engagement and questioning. But we also frame the material, the texts, and the discussions in a particular way so that the course coheres. There must be a narrative unity to the course—some organizing themes or questions that provide a framework for the different characters that appear throughout the term. And yet, true learning most often happens when students make the script their own and not only participate in the course but actually alter its structure by putting the pieces together in a way that faculty members had not anticipated. This "creative interaction" between student and syllabus is analogous to that described by Orit Kamir as occurring between text and reader/viewer: "Believing that a text both constitutes its reader/viewer and is simultaneously created by him or her in the process of reading/viewing, I look at both text and reader/viewer as active participants in the creative interaction that occurs at their meeting" (2006, xvi).

This kind of creative interaction can no doubt occur in classes that do not use movies. Nevertheless, I have found film to be such an empowering medium for students that it more readily prompts their interaction with and sense of ownership of the course material. In other words, using a medium that students are particularly comfortable with facilitates their claim to subjectivity.

In "The Moral Agency of Women," this claim to subjectivity took concrete form as students wrote about and then analyzed a moral moment from their own lives. The nature and intensity of these moments ranged from silencing a cursing father during a little league baseball game, to challenging cultural traditions in order to establish a more egalitarian household, to coming out as a lesbian and leaving the ordination process. These stories regularly made their way into our discussions, adding texture and complexity. Moreover, because students were speaking for themselves rather than for all women, they usually avoided essentialism. Representation persisted, for the most part, as they ordered the experience and characters in a certain way.

The persistence of representation in our writing and teaching does not mean that we must abandon storytelling altogether and thereby refuse to structure a narrative or present material in a coherent way. However, it does mean that we should strive to let others speak for themselves whenever we can.

As I have said, one could move through this learning process from essentialism and representation to subjectivity without the use of film. Still, in my experience, film accelerates the process. It is a catalyst because students not only engage it readily but also respond vigorously to essentialism and representation broadcast on the silver screen. In this particular course they responded by asserting their own subjectivity and narrating their own moral experiences with honesty, care, and thoughtfulness. This teaching experience, therefore, convinced me that film can indeed enhance the moral agency of women.

NOTES

1. The majority of students in this graduate-level seminar course were women. Some were seeking ordination, while others were either preparing for or pursuing doctoral work in ethics or women's studies.

2. These are the terms H. Richard Niebuhr uses for the teleologist and the deontologist throughout chapter 1 of *The Responsible Self: An Essay in Christian Moral Philosophy* (New York: Harper and Row, 1963).

3. I have also used the short film *Jury of Her Peers* for this purpose. Susan Glaspell first wrote this story as a play in 1916 (titled *Trifles*) and then rewrote it as a short story in 1917 (titled *Jury of Her Peers*). In 1981 Sally Heckel adapted it for the screen as a short film. Orit Kamir includes a discussion of this film in her text *Framed* (2006).

4. *Daughters of the Dust* also addresses the issue of essentialism by presenting a "whole range" of African American women and allowing the camera to linger on their different features. The "camera really zooms in on black women's faces," says hooks. "And lingers for a period of time," continues Dash, with "[e]xtreme close-ups and different angles" (1992, 52).

REFERENCES

Aristotle. 1962. *Nicomachean Ethics.* Trans. with an introduction and notes by Martin Ostwald. Englewood Cliffs, N.J.: Prentice Hall.

Benhabib, Seyla. 1992. *Situating the Self: Gender, Community, and Postmodernism in Contemporary Ethics.* New York: Routledge.

Cannon, Katie Geneva. 1996. *Katie's Canon: Womanism and the Soul of the Black Community.* New York: Continuum.

Dash, Julie. 1991. *Daughters of the Dust.* American Playhouse.

———. 1992. *Daughters of the Dust: The Making of an African American Woman's Film.* New York City: New Press.

Eugene, Toinette. 1994. "Moral Values and Black Womanists." In *Feminist Theological Ethics: A Reader,* ed. Lois K. Daly, 160–71. Louisville: Westminster John Knox Press.

Gentile, Mary C. 1985. *Film Feminisms: Theory and Practice.* Contributions in Women's Studies 56. Westport, Conn.: Greenwood.

Gilligan, Carol. 1982. *In a Different Voice: Psychological Theory and Women's Development.* Cambridge, Mass.: Harvard University Press.

———. 1995. "Moral Orientation and Moral Development." In *Justice and Care: Essential Readings in Feminist Ethics,* ed. Virginia Held, 31–46. Boulder, Colo.: Westview.

Hartsock, Nancy. 1979. "Feminist Theory and the Development of Revolutionary Strategy." In *Capitalist Patriarchy and the Case for Socialist Feminism,* ed. Zillah R. Eisenstein, 56–77. New York: Monthly Review Press. Quoted in Gentile, *Film Feminisms,* 13n2.

Hoagland, Sarah. 1991. "Some Thoughts about 'Caring.'" In *Feminist Ethics,* ed. Claudia Card, 246–63. Lawrence: University Press of Kansas.

hooks, bell. 1990. "Representations: Feminism and Black Masculinity." In *Yearning: Race, Gender, and Cultural Politics,* 65–77. Boston: South End Press.

Kamir, Orit. 2006. *Framed: Women in Law and Film.* Durham, N.C.: Duke University Press.

Makarushka, Irena. 1995. "Women Spoken For: Images of Displaced Desire." In *Screening the Sacred: Religion, Myth, and Ideology in Popular American Film,* ed. Joel W. Martin and Conrad E. Ostwalt Jr., 142–51. Boulder, Colo.: Westview.

Marshall, Ellen Ott. 2003. "Making the Most of a Good Story: Effective Use of Film as a Teaching Resource for Ethics." *Teaching Theology and Religion* 6(2): 93–98.

McGee, Scott, and David Siegel. 2002. *The Deep End.* Fox Searchlight Pictures.

Richards, Lloyd. 1995. "The Making of 'The Piano Lesson.'" In *August Wilson's The Piano Lesson.* Hallmark Hall of Fame Productions.

Rosenberg, Jan. 1983. *Women's Reflections: The Feminist Film Movement.* Studies in Cinema series 22, ed. Diane M. Kirkpatrick. Ann Arbor: UMI Research Press.

Spelman, Elizabeth V. 1988. *Inessential Woman: Problems of Exclusion in Feminist Thought.* Boston: Beacon.

Testaferri, Ada. 1995. "Introduction." In *Feminisms in the Cinema,* ed. Laura Pietropaolo and Ada Testaferri. Bloomington: Indiana University Press.

Thumin, Janet. 1992. *Celluloid Sisters: Women and Popular Cinema.* New York: St. Martin's.

Townes, Emilie M. 1995. *In a Blaze of Glory: Womanist Spirituality as Social Witness.* Nashville: Abingdon.

Welch, Sharon. 2000. *A Feminist Ethic of Risk,* rev. ed. Minneapolis: Fortress.

Williams, Delores S. 1990. "August Wilson's Women." *Christianity and Crisis* 50 (October 22): 331–32.

Wilson, August. 1990. *The Piano Lesson.* Plume Drama series. New York: Penguin.

17

Searching for Peace in Films about Genocide

Jolyon Mitchell

I recently began a film and religion class by asking the participants what their favorite movie was. I was genuinely surprised when several, out of about fifty students, put *Shooting Dogs* (directed by Michael Caton-Jones, 2005) at the top of their list. I was intrigued to find out from this group (mostly British nationals in their twenties studying religion or theology) why they rated a film about the Rwandan genocide so highly. A fascinating discussion ensued on the merits and difficulties of making a film about genocide. In this conversation several other students named *La vita è bella* ([Life Is Beautiful]; Roberto Benigni 1997), a comedy partly set in a concentration camp, as one of their favorite films. While for some genocide was a depressing topic and made for a difficult viewing experience, for many others films such as *Shooting Dogs* (also known in the United States as *Beyond the Gates*) raised profound ethical and religious issues. In this chapter I discuss whether films that tackle such difficult topics can provide rich resources for reflecting not just on genocides but also on the relationships between violence, peacemaking, and religious belief in our world.

Filming Genocide and Religion

*You cannot respond to such a determined and terrible crime . . . except
with an equal determination to bear witness.*
  —*Film education CD-ROM material on "Rwanda and the
    Genocide," on* Shooting Dogs *DVD (BBC Films 2005)*

To what degree can a film bear witness to genocide? This is a significant topic for students and film scholars to consider. Many filmmakers have tried to bear witness to the mass killing of Jews during the Second World War, from the simple testimonies in *Shoah* (Claude Lanzmann, 1985)[1] to the black-and-white drama of *Schindler's List* (Steven Spielberg, 1993).[2] Bearing witness is an important practice in a number of religious traditions, but it can be a difficult undertaking when the subject matter is distressing. Recalling mass murder through the visually powerful medium of film can be a painful task, especially as telling or showing may reopen old wounds. Nevertheless, in the shadows of the attempted extermination of the Jewish people, remembering genocide through film has become a topic that filmmakers regularly attempt.[3] When handled with sensitivity and skill, both documentaries and feature films can provoke profound questions. Even less well received films such as Atom Egoyan's complex *Ararat* (2002), which explores the Armenian genocide and its impact on several contemporary lives,[4] has the potential to bring about critical questioning and lively debate.

In this chapter I consider the extent to which the religious and theological questions raised by the attempted extermination of a people can be represented cinematically. To answer this question I examine a single film: Caton-Jones's *Shooting Dogs*, which was filmed some ten years after the genocide in Rwanda. More specifically, I consider aspects of the film itself, the filmmakers' reflections, and various critiques. My aim is to demonstrate that considering the film from these different perspectives provides further educative opportunities. While the central characters are fictional, *Shooting Dogs* is based upon the true story of a large group of Tutsis who sought refuge in a Kigali secondary school (*école technique officielle*), which was briefly protected by UN troops. Once the Belgian soldiers withdrew, leaving the group defenseless, nearly all of the twenty-five hundred men, women, and children were massacred by the waiting militia or *interhamwe*.

Absence, Ritual, and Presence

The 1994 Rwandan genocide, where more than eight hundred thousand people were killed, has already inspired several other films, including *Sometimes in April* (directed by Raoul Peck 2005), *Hotel Rwanda* (directed by Terry George 2004), and *100 Days* (directed by Nick Hughes 2000). Because the central character of *Shooting Dogs* is a white priest (played by John Hurt), many of the religious questions that are latent in other such films are brought to the fore. In this section I consider some of the religious and ethical questions that arise in this film by considering the three themes of absence, ritual, and presence.

First, *Shooting Dogs* depicts several different kinds of absence. After witnessing the brutal murder of a young mother and her baby as the woman tried to flee, the young teacher, Joe (played by Hugh Dancy) asks, "How much pain can a human being take? If you feel enough pain, does everything just shut down before you die?" Father Christopher replies, "I don't know." Looking into the middle distance Joe says, "God knows.... Maybe we should ask him. If he's still around." Joe, who earlier in the film had struggled to explain to the children in his class whether Jesus was actually in the bread during communion, highlights a more profound struggle with the perceived absence of God. This is some distance from a formal discussion of *Deus absconditus* ("the hidden God") and perhaps resonates more with Elie Wiesel's account of "those flames which consumed my faith forever" in his memorable book about life, death, and a "world without God" at Auschwitz and Buchenwald (1960, 32).

While Wiesel takes the reader into a world where children's faces are erased and their bodies are "turned into wreaths of smoke beneath a silent blue sky," *Shooting Dogs* takes the viewer into a world reeking of death, where law and order are absent. Gradually the horror of what is happening beyond the school gates is revealed. When Joe or Father Christopher venture beyond the gates and outside the apparent safety of the compound, they encounter bodies littering the roads and checkpoints, and, in the midst of gangs who kill without hesitation, they see former pupils wielding machetes. When Father Christopher pays his weekly visit to a nearby convent, he discovers the door off its hinges and is overcome by a smell that makes him retch. He finds the bloodied corpses of the nuns, who appear to have been raped. Soon afterward, back in his chapel in the compound, he begins to question the absence of understanding among those he has served:

> People have been coming to Mass here for God knows how long.
> They get up, they go to church, they sing, they genuflect, they kneel,
> they leave. Do you know why? Because they're told to. They just go
> through the motions without the slightest understanding of what it
> is they're engaged in. Whether they're being told to eat a wafer or hack
> their own flesh and blood to death.

He begins to question the value of his thirty years of missionary work in Africa. What has sustained him for many years is increasingly absent, and in the face of so much killing hope is "running dry." When there is no more fuel for people's cooking fires, he suggests that they "use the Bibles," as they can share those that are left over. This moment is symbolic of his growing sense of despair, which is reflected later in the distracted way in which he performs a baptism.

At least one critic observed another absence depicted in this film. In the context of a largely positive review, Geoff Andrew observed that *Shooting Dogs* "doesn't entirely avoid the pitfalls traditional to heroic drama (occasional expository dialogue, the odd tidily convenient climax)" but that the director Michael Caton-Jones:

> orchestrates the spiralling violence with considerable dexterity, re-
> vealing a keen understanding of how, in the wrong circumstances,
> human beings can and do inflict the most barbaric cruelties upon
> one another. Crucially, however, the Hutu are not presented as pan-
> tomime villains; nor are the UN troops. Rather, we're kept aware
> of an absence: the rest of the world, abandoning the Rwandans to
> their fate.[5]

This observation moves from questions about "absence" to a second set of reflections, this time about the place of "ritual." In *Shooting Dogs* the liturgical practices of the priest, whether he is performing a baptism or celebrating the Eucharist, stand in sharp contrast to what is happening both inside and outside the compound. At the end of the baptism, following the signing of the cross on the baby's forehead, Father Christopher's admonition to fight against "sin, the world and the devil . . . unto his life's end" is poignant because of the context in which it is uttered. As the young Joe becomes increasingly distanced from these religious rituals, he prefers to offer concrete help, such as providing fire-wood for fires.

While Father Christopher also attempts to help through action (e.g., by risking his life to obtain drugs for this sick baby), in the final sequence his concern is to ensure that these "children do not die without taking commu-nion." Scenes of the communion are juxtaposed with pictures of the Belgian peace monitors lowering their flags, packing up their equipment, and prepar-ing to leave as quietly as they can. On one level the liturgy acts as a distraction to the men, women, and children, who are relying on the soldiers' protection, while on another it highlights the divide between what is said and what is happening.

When Father Christopher says, "Happy are those who are called to this supper," the faces of his communicants look more pensive than joyful. His closing statement—"the burden we have set down at the door of the Church for this Eucharist, we know we must bear again"—resonates more closely with the actual situation. His final words, spoken with his arms raised, carry much dramatic irony: "Go in peace." This is highlighted by the fact that he imme-diately looks down and appears lost in thought, presumably as to what is likely to happen to those in the church. These scenes raise questions such as the following: What place does worship have in the midst of so much violence? How can religious leaders speak words of peace in the presence of so much embodied hatred? Why turn to ritual in such a situation? These questions might also provide an incentive for further reading beyond the usual film and religion literature for students who wish to reflect more on the place of ritual in the midst of violence.[6]

Alongside questions about absence and ritual, a third set of questions also emerges from a consideration of these themes, the narrative, and the dialogue, particularly those moments that emphasize "presence." As we have seen, both the plot and the script touch on the absence of God and the value of ritual. In a sense, this film is about leaving. The French soldiers leave, the journalists leave, the white Europeans leave, the UN peace monitors leave, and even the young, idealistic Joe leaves in one of the last lorries to depart the compound. Outside the gates, the presence of a gang of youths waving machetes, blowing whistles, and shouting drunkenly is a visual reminder of the attendance of evil. By contrast, the fact that Father Christopher remains almost to the very end expresses a different kind of presence. His staying highlights the departure of so many others and raises the question of why he stayed while so many others left.

Father Christopher's parting words to Joe articulate his own experience of moving on from despair at the absences he has observed: "You asked me, Joe, where is God in everything happening here in all this suffering? I know exactly where he is. He's right here, with these people, suffering, his love is here, more intense and profound than I have ever felt." Even staring directly into the sun, John Hurt delivers these lines with understated force, and it is hard not to believe him when he goes on to say," "And my heart, my soul is here. . . . If I leave, I think I might not find it again." Father Christopher's loyalty to his "flock" is manifested by his continued presence even when all of the other Europeans have left.

Some of the religious questions are made explicit in David Wolstencroft's script. In an informal catechism class a young Rwandan girl named Marie (played by Claire-Hope Ashitey) first affirms her belief in God and then asks, "Does he love everyone? Does he even love those men on the roads outside?" This is a incisive couplet of questions and, given what these men have done and will do, is well put. Father Christopher replies, "God doesn't always love everything we do, that's our choice, but he loves all his children." This affirmation of compassionate love is embodied in his final actions—for instance, when he is stopped and confronted at a roadblock by a drunken and enraged former pupil. Instead of fighting or running away, he affirms, "When I look into your eyes, the only feeling I have is love." These scenes provoke other questions about how compassion can be expressed and what kinds of love can be embodied in a place overrun by killing? Unlike in *Hotel Rwanda,* where the protagonist, Paul Rusesabagina (played by Don Cheadle), acts like a Rwandan Oscar Schindler by providing a safe haven for endangered Rwandans, Father Christopher's presence operates at several different levels. For this priest, action is partly about being present with those who suffer, performing the liturgies of the church, welcoming hundreds of strangers into his school, trying to organize their protection, and then, when all else fails, attempting to help several children to escape.

In this section I have discussed a range of religious and ethical questions that surface from consideration of the themes of absence, ritual, and presence. A rich classroom conversation about a film such as *Shooting Dogs* could usefully consider the tension between absences and presences. What is missing from the narrative? What is left outside the frame? How valuable is the presence of ritual in the face of violence? In a pedagogical context these themes and related questions can naturally lead viewers to reflect, critique, and discuss not only questions of theodicy but also ethical issues related to the international community's responsibility in the face of genocide. Why did many Western countries initially fail to describe this as genocide? Why were so few leading journalists initially willing to cover the Rwanda story? What economic and environmental factors have been left out of this film account? What role did the local majority Catholic Church play during the genocide, and what role *should* it have played? In other words, a fictional film that is based upon actual events can lead students to reconsider historical, ethical, religious, and theological questions. Given many films' emotional potential and power, it is not surprising that some of them can do far more than a simple news report to awaken viewers' consciences.

Witnesses, Receptions, and Memories

In this section I discuss the way in which *Shooting Dogs* raises significant questions about witnessing, viewing, and remembering. There is a passive form of observation or witness, which sees but does nothing to alleviate suffering. Another form of viewing, however, involves the spectators being changed by what they see. Such transformations may be facilitated when a viewer learns a film's historical background. A viewer can change from being a passive observer to an active witness: someone who is willing to support peacemaking and reconciliation. Witnessing real violence can be a traumatic experience. Viewing cinematic violence, especially if it depicts historical events, can evoke painful memories. For instance, some survivors from the 1944 D-day landings found that watching the carefully crafted opening sequence in *Saving Private Ryan* (directed by Stephen Spielberg, 1998) resurrected many difficult, buried memories.[7] This has also been the case with several films that portray the Rwandan genocide. This is not surprising, given what was witnessed during those one hundred days in 1994.

At the peak of the genocide more than five deaths occurred every minute in Rwanda: the rate of killing was three times as rapid as the murder of Jews in the Second World War.[8] Unlike in Germany, where people were mostly transported away from their communities and murdered in gas chambers, many Rwandan women, children, and men died from *masu* (nail-studded clubs) or machete blows at the hands of neighbors in their own homes or nearby in local churches, hospitals, and schools and at roadblocks. Numerous local survivors supported the making of *Shooting Dogs* on the grounds that they wanted to help both to preserve the memory and spread the knowledge of what had happened during the genocide beyond Rwanda. For many local people who lost relatives, friends, or their own limbs, these are memories that can never be fully erased. For instance, some of the extras who participated in the filming of *Shooting Dogs* in Kigali were traumatized by the process and had to receive medical attention.[9] What the producers described as the "world premiere" of the film took place on March 27, 2006, at the Amahoro National Stadium in Kigali. In spite of a heavy rainstorm, more than fifteen hundred people saw the film, and, according to some observers, the movie provoked strong emotional responses among many of the survivors. For instance, after seeing *Shooting Dogs,* Speciose Kanyabugovi, a fifty-five-year-old, told an Associated Press journalist that "I have no words to explain what I feel. We were abandoned. I hope this film explains the reality to the world."[10] This statement is rooted in vivid memories and the belief that a film can tell the rest of the world what happened in Rwanda.

This hope was shared by many members of the production team. Some of the British filmmakers had made earlier research visits to Rwanda. Unsurprisingly, these forays also had an impact upon the final production. Unlike *Hotel Rwanda,* which was filmed in South Africa, *Shooting Dogs* was filmed in the Kigali school where the events actually happened during the first few days of the genocide. In much the same way that the production location significantly influences a film's form and content, so the point of reception can shape viewers' responses to cinematic narratives of violence. Therefore, not only can films hide certain kinds of violence, but they can also try to bring distant violence, such as the Rwandan genocide, closer to viewers who are watching in more secure situations. My argument is that the place of reception matters. Where a film is seen is a significant variable. While it is obvious that the responses evoked in a stadium in Kigali will be different from the comments of students watching in a European or North American classroom, this fact can usefully be drawn out in different pedagogic contexts. Encouraging students to imagine different points of reception and ways in which they might transform the viewing experience is a productive method for encouraging reflection.

So too is the distinction between actual historical remembering and cinematic remembering. The screenwriter of *Shooting Dogs,* David Wolstencroft, based his characterization of Father Christopher on an actual Franciscan priest, Croatian Vjeko Ćurić (1957–1998). He was one of the few Europeans who refused to leave the country during the genocide, despite his superiors' orders to do so. Ćurić sheltered numerous Tutsis and saved hundreds of lives. His actual practices were more nuanced than his cinematic counterpart. For example, during "the genocide and a number of months later, he refused to provide the sacraments to his flock, finding it inappropriate to do so while they were in the throes of madness; and then after the genocide, only once they had undertaken such acts of collective penance and reconciliation as, for example, rebuilding the houses of their victims."[11]

Ćurić himself survived the genocide, only to be shot to death by unknown assailants in 1998 in Rwanda. His life story illustrates how some religious leaders neither fled nor supported the genocide but chose instead to stand up against the mass killing.[12] By drawing this historical reality to the attention of viewers who are intrigued by Father Christopher's brave actions in *Shooting Dogs,* the film can encourage students to think through the diversity of responses (including those of religious leaders) to the genocide. It might also encourage some to consider the difference between Ćurić's actual life and John Hurt's fictional depiction of Father Christopher.

It almost goes without saying that films can provide windows onto the worlds of not only the few rescuers and the many victims but also the perpetrators. What motivated them to acts of such evil? Why did they kill their neighbors? There are several moments in *Shooting Dogs* in which the perpetrators are portrayed listening attentively to the radio. Again, this has its roots in historical fact. Some of the most chilling broadcasts in the history of radio emerged from Rwanda in the 1990s. Radio-Télévision Libre des Mille Collines (RTLM) [One Thousand Hills Free Radio] is frequently blamed for inciting the genocide that claimed more than eight hundred thousand lives during a hundred-day period in 1994.[13] In "its scale and apparent impact, hate radio in

Rwanda seemed to have no parallel since the Nazi propaganda for genocide."[14] But what role did radio actually play in these localized mass murders? Although some early accounts claim that much "of the responsibility for the genocide in Rwanda can be blamed on the media,"[15] this appears to be an oversimplification. Most scholars agree that the Rwandan genocide would have happened without the RTLM broadcasts and that blaming radio is one way of denying responsibility for what was an ethnocide.[16]

Nevertheless, the precise role of radio in the genocide is a contested phenomenon, and while it is neither a new nor a unique occurrence, the use of radio to express racial hatred and to inspire ethnic violence remains a disturbing abuse of the medium. In *Shooting Dogs* the radio makes few appearances and primarily adds to the atmosphere of the film. Nonetheless, it can serve as a discussion point of the role of the news media in propagating hatred and reinforcing the ethnic divides that were strengthened through the work of German and Belgian missionaries earlier in the twentieth century.

Unlike radio, a film can communicate far more visual information in a short period of time. For teaching, this provides both opportunities and difficulties. To actually see the *interhamwe* listening attentively to the radio is a powerful visual catalyst for thinking about the role of the local media during the genocide. A film will inevitably, however, simplify the complex causes behind the genocide. It cannot do justice to the complete communicative environment, where extremist local papers such as *Kangura* were also promoting hate speech in the months leading up to the slaughter. I suggest that using a film as the only witness to genocide will create a distorted memory, whatever the reception context. Like an increasing number of DVDs, the *Shooting Dogs* DVD provides useful additional teaching material, but this may not be enough. Educators can go further.

The range of film reviews of *Shooting Dogs* found on websites such as Rotten Tomatoes provides additional information on the multiple receptions this film received.[17] Of fifty-two reviews cited, more than forty-three were largely positive. Nevertheless, the less favorable responses are also worth considering. For instance, several reviewers were uncomfortable with the fact that the story was told through the eyes of two white characters. According to Kirk Honeycutt, writing for *The Hollywood Reporter*, "the greatest failure" of the film is "its inability to enter into the lives of the Rwandans, Tutsi and Hutu alike. The movie never moves beyond the tragic facts to show us the human face of either victims or perpetrators. All we get are white people shaking their heads and cursing Western governments."[18]

This overstated criticism does not do justice to the film's narrative and characterizations. Such critical responses, however, can provoke valuable discussions among students who have also seen the film and have been encouraged to develop their own independent judgments before reading published critics. Some websites even follow a review with a set of questions intended to bring about thoughtful discussion.[19] For students and other viewers, when a powerful film like *Shooting Dogs* becomes integrated into wider critical, historical, and social accounts, as well as theological and religious debates, it has the potential to become an even more valuable catalyst for further reflection, discussion, and even action.

Conclusion

Elsewhere I have argued that, from the earliest days of film, many viewers have been mesmerized by moving images of conflict and violence. Directors and producers have also found brutality an irresistible topic for their craft. From comedy to tragedy, from war films to Westerns, and from historical dramas to fantasy epics, violence is often close to the heart of the story. This is the case in *Shooting Dogs*, which is unafraid of showing actual machete blows. This is not done gratuitously. It highlights the reality of a particularly savage moment in history but without savoring the blood spilling. Placed along side some of the films I discuss in detail in *Media Violence and Christian Ethics* (2007), *Shooting Dogs* is at first sight comparatively easier on the viewer. The central topic, however, makes watching unsettling, and this can be usefully explored in the classroom. While watching the movie, if it is hard not to believe that this event actually occurred and was allowed to happen partly due to the inaction of the West, it is reasonable to discuss similar incidents in regions such as Darfur in Sudan.

My aim through this brief study of *Shooting Dogs* is to suggest that film provides a rich resource for thinking about what we value in our world. As producer, cowriter, and former Rwanda-based BBC journalist David Bolton states in the commentary on the DVD, this film does not intend "to give all the answers," and he hopes that the audience will "go away with further questions" about what actually happened in Rwanda. Several scenes in the film do this particularly effectively. Take, for example, the conversation between Joe, the young teacher, who hopes to "make a difference," and Rachel, the seasoned television journalist (played by Nicola Walker) who admits that she felt far more emotion in Bosnia seeing bodies of European women than she did in Rwanda witnessing the massacre of Africans. This memorable discussion explores motivations, memories, and responsibilities through a brief conversation. It could be used to good effect in a class setting, for example, to explore the journalist's role in covering genocide, the ethics of portraying distant suffering, and the responsibilities of those who watch it in comparative comfort and safety. Or consider the "end credit sequence," which "bears witness to the number of crew members whose lives were directly affected by the genocide."[20] This sequence, easily overlooked by viewers, connects those locals involved in making the film and the actual historical events that inspired the narrative. It also raises questions about what Avishai Margalit describes as the "ethics of memory": Is there ever a time to forget, or will making a film about genocide ensure that there is perpetual remembering?[21]

In this chapter I have investigated some of the pedagogical opportunities and difficulties of teaching through a film that focuses upon a particularly violent episode in one country's history. I have intentionally sidestepped the extensive research that investigates whether violent film makes viewers more aggressive. In the classroom, to focus purely on the violent-effects debate misses another set of highly significant questions about presences and absences, rituals and memories, viewing and hearing. Like other genocide films such as *Shoah* or *Schindler's List*, these movies—when handled wisely—can help students think critically about the nature of violence and evil and even whether the apparent absence of peace and peacemaking in many films is something to be concerned about.

The peacekeepers in *Shooting Dogs* are accurately portrayed as ineffective and powerless. The European title points to the fact that the UN soldiers were allowed to shoot the local dogs that fed on the decomposing bodies of the genocide victims. In the film, this action infuriates Father Christopher, especially given that the UN troops are not permitted to use their guns against the threatening gangs outside the compound. They are bound by UN directives and constrained by governmental apathy. Is there ever a time to use force to protect the defenseless?

A further set of more general questions emerges: Why do many films undervalue peacemaking? Where is real peace to be found in films about violence? Why is peace so hard to depict cinematically? In light of these and the other questions raised earlier, my contention is that film education, at its best, can assist students in developing a more critical understanding of the difficulties of attempting to depict genocide cinematically, the related religious and theological issues, and the wider problems and values of cinematic brutality. Undertaken in a creative, supportive, and imaginative environment, film education that focuses on understanding films about genocide may even inspire students to consider ways of living that will promote a more peaceful world.

NOTES

1. See Felman (1994).

2. See Loshitzky (1997).

3. For an extensive, annotated list of films and documentaries, see the videography prepared by William Schulman et al. at *A Teacher's Guide to the Holocaust,* http://fcit.usf.edu/holocaust/resource/films.htm.

4. Not all of the reviews of *Ararat* were negative; see, for example, Frederic Brussat and Mary Ann Brussat, who believe that "Atom Egoyan's thought-provoking film compels us to experience the toxicity of genocide and the ways it continues to cast shadows on the lives of Armenians and others years after its bloody unfolding." See "*Ararat:* Film Review" at *Spirituality and Practice,* http://www.spiritualityandpractice .com/films/films.php?id=5342. By comparison to *Shoah,* far fewer films or documentaries have been made about what is often described as the Armenian genocide. For recent research on this controversial topic see Lewy (2005) and Bloxham (2005).

5. Geoff Andrew, "*Shooting Dogs,*" review in *Time Out* (London) 1858 (March 29–April 5, 2006).

6. For theologians, see, for example, the work of Cavanaugh (1998) and Anderson and Foley (1998). For students of religion see the work of Rappaport (1999) and Grimes (1994).

7. For a discussion of the skillful aestheticization of violence in *Saving Private Ryan* see Prince (2000), 29.

8. Cohen (2001), 284; Gourevitch (1998).

9. Alice O'Keefe (2006), "Anger at BBC Genocide Film," *Observer* (19 March). See also Linda Melvern (2006), "History? This Film Is Fiction," *Observer* (19 March).

10. See *MSN Movie News*, "Hurt Says Genocide Film a Wake-up" at http://movies .msn.com/movies/article.aspx?news=219603.

11. Petrie (2004), 87–88.

12. See Ritner, Roth, and Whitworth, eds. (2004).

13. Estimates range from half a million to one million victims. See Prunier (1997), "How Many Were Killed?" in *Rwanda Crisis*, 259–65. Prunier makes a strong case for there being about 850,000 victims.

14. Carver (1996), 3.

15. Carver (2000), 189. Carver cites journalist Ed Broadbent in the Montreal *Gazette* (May 3, 1994).

16. Carver (1996), 190–91.

17. See http://uk.rottentomatoes.com/m/beyond_the_gates/.

18. Kirk Honeycutt, "*Beyond the Gates*: Bottom Line: Saga of the Rwandan Genocide Takes the Tired Point of View of White Westerners," at http://www.hollywood reporter.com/hr/film/reviews/article_display.jsp?andrid=8883.

19. See, for example, http://www.christianitytoday.com/movies/reviews/2007/ beyondthegates.html.

20. Joe Utichi, "Review: *Shooting Dogs*" at http://www.Film Focus.co.uk.

21. See also Volf (2007) and Margalit (2002).

REFERENCES

Anderson, Herbert, and Edward Foley. 1998. *Mighty Stories and Dangerous Rituals*. San Francisco: Jossey-Bass.

Bloxham, Donald. 2005. *The Great Game of Genocide: Imperialism, Nationalism, and the Destruction of the Ottoman Armenians*. New York: Oxford University Press.

Carver, Richard. 2000. "Broadcasting and Political Transition." In *African Broadcast Cultures: Radio in Transition*, ed. Richard Fardon and Graham Furniss, 188–97. Oxford, UK: James Currey.

———. 1996. "Introduction." In *Broadcasting Genocide: Censorship, Propaganda, and State-sponsored Violence in Rwanda, 1990–1994*, Article 19, Linda Kirschke, Richard Carver, and Sandra Coliver (October).

Cavanaugh, William. 1998. *Torture and Eucharist: Theology, Politics, and the Body of Christ*. Malden, Mass.: Blackwell.

Cohen, Stanley. 2001. *States of Denial: Knowing about Atrocities and Suffering*. Cambridge, UK: Polity.

Felman, Shoshana. 1994. "Film as Witness: Claude Lanzmann's *Shoah*." In *Holocaust Remembrance: The Shapes of Memory*, ed. Geoffrey Hartman. Oxford, UK: Blackwell.

Gourevitch, Philip. 1998. *We Wish to Inform You That Tomorrow We Will Be Killed with Our Families: Stories from Rwanda*. New York: Farrar, Straus, and Giroux.

Grimes, Ronald L. 1994. *The Beginnings of Ritual Studies*. Columbia: University of South Carolina Press.

Lewy, Guenter. 2005. *The Armenian Massacres in Ottoman Turkey: A Disputed Genocide*. Salt Lake City: University of Utah Press.

Loshitzky, Yosefa. 1997. "Holocaust Others: Spielberg's *Schindler's List* versus Lanzman's *Shoah.*" In *Spielberg's Holocaust: Critical Perspectives on* Schindler's List, ed. Yosefa Loshitzky. Bloomington: Indiana University Press.

Margalit, Avishai. 2002. *The Ethics of Memory.* Cambridge, Mass.: Harvard University Press.

Mitchell, Jolyon. 2007. *Media Violence and Christian Ethics.* New York: Cambridge University Press.

Mitchell, Jolyon, and S. Brent Plate, eds. 2007. *The Religion and Film Reader.* New York: Routledge.

Mitchell, Jolyon. 2007. *Remembering the Rwandan Genocide: Reconsidering the role of Local and Global Media* 6(11). http://lass.calumet.purdue.edu/cca/gmj/fa07/gmj-fa07-mitchell.htm

Petrie, Charles. 2004. "The Failure to Confront Evil: A Collective Responsibility." In *Genocide in Rwanda,* ed. Rittner, Roth, and Whitworth, 83–91.

Prince, Stephen. 2000. "Graphic Violence in Cinema." In *Screening Violence,* ed. Stephen Prince, 1–44. New Brunswick, N.J.: Rutgers University Press.

Prunier, Gérard. 1997. *The Rwanda Crisis: History of a Genocide.* London: Hurst.

Rappaport, Roy. 1999. *Ritual and Religion in the Making of Humanity.* New York: Cambridge University Press.

Rittner, Carol, John K. Roth, and Wendy Whitworth, eds. 2004. *Genocide in Rwanda: Complicity of the Churches?* Saint Paul: Paragon.

Volf, Miroslav. 2007. *The End of Memory: Remembering Rightly in a Violent World.* Grand Rapids, Mich.: Eerdmans.

Wiesel, Elie. 1960. *Night,* trans. Stella Rodway. New York: Hill and Wang.

Index